Sustainable Development Across Pacific Islands

Edoardo Monaco · Masato Abe
Editors

Sustainable Development Across Pacific Islands

Lessons, Challenges, and Ways Forward

Springer

Editors
Edoardo Monaco
Department of Social Sciences,
Globalisation and Development (GAD)
Programme
Beijing Normal University-Hong Kong
Baptist University United International
College (BNU-HKBU UIC)
Zhuhai, Guangdong Province, China

Masato Abe
United Nations Multi-Country Office for
Micronesia
Kolonia, Pohnpei
Federated States of Micronesia

ISBN 978-981-97-3628-7 ISBN 978-981-97-3629-4 (eBook)
https://doi.org/10.1007/978-981-97-3629-4

This Springer imprint is published by the registered company Springer Nature Singapore Pte Ltd.
The registered company address is: 152 Beach Road, #21-01/04 Gateway East, Singapore 189721, Singapore

To Lina, Marina, Michele, and Antonietta

Foreword by Izumi Kobayashi

In the early 1970s, the United States, the administering authority of the United Nations Trust Territory of the Pacific Islands (Micronesia), decided to terminate their trusteeship by transitioning Micronesia into a self-governing or independent country. The necessary steps to achieve this transition were to develop industries and generate self-sustaining economic activities in the Micronesian islands. Micronesian people under the trusteeship lived on administrative funds provided by the United States while relying on traditional subsistence economies in which they enjoyed the blessings of nature.

To attract external industrial investment to Micronesia, the United States introduced the "Foreign Investment Permit Law", shifting from a previous policy of regional closure to an open policy allowing the free entry of foreigners to the islands. At that time, the United States had high expectations for Japan's role in the economic development of Micronesia. The central reason for this was that Japan was one of the most rapidly growing economies in the world at the time and was the closest economic power to the islands. Before the United States trusteeship, Japan had governed the region. In the roughly 30 years of its mandated administration granted by the League of Nations, Japan achieved Micronesia's industrial development. Various industries were established in Micronesia, including agricultural produce such as sugarcane, pineapple, and copra and processed products such as bonito flakes, canned goods, charcoal, and crafts made from shells and tortoiseshells. Mineral resources such as bauxite and phosphate were also produced in the region. These industrial activities made Japan's governance of Micronesia profitable, resulting in trade surpluses.

As Micronesia approached independence, many believed that economic self-reliance was possible by emulating Japan's past success. Many also thought that the Micronesian economy would readily flourish if Japan once more became significantly involved in its development. Around this time, investment solicitation missions comprising Trust Territory Government officials and Micronesian Congress members began frequently visiting Japan. My engagement and research in Micronesia also started in response to these island movements.

Fifty years later, the former United Nations Trust Territory of Micronesia became three independent nations and one United States territory: Palau, Federated States of

Micronesia, Marshall Islands, and the Commonwealth of Northern Marianas. While tourism has developed in some islands, such as Palau and Saipan, there has been no fundamental change in the economic structure of Micronesia. Livelihoods still depend primarily on United States aid and on subsistence economies.

So why has economic development not advanced in the Micronesian islands? I believe it is mainly because the United States and all of the aid-giving developed countries, international organizations, and development experts for the island nations have pursued development without conducting detailed investigations into local conditions. They have applied the same methods that had succeeded elsewhere to the small islands without considering the people's traditional subsistence economies and ways of life, leading to the failure of development.

My responses to visitors from Micronesia have been discouraging, as the socioeconomic circumstances surrounding the islands and the needs of the islanders are now entirely different from those of the pre-Second World War time. According to a historical document of Japan's Territorial Government of the South Seas (the 1940 edition of the *Southern Pacific islands handbook*, published in Tokyo), Saipan, where industrial development was most advanced, had a Japanese population ratio of 91 per cent, followed by Palau with 78 per cent. These two islands contributed to over 70 per cent of the overall production in the Micronesia region. In contrast, the Japanese ratio decreased in Ponape (present-day Pohnpei) to 46 per cent and in Truk (present-day Chuuk) to 22 per cent, corresponding to a decline in production. While the resident Japanese population ratio differed across the islands, in the entire Micronesia region nearly 85,000 Japanese settled (excluding military personnel) compared with only 51,000 native Micronesians. The data reveals that the main contributors to production on the islands were not Micronesians but Japanese. Moreover, these Japanese residents were working to produce goods demanded by mainland Japan. In other words, the industrial structure that had thrived in Micronesia was a typical colonial industrial structure where all three essential elements—capital, labour, and market—were Japanese.

The industrialization of the Japanese era could not be revived or re-established in present-day Micronesia. Today's Micronesian islands have unique national laws, cultural customs, and people's needs. Meanwhile, markets that could accept the islands' products do not exist readily among neighbouring countries. Additionally, thanks to economic cooperation and aid from the United States and other regional powers, the living conditions of Micronesians today are far more prosperous than those of the Japanese who migrated to the islands. Considering these socioeconomic changes, it is meaningless to reference the forms of industry of over 80 years ago. The islands' lack of significant industrial development over the past half-century supports this point.

No one who once considered industrial development in Micronesia has fully replicated the successful cases of the Japanese administration era in their development plans and implementation. We should thus face the reality that almost no industrial development initiatives have succeeded in the Micronesia countries. This is because most economic development plans, including those of aid countries, international organizations, and development experts and researchers, have been driven primarily by best practices or development methods that are based not on local conditions but on existing theories, as I pointed out earlier. These aid countries and organizations have typically imposed economic development in Micronesia by importing the development model of injecting capital and labour into a region or a country without considering local cultural traditions and ways of life. This development strategy has been impractical and has not led to sustainable development in Micronesia. Many insights gained from the development failure in Micronesia can also apply to other Pacific island nations in similar conditions. However, a lack of awareness of these issues has persisted for a long time, and development economists must bear some responsibility.

Young researchers interested in the small islands in Micronesia or the Pacific often find a limited number of papers available to explore when looking for advanced economic studies on the development issues of such small island worlds. Researchers in various disciplines, including cultural anthropology, sociology, and political science, often apply existing economic theories to their island studies without fully understanding the islands' actual situation or the danger of replicating the existing theories. This lack of economic studies is probably a result of the fact that the islands' tiny economies have not reasonably attracted the interest of modern development economists. Constructing practical economic insights that work effectively for sustainability in the small islands is essential in order to improve development plans and policies. In addition to economists, investigating island economic issues requires the distinct knowledge and insights of regional studies encompassing cultural anthropology, sociology, political science, and others.

From this perspective, this book's aim of facilitating multidisciplinary researchers to discuss sustainable island development is a highly timely endeavour. As no similar preceding works exist, this United Nations-led publication could become a monumental work on the discourse of sustainable development issues in the small islands of Micronesia and the Pacific. I sincerely hope that the discussions in this book will serve as a significant stimulus, fostering increased interest in small island nations among young researchers.

Translated by Miri Asano

November 2023

Prof. Izumi Kobayashi
Osaka Gakuin University
Suita, Japan

Foreword by Jaap van Hierden

The development patterns of Pacific island countries and territories (PICTs) across the Pacific Ocean have long been hampered by severe, unique constraints and challenges, which include, but are not limited to, geographical remoteness; small landmass and population; narrow resource base; vulnerability to exogenous economic shocks, climate change, and ecosystem fragility; limited institutional and financial capacity; and the high cost of imports and exports. In addition, from 2020 onwards, converging crises such as the lingering COVID-19 pandemic, the Russia–Ukraine conflict, and large price hikes in commodity and energy markets have been posing additional daunting, if not existential, threats to small island nations that are structurally less capable of dealing with economic, social, and environmental shocks.

The United Nations Multi-Country Office for Micronesia was established on 1 October 2021 and is based in Kolonia, Pohnpei Island, Federated States of Micronesia (FSM). This Office covers Micronesia, a northern subregion of the Pacific encompassing over 2000 islands and five independent states: Palau, FSM, Marshall Islands, Nauru, and Kiribati. Under this Office's close coordination, the United Nations Country Team in Micronesia, which comprises over 20 United Nations organizations, has supported the countries in meeting national development priorities and achieving the United Nations 2030 Agenda for Sustainable Development, or the Sustainable Development Goals (SDGs). The United Nations entities are implementing their projects and activities under the *United Nations Pacific sustainable development cooperation framework 2023–27* (United Nations in the Pacific, 2023). I am honoured to be the first United Nations Resident Coordinator to lead the Office.

This timely edited volume explores the most pressing sustainable development challenges that PICTs face, and the governance practices being implemented to realize national development priorities successfully at both national and transnational levels. By inviting analytical contributions from expert researchers and practitioners in the region and beyond, the book sheds light on a selection of key issues—and related responses—in five broad dimensions of sustainable progress, fully aligning with the SDG framework, namely socioeconomic inclusion, diversified and sustained economic growth, sound environmental management, stabilized regional geopolitics, and enhanced international cooperation: "people", "prosperity", "planet", "peace", and "partnership". While the scope of the analysis covers small island nations throughout the Pacific Ocean, particular attention is dedicated to Micronesia, which, in many crucial aspects, is highly representative of the circumstances shared by other small island nations elsewhere in the Pacific and beyond.

I sincerely hope that this intellectual endeavour will contribute to conducting concrete and practical policy advocacy and providing relevant technical assistance in the Pacific while facilitating effective coordination within the United Nations system and with all partners, donors, and stakeholders. My office will continue to sponsor substantive research and fact-finding initiatives to realize the SDGs in the region.

Jaap van Hierden
United Nations Resident Coordinator
for Palau
Federated States of Micronesia
Marshall Islands
Nauru, Kiribati
Kolonia, Pohnpei
Federated States of Micronesia

Reference

United Nations in the Pacific (2022). *The United Nations Sustainable Development Cooperation Framework 2023–27* [Online]. Available at: https://micronesia.un.org/en/236410-un-sustainable-development-cooperation%C2%A0framework-unsdcf-2023-27. (Accessed: 5 March 2024)

Acknowledgements

Many are the organizations and individuals that played a role in this ambitious edited book project. Edoardo Monaco wishes to acknowledge in particular the support received over the years from the Beijing Normal University–Hong Kong Baptist University United International College (BNU-HKBU UIC) and its leadership and in particular Prof. Chen Zhi, Prof. Tang Tao, Prof. Ng Ching Fai, Prof. Tzeki Hon, and Professor Simon Zhao Xiaobin. At BNU-HKBU UIC, the Department of Social Sciences (DSS) and its Globalisation and Development (GAD) Programme deserve a special mention for the nurturing and thought-provoking environment they have represented all along. Sincere thanks go to the United Nations Multi-Country Office for Micronesia, for the fruitful and meaningful research collaboration that has, quite simply, made this volume possible. Crucial in many ways have been the resources of United Nations Volunteers, the Pacific Island Forum, the Alliance of Pacific Island States, and the Club of Rome network (and in particular its China Association), as well as the advice of countless more experts, friends, and colleagues in the Pacific and beyond.

Disclaimers

The opinions, figures, and estimates outlined in this study are the authors' responsibility and should not necessarily be considered as reflecting the views or carrying the endorsement of the United Nations. Any errors are the responsibility of the authors. The designations employed and the presentation of the material in this publication do not imply the expression of any opinion whatsoever on the part of the secretariat of the United Nations concerning the legal status of any country, state, territory, city, or area, or its authorities, or concerning the delimitation of its frontiers or boundaries. Mentioning firm names and commercial products does not imply the endorsement of the United Nations. References to dollars ($) are all to United States dollars. Bibliographical and other references have, wherever possible, been verified. The United Nations bears no responsibility for the availability or functioning of URLs. This study was prepared, for most chapters, with the latest available data as of November 2023.

Introduction

This volume is timely and ambitious: it is in fact conceived as a holistic "journey" across various domains of progress in a region that, despite fundamental common traits, remains vast and diverse.

Pacific island countries and territories (PICTs) have often been identified with elements of vulnerability, whether these be social, economic, or environmental in nature. This tendency has only been exacerbated given the PICTs' position on the frontline of challenges related to climate change, both as they navigate impacts that are already being felt as a result of increased volatility in weather patterns and other changes and as they contemplate a future that may involve the migration of entire populations in the face of sea level rises rendering some locations uninhabitable.

While these factors cannot be overlooked, this volume aims to showcase not only the long-standing and emerging challenges but perhaps more importantly, the opportunities, the resilience, the resourcefulness, and the ambition that local socioeconomic development patterns in the Pacific already encompass.

And beyond the PICTs themselves, we hope that the analyses collected in this volume will contribute to highlighting the global significance of the human–nature nexus in the current Anthropocene. Often captured in the concept of "small islands, big oceans", the importance of the region and its islands and peoples transcends the geographical remoteness and small size of many PICTs.

Although the themes, the challenges, and the solutions overlap considerably among the PICTs and therefore, correspondingly, among the contributions to this volume, we divide the chapters between four themed parts depending on their specific areas of focus, in turn reflecting the "5Ps" of the United Nations' 2030 Agenda for Sustainable Development.

In Part I: People, we concentrate on the communities of the PICTs, and in particular those of Micronesia. How are these communities faring in relation to the United Nations' Sustainable Development Goals (SDGs)? How are they responding to and coping with global economic trends and conditions? And, crucially, how are islanders responding to climate change and sea level rise, not only in terms of projected future threats but as they are already making their impact felt in these especially vulnerable locations?

Climate change is expected to drive increases in, and increasingly complex patterns of, migration in the remainder of the twenty-first century and beyond. Yet migration has already long been a central fact of life in Micronesian communities, with many seeking to improve on limited educational, healthcare, and employment opportunities available at home by moving elsewhere, particularly to the United States. In Chap. 1, Masato Abe and Agnieszka Wang delineate some of these dynamics through a consideration of the "freely associated states" of Palau, Federated States of Micronesia (FSM), and Marshall Islands and the Compact of Free Association (CoFA) agreements that have enabled many Micronesians to study, work, and live in the United States. The CoFAs removed visa restrictions, affording citizens of the freely associated states opportunities to seek the kind of decent, well-paying work that is in short supply at home. The authors consider in detail the factors that push citizens of Micronesia to pursue such opportunities, as well as downsides such as the discrimination, poverty, and lack of assistance that they often experience in the host country, before outlining the significant migration-related policy challenges facing the three states in the future.

The global importance of meeting the United Nations' SDGs is reflected in the PICTs. Chapter 2 focuses attention on one factor in these goals, gender equality—addressed both in its own right as Goal 5 and as a cross-cutting factor affecting outcomes under all of the other goals. Taking FSM as her case study, Sabrina Regmi looks at the extent to which the country has committed to achieving SDG 5, what structures and initiatives it has put in place to do this, and both the successes and limitations of its approach so far, concluding with clear recommendations for future action on gender-based violence, protection and justice for young girls who have been or are at risk of being trafficked, closing economic gender gaps, improving capacity and data collection, political participation, and how gender equality intersects with resilience to climate change.

In Chap. 3, authors Valentine Hazelman, Sandy O'Brien, Marieta Tekabu, Bannau Tiiata, and Jason Flello turn their attention to aged care training in Kiribati. As one of the sectors in which many Pacific islanders seek employment opportunities abroad, particularly in Australia and New Zealand, and given the ageing population in such countries, aged care is likely to represent one of the "golden opportunities" for I-Kiribati workers to access skilling and employment beyond their home shores. The chapter offers a close consideration of an in-island training programme that seeks to equip islanders to meet the relevant skills needs and access such opportunities.

Finally in Part I, in Chap. 4 Nikisha Smith undertakes a thorough review of one of the major secondary impacts of climate change—its serious negative effects on mental health, particularly among those for whom it is already threatening to uproot their traditional systems and culture. Focusing on Kiribati, Tuvalu, and Marshall Islands, Smith explores phenomena such as solastalgia—the negative emotions experienced over the loss of livelihoods and of the environment as it once was—eco-anxiety about the future, and the wholesale relocation that some societies are now considering as their current locations become unliveable, along with the serious consequences this is likely to have on mental health. Smith concludes by looking at policy implications, including the role that other countries should play given that the islands under study are facing the worst impacts of climate change while bearing very little responsibility for causing it.

Our attention turns to economic issues in Part II: Prosperity. How to build and maintain prosperity in a way that is environmentally sustainable is a pressing concern for all nations, but particularly for those on the frontline of climate change. In Chap. 5, Masato Abe and Nick Freeman review current challenges and approaches to development before going on to outline the "BlueEARTH" development model as a more sustainable and resilient approach than those that have been proposed and implemented from the mid-1980s onwards.

Adrian J. Bailey and Jialing Zou then, in Chap. 6, address a fundamental aspect of any contemporary approach to development: digitalization. They consider the potential for digitalization to fuel a more sustainable approach to development across the PICTs, with a particular focus on how migration patterns have changed and may change further in the future in light of the increasing integration of digital data and technologies into daily life.

One of the most critical industries for sustainable socioeconomic development in the Pacific has been tourism, and particularly "blue ocean tourism", focusing on the appeal and advantages of the vast ocean expanse to which the PICTs can potentially provide access for tourists. In Chap. 7, Masato Abe and Luisa Pischulti respond to this by considering the concept of "friendship islands". Based on three case studies (Nadi and Suva in Fiji; Samoa and American Samoa; and Palau and the Yap State of FSM), the authors review different models for the "friendship islands" relationship as a starting point for collaboration between countries and territories to more effectively and sustainably promote blue ocean tourism.

In Chap. 8, Tan Farlynda then undertakes a comparative analysis of Bali and Palau to look at how certain small island states have pioneered unique approaches to sustainability that incorporate eco-friendly practices in a range of sectors, including tourism, agriculture, and waste management. These approaches are reviewed with a view to capturing their value both as case studies that can inform action in other island states and for their potential to provide a holistic blueprint for sustainable development more broadly that could be applied in other regions.

Part II closes, in Chap. 9, with a focus on infrastructure development. Scott M. Hook looks particularly at the concept of resilience and what it means in the context of sustainable infrastructure development, concluding with clear recommendations to ensure resilient infrastructure in the face of climate change and natural disasters.

Part III: Planet comprises a series of chapters concentrating directly on the natural environment. Central to the environment in the Pacific island context is, of course, the ocean, and in Chap. 10, M. James C. Crabbe, George R. Barker, Linda Wong, and Jinfeng Zhou take up concerns about the fragility of ocean ecosystems and habitats. Their thorough review addresses the full breadth of threats posed by climate change and human activity, with particular attention paid to the growing fragility of coral reefs and to both the opportunities and the serious environmental concerns associated with deep-sea mining. In relation to the latter, they carefully outline approaches to cost–benefit analysis that account for risk, uncertainty, ignorance, and reversibility, thus offering a way to assess the potential pressures of any human activity that potentially threatens already fragile ocean environments.

In Chap. 11 we turn to another more specific issue that acts as a case study illuminating wider environmental damage and changes, as Kiyoshi Fujimoto, Shin Watanabe, Kenji Ono, and Keita Furukawa look at the present situation of and future threats to mangrove forests resulting from sea level rises. They delineate the factors that have enabled mangrove communities to withstand potential anthropogenic disturbance, at least in some locations, underlining their climate change mitigation value in terms of carbon capture and preventing erosion, and in turn the need for developed-country assistance to protect mangrove plantations going forward.

The concept of Nature-based Solutions, or NbS, has been proposed as the best way to ensure coastal resilience and sustainability, combining natural and engineering counter-measures. In Chap. 12, Akihiko Nonaka, Yoshimitsu Tajima, Tatsuhito Kono, Hiroya Yamano, Tomonori Orita, and Hajime Kayanne offer a comprehensive review of the needs of coastal environments and societies in light of climate change and the potential for NbS to address these needs.

In Part IV: Peace and Partnership, we conclude the volume with two chapters concerned with very different aspects of political cooperation in the Micronesian context. In Chap. 13, Maho Inomata and Masato Abe examine the process through which the former Trust Territory of the Pacific Islands (TTPI) was "decoupled" from United States trusteeship into the five sovereign states (Palau, FSM, Marshall Islands, Nauru, and Kiribati) of Micronesia today. This informs a consideration of how the Micronesian states can both maintain unity at the intra- and inter-state level and cooperate beyond their borders to the benefit of their future resilience and prosperity.

Finally, Chap. 14 revisits a fundamental aspect of the past of Marshall Islands, as Yoshiki Narita and Masato Abe outline the history of nuclear weapons tests in the islands and their legacy, which continues to affect the Marshallese today. The chapter provides a case study of a small nation's attempts to obtain recognition and justice via the United Nations for the harms done in the course of the nuclear tests of the 1940s–1960s and the resulting forced displacement of islanders.

The contributions to this book bring to light the wide range of innovative approaches to development, ways of contending with history, and, of course, responses to current pressing socioeconomic and environmental challenges and those of the future that are deployed across the PICTs. These are important aspects of the past and the future of the Pacific region in and of itself. But beyond that, at a time of rising global geopolitical tensions, "planetary boundaries" that are approaching dangerously fast, the ever more intense quest for inclusive prosperity, and the increasing interdependence among peoples and places, they potentially provide multiple examples of good practice from which other regions and states can learn.

Zhuhai, China

Edoardo Monaco
emonaco@uic.edu.cn

Kolonia, Federated States of Micronesia

Masato Abe

Contents

Editors and Contributors

About the Editors

Edoardo Monaco is an Asia-based international development and sustainability specialist. He currently serves as an associate professor and the acting head of the Department of Social Sciences (DSS), Faculty of Humanities and Social Sciences (FHSS), at the Beijing Normal University–Hong Kong Baptist University United International College (BNU-HKBU UIC) in Zhuhai, Guangdong Province, China. His interests lie in comparative development and the rise of the Global South, with particular regard to innovation for sustainable development; economic growth, diversification, and inclusion; South–South cooperation; Small Island Developing States (SIDS); and Least Developed Countries (LDCs). Edoardo regularly collaborates with intergovernmental organizations, prominent think tanks, and global media platforms. He has been a member of the China Association of the Club of Rome since 2021 and a research fellow at the United Nations Multi-Country Office for Micronesia since 2023.

Masato Abe is the economist of the United Nations Multi-Country Office for Micronesia, Kolonia, Pohnpei, Federated States of Micronesia (FSM). He has extensive experience in enterprise development and financing for development with a special emphasis on the micro, small, and medium-sized enterprise (MSME) sector, global value chains, disaster risk reduction, and access to finance. Before joining the secretariat of the United Nations, he worked in the global automotive, electronics, and high-technology industries. He has published numerous books, book chapters, journal articles, policy papers, and other writings for various outlets. He holds marketing, business administration, and economics degrees and is a research fellow at Thammasat University, Bangkok; a visiting lecturer at Waseda University, Tokyo; and a special lecturer at Naresuan University, Phitsanulok.

Contributors

Masato Abe United Nations Multi-Country Office for Micronesia, Kolonia, Pohnpei, Federated States of Micronesia

Adrian J. Bailey Beijing Normal University–Hong Kong Baptist University United International College, Zhuhai, China

George R. Barker Wolfson College, Oxford University, Oxford, UK

M. James C. Crabbe Wolfson College, Oxford University, Oxford, UK

Tan Farlynda Murdoch University, Murdoch, Australia

Jason Flello Kiribati Institute of Technology, Betio, Kiribati

Nick Freeman Lafayette, California, United States

Kiyoshi Fujimoto Nanzan University, Nagoya, Japan

Keita Furukawa Association for Shore Environment Creation, Yokohama, Japan

Valentine Hazelman Kiribati Institute of Technology, Betio, Kiribati

Scott M. Hook Principal Economist, Economics, Policy and Ideas, Brisbane, Australia

Maho Inomata Embassy of Japan, Federated States of Micronesia, Kolonia, Micronesia

Hajime Kayanne The University of Tokyo, Tokyo, Japan

Tatsuhito Kono Tohoku University, Sendai, Japan

Yoshiki Narita United Nations Multi-Country Office for Micronesia, Kolonia, Micronesia

Akihiko Nonaka Nikken Sekkei Ltd., Tokyo, Japan

Sandy O'Brien Kiribati Institute of Technology, Betio, Kiribati

Kenji Ono Tohoku Research Center, Forestry and Forest Products Research Institute, Morioka, Japan

Tomonori Orita Ministry of the Environment of Japan (MOEJ), Tokyo, Japan

Luisa Pischulti Waseda University, Tokyo, Japan

Sabrina Regmi New York, USA

Nikisha Smith United Nations Multi-Country Office for Micronesia, Kolonia, Micronesia;
Charles Darwin University, Darwin, Australia

Yoshimitsu Tajima The University of Tokyo, Tokyo, Japan

Marieta Tekabu Kiribati Institute of Technology, Betio, Kiribati

Bannau Tiiata Kiribati Institute of Technology, Betio, Kiribati

Agnieszka Wang United Nations Multi-Country Office for Micronesia, Kolonia, Pohnpei, Micronesia

Shin Watanabe Tropical Biosphere Research Center, University of the Ryukyus, Taketomi, Japan

Linda Wong China Biodiversity Conservation and Green Development Foundation, Beijing, China

Hiroya Yamano The University of Tokyo, Tokyo, Japan;
National Institute for Environmental Studies (NIES), Tsukuba, Japan

Jinfeng Zhou China Biodiversity Conservation and Green Development Foundation, Beijing, China

Jialing Zou Guangdong University of Foreign Studies, Guangzhou, China

Part I
People

Chapter 1
Migration Among the Freely Associated States in Micronesia: Trends, Drivers, and Implications

Masato Abe and Agnieszka Wang

Abstract According to their Compact of Free Association agreements with the United States, citizens of Palau, Federated States of Micronesia, and Marshall Islands are allowed to enter the United States and live, study, and work there as if they were Americans. Despite the impediments and threats of living abroad, many Micronesians have emigrated. This chapter analyses economic, educational, healthcare, and other migration drivers that push many citizens of the "freely associated states", including the youth, out of their home countries to pursue better income and life opportunities. The chapter describes Micronesians' life in the United States, often characterized by poverty, discrimination, and lack of assistance from the host country. We also discuss the measures that the three freely associated states could take to mitigate the outflow of their citizens.

1.1 Introduction

Outflows of Micronesians, including many young people, have been a severe issue. Palau, Federated States of Micronesia (FSM), and Marshall Islands are "freely associated states" (FASs) under Compact of Free Association (CoFA) agreements with the United States. The three countries share the everyday challenges of Small Island Developing States (SIDS) and face other challenges specific to their histories, geographies, societies, and economies. Their development opportunities are challenged by size, isolation, distance, infrastructure, and climate. They struggle to deliver quality education, and the healthcare systems and their coverage are inadequate, particularly given the prevalence of non-communicable diseases (NCDs) in Micronesia. Poverty is widespread, and the region has limited social protection programmes. Well-paying jobs and decent work are absent, particularly in the private sector. All of these factors contribute to growing outward migration in Micronesia.

M. Abe (✉) · A. Wang
United Nations Multi-Country Office for Micronesia, Kolonia, Pohnpei, Micronesia
e-mail: abem@un.org

E. Monaco and M. Abe (eds.), *Sustainable Development Across Pacific Islands*,
https://doi.org/10.1007/978-981-97-3629-4_1

The citizens of the three FASs often search for better living conditions and options in the United States. One apparent reason is the CoFA agreements since the end of the 1980s. Under the CoFAs, Micronesian people can freely move to the United States, without a requirement to obtain a visa, and access study and employment on par with American citizens. Once this arrangement was in place, people quickly took the opportunity to migrate to the United States and pursue their lives there, with remittances being sent back to their families at home. As a result, the FASs have experienced depopulation. In this context, the FASs must better understand the situation with regard to migration and consider what they can do to bring renewed perspectives to people and incentivize them to contribute to the future of their countries from within. This may require improvements in various socioeconomic and environmental domains within the nations, to lessen their citizens' desire to move overseas. However, these issues do not currently appear to be well debated.

This chapter assesses the FASs' history, population, and migration, which show distinct characteristics.[1] It addresses the crucial attributes that encourage citizens' outward migration, before presenting policy and practical implications.

1.2 The Freely Associated States of the Northern Pacific: Palau, Federated States of Micronesia, and Marshall Islands

Palau, FSM, and Marshall Islands, three of 57 countries and territories classified by the United Nations as SIDS, encompass a maritime expanse surpassing the land area of the continental United States. Between them they govern more than 1000 islands and atolls, sustaining a population of approximately 170,000. Like numerous other Pacific island countries and territories (PICTs), these states encounter structural challenges such as insufficient economies of scale, compact land area, restricted natural and human resources, remote location, inadequate infrastructure, and susceptibility to climate change. In 2021, Palau, Marshall Islands, and FSM rank 118th ($12,084), 162nd ($6728), and 192nd ($3741) out of 229 countries by gross domestic product per capita (Congressional Research Services 2023; World Bank 2023). Palau and Marshall Islands are categorized as upper-middle-income countries, while FSM is a lower-middle-income country. Like many other PICTs, they heavily rely on grants and loans from other countries and organizations, especially from the United States. The countries' primary income comes from selling fishing licences (FSM and Marshall Islands) and from tourism (Palau). Due to the small production base, they heavily depend on imports of food, clothes, and other goods, leading to a large and constant trade deficit. After the Second World War, the United Nations granted the United States administrative authority over Micronesia, formerly under Japan's control, as the Trust Territory of the Pacific Islands (TTPI), whereby the three FASs

[1] Jaap van Hierden suggested this study. Christian Viegelahn and Maryann Eperiam provided useful information for the study.

were administered until their independence in the 1980s/90s. Unlike under Japanese rule, this time there was no significant emphasis on developing the infrastructure and private sector that could sustain the countries' growth and reduce their dependence on foreign aid. The so-called "zoo policy" allowed local people to maintain their culture and ways of life while the islands were closed to international trade and direct foreign investment (FDI) (Hezel 1995). Consequently, Micronesian living standards dropped quickly (Andrews 2017). Development policies were based predominately on the security interests of the United States (Andrews 2017).

The three countries separately signed the original CoFAs with the United States, establishing formal dependency ties as the FASs of the Northern Pacific. The CoFAs came into effect in 1986 for FSM and Marshall Islands and in 1995 for Palau. Each CoFA granted economic assistance for a 15-year duration. In 2003, FSM and Marshall Islands entered into agreements to extend Compact assistance from the United States for an additional 20 years. Regarding Palau, an agreement in 2010 stipulated ongoing support from the United States, but the formal authorization for total funding was signed only in 2018 (Congressional Research Services 2023). The latest (third) CoFAs were signed in 2023, with financial assistance of $7.1 billion for the three nations' development over the next 20 years, assuring slightly over $2000 per capita annually (Guardian 2023). Under the CoFAs, the three countries are granted permission for their citizens to enter the United States and live, study, and work there without needing visas and for an indefinite period (US Government Accountability Office 2020). In return, the United States takes full responsibility for the security and defence of the FASs. This entitles the United States to deny third countries access to or use of FAS territories, airspace, and territorial seas, and to retain the option to establish military bases on the islands (USIP 2022). In the past four decades, the unique relationship and permitted emigration have significantly influenced the island countries' population, society, and economy.

1.3 The Population

During the US administration of the TTPI, the FAS population grew rapidly until the end of the 1990s (Fig. 1.1). The high birth rate and plummeting death rate contributed to the population growth (Hezel 2010). This is mainly attributed to the introduction and widespread availability of contemporary medical advancements and healthcare technology and improved dietary practices during the immediate aftermath of the Second World War. These factors collectively played a pivotal role in enabling the FASs to manage numerous diseases endured before the war (Grieco 2003). During this period, however, NCDs became prevalent in the FAS due to changed diets and the dominance of imported low-nutrition foods (Hezel 2010).

Palau saw an increase in its population from fewer than 10,000 in 1960 to nearly 20,000 in 2004. Since 2004, the nation has experienced stagnating or declining trends, and the current population is around 18,000. The population of FSM increased from 43,000 in 1960 to 112,000 in 2002. During the 2000s, the country recorded

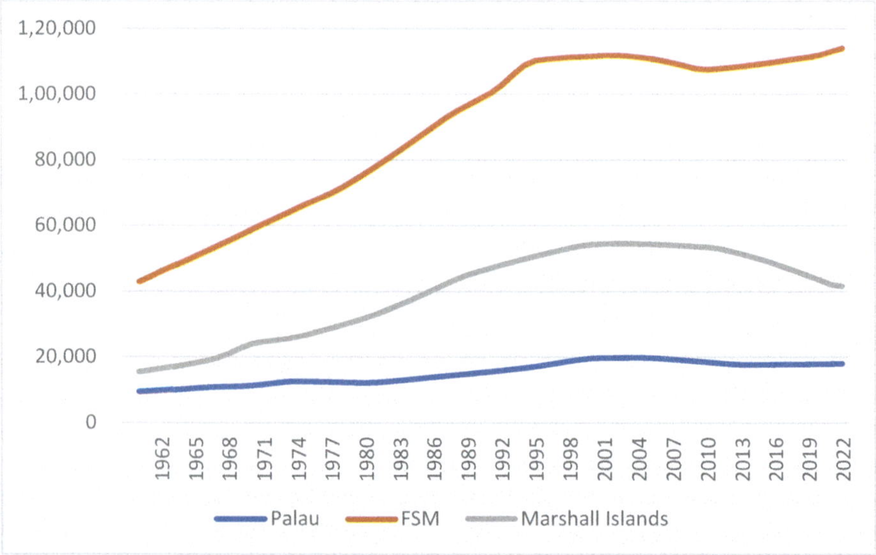

Fig. 1.1 FAS population, 1960–2022. *Source* Authors' illustration based on World Bank (2023)

negative population growth caused mainly by out-migration, with the population decreasing to 108,000 in 2010 before growing to an estimated 114,000 in 2022. After population growth until the early 2000s, reaching nearly 55,000, Marshall Islands also experienced stagnation and decline, losing over 20% of its population in the last decade (to 42,000 in 2022). This shared trend among the three countries is partially due to decreasing birth and fertility rates (Fig. 1.2). However, migration has also significantly impacted populations, rapidly decreasing demographic dividends in the future.

Many FAS households live in poverty, while inequality is less observed.[2] For example, the most recent national data for FSM shows that in 2019, approximately 40% of the population lived below the national poverty line while 15% lived below the international poverty line of $1.90 per day (purchasing power parity—PPP; World

[2] The Gini index measures the extent to which the distribution of income or consumption among individuals or households within an economy deviates from a perfectly equal distribution. A Gini index of 0 represents perfect equality, while an index of 100 implies perfect inequality. The Gini index is 40.1 for FSM (2013 data), 35.5 for Marshall Islands (2019 data); Gini is not available for Palau.

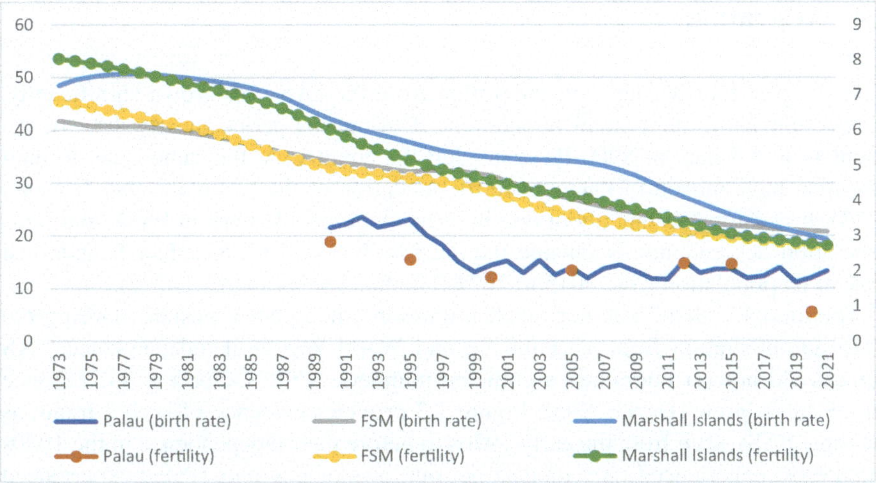

Fig. 1.2 Birth and fertility rates of FAS. *Note* Birth rate is per 1000 people; fertility rate is the number of births per woman. *Source* Authors' illustration based on World Bank (2023)

Bank 2019).[3] In Marshall Islands, the high levels of poverty and hunger are considered the main reasons for the most recent migration wave. About 40% of households indicate that they have "run out of food" and have "skip[ped] a meal". With over one in three households reporting that they "go without eating for a whole day", it is unlikely that the pace of out-migration will decline soon (Pacific Community and Marshall Islands EPPOSO 2022, pp. 74–75).

Across the FASs, nearly 80% of the entire population live in rural areas and support themselves through subsistence. In towns, employment centres around the government and the small commercial sector (US Department of State 2022). Subsistence farming remains a standard means of livelihood. However, the growing volume of and dependence on imported commercial goods suggests that people want more than a subsistence lifestyle. But such spending on imported goods requires substantial additional income, creating another migration pressure.

[3] The national poverty statistics for FSM for 2013/14 used a "cost of basic needs" approach to establish a welfare benchmark for the national poverty line, which comprises a food poverty line (FPL) and a non-food poverty line (NFPL). The FPL is estimated using a basket of goods based on the consumption of the bottom four deciles in the distribution. The NFPL uses the average non-food consumption of households. The international poverty line is a monetary threshold. It is calculated by taking the poverty threshold from each country—given the value of goods needed to sustain one adult—and converting it into US dollars.

1.4 Migration

Over the past four decades, out-migration from the FASs has grown significantly, heavily impacting their small populations. During this period, nearly 40% of the population of Palau, or 8000 Palauans, left the country. At the same time, foreign labourers have moved to Palau since the inception of the CoFA in 1994 (Kesolei 2023). It is estimated that about one in every three people born in FSM (and first-generation descendants) is outside the islands (IOM 2016). Marshall Islands lost 15% of its population from 2015 to 2021 (Graduate School USA 2022a).

Traditionally, there was not much migration among Micronesians. During the TTPI administration from after the Second World War until independence, FAS citizens did not yet migrate in significant numbers, while socioeconomic reliance on US funds grew (Hezel 1995). Figure 1.3 provides evidence of such a trend, as the three FASs, seen from the early 1970s to before their independence in the 1980s and 1990s, experienced only modest net outflows of migrants (Palau experienced positive inflows after 1981 due to its tourism boom).

All three countries experienced the temporary migration of their youth during the 1970s, thanks to US scholarships for college education under the Basic Educational Opportunity Grant or the Federal Pell Grant (Hezel 1995). As shown in Fig. 1.3, during this period most of the Micronesian students returned to their home countries after graduation, against the common belief that college graduates tend not to return

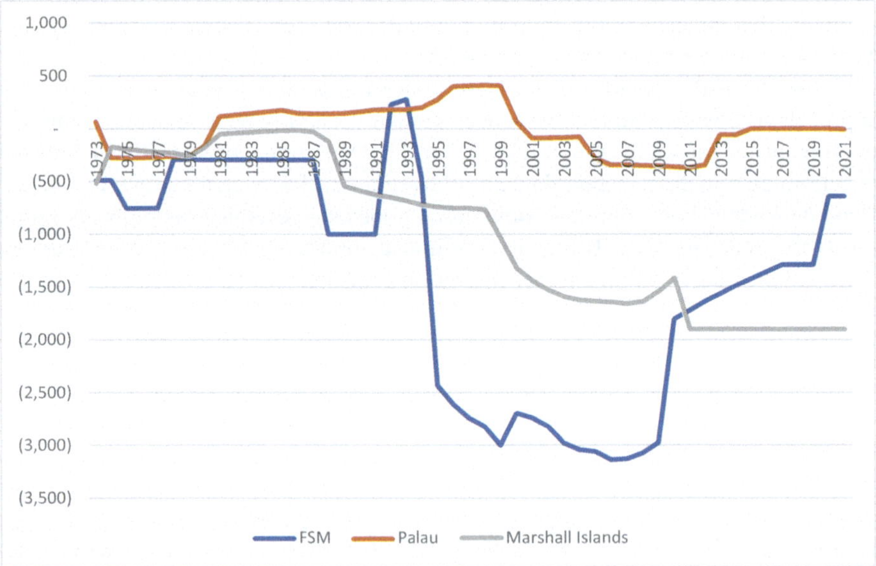

Fig. 1.3 FAS net migration, 1973–2021. *Note* Net migration is the number of emigrants minus the number of immigrants, including citizens and non-citizens. *Source* Authors' illustration based on World Bank (2023)

(Hezel 2001). Education abroad also created an over-education problem in that the number of educated FAS citizens abroad is higher than the number of formal wage jobs that governments and the private sector can offer within the FAS (Hezel 2001).

The noticeable growth in out-migration occurred after the signing of the first CoFAs for FSM and Marshall Islands in 1986 (Fig. 1.3). For example, Hezel (2013) reports that emigration from FSM was intensified after the CoFA came into effect in 1986, initially to Guam and the Commonwealth of Northern Mariana Islands (CNMI) and later to Hawaii and the mainland United States. In addition to the CoFA's free migration policy, two other US policies were essential in creating this mobility (Grieco 2003). First, the infusion of US funds to develop a wage economy undermined the subsistence economy that predominated in the FASs until the 1960s. This increased the importance of wage jobs and encouraged labour mobility, and thus emigration under the CoFA. Second, the policy of universal education and the development of the education infrastructure led to an education explosion in the 1980s and 1990s, dramatically increasing the number of high school and college students who sought opportunities for further education and paid jobs. Thus, although well intentioned, these two policies of the United States helped to create a FAS population that was increasingly wage dependent, educated, unemployed or underemployed, and mobile (Grieco 2003). Combined with the slow economic development of the FASs, these trends created a "surplus" population and, for the countries, a difficulty in discouraging their labour from international migration (Rajaram 2018).

During the early 1990s, however, the level of out-migration was stable, and fewer people moved to the United States. FSM's temporary inward migration hike in 1992/93 was mainly due to the economic slowdown in Guam and CNMI (i.e., there were fewer visitors and fewer exports in the tourism and garment sectors) (Laney 2008; US Government Accountability Office 2000). The record shows a massive increase in out-migration since 1995 in FSM and after 1999 in Marshall Islands. Over 4,000 people left the two countries combined in the year 2000, when the Compacts were about to come to an end and people were unsure what the result of the new CoFA negotiations would be. Figure 1.3 also illustrates that the 1997/98 Asian financial crisis impacted FSM's outward migration briefly, and the 2007/08 global financial crisis reduced outward migration from FSM and Marshall Islands while modest emigration was maintained in Palau due to slowdowns in its tourism sector, which were caused by the recession in regional and global markets. FSM's numbers of emigrants continuously decreased during the 2010s owing to the economic sluggishness of their primary destinations, Guam, Hawaii, and CNMI, and further dropped during the COVID-19 pandemic in 2020 when travel became more difficult or impossible. Figure 1.4 presents the emigration stock of the three FASs, illustrating the gradual growth in numbers of outward migrants since the early 1990s with a further increase in the last decade.

Figure 1.5 illustrates the significance of the FASs' outward migration as a share of their population. While in Palau the emigration share in the population gradually decreased and was then maintained at less than 15% after 2005, in FSM and Marshall Islands the volume of emigration in proportion their populations gradually increased. It is particularly noticeable that after an initial hike during the 1990s and early 2000s,

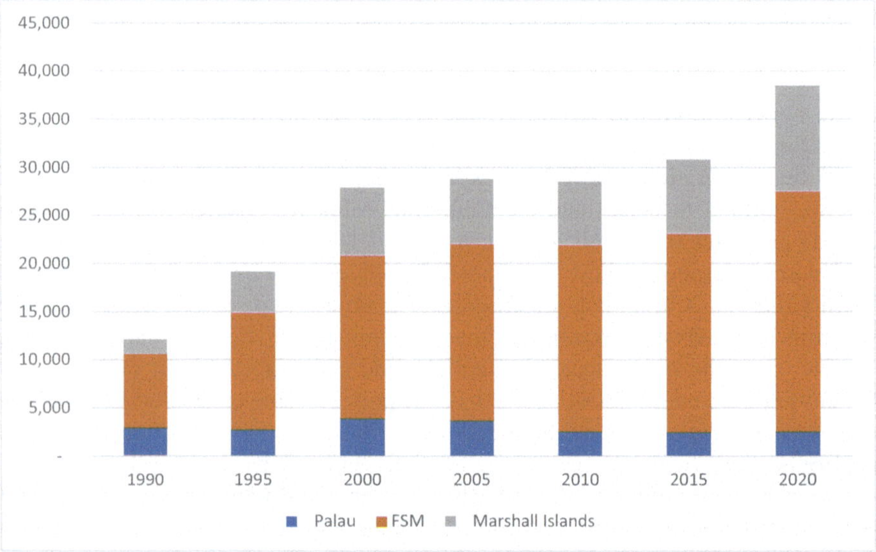

Fig. 1.4 FASs' emigration stocks. *Source* Authors' illustration based on UNDESA Population Division (2020)

Mashall Islands saw drastically increased numbers of outward migrants while its population decreased (see Fig. 1.1 again).

It is predominantly young people who migrate. For example, in 2020 and 2021 the average age of migrants from FSM was 25 and the median was 28 (Government of FSM 2023). In 2019, 66% of survey participants at the College of Micronesia-FSM expressed a desire to migrate (Moriya 2019).[4] Also in 2019, 44% of students at the University of the South Pacific (USP) campus in Marshall Islands indicated an aspiration to move abroad (Yoshioka et al. 2019). The eagerness to migrate among the younger generation is particularly worrisome for the FASs. It has been argued that the brain drain, or loss of many of the most productive citizens as they move and remain overseas, may be the most noteworthy development challenge for the FASs (Grieco 2003).[5]

Owing to the convenient regulations that allow FAS citizens to establish residency in the United States, the latter became a top destination for migration. In 2018, more than 94,000 migrants from all FASs and their US-born children and grandchildren younger than 18 lived and worked in the United States and its territories (US Government Accountability Office 2020). Historically, many CoFA migrants lived in US territories, such as Hawaii, Guam, and CNMI, closer to their home islands. This has changed and in 2018, it was estimated that half of FAS migrants were living on the US mainland (Fig. 1.6). The total number of FAS migrants in the United States

[4] The survey included approximately 200 respondents.

[5] Brain drain occurs when migrants take their skills and initiative to their new countries of residence.

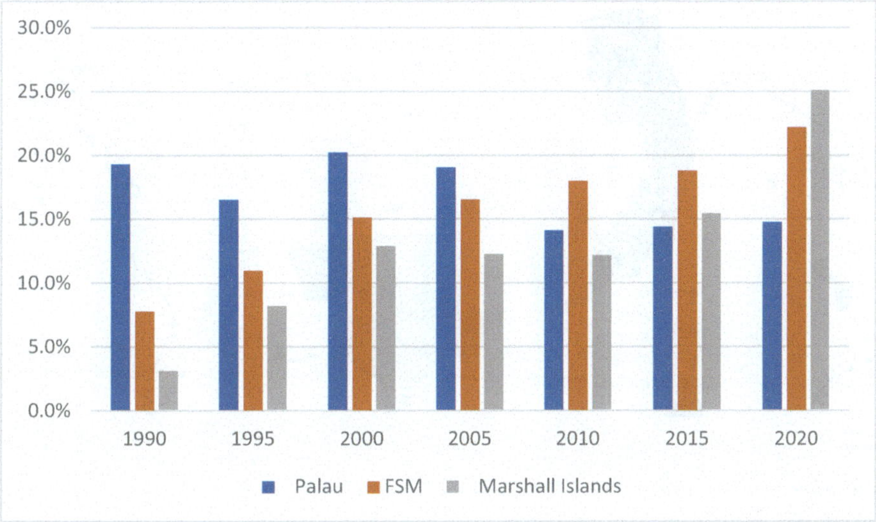

Fig. 1.5 FASs' emigration stocks as a percentage of the population. *Source* Authors' illustration based on UNDESA Population Division (2020)

has grown by about 70% in the last decade (US Government Accountability Office 2020). Figure 6 also presents the population of FAS migrants in the states and territories of the United States. Four clusters emerge: (i) Guam, Hawaii, and CNMI; (ii) West Coast; (iii) Arkansas and its neighbouring states; and (iv) South East. Arkansas has attracted nearly 6,000 Marshallese low-skilled labourers (mainly for the poultry industry) and their family members (US Government Accountability Office 2020).

The FASs have also received many foreign migrants compared with their small populations (Fig. 1.7). Palau has a high percentage of foreign population due to its tourism and services sectors: in 2020, foreigners accounted for nearly a third of the country's population, nearly two-thirds of them Filipinos (Graduate School USA 2023). The trend of foreign migration aligns with Palau's economy and is driven mainly by tourist receipts. FSM received foreign migrants from various countries, including other Compact states, neighbouring small island states, and the United States, but numbers have gradually declined, suggesting that FSM has become less reliant on immigrants. Marshall Islands, on the other hand, has rapidly increased its dependence on foreign labourers, filling the gap created by the reducing population in the past decades. Americans and Filipinos are the major nationalities, besides Chinese and other neighbouring islanders.

It is expected that the third CoFAs (2023–2043) will maintain the present outward migration levels while increasing inflows of foreign workers (Asian Development Bank 2023a, b, c). This is because: (i) the newly agreed Compact assistance will increase the number of government-related formal wage jobs; (ii) such new jobs will require skilled-labourer posts which cannot be quickly filled locally; (iii) the Compact assistance (both financial and technical) will not greatly impact real economic or

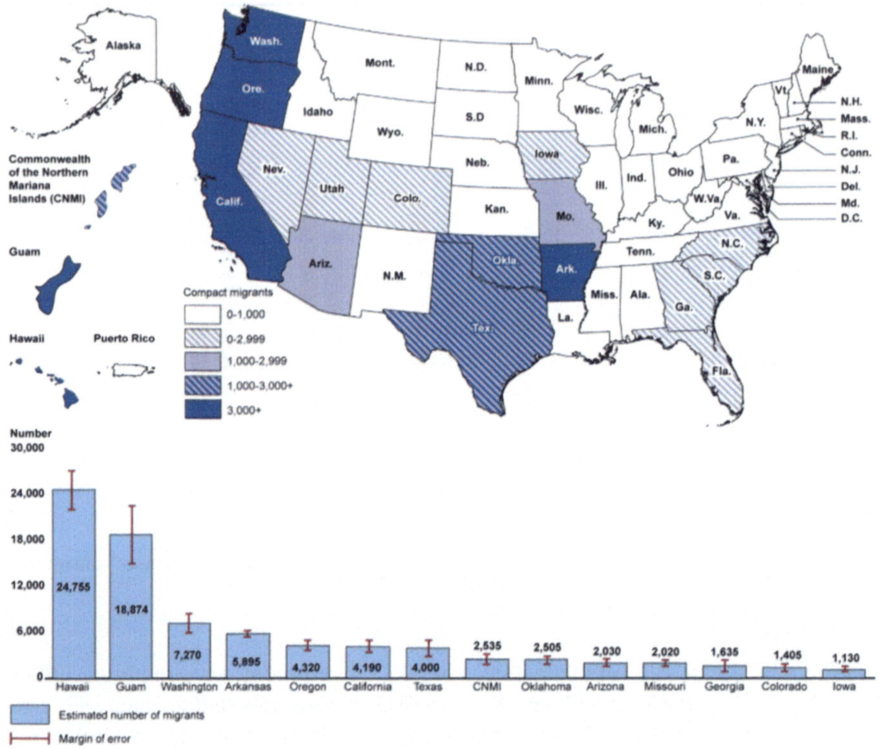

Fig. 1.6 FAS migrant populations in US territories, 2013–18. *Source* Reproduced from US Government Accountability Office (2020, p. 16)

private sector growth and development while further expanding the government's role in the economy, something which has been observed in Micronesia in the past 40 years; and (iv) as a result, FAS citizens in disadvantaged positions (e.g., people in rural and outer islands and low education attainers) will continue to face relative poverty and widening inequality, which will drive outward migration. There is an urgent need to dismiss this vicious cycle under the CoFAs.

1.5 The Drivers

The drivers associated with the decision to migrate and the process of migration are divided into the following four categories: (i) factors associated with the country of origin; (ii) factors associated with the country of destination; (iii) intervening obstacles; and (iv) personal factors. In each driver, there are numerous factors that act to drive people away from the country, hold people in the area, or attract people

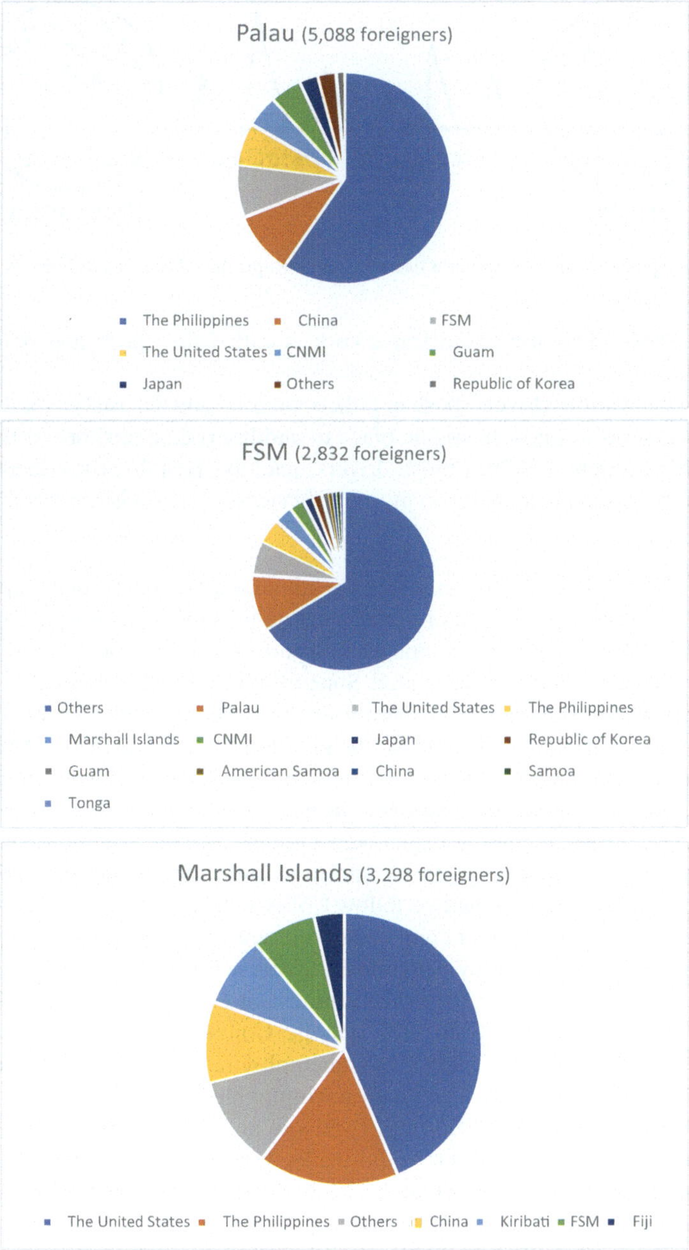

Fig. 1.7 Foreign immigrants in the FASs, 2020. *Source* Authors' illustration based on UNDESA Population Division (2020)

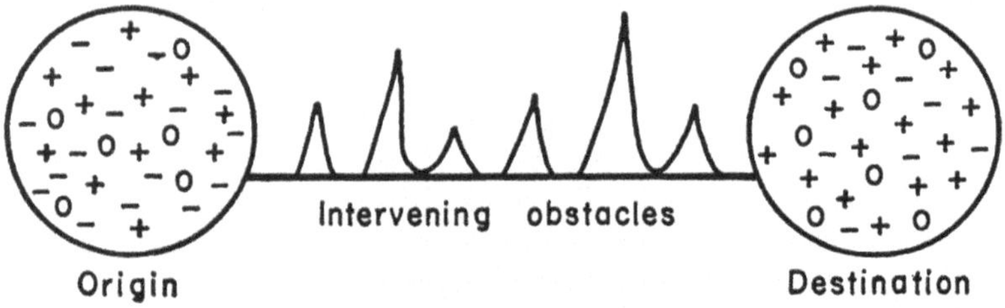

Fig. 1.8 The "push and pull" migration theory. *Source* Reproduced from Lee (1966, p. 50)

to it (Lee 1966). This migration framework is called the "push and pull" theory (Fig. 1.8).

In the FASs, various drivers (push or pull, or internal and external) have influenced people's decisions to move from one place to another (i.e., a territory of the United States). This section describes those drivers, namely: (i) jobs; (ii) education; (iii) healthcare; (iv) climate change; (v) military services; (vi) gravity; and (vii) family.

A. **Jobs**

In the FASs, the public sector dominates the labour market and formal employment, struggling to foster a private sector that can create jobs in the economy. This lack of formal wage jobs has been the single most significant factor encouraging people's migration predominantly to the United States. Figure 1.9 illustrates this trend by comparing the government's contribution to the economy with that of the neighbouring countries in the Pacific. While the private sector of the three FASs is more active than in some neighbouring countries, such as Kiribati, Nauru, and Tuvalu, governments play a more dominant role in the FASs' economies than in those of many other countries, including Papua New Guinea, Samoa, Solomon Islands, Fiji, and Tonga. Understandably, given its vital tourism sector, Palau has more active private sector activities than the two fellow CoFA states.

High levels of unemployment and underemployment have encouraged people to migrate outward. The unemployment rate for adults in FSM has gradually decreased, from 22% in 2005 to 16% in 2019 (Government of FSM 2020). Marshall Islands' unemployment rate was 10% in 2021 (Pacific Community and Marshall Islands EPPOSO 2022). Palau has a stable, low unemployment rate of about one percent (Government of Palau 2020). The youth unemployment rate in FSM and Marshall Islands remains high at 25% (ILO 2021; Clarke and Azzopardi 2019), while it is three percent in Palau (ILO 2021). Additionally, 32% of young people aged 15 to 24 in Marshall Islands, 29% in FSM, and 17% in Palau are not engaged in education, employment, or training (NEET) (Clarke and Azzopardi 2019; Pacific Community and Marshall Islands EPPOSO 2022). If NEET-Plus[6] is applied, the rate increases to 54% in FSM and 13% in Palau. Because of difficulties finding satisfactory wage

[6] NEET-Plus is a youth category comprising NEET and other "youth who work in unpaid employment and who are looking for paid work and are able and willing to take such work if it is available" (Clarke and Azzopardi 2019, p. 97).

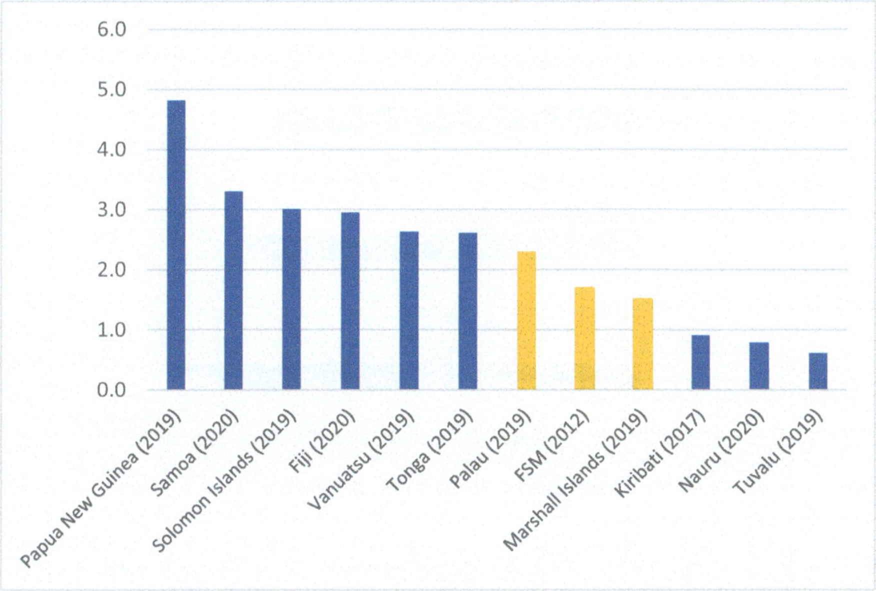

Fig. 1.9 The government's contribution to the economy. *Note* The figure shows how many times larger than GDP the national budget is. The higher this number, the larger the private sector. *Source* Authors' illustration based on World Bank (2023)

work, people take the opportunity to search for more reliable jobs and higher wages in the United States. Weak job creation in the private sector has pushed FAS citizens to choose to migrate to the United States.

The FAS labour market has three distinct characteristics. First, it is a mixture of formal employment (i.e., salaried jobs with various benefits and protection), a large informal sector (often part-time or seasonal jobs without benefits and protection), and a persistent subsistence economy (often drawing on non-paid family or kinship labour). Such a structure cannot be changed quickly, as it is based on culture, norms, and values (Hezel 2013). Second, there are considerable gender disparities in job opportunities and salaries (e.g., numbers, quality, and skill requirements). Often, women undertake unpaid and traditionally assigned family care obligations and responsibilities. They remain under-represented in the national congress, cabinet, and senior leadership positions, earn less than men,[7] and have limited career choices (UN Women 2022a, b, c). Third, while the government has been the primary employer for many years, significant sectoral disparities exist among government offices, businesses, and others (e.g., non-governmental or civil society organizations). The

[7] Palau is an exception regarding salary equality. According to the census, women earn six percent more than men in higher positions and eight percent more in medium-level positions (Pacific Community 2023a).

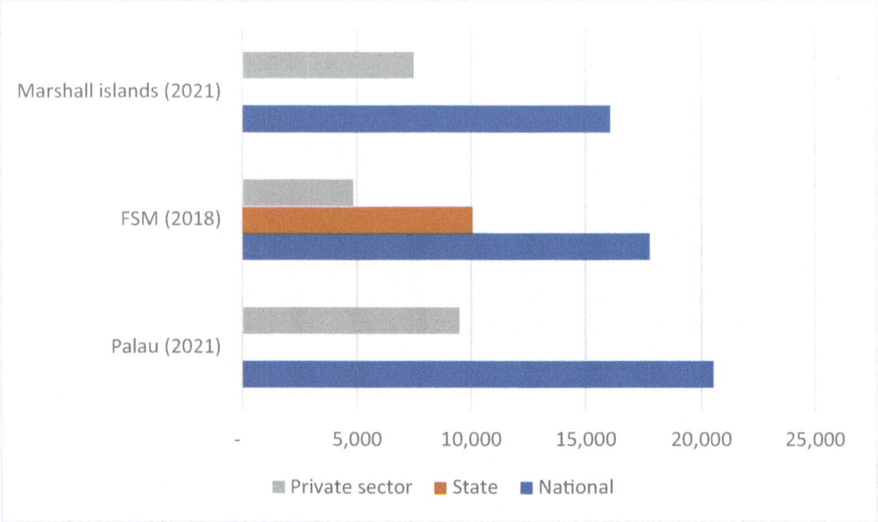

Fig. 1.10 Latest average wages in the public and private sectors, Palau, FSM, and Marshall Islands. *Source* Authors' illustration based on Graduate School USA (2019, 2021b, 2023)

Table 1.1 FSM's minimum wages

Sector	Hourly minimum wage
Private sector on Pohnpei	$1.75
Federal government	$2.65
Pohnpei State government	$2.00
Chuuk State government	$1.25
Kosrae State government	$1.42
Yap State government	$1.60

Note When interviewed on the private sector minimum wage, some local business owners said $3.00 per hour on Pohnpei (October 2023); the interviews suggested that an ordinal worker in Kolonia, Pohnpei, could get $10 to $25 per day depending on their work and employer.
Source US Department of State (2022)

government's pay is estimated to be two to three times higher than that of the private sector, given the abundant Compact money (Fig. 1.10).[8]

Minimum wages are often considered a tool to reduce income gaps among different socioeconomic groups and reduce the desire to migrate. Table 1.1 presents FSMs' minimum hourly wages, adjusted on 1 January 2015 (US Department of State 2022).

[8] In the United States, federal workers earned nearly a quarter less than their private sector counterparts in 2021 (Wagner 2022).

Raising the minimum wage appears to be a crucial policy option, as workers in the private sector typically neither receive health benefits nor take sick, family, or maternity leave, and they do not participate in the social security system. In this context, the Pohnpei State Legislature has passed a bill to increase the minimum wage on Pohnpei by 45% as of November 2023. The bill is waiting for the governor to sign it into law. Palau also plans to increase its minimum wage, from $3.50 to $5.00 or more, in the public and private sectors (Graduate School USA 2021a). However, this minimum wage increase is expected to raise the prices of items consumed in Palau and the cost of tourism, leading to reduced market demand (Graduate School USA 2021a).

In Palau, tourism and related services sectors (e.g., accommodation, retailing, and construction) dominate private businesses, making it an important economic centre besides the government. For example, the growth of tourist receipts significantly impacts employment in the private sector (Fig. 1.11). This situation strongly suggests that Palau's job markets are divided into two sectors: public jobs and tourism-related work.

B. **Education**

FAS migrants' profile suggests that there is not a brain drain. An estimate shows that almost 30% of them had no diploma, while only 12% held associate's, bachelor's, graduate or professional degrees (US Government Accountability Office 2020). Among FSM migrants in Hawaii in 2012, five per cent held a bachelor's degree or higher, while on the mainland, six percent had a full college degree (Hezel and Levin

Fig. 1.11 Tourist receipts and private sector employment. *Source* Authors' illustration based on Graduate School USA (2023)

2012). Rather, the FASs have lost many low-skilled labourers, especially younger generations, to the United States.

Those labourers who have emigrated from the FASs have attained substandard academic training. The education system in the FASs, following the American academic curriculum, has faced various challenges that can result in subpar academic achievements and constrain individuals' future opportunities (US Commission on Civil Rights 2019). Public schools tend to exhibit lower academic performance than private schools, leading to a significant discrepancy in the quality of education offered (Hezel 2001; Ministry of Education of Marshall Islands 2014). Attaining a minimum proficiency level in numeracy and literacy presents a formidable challenge for students in FASs. Test outcomes in both primary and secondary schools consistently underscore the limited knowledge and skills of the students in these crucial areas (Pacific Community 2018). Many teachers are not certified to teach at the global standards. While the three countries have some teachers with higher qualifications, these comprise a relatively small percentage of the teaching population. This situation suggests that the United States has accepted FAS migrants mainly for entry-level or unskilled low-paid labour jobs which require neither an academic diploma nor vocational training. FAS families also move to the United States in order that their children can access better education on all levels than is offered in their home countries (US Government Accountability Office 2020).

In 2013 and 2014, as many as 7.9% of FSM's population aged six or above had never attended school. Only 43.0% of those aged 21 or above had completed secondary education, while only 10.6% had graduated from tertiary or vocational schools (Government of FSM n.d.).[9] In Yap State, many teachers possess only a high school diploma, while only one teacher across all four FSM states has a degree in early childhood education (Government of FSM 2020, 2022). In Marshall Islands (2021), about 61% of the population have finished secondary education, and only five per cent have completed tertiary education at the highest level (Pacific Community, 2023b). In Palau, five per cent of the population above the age of 25 have only elementary educational attainment, 48% have a high school diploma or vocational education, and 43% have college education or associate's, bachelor's, or professional degrees (Government of Palau 2020).

The lack of fully fledged higher education encourages FAS students to migrate for their advanced studies. The FASs' higher education comprises three post-secondary national colleges (comparable to community colleges in the American education system) that offer only associate degrees (and select bachelor's degrees in business and nursing).[10] These colleges were developed based on the higher education structure designed and implemented during the TTPI era. Since its establishment in 1952, the University of Guam a US public university, has been a focal-point higher education institution as the regional university in Micronesia, while the three community colleges send their well-performing students to Guam and other US territories.

[9] FSM conducted a household income and expenditure survey in 2013 and 2014.

[10] In addition, the USP has a satellite campus on Majuro, Marshall Islands, offering select bachelor's degrees and vocational training courses (mainly online).

Figure 1.12 gives an overview of the current education structure of the seven former TTPI districts (i.e., Northern Mariana Islands; Palau; Yap; Truck, now Chuuk; Ponape, now Pohnpei; Kusaie, now Kosrae; and Marshall Islands) and Guam under the US administration. The academic programmes of their colleges are still limited; hence, wealthier students often choose to study abroad, usually at universities in Guam, Hawaii, or the mainland United States. High-performing students can also apply for abundant US and local scholarships. Various bilateral and private scholarships and training programmes are also sponsored by Australia, China, Japan, New Zealand, Republic of Korea, the United States, Taiwan Province of China, and others. While these students can choose to stay and work abroad after graduation, the number of such students has not been as high as people believe unless other factors are considered, such as family reasons (e.g., group migration and healthcare needs) and marriages (Hezel 2013).

C. **Healthcare**

The FASs face massive challenges in providing decent healthcare services to their citizens, forcing them to seek such services outside their countries and pressuring them to consider outward migration (US Government Accountability Office 2020). Elderly FAS citizens often need to find necessary healthcare services in Hawaii, Guam, the Philippines, Fiji, or Singapore, depending on their illnesses, budgets, convenience, and, most importantly, access to public health insurance—for example, under the US

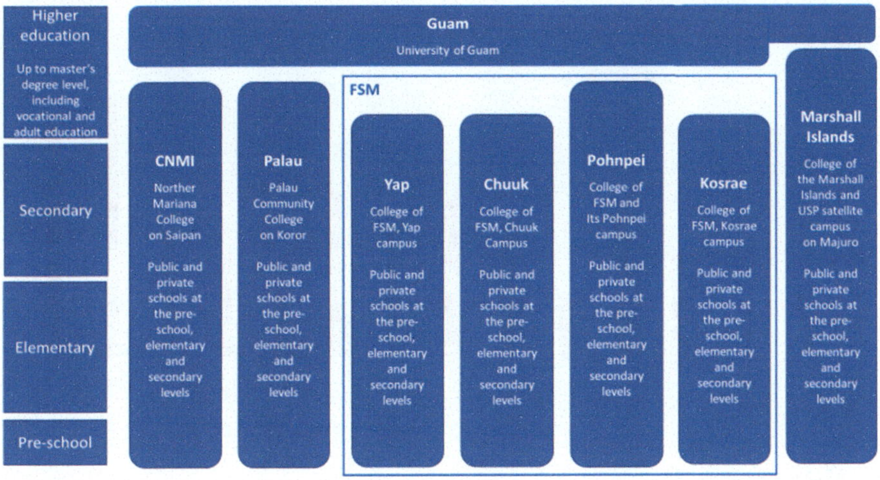

Fig. 1.12 The education structure of the former TTPI districts and Guam. *Notes* In relation to Guam, only its four-year public college, the University of Guam, which offers limited undergraduate and graduate degrees, is shown; the University of Guam neither has professional schools (e.g., medicine and law) nor offers doctorate degrees, for which students must attend schools in Hawaii and the mainland United States; two small and relatively new private colleges in Guam—Guam Community College and Pacific Islands Bible College—are excluded. *Source* Authors' illustration based on the websites of the institutions mentioned in the figure

Patient Protection and Affordable Care Act (Ng Kamstra et al. 2021). Some medical procedures, e.g., dialysis and computed tomography scans, are available only outside the FASs. Some family members also accompany those sick people, increasing the number of migrants (US Government Accountability Office 2020). Many FAS citizens must, even if temporarily, migrate to the United States to obtain medical treatment for themselves or family members, and healthcare is the most frequently cited reason for migrating to Hawaii and other US territories (US Commission on Civil Rights 2019).

Healthcare services are still poor in the FASs, in terms of the number of medical professionals (doctors, nurses, technicians, and researchers) and limited financial resources (Fig. 1.13). Hospitals, clinics, and dispensaries require massive upgrades and renovations to provide more space and new equipment. Medical supplies are always constrained due to the FASs' remoteness, the resulting high logistical costs, and lack of infrastructure such as cold storage warehouses and specialized transportation. Isolated outer islands and atolls exacerbate the difficulties of the issues, as their extra remoteness poses a significant challenge to accessing hospitals and other healthcare service providers (e.g., pharmacies) (Person 2014).

This situation has also been worsened with the increase in NCDs; the FAS populations have among the highest rates of overweight and obesity in the world, leading to tuberculosis, diabetes, and hypertension (WHO 2017). In Marshall Islands, despite the cessation of nuclear bomb testing over six decades ago, the population still grapples with abnormally high incidences of thyroid disorders, birth defects, and cancers

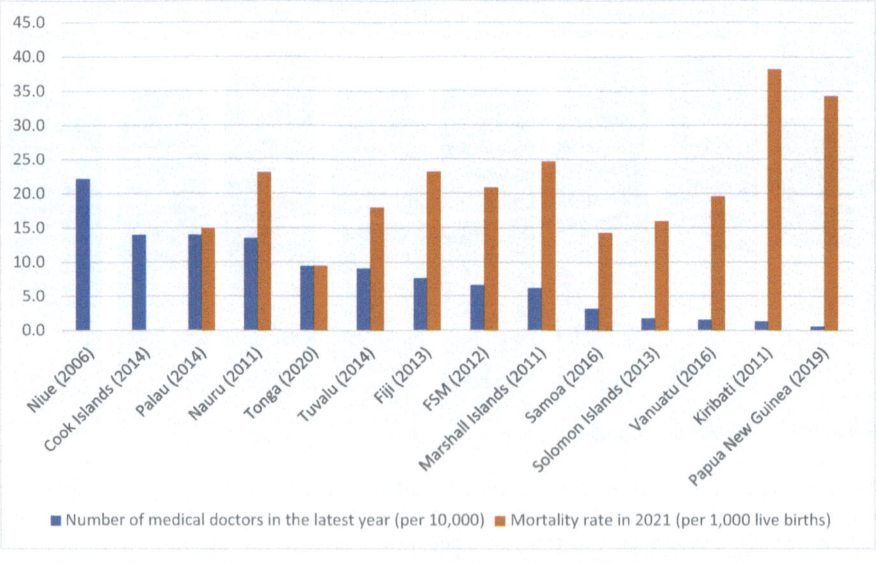

Fig. 1.13 The status of healthcare services in the Pacific. *Note* Years shown are the most recent for which data is available. *Source* Authors' illustration based on World Bank (2023)

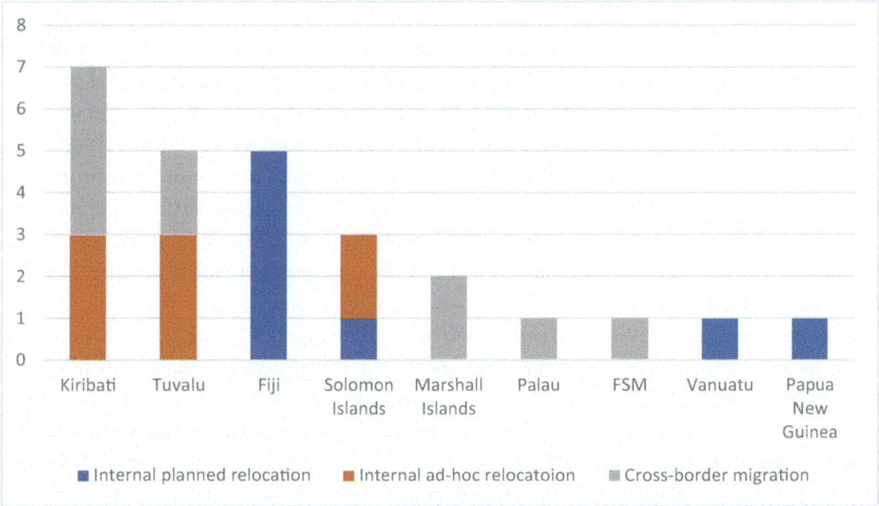

Fig. 1.14 Peoples' displacements in the Pacific, 26 cases. *Note* Each case represents a group migration or relocation with a different origin or destination, captured in various studies published between 1990 and 2019. *Source* Authors' illustration based on Yates (2022)

(Duke 2014). Life expectancy in Marshall Islands is approximately five years lower than in the other two FASs (Duke 2014).

D. **Climate change**

Climate change and its impacts have caused displacement of populations in the Pacific, including some cases in the FASs. Figure 1.14 provides the latest and most comprehensive view of such movements in the Pacific, including Palau, FSM, and Marshall Islands. In the past 30 years, people have been displaced because of the ongoing climate change and other factors, such as employment, education, healthcare, and family. The FASs recorded a small number of such (cross-border) mobilities (two cases in Marshall Islands, one each in Palau and FSM). Climate change impacts such as rising sea levels and more frequent natural disasters are expected to increase migration, particularly for low-lying atolls, although evidence is not fully available. More scientific and socioeconomic studies are required.

Neither slow- nor rapid-onset impacts of climate change can be overlooked, as they pose numerous threats in FASs now and in the future.[11] Sea level rises, which are most dangerous to low-lying atolls, cause infrastructure flooding and critical threats to drinking water supplies and food security, as they increase the risk of saltwater infiltration into the groundwater, hampering irrigation and poisoning the soil for years (Bilsky 2010).

[11] Slow-onset events evolve gradually from incremental changes occurring over many years or from an increased frequency or intensity of recurring events, whereas a rapid-onset event may be a single, discrete event that occurs in a matter of days or even hours. See UNFCCC (2012).

Over 50,000 people in the Pacific are forced to move annually due to the devastating impacts of disasters and climate change (United Nations 2021). In neighbouring Kiribati, for example, 73% of households agreed that if agricultural production becomes more complex, sea levels rise, or flooding or saltwater intrusion worsen, migration would be a likely choice (ILO 2019). Reduced food resources, typhoons, coral reef bleaching, and fish stock decrease have already contributed to migration from the FASs (US Government Accountability Office 2020). Fifteen per cent of Chuukese living in Oregon in the United States report climate change as one of the factors in their relocation, and 18% cite it as a reason for not returning to FSM (Drinkall et al. 2019).

Climate change is having not only environmental impacts but also socioeconomic consequences throughout nations. It is affecting migration patterns within countries, with inhabitants of outer low-lying islands and atolls, especially, increasingly moving to urban or higher-level areas in search of livelihood security, increasing urban population density (IOM 2016). Disastrous events, such as Typhoon Wutip, which hit areas of Yap and Chuuk in February 2019, are becoming more common (IOM 2019). Typhoon Maysak tore through the islands of FSM in March 2015, causing fatalities and doing millions of dollars' worth of damage to houses, crops, and public infrastructure (United Nations Office for the Coordination of Humanitarian Affairs 2015). The potential for category 4 and 5 typhoons in the FASs has been increasing.

Droughts, which directly impact subsistence in agriculture, are expected to occur less frequently but with more severity in the future (Government of FSM 2018). Rising ocean temperatures and acidification cause coral reef damage and bleaching, contributing to coastal erosion and leaving the islands more vulnerable to storm surges and floods (United Nations Children's Fund 2017). These rising temperatures also pose a direct threat to tuna supplies, the most profitable source of income in the FASs. The reduction in fishing opportunities will result in declining national revenue generated from fishing licences and curb subsistence for local households (United Nations Office for the Coordination of Humanitarian Affairs 2023).

Despite the evidence of climate change impacts, however, only four per cent of College of FSM students recently gave "climate change" and "natural disaster" as their primary reasons for possible migration (Moriya 2019). Also, students in Marshall Islands indicated these reasons as the least important factors for them in relation to migration (Yoshioka et al. 2019). Migration drivers, such as education, jobs, healthcare, and family, were reported by Chuukese living in Oregon as significant reasons for future migration (Drinkall et al. 2019).

E. **Military services**

Many young FAS migrants move to the United States to join the US military. According to the US Department of Defense, 1500 FSM citizens voluntarily serve in the US armed forces (Cronk 2019). Regarding per capita representation, FSM citizens in the US military surpass those from any other nation. Approximately 500 Palauans currently serve in the US armed forces (Regina 2023). Many Marshallese have also served in the US forces (Garamone 2022). Those enrolled in the US forces feel a sense of duty to defend Palau, they gain training, education, and experience away from home, and they consider it an option for upward mobility (Diaz 2012). The CoFA enables a high level of military enlistment by Compact citizens in the US forces.

Apart from feelings of prestige and pride engendered by serving in the military, joining it is a way for Micronesians to support themselves and their families. Enlisted infantry personnel in the US Army have the potential to earn salaries comparable to those of senior officials in FSM (Round 2018). Also, young men and women who join the army can become US citizens and have full access to all benefits offered to US soldiers and veterans. However, obtaining US citizenship is not easy and requires adequate preparation. If FAS citizens do not secure citizenship after serving the US forces, they return to their home islands. There are a few hundred veterans living in the FASs (Ordonio 2023). These veterans, who often carry physical trauma or post-traumatic stress disorder (PTSD), have difficulty accessing the benefits they are entitled to, such as access to Veteran Administration hospitals, mental health treatment, loans, etc. (Pacific Waves 2018).

It should not be forgotten that people serving in the US forces and deployed to war zones risk their lives. Since 2001, 16 soldiers from FSM, five from Palau, and one from Marshall Islands have died, mainly in Afghanistan, Iraq, and Kuwait (US Department of the Interior 2023).

F. **Gravity**

The gravity theory can, at least partially, explain the flow of migrations from the three FASs to the United States. The gravity theory for migration is based on Newton's law of universal gravitation, which states that every object in the universe pulls on every other object (Heath 2007). The gravity theory can assess migration patterns between two countries and the attraction of one country's people to another (cf. Carey 1858). Many factors, including politics, language, culture, and taxation, affect how far individuals perceive the attractiveness of a country. These characteristics are influenced by free trade agreements and, more broadly, by the size of the countries (population, GDP, or income) (Capoani 2023). Migration flows between two countries are directly proportional to their size and inversely proportional to the physical distance between them (Ramos 2016). Migrants tend to move to the great commerce and industry centres to seek job opportunities, so economic factors are the leading cause of the migration.

FAS citizens migrated first to the closest destinations such as Guam and CNMI (especially Saipan) and later to Hawaii and the mainland United States (US Government Accountability Office 2020). Figure 1.15 illustrates the size of the respective economies, which supports the impact of the gravity theory.

G. **Family**

For Micronesians, family is the most essential element in their lives. In addition to the migration drivers associated with the country of origin and destination, intervening obstacles, and personal factors, family perceptions significantly influence the actual act of migration (Hezel 2001, 2013; Lee 1966). This issue is evident in migration

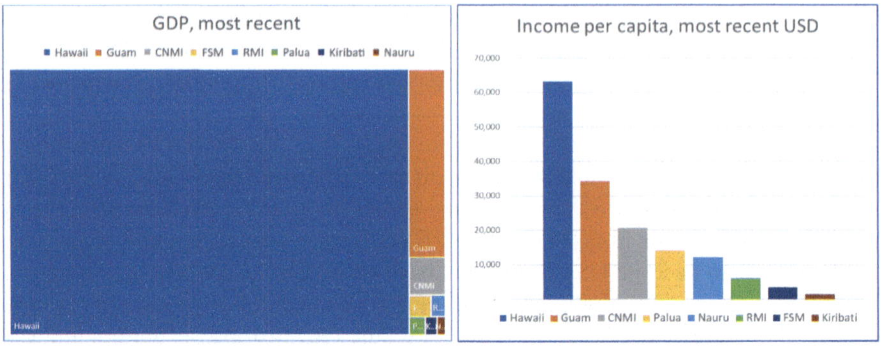

Fig. 1.15 Economy sizes of Micronesia and Hawaii. *Source* Authors' illustration based on World Bank (2023), Graduate School USA (2019, 2021b, 2022b), and State Government of Hawaii (2022)

patterns through kinship linkages to popular destinations, such as Arkansas, Guam, Hawaii, Oregon, and Southern California (Hezel and Samuel 2006). A typical pattern has been that after a young male family member finds a stable job in a US territory, he will bring his siblings and/or wife and children. Then their parents and relatives will join them later in building an offshore family base (Hezel 2001, 2013).

Migrant family members representing different generations usually live under the same roof, and even limited space does not deter migrants from joining close or distant relatives. In such households, special attention is paid to the culture which the family comes from and the customs that they know. They speak their first language with each other and prepare food that is common back in the islands. Family ties are strong, and the necessity of helping one's own family is natural. New members are supported not only by their own families but also by diasporas, churches, and other social groups which preserve the culture and customs of the island people and uphold solid cultural belonging (Hezel and Samuel 2006).

1.6 Life After Migration

Although FAS migrants move to foreign countries for their betterment (and often for their families' future gain), they may not achieve it quickly. An earlier survey reveals that in 2012, 74% of FAS households in the US territories lived below the poverty line (Hezel and Levin 2012). In the same year, as many as 58% of the migrants in Guam, 46% in Hawaii, and 35% in the continental United States received food stamp assistance for low-income households (Hezel and Levin 2012). Staggeringly, 20 to 25% of the population using the state's homeless services in Hawaii self-identified as part of the FAS communities in 2020 (US Government Accountability Office 2020).

It is challenging for FAS migrants to find and keep a job (Drinkall et al. 2019). They take primarily entry-level jobs in industries such as meat processing, restaurants, hotels, construction, manufacturing, security, and warehousing (US Government Accountability Office 2020). Previous research has revealed that challenges result from insufficient preparation, including lack of English language proficiency, inadequate education, and poor vocational skills (Drinkall et al. 2019; Hawaii Advisory Committee to the US Commission on Civil Rights 2019). Limited knowledge of local laws and rules can also prevent FAS migrants from attaining better-paying jobs. They often find that they must hold multiple menial jobs to make ends meet (Hawaii Advisory Committee to the US Commission on Civil Rights 2019).

Although FAS migrants are entitled to live, study, and work in the United States, they still do not have full access to all of the social benefits available to US citizens. One of the most essential among these is healthcare coverage. In 1996, the Personal Responsibility and Work Opportunity Reconciliation Act stripped FAS citizens of eligibility for most federal benefits, including Medicaid (Asian and Pacific Islander American Health Forum 2020).[12] In 2020, the United States reinstalled full Medicaid eligibility for FAS citizens. However, several states have yet to update their policies or are unclear whether the FAS citizens can receive healthcare services (Embassy of the Federated States of Micronesia 2022).[13] Furthermore, problems with Medicaid application and enrolment processes and other barriers prevent FAS citizens from receiving adequate healthcare services in the US territories (Stephens 2022). The 2020 legislation does not apply to other benefits such as the Children's Health Insurance Programme (CHIP), and it gives states the freedom to decide whether FAS citizens should be included (Centers for Medicare and Medicaid Services 2023). Medicare, a federal health insurance for people aged 65 or older, also has various requirements which FAS citizens may not meet quickly. It is evident that although access to the US healthcare system for FAS migrants has improved over the years, there are various eligibility constraints.

Often, FAS emigrants support their families back home. Emigrants' remittances increase household income, assets, savings, educational attainment, and knowledge while reducing the proportion of the impoverished population (ILO 2019). Remittances support a significant number of families—for example, about 40% of households in FSM—although they still account for less in the FASs than in other Pacific countries (EU Global Diaspora Facility 2020). Figure 1.16 illustrates the status of remittance inflows to the Pacific, including the three FASs.

The transition from living in one of the FASs to the United States is a demanding process mentally and socially for most migrants. Differences of custom and culture are significant. FAS migrants face discrimination, mistreatment, or abuse from landlords, employers, and fellow employees (Hawaii Advisory Committee to the US Commission on Civil Rights 2019). Most continue to speak their first languages at

[12] Medicaid is a joint federal and state programme that provides healthcare coverage to eligible people with limited incomes and resources.

[13] CNMI and Guam provide all FAS migrants with Medicaid services if they meet the territories' eligibility requirements.

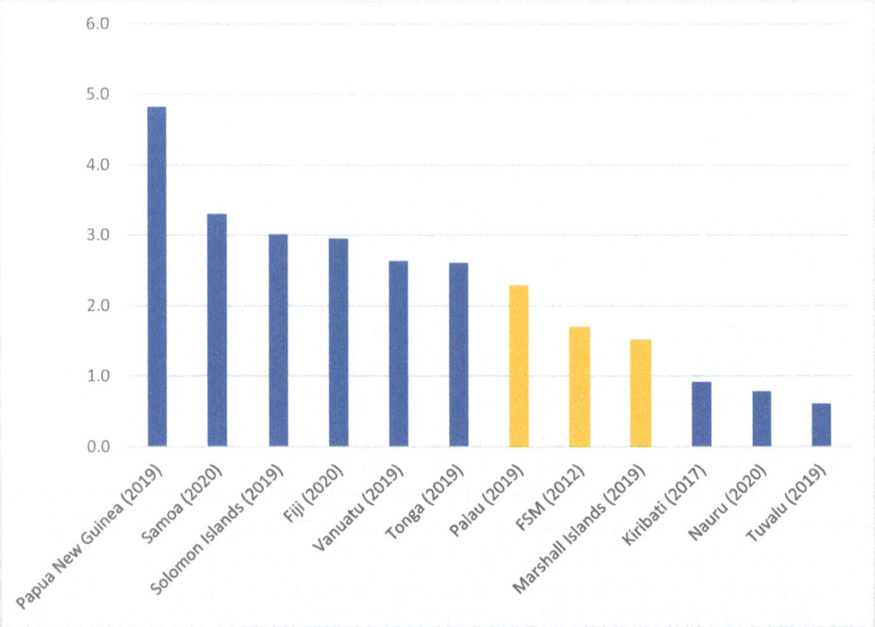

Fig. 1.16 Remittance in the Pacific (percentage of GDP). *Source* Developed based on the World Bank (2023)

home, and about two out of every three retain their home citizenship. It has been found that the farther away from Micronesia migrants settle, the greater their attachment is to traditions (IOM 2016).

1.7 Policy and Practical Implications

This chapter has identified several drivers for FAS citizens' outward migration, mainly to the United States. These diverse drivers have encouraged many people to take the risk in the hope of finding better lives (for themselves and their families) in a foreign country in the future. However, emigration poses a significant threat to the FASs' ability to maintain a healthy future for themselves, in addition to growing inequality between urban areas and outer islands, a heavy reliance on foreign capital and supplies, and intensifying natural hazards. This section seeks to identify critical gaps that the FASs confront and to make practical policy recommendations to directly and indirectly alleviate migration challenges. This part of the study is based on the previously presented information and data. It is not an exhaustive checklist, nor does it seek to go into great depth. Instead, it attempts to delineate and prioritize the most pressing challenges confronting Palau, FSM, and Marshall Islands.

A. **Develop a holistic policy approach**

The three FASs will benefit from a holistic approach to addressing interlinking migration drivers for the islands' future prosperity. With competing demands for finite funds and resources, as well as limited institutional capacity, strategic and practical prioritization becomes critical in seeking to achieve the most significant net positive impact. While it is helpful to clearly define each of the migration drivers, for clarity and a strategic allocation of resources, coping with these issues necessitates taking a holistic approach, and, conversely, avoiding the temptation to adopt a "silo approach". Gains made in one field may have a positive (or negative) knock-on effect in another area, while a lack of progress in one area could create a negative drag on another. There is also a need to prioritize and pursue a strategy likely to bring about the most significant desirable impact, relative to the funds, resources, and institutional capacities available. A holistic approach to mitigating the issues that FASs face can be categorized into: (i) jobs; (ii) education; (iii) healthcare; (iv) climate change; (v) military services; (vi) gravity; and (vii) family. Some of these components are interdependent and overlapping in focus and intent. This is a good thing, as it suggests that there are areas where efficiency gains ("two—or three or more—for the price of one") can be achieved by adopting a holistic approach. Indeed, these areas mutually rely on progress attained elsewhere for their improvement. This underlines the necessity of what is sometimes called "joined-up government", where state agencies work in close coordination and resist the temptation to focus only on their particular mandates, resulting in a "siloed government". The latter tends to lead to duplication of effort, a potential wastage of finite resources, and, most importantly, an inability to make substantive gains across the full spectrum of socioeconomic and environmental priorities, as any initiatives undertaken will come up against, and be constrained by, the boundaries of their respective silo.

B. **Develop a dedicated migration and mobility policy**

The FASs must develop a comprehensive policy framework to deal with growing outward migration and the resulting recent, significant population drop in the region, while intensifying engagement with the Compact diaspora so that they can better contribute to local development, perhaps through increased remittances. Such a policy framework will help the countries to seize the demographic dividends, retaining more of the young generation within their borders. This can be achieved through improving a combination of public services, such as education, healthcare, and job creation, in collaboration with various stakeholders, such as businesses, civil society organizations, and donors. The policy framework must be developed based on changing national culture and social norms. In this context, the FASs must also consider developing policy frameworks to support foreign immigrants who contribute to socioeconomic development in a depopulating society.

C. **Create jobs in the homelands**

There is no single solution to the migration problems in the FASs. However, domestic job creation is perhaps one of the most significant policy options, as emigrants primarily move to their destinations for better work opportunities. Increased job opportunities in their home islands would make it more likely that people who had studied or lived abroad would return and add value to the FASs. Among the FASs, private sector development has progressed little, with the exception of Palau's tourism sector, and is still at the nascent stage with many obstructions, such as traditional clanship land ownership, poor entrepreneurship, and frequent public intervention. In this area, a comprehensive private sector development (PSD) strategy could help to cover multiple issues such as access to markets and finance, skilled labour development, and foreign direct investment (FDI). The PSD strategy also requires long-term planning, adaptation, and capacity-building. In this context, as the public sector dominates the FAS economies, their second option is to develop state-owned enterprises (SOEs) to implement public schemes aimed at income redistribution (e.g., foreign aid, fishery licences, and tourism income) and poverty alleviation (e.g., copra subsidies to outer island farmers). Tourism promotion must also be prioritized, including historical and blue ocean tourism.

D. **Enhance education offerings**

To provide better opportunities for the Compact countries' future generations, it is crucial to overhaul the education system. There is a need for a quality education system at various levels and fields to reduce the level of NEET, spanning academic (elementary, secondary, and tertiary), vocational, and adult/further education. A greater emphasis on quality technical and vocational education and training (TVET) is also recommended, to equip FAS citizens—particularly young people and women—with the skills needed to be employable. These actions will not only enhance school performance but also enable young people to secure better future lives and careers within the country, thereby decreasing the rate of outward migration while reducing the nation's dependence on foreign workers to fill specialized roles. Such a reform process must encompass improved governance structures, physical facilities, and curricula, and well-trained educators and administration personnel. In particular, it is strongly recommended to establish fully fledged, four-year, national universities (e.g., liberal arts colleges) with vocational and further education streams in the region.

E. **Strengthen national healthcare services**

In the Compact countries, the coverage and outcomes of healthcare services have been suboptimal, often forcing those who are ill and old to move out. FAS citizens struggle with one of the highest obesity levels globally, leading to NCDs and premature deaths. Enhancing healthcare services should be one of the top development priorities for the islands in seeking to mitigate outward migration. To tackle health problems, the government should consider applying a comprehensive approach to strengthening public health while focusing on mortality reduction by providing better healthcare services for pregnant people, babies, and mothers.

In the United States, access to healthcare services for Compact migrants is a fundamental human right acknowledged in numerous international agreements and instruments, as evidenced by its inclusion in the United Nations Sustainable Development Goals (SDGs). In accordance with established international norms governing the fundamental rights of migrants, and on behalf of all of them, the Compact countries should actively lobby the US administration to provide their migrants with sustained access to healthcare services readily available to American citizens in the US territories.

F. **Maintain ecology, biodiversity, and marine resources**

Ongoing climate change and its intensifying impacts, such as rising sea levels, high temperatures, and extreme weather events, suggest a clear need to develop various initiatives in adaptation, mitigation, and resilience. Such initiatives will protect the islands' ecology, biodiversity, and marine resources and will help to implement disaster risk reduction and a circular economy. Considering the future landscape, in which slow-onset climate events are anticipated to intensify, suitable migration management policies and practices must be applied. The migration process has been accelerated by the negative consequences of climate change on a country's economy and overall people's livelihood. In general, the Compact governments expressed the desire to focus first and foremost on the climate drivers for migration, so that people can remain and live in their own countries. This, however, requires financial assistance from developed countries, to invest in climate resilience and adaptation measures to prevent displacement and facilitate preparedness for climate-induced migration.[14]

G. **Maintain national culture and family values**

In destination countries, FAS immigrants lack adequate preparation for many aspects of life in the new place. The countries should invest in more comprehensive planning and training for those willing to leave. Such planning and training should emphasize the importance of distinct national cultures and traditional family values to deal with challenges in a foreign destination. In the end, this could improve transition and overall quality of life. Migrants' solid connections with Micronesian culture, languages, and families back in their country of origin will also facilitate a smooth return process.

H. **Foster regional cooperation**

The FAS countries should strengthen collaboration with regional partners such as the Pacific Island Forum (PIF), the Pacific Community (SPC), and the Secretariat of the Pacific Regional Environment Programme (SPREP). They should jointly develop comprehensive regional strategies for socioeconomic and environmental issues to help people live in their home countries without displacement or migration.

---

[14] Developed countries, which could be directly impacted by climate migration, have started preparing for financial assistance—e.g., New Zealand's displacement and migration action plan (2018) includes ODA (Official Development Assistance) for creating regular migration pathways (Chazalnoël and Randall 2021).

1.8 Conclusion

To summarize, the CoFAs have enabled expanded migration from the FASs to the United States for nearly the last four decades. Out-migration from the three CoFA countries is related primarily to the young generation seeking better lives outside their homes. Such movements are particularly encouraged by inadequate employment or lack of jobs, underdeveloped education systems, and poor healthcare services in migrants' home islands. Given the limited development potential of the countries and with free movement assured for another 20 years by the latest CoFAs with the United States, the migration is likely to continue. Ultimately, the FASs need to find ways to slow down migration and take action to attract back those who have already left while also attracting foreign labour. This requires vast changes in the countries regarding the economy, jobs, education, healthcare, and other essential areas that provide income and wellbeing to the people. Given the most recent CoFAs signed for new development funds, the countries would be wise to focus on areas such as private sector development, job creation, income redistribution, and educational and healthcare improvements. Investing in human capital will also accelerate the countries' overall development and alleviate the threats from migration outflows.

References

Andrews CJ (2017) Micronesia in modern geopolitics. Plan II Honors Program, University of Texas at Austin. Available at: https://repositories.lib.utexas.edu/bitstream/handle/2152/63613/andrewscameron_3867643_44267389_CameronAndrewsThesis.pdf?sequence=2&isAllowed=y. Accessed 13 Dec 2023

Asian and Pacific Islander American Health Forum (2020) COVID-19 relief bill restores Medicaid access for COFA community [Online]. Available at: www.apiahf.org/press-release/covid-19-relief-bill-restores-medicaid-access-for-cofa-community. Accessed 13 Dec 2023

Asian Development Bank (2023a) Economic impact of the compact and renewal for the Federated States of Micronesia [Online]. Available at: https://pitiviti.org/storage/dm/2023/09/adb-fsm-countryfocus-sep2023-digital-20230911234558831.pdf. Accessed 13 Dec 2023

Asian Development Bank (2023b) Economic impact of the compact and renewal for the Republic of the Marshall Islands [Online]. Available at: https://pitiviti.org/storage/dm/2023/09/adb-rmi-countryfocus-sep2023-digital-20230905220951987.pdf. Accessed 13 Dec 2023

Asian Development Bank (2023c) Economic impact of the compact and renewal on the Republic of Palau [Online]. Available at: https://pitiviti.org/storage/dm/2023/06/adb-palau-countryfocus-may2023-digital-20230609022330965.pdf. Accessed 13 Dec 2023

Bilsky P (2010) 'Water woes', Deutsche Welle, 20 April [Online]. Available at: https://p.dw.com/p/MzWg. Accessed 13 Dec 2023

Capoani L (2023) Review of the gravity model: origins and critical analysis of its theoretical development. SN Bus Econ 3:95

Carey HC (1858) Principles of social science. J.B. Lippincott & Co., Philadelphia, PA

Centers for Medicare and Medicaid Services (2023) Health coverage options for COFA Migrants, Version August 2023 [Online]. Available at: www.cms.gov/marketplace/technical-assistance-resources/health-coverage-options-cofa-migrants.pdf. Accessed 13 Dec 2023

Chazalnoël MT, Randall A (2021) Migration and the slow-onset impacts of climate change: taking stock and taking action. In: McAuliffe M, Triandafyllidou A (eds) World migration report 2022. International Organization for Migration (IOM), Geneva, pp 223–252
Clarke D, Azzopardi P (2019) State of Pacific youth. United Nations Population Fund Pacific Sub-Regional Office, Suva
Congressional Research Services (2023) The compacts of free association. In: Focus, 13 November [Online]. Available at: https://crsreports.congress.gov/product/pdf/IF/IF12194#:~:text=The%20Compacts%20of%20Free%20Association%20govern%20the%20relationships%20between%20the,)%2C%20and%20Republic%20of%20Palau. Accessed 13 Dec 2023
Cronk TM (2019) Esper welcomes Micronesia's president to Pentagon [Online]. Available at: www.defense.gov/News/News-Stories/Article/Article/1988044/esper-welcomes-micronesias-president-to-pentagon/#:~:text=Published%20reports%20indicate%20up%20to%201%2C500%20Micronesian%20citizens%20serve%20in%20U.S.%20forces. Accessed 13 Dec 2023
Diaz KK (2012) The compact of free association (COFA): a history of failures [Online]. Available at: https://scholarspace.manoa.hawaii.edu/server/api/core/bitstreams/a0e512d7-02d5-419d-9623-3f184dfa1839/content. Accessed 13 Dec 2023
Drinkall S, Leung J, Bruch C, Micky K, Wells S (2019) Migration with dignity: a case study on the livelihood transition of Micronesians to Portland and Salem, Oregon. J Disaster Res 14:1267–1276
Duke MR (2014) Marshall islanders: migration patterns and health-care challenges. Migration Policy Institute (MPI), Washington, DC
Embassy of the Federated States of Micronesia (2022) FSM medicaid eligibility guide by state [Online]. Available at: https://fsmembassy.fm/wp-content/uploads/2022/06/Medicaid-Eligibility-by-State.pdf. Accessed 13 Dec 2023
EU Global Diaspora Facility (2020) Diaspora engagement mapping: Federated states of Micronesia [Online]. Available at: https://diasporafordevelopment.eu/wp-content/uploads/2020/04/CF_FSM-v.1.pdf. Accessed 13 Dec 2023
Garamone J (2022) Austin welcomes Marshall Islands president to Pentagon [Online]. Available at: www.safia.hq.af.mil/IA-News/Article/3176162/austin-welcomes-marshall-islands-president-to-pentagon. Accessed 13 Dec 2023
Government of FSM (2018) Federated states of Micronesia state of environment report 2018. Secretariat of the Pacific Regional Environment Programme (SPREP), Apia
Government of FSM (2020) FSM education indicators report November 2020, version 3 [Online]. Available at: https://pacific-data.sprep.org/dataset/fsm-education-indicators-2020-version-3. Accessed 13 Dec 2023
Government of FSM (2022) FSM education indicators report September 2022, version 1 [Online]. Available at: www.national.doe.fm/wp-content/uploads/2023/03/National_JEMCO_25_Indicators_21-22.pdf. Accessed 13 Dec 2023
Government of FSM (2023) Address by H.E. David W. Panuelo, on the occasion of the State of the Nation. FSM Information Services Press Release, 13 January
Government of FSM (n.d.) Federated states of Micronesia 2013/2014 HIES education [Online]. Available at: www.national.doe.fm/wp-content/uploads/2023/03/FS-FSM-Education.pdf. Accessed 13 Dec 2023
Government of Palau (2020) 2020 census of population, housing and agriculture. Office of Planning and Statistics Republic of Palau, Koror [Online]. Available at: www.palaugov.pw/wp-content/uploads/2022/07/2020_Census-of-Population-Housing-and-Agriculture-Basic-Tables.pdf. Accessed 13 Dec 2023
Graduate School USA (2019) Federated states of Micronesia: fiscal year 2018 statistical appendices [Online]. Available at: https://pitiviti.org/storage/dm/2021/08/fsm-econstat-tabs-fy18-pub2-20210825004607683.pdf. Accessed 13 Dec 2023
Graduate School USA (2021a) October 21 economic brief: FSM, FY 2021. Economic Monitoring and Analysis Program (EconMAP), Koror

Graduate School USA (2021b) Republic of the Marshall Islands: fiscal year 2021 statistical appendices (preliminary) [Online]. Available at: https://pitiviti.org/storage/dm/alternate/2022/10/rmi-econstat-tabs-fy21-prelim-pub1-20221030020126721.pdf. Accessed 13 Dec 2023

Graduate School USA (2022a) Economic brief: Republic of the Marshall Islands, November 2022. EconMAP, Koror

Graduate School USA (2022b) Economic brief: Republic of Palau, June 2022. EconMAP, Koror

Graduate School USA (2023) Palau FY22 economic statistics (preliminary) [Online]. Available at: https://pitiviti.org/palau. Accessed 27 Dec 2023

Grieco E (2003) The federated states of Micronesia: the 'push' to migrate. Migration Policy Institute, Washington, DC

Guardian (2023) US set to open Tonga embassy in May as Pacific push ramps up. Guardian, 3 May 2023 [Online]. Available at: www.theguardian.com/world/2023/may/03/us-set-to-open-tonga-embassy-in-may-as-pacific-push-ramps-up. Accessed 13 Dec 2023

Hawaii Advisory Committee to the US Commission on Civil Rights (2019) A Micronesians in Hawaii: migrant group faces barriers to equal opportunity [Online]. Available at: www.usccr.gov/files/pubs/2019/08-13-Hawaii-Micronesian-Report.pdf. Accessed 13 Dec 2023

Heath JE (2007) Newton's universal law of gravity [Online]. Available at: www.austincc.edu/jheath/Solar/Hand/NULOG/nulog.htm. Accessed 13 Dec 2023

Hezel FX (1995) Strangers in their own land: a century of colonial rule in the Caroline and Marshall islands. University of Hawaii Press, Honolulu

Hezel FX (2001) The new shape of old island cultures: a half century of social change in Micronesia. University of Hawaii Press, Honolulu

Hezel FX (2010) Disease in Micronesia: a historical survey. Pac Health Dialog 16(1):11–25

Hezel FX (2013) Micronesians on the move: eastward and upward bound. East-West Center, Honolulu

Hezel FX, Levin MJ (2012) Survey of Federated States of Micronesia migrants in the United States including Guam and the Commonwealth of Northern Mariana Islands (CNMI) [Online]. Available at: https://prd.isr.umich.edu/wp-content/uploads/2019/12/Resources_Report-on-PI-Jurisdictions.pdf. Accessed 13 Dec 2023

Hezel FX, Samuel E (2006) Micronesians abroad. Micronesian Counselor, 64 (10 November)

ILO (International Labour Organization) (2019) Labour mobility in the Pacific countries [Online]. Available at: www.ilo.org/wcmsp5/groups/public/-asia/-ro-bangkok/-ilo-suva/documents/publication/wcms_712549.pdf. Accessed 13 Dec 2023

ILO (2021) ILOSTAT explorer [Online]. Available at: www.ilo.org/shinyapps/bulkexplorer44/?lang=en&id=SDG_0852_SEX_AGE_RT_A. Accessed 13 Dec 2023

IOM (International Organization for Migration) (2016) Migration in the Federated States of Micronesia: a country profile 2015 [Online]. Available at: https://publications.iom.int/books/migration-federated-states-micronesia-country-profile-2015. Accessed 13 Dec 2023

IOM (2019) Typhoon wutip destruction: federated states of Micronesia, Republic of the Marshall Islands, Republic of Palau. IOM UN Migration Newsletter, July 2018–April 2019 [Online]. Available at: www.iom.int/sites/g/files/tmzbdl486/files/mission_newsletter/file/micronesia_mn_201807-201904.pdf. Accessed 13 Dec 2023

Kesolei OK (2023) Looking at Palau's approach to the compact negotiation. Pacific Island Times, 7 February [Online]. Available at: www.pacificislandtimes.com/post/looking-at-palau-s-approach-to-the-compact-negotiation. Accessed 13 Dec 2023

Laney LO (2008) Economic forecast: 2008 Guam-CNMI edition. First Hawaiian Bank, Honolulu

Lee ES (1966) A theory of migration. Demography 3(1):47–57

Ministry of Education of Marshall Islands (2014) Education for all 2015 national review report: Marshall Islands [Online]. Available at: https://unesdoc.unesco.org/ark:/48223/pf0000229722/PDF/229722eng.pdf.multi. Accessed 13 Dec 2023

Moriya K (2019) Motivations for students in the Republic of the Marshall islands and the federated states of Micronesia to emigrate abroad. J Disaster Res 14(9):1293–1296

Ng Kamstra JS, Molina T, Halliday T (2021) Compact for care: how the Affordable Care Act marketplaces fell short for a vulnerable population in Hawaii. BMJ Glob Heal 6:e007701

Ordonio C (2023) For COFA veterans seeking health care, living at home in Micronesia isn't an option. Hawai'i Public Radio, 26 June [Online]. Available at: www.hawaiipublicradio.org/local-news/2023-06-26/for-cofa-veterans-seeking-health-care-living-at-home-in-micronesia-isnt-an-option. Accessed 13 Dec 2023

Pacific Community (2018) Pacific islands literacy and numeracy assessment (PILNA) [Online]. Available at: https://eqap.spc.int/PILNA. Accessed 13 Dec 2023

Pacific Community (2023a) Palau gender factsheet [Online]. Available at: https://spccfpstore1.blob.core.windows.net/digitallibrary-docs/files/e1/e1a4a1fc3740bb29583349c896e79520.pdf?sv=2015-12-11&sr=b&sig=%2FFKnJmZ0QIv1ukufq4S%2B%2BATnAbzB4C99wH347Aw%2BLQQ%3D&se=2024-05-09T13%3A39%3A04Z&sp=r&rscc=public%2C%20max-age%3D864000%2C%20max-stale%3D86400&rsct=application%2Fpdf&rscd=inline%3B%20filename%3D%22Palau_2023_Gender_factsheet.pdf%22. Accessed 13 Dec 2023

Pacific Community (2023b) RMI census report 2021, volume 1: basic tables and administrative report. Pacific Community, Noumea

Pacific Community and Marshall Islands EPPOSO (Economic Policy, Planning and Statistics Office) (2022) Republic of the Marshall Islands 2021 census report, volume 1: basic tables and administrative report. EPPOSO, Noumea

Person DA (2014) The Pacific island health care project. Front. Public Health 2:175 [Online]. Available at: https://doi.org/10.3389/fpubh.2014.00175/full. Accessed 13 Dec 2023

Pacific Waves (2018) Film shines light on Micronesians in US military. Radio New Zealand, 26 April [Online]. Available at: www.rnz.co.nz/international/programmes/datelinepacific/audio/2018642185/film-shines-light-on-micronesians-in-us-military. Accessed 13 Dec 2023

Rajaram PK (2018) Refugees as surplus population: race, migration and capitalist value regimes. New Polit. Econ. 23(5):627–639

Ramos R (2016) Gravity models: a tool for migration analysis. Institute of Labor Economics (IZA), Bonn

Regina P (2023) Palau honors its US military veterans for their legacy of service [Online]. Available at: www.army.mil/article/248418/palau_honors_its_u_s_military_veterans_for_their_legacy_of_service#:~:text=Approximately%20500%20Palauans%20currently%20serve,why%20Palauans%20choose%20to%20serve. Accessed 13 Dec 2023

Round S (2018) Island soldier brings hope in FSM. Radio New Zealand, 26 April [Online]. Available at: www.rnz.co.nz/international/pacific-news/355931/island-soldier-brings-hope-in-fsm. Accessed 13 Dec 2023

State Government of Hawaii (2022) Statistics and data. Department of Business, Economic Development & Tourism, Honolulu. [Online]. Available at: https://dbedt.hawaii.gov/economic/statistics-data. Accessed 8 Dec 2023

Stephens J (2022) Micronesian migrant communities face barriers to health care access, insurance, Medicaid. Pacific Daily News, 13 November [Online]. Available at: www.guampdn.com/news/micronesian-migrant-communities-face-barriers-to-health-care-access-insurance-medicaid/article_910d0bf8-5122-11ed-a414-4f70b93cf59c.html. Accessed 13 Dec 2023

UN Women (United Nations Entity for Gender Equality and the Empowerment of Women) (2022a) Gender equality brief for Federated States of Micronesia [Online]. Available at: https://asiapacific.unwomen.org/en/digital-library/publications/2022/12/gender-equality-brief-for-federated-states-of-micronesia. Accessed 13 Dec 2023

UN Women (2022b) Gender equality brief for the Republic of Marshall Islands [Online]. Available at: https://asiapacific.unwomen.org/en/digital-library/publications/2022/11/gender-equality-brief-for-the-republic-of-marshall-islands. Accessed 13 Dec 2023

UN Women (2022c) Gender equality brief for Palau [Online]. Available at: https://asiapacific.unwomen.org/en/digital-library/publications/2022/11/gender-equality-brief-for-palau. Accessed 13 Dec 2023

UNDESA (United Nations Department of Economic and Social Affairs) Population Division (2020) International migrant stock 2020 [Online]. Available at: www.un.org/development/desa/pd/content/international-migrant-stock. Accessed 13 Dec 2023

UNFCCC (United Nations Framework Convention on Climate Change) (2012) Synopsis series: slow onset events [Online]. Available at: https://unfccc.int/files/adaptation/application/pdf/soe_synopsis.pdf. Accessed 13 Dec 2023

United Nations (2021) Pacific regional consultation on internal displacement [Online]. Available at: www.un.org/internal-displacement-panel/events/pacific-regional-consultation-internal-displacement. Accessed 13 Dec 2023

United Nations Children's Fund (2017) Situation analysis of children in the Federated States of Micronesia [Online]. Available at: www.unicef.org/pacificislands/media/1101/file/Situation-Analysis-of-Children-Micronesia.pdf. Accessed 13 Dec 2023

United Nations Office for the Coordination of Humanitarian Affairs (2015) Tropical cyclone Maysak: Federated States of Micronesia, Philippines (ECHO daily map 2/4/2015) [Online]. Available at: https://reliefweb.int/map/micronesia-federated-states/tropical-cyclone-maysak-federated-states-micronesia-philippines-echo. Accessed 13 Dec 2023

United Nations Office for the Coordination of Humanitarian Affairs (2023) Climate change in the Federated States of Micronesia: indicators and considerations for key sectors [Online]. Available at: https://reliefweb.int/report/micronesia-federated-states/climate-change-federated-states-micronesia-indicators-and-considerations-key-sectors. Accessed 13 Dec 2023

US Commission on Civil Rights (2019) Micronesians in Hawaii: migrant group faces barriers to equal opportunity [Online]. Available at: www.usccr.gov/files/pubs/2019/08-13-Hawaii-Micronesian-Report.pdf. Accessed 13 Dec 2023

US Department of State (2022) Investment climate statements: Micronesia [Online]. Available at: www.state.gov/reports/2022-investment-climate-statements/micronesia. Accessed 13 Dec 2023

US Department of the Interior (2023) Island military heroes [Online]. Available at: www.doi.gov/oia/islanders_in_the_military/heroes. Accessed 13 Dec 2023

US Government Accountability Office (2000) Northern Mariana Islands: garment and tourist industries play a dominant role in the Commonwealth's economy. Government Accountability Office, Washington, DC

US Government Accountability Office (2020) Compacts of free association: populations in US areas have grown, with varying reported effects. Government Accountability Office, Washington, DC

USIP (United States Institute of Peace) (2022) China's influence on the freely associated states of the Northern Pacific. USIP Senior Study Group Report, 5 (September)

Wagner E (2022) New data suggests the federal pay gap with the private sector is widening. Government Executive, 1 November [Online]. Available at: www.govexec.com/pay-benefits/2022/11/new-data-suggests-federal-pay-gap-widening/379181. Accessed 13 Dec 2023

WHO (World Health Organization) (2017) Overweight and obesity in the Western Pacific region. WHO Regional Office for the Western Pacific, Manila [Online]. Available at: https://iris.who.int/bitstream/handle/10665/255475/9789290618133-eng.pdf?sequence=1. Accessed 13 Dec 2023

World Bank (2019) Poverty and equity brief: Federated States of Micronesia [Online]. Available at: https://databankfiles.worldbank.org/public/ddpext_download/poverty/33EF03BB-9722-4AE2-ABC7-AA2972D68AFE/Archives-2019/Global_POVEQ_FSM.pdf. Accessed 13 Dec 2023

World Bank (2023) World development indicators [Online]. Available at: https://databank.worldbank.org/source/world-development-indicators. Accessed 13 Dec 2023

Yates OET (2022) Stories of neighbours and navigators: perceptions and implications of climate mobility from Tuvalu and Kiribati to Aotearoa New Zealand. DPP thesis, University of Auckland

Yoshioka N, Taafaki I, McKay J (2019) Higher education and destination of the youth in the Republic of the Marshall Islands: implication for climate-induced migration. J Disaster Res 14(9):1287–1292

Chapter 2
Current Issues and Challenges Affecting Gender Equality and Sustainable Development in Federated States of Micronesia

Sabrina Regmi

Abstract Federated States of Micronesia (FSM), situated in the North Pacific region, is facing diverse challenges in attaining the Sustainable Development Goals (SDGs). One of the major challenges that intersects with almost all of the goals is gender (in)equality. Members of the development community consisting of local, national, and international agencies and actors have been trying to promote gender equality through their own mandates and work, but with very little positive impact and progress on the ground. Hence, there is a need to understand on-the-ground social, economic, environmental, legal, and political issues that often intersect to create gender inequality, which ultimately hampers sustainable development. This chapter illuminates some of the main issues affecting gender equality and their implications for achieving the SDGs by 2030. In doing so, it identifies and synthesizes four major challenges, addresses the gaps, and provides recommendations that can also serve as opportunities for local, national, and international development agencies and actors towards overcoming the current challenges and filling the current gaps.

2.1 Introduction

Gender equality may be addressed specifically as the fifth goal among the Sustainable Development Goals (SDGs) that are expected to be met by the year 2030. However, it intersects with every other goal in the list and is integral to each stage of the development process. In Federated States of Micronesia (FSM), the government and development partners including national, local, and international development agencies working on gender equality and the SDGs are putting efforts into realizing these goals, through progressive dialogues and conventions as well as through the implementation of both short-term and long-term initiatives to address gender inequality issues in sustainable development. These efforts, however, have shown

S. Regmi (✉)
New York, USA
e-mail: sabrgi@yahoo.com

E. Monaco and M. Abe (eds.), *Sustainable Development Across Pacific Islands*,
https://doi.org/10.1007/978-981-97-3629-4_2

little progress on the ground. Hence, this chapter will explore current on-the-ground social, economic, environmental, legal, and political issues contributing to gender inequality and challenges in meeting gender goals and the SDGs in FSM. The chapter draws information from a desk review as well as from a consultation carried out with relevant people from government agencies, non-governmental organizations (NGOs), civil society organizations (CSOs), women in communities, and women-led church groups which hold knowledge on gender and sustainable development issues in FSM. It outlines and synthesizes some of the key gender issues affecting sustainable development goals in the FSM context, with a primary focus on the challenges. Based on the critical issues and challenges identified from the synthesis, the chapter further outlines the major gaps and provides recommendations that also serve as opportunities for local, national, and international development agencies and actors to accelerate gender equality in order to achieve sustainable development goals in FSM.

2.2 Country Context

FSM is situated in the North Pacific region. Although there is a national government, it consists of four states—Pohnpei, Chuuk, Yap, and Kosrae. Each state has distinct government, constitution, culture, and gender issues.

The country has a Compact of Free Association with the United States, which was signed into law in 1986 and amended in 2003. Under the Compact, FSM has the sovereign right to self-determination and the capacity to conduct foreign affairs, including to sign treaties and other international agreements.

FSM had an estimated total population of 105,754 in 2020, 48.8% of whom were female. Of the overall population, 31.4% were below the age of 15 in 2020 (SPC Pacific Women 2013). Most of the population resides in rural areas: according to the most recent data, 22.3% of the population was living in urban areas in 2010. In 2013, 19.9% of households were headed by women. The average size of female-headed households was 9.0 people in 2013, with an average of 3.3 children; for male-headed households, the average size was 8.5 with an average of 3.1 children (SPC Pacific Women 2013). In the recent years, a growth in the number of female-headed households, particularly in communities where male migration is increasing, has become a trend.

2.3 National and International Laws and Policies

FSM has pledged to bring gender parity to its population through its ratification of the Convention on the Elimination of All Forms of Discrimination against Women (CEDAW) in 2004 and the Pacific Leaders Gender Equality Declaration in 2012. Similarly, in 2018 it endorsed its first national gender policy, which ends in 2023.

Pacific Women (part of the Pacific Community, SPC) provided technical support in the design and implementation of the gender policy for the years throughout its lifespan. The policy notes that its implementation will incorporate high-level accountability, along with designated "Gender Focal Points" in every FSM department. However, except for the Department of Health and Social Affairs, which includes a Gender Unit, other departments in Pohnpei still do not have Gender Focal Points, even approaching the end of the implementation period. While the Gender Unit in Pohnpei looks after national-level matters including sector-specific issues and issues of all four states, there are subnational-level Gender Focal Points. Only one member of staff is appointed to cover gender issues in each of the three other states, barely providing sufficient technical capacity on gender mainstreaming. Since sectoral departments at both national and subnational levels do not have a gender expert or even a Gender Focal Point appointed to look after each sector's issues, gender-disaggregated data and information is so far not collected, updated, and managed. Even the Gender Unit in Pohnpei (the national-level head office) consist of only a few staff with limited skills on gender mainstreaming, who are struggling to develop a new gender policy for the next term (2024–29). The unit also needs support in implementing the Gender Equality Framework which was developed at the beginning of 2023.

The law and services relating to social matters are largely the responsibility of the states and need development and funding. From 2018 to 2023, FSM education and health services were supported by US funding through the Compact of Free Association. The education and health sectors include services for disabled students. Outside of these two sectors, there are few state-initiated policies and social services.

Although, the provisions of the constitutions of the country at both national and state levels do not discriminate against women and girls, there are still gender gaps between women/girls and men/boys. Despite the government's commitments to address the prevailing gender inequality issues, progress in meeting these commitments has been slow. One of the major constraints is lack of resources and capacity within the national gender machinery, greatly inhibiting the ability to promote protect and fulfil the rights of women and girls.

2.4 Gender Equality and Sustainable Development Goals in FSM: Current Issues and Challenges

The main issues affecting gender equality and the achievement of the SDGs in FSM, which have more negative implications for women and girls' than men and boys, are identified as follows:

1. Health, protection, and justice;
2. Economic empowerment;
3. Climate change and disaster resilience;
4. Leadership and political participation.

A. **Health, protection, and justice**

Consultation with stakeholders and information from the desk review reveal that one of the pressing gender issues impacting health, protection, security, and justice in Micronesia is gender-based violence (GBV), and that this is prevalent in all four states.

In the *FSM Family Health and Safety Study* (FHSS) undertaken in 2014, 28.6% of women with long-term partners reported that they had experienced physical violence from an intimate partner in their lifetime (UNFPA 2014). Among women with long-term partners, 18.1% reported having experienced sexual violence from a partner in their lifetime, with 12.9% having experienced this violence in the previous 12 months. Overall, 32.8% of women with long-term partners had experienced physical or sexual violence from an intimate partner in their lifetime, and 24.1% had experienced this violence in the 12 months prior to the study. The study also revealed that women were facing emotional violence, with 32.8% of women with long-term partners having faced this form of violence from an intimate partner in their lifetime, including having been insulted, belittled, humiliated, threatened, scared, and intimidated. Moreover, 14.9% of women with long-term partners reported that they had experienced economic violence from a partner, including taking away money that they had earned or saved (9.3%) and refusing to give them money for household expenses despite money being available for other things (11.7%).

According to the same survey, the highest rate of GBV was found in Kosrae (57.8%), followed by Chuuk (49.9%), Yap (27.0%), and Pohnpei (18.9%) (UNFPA 2014). There is no GBV support centre in Kosrae, nor are there any functional referral pathways. Although the government of Kosrae passed the Family Protection Act in 2004, the impact of its implementation on the ground is unknown. Consultation with the Gender Focal Point in Yap revealed that the issue has not been addressed so far by the state government, although recently a short-term Australian Volunteer Programme provided GBV response training to responders.

Chuuk has a more functional GBV centre, the Tongen Inepwineu Counseling Center (TICC), which has been instrumental in providing free confidential counselling and referral support through trained, safe counsellors to survivors of domestic violence, rape, sexual harassment, and child sexual abuse. The centre is operated by Chuuk Women's Council, its building was funded by the Japanese government, and operational services are funded by the Australian government with technical support from SPC.

In 2020, the FSM Protection Cluster Group was established at the national level. This aims to support stakeholders' coordination of prevention efforts, response, and access to services and justice in relation to GBV. The group was not functional for some time but with technical support from Pacific Women (SPC) and the International Organization for Migration (IOM), it became active from 2023 and now holds monthly meetings. At this stage, it is developing a terms of reference document and is hoping to endorse it. This would enable it to provide support to GBV victims, particularly in Pohnpei. However, the group is still short of funding, as the annual amount ($1000) received from the government is barely enough to allow it to hold regular meetings.

State-level efforts focused on reducing violence against women and girls include the Kosrae Family Protection Act 2004 and the Pohnpei Domestic Issues Act 2017. However, these pieces of legislation remain largely unenforced. Other programmes in Pohnpei include the Pohnpei Domestic Violence Act Taskforce established in 2014, training of the Pohnpei Police Domestic Violence Unit, and training of health workers on the Standard Operating Procedures (SOPs) on clinical management of rape and sexual assault in Pohnpei. In the context of the COVID-19 pandemic, Chuuk developed an animated video, "Staying safe at home", aimed at raising awareness of the heightened risk of gender-based violence and offering information on assistance available.

Despite support from both national and international development agencies and actors, as well as efforts made by the national government, CEDAW has identified several weaknesses in terms of prevention, protection, and overall response and has recommended that the government give high priority to ensuring that policy, legislation, and support services are in place (CEDAW 2017). Similarly, the unavailability of qualitative research or recent statistical information on GBV has made it difficult to understand the impact of any development work aimed at reducing GBV, at national and local levels.

Consultation with a female advocate against domestic violence faced by women revealed that GBV is a complex issue in FSM. Not only women who are underprivileged, such as those with less education and low incomes, but also privileged women with higher education who are financially and economically independent, such as the advocate herself, often find it difficult to report against GBV. This is mainly due to childcare responsibilities, and fear of stigma and negative impact on children. A Gender Focal Point consulted in Yap echoed this, sharing the similar story that even those who somehow find the courage to file a GBV report against their husbands later drop the case and return to their husbands due to the fear that the separation will negatively impact their children.

In addition to the above, an emerging issue affecting access to justice and protection of young women and girls is trafficking, particularly in the state of Pohnpei. There are cases of internal trafficking, where girls as young as 12 or 13 years old are trafficked to foreign marine workers. At national level, there are laws and policies against traffickers. The national anti-trafficking law criminalizes sex and labour trafficking and prescribes penalties of up to 15 years' imprisonment, a fine of $5000–25,000, or both for offences involving adult victims; and up to 30 years' imprisonment, a fine of $5000–50,000, or both for offences involving child victims (US Department of State 2023). Each of Micronesia's four states has its own laws that criminalize trafficking crimes; however, Pohnpei and Chuuk do not explicitly prohibit adult sex trafficking. Cases prosecuted at the state level may be heard subsequently at the national level, under national anti-trafficking law, depending on which court hears a case. Although laws and policies against perpetrators are in place, they have not had positive impacts in the case of trafficking of young girls. According to a national protection officer, in the state of Pohnpei, parents of young girls are also involved in the trafficking along with other local people and agents who act as links to foreign marine workers; this contributes to cases going unnoticed and unreported. Moreover, anti-trafficking policies and laws are quite weak and gender-irresponsive, as they do not support the victims/survivors.

The IOM has initiated awareness activities such as putting up posters on human trafficking at and around the port and at the local and international airports and producing YouTube videos involving college students in messaging. Till date, there are no evidences to support if these efforts have shown any positive impact on the ground.

B **Economic empowerment**

Typically, FSM gender roles assign women to agricultural food production, seafood collection, and artisan crafts (e.g., loom-woven clothes, oils, and medicine). Earnings from selling crafts are often used to procure canoes, which are an important means of transport. Meanwhile, men are usually assigned to coconut tree cultivation and aquatic activities such as fishing.

Wages in FSM remain low, particularly in the private sector, where both skilled and unskilled workers often make $1.25 to $4.00 per hour. In 2015, women in the formal sector earned on average 13% less than their male counterparts (SPC Pacific Women 2013). Pohnpei has legislation prohibiting wage discrimination based on gender. Kosrae, Chuuk, and Yap have no equal pay legislation. Discrimination in employment based on gender is prohibited under the national and state code in all four states, although this applies only to public service employees.

The labour force participation rate was 46.2% for women and 67.8% for men according to the 2013–14 Household Income and Expenditure Survey (HIES; SPC Pacific Women 2013). The unemployment rate was 13.9% for women and 5.4% for men aged 15 and over. An estimated 29.1% of young women and 18.3% of young men aged 15–24 were not in education, employment, or training.

In the 2013–14 HIES, the incidence of poverty was found to be higher in female-headed households (50.5%) than male-headed households (38.9%) (SPC Pacific Women 2013). In all states, female-headed households were poorer than male-headed households. Although no statistical data is available on current trends, consultation with government officials and with women in some communities in Pohnpei revealed that the migration of men has increased recently, particularly among rural households, with an accompanying increase in both temporary and permanent female-headed households. This has further impacted women's economic status, with increased economic responsibilities and material poverty. Young women are more impacted, with increased family responsibilities.

Currently, one of the main sources of income for women is sewing clothes, which generates more income than selling surplus produce from their garden. However, women are engaged in sewing clothes mostly on a part-time basis due to their reproductive and subsistence work such as childcare, elderly care, cleaning, cooking, gardening/farming, and other household work. Some women also generate income through fundraising activities in their communities.

The IOM has provided technical and funding support for women's economic empowerment (e.g. income generation projects). This support was provided to women entrepreneurs who met the criteria set by the initiative. Funding support provided $5000 dollar to selected women while the technical support consisted of training on financial literacy and on business development and management. Since both technical and funding support were provided to only a few women entrepreneurs, it excluded other women who were new to entrepreneurship ventures or who did not meet the eligibility criteria, particularly young women in rural areas.

In terms of policies and instruments, FSM is not a member of the International Labour Organization (ILO) and therefore has not signed any ILO conventions on equality of economic opportunity and equal treatment at work. Government policies and laws on employment are also gender blind: there are no laws and policies against discrimination based on gender and no gender-responsive provisions or enabling environment for informal or informal employment, although there are a few women-friendly policies (e.g. provision of maternity leave).

Maternity leave is available for women employees working only in the public sector (government agencies). This was increased from 6 to 12 weeks by a Congressional Act in November 2021. There are currently no paternity or parental leave provisions available to male government employees, and there is no national legislation on parental leave in the private sector. Similarly, there is no national legislation against sexual harassment in employment. There is also no legislation to guarantee the provision of childcare by either employers or the state.

UNDP implemented a project on "Strengthening national gender machinery" in FSM from 2019 to 2023. The project was intended to implement key gender policies such as tackling sexual harassment; however, such policies have not been designed or implemented to date. According to the National Child Protection Officer, there are no workplace policies on sexual harassment in place yet., although cases of sexual harassment, particularly faced by women, certainly exist. Cases have been informally reported, but, have not been addressed yet due to lack of formal reporting mechanisms and provisions to address the issue.

C **Climate change and disaster resilience**

The link between gender, climate change, and disaster resilience is not understood clearly in the FSM context. Only recently, in 2018, was a study, undertaken by the IOM, able to explain the gendered nature of the impacts of disasters on the health and safety of women and girls, with a call for more gender-responsive practices and women's and girls' participation in disaster resilience (IOM 2018). Similarly, in 2019 a project implemented by the Green Climate Fund (GCF) titled, "Climate change adaptation solutions for local authorities in the Federated States of Micronesia", undertook gender analysis to understand the gendered impact of climate change and disaster, particularly in Pohnpei (GCF 2019). The project's gender analysis reveals that women in Pohnpei embrace their gender roles in climate change adaptation and disaster resilience and do not expect any changes in the roles. They are more interested in strengthening their roles in building resilience to protect themselves, their families, and their assets from the adverse impacts of climate change and disaster.

In 2017, a workshop was conducted by the Nature Conservancy in collaboration with the Micronesia Conservation Trust to provide a platform for women from the Micronesia region, including FSM, to discuss relevant issues and identify the gaps that need to be addressed in different contexts. From FSM, women mentioned that in Chuuk, violence was reported by some women and girls because of droughts (Mcleod et al. 2018). Similarly, a government official from Pohnpei discussed the need for an analysis of existing climate and gender policies from local to global levels to determine where they can be harmonized by integrating climate considerations into CEDAW and by integrating gender equity into national adaptation plans. Women also pushed for stronger collaboration among local women's groups, national gender development offices, and CEDAW.

Consultation with women in communities in Pohnpei revealed that women are equally involved in farming activities together with men. They usually grow vegetables and crops in their garden, mainly for subsistence. Women often face challenges when their crops are destroyed by climate change impacts such as flooding, which is frequent in Pohnpei. They do not know where to seek climate-related information to protect their crops from such impacts. They also have limited access to information on how to protect their crops from new types of fungus that are affecting their subsistence production and food security. Agriculture extension services and climate-/disaster-related information rarely reach them.

Although social and gender considerations are found in high-level policies on climate change, disaster, fisheries, and agriculture at both national and state levels, the potential of women and the importance of their participation is not generally highlighted. Policies on climate change and disaster mitigation such as the Nationally Determined Contribution (NDC) 2022, National Disaster Response Policy 2016, and Nationwide Climate Change and Disaster Risk Management Policy 2013, mention the importance of gender integration, but, lack contextual gender analysis and evidence.

D **Leadership and political participation**

The importance of women's participation in public life is reiterated in the SDGs, which state that women's full and effective participation and equal opportunities for leadership at all levels of decision-making in political, economic, and public life are critical for the attainment of gender equality and the empowerment of all women and girls. In 2021, the 65th Commission on the Status of Women (CSW65) adopted agreed conclusions on the topic of women's full and effective participation in decision-making and public life, including the encouragement of the implementation of measures and mechanisms to achieve the goal of 50/50 gender balance at all levels of elected positions.

Nonetheless, women's participation in politics and involvement in leadership positions as decision-makers in FSM is very low, at 7.1% (Inter-Parliamentary Union 2022). Following the 2020 State Congress elections, just 5 of the 85 members (six per cent) of state legislatures were women. As of 2022, there are nine women elected to local municipal councils, with women therefore holding one per cent of seats in local government.

In terms of leadership, at community level, three states (excluding Yap) have a matrilineal society where women have decision-making power as heads of the clan. However, as societies are changing and with nuclear households becoming more common, men have more hold over household matters. At institutional level, services in the security sector, such as the police, are male dominated: so far there are no women police officers, although, there are women's associations which are strong. There are women's councils in every state which come together to collectively voice their issues and provide support to women and other marginalized groups in their communities. The Chuuk Women's Council, for example, has played an instrumental role in providing GBV services and has a strong support system for women and girls who are GBV survivors. Similarly, Pohnpei Women's Council, while it does not have any technical capacity, provides its office as a house for GBV survivors—although it is unable to take charge of their protection and security.

2.5 Gaps and Recommendations/opportunities

The above discussion of the issues and challenges clearly shows that there are gaps not only in research and data but also in the clear comprehension of (often complex) on-the-ground issues surrounding gender equality and the SDGs in FSM, which ultimately is affecting the work and efforts of the development community to address the challenges.

Based on the synthesis of issues and challenges presented above, the chapter concludes by briefly outlining below some of the major gaps and provides recommendations for the development community (local, national, and international) on how it can overcome these challenges and increase efforts to accelerate gender equality as a part of achieving the SDGs in FSM.

GBV is the pressing issue affecting the health and safety particularly of women and girls, as identified by the desk review and stakeholder consultations, with huge gaps in the enforcement of policy and law and in response, protection, and prevention, as well as gaps in qualitative research and availability of data. There is an opportunity for national and international development agencies and actors working in the FSM development sectors to provide support to capacity-building for the first responders and service providers, including health service providers, the police force, and women's associations. Further, prevention strategies are recommended, such as dialogues with those holding power in communities, including men, boys, village kings, and religious leaders, as well as those in the government, such as human rights advocates, judges, lawyers, law enforcement personnel, social workers, and policymakers. Such strategies should be accompanied by gender-responsive advocacy for the effective enforcement of policy and law. Additionally, data on GBV is outdated. Currently, the only available data is from 2011. A collaboration of local, national, and international development communities should be envisaged to provide support in collecting and managing GBV data, ensuring this reflects intersectional concerns of diverse groups of women and girls. Further research studies to understand more deeply the connection between GBV and complex relationships existing among women victims, family members, and those in the wider community are critical for gender-responsive policymaking, advocacy, and better programming.

Gender inequality in terms of protection and justice has also hampered the sustainable development of FSM, as trafficking of young girls has become a challenge. Among these young girls, those from low-income households in Pohnpei are particularly at greater risk. Although there are laws and policies against the perpetrator, better laws and policies need to be designed and implemented taking into account the complex nature of trafficking where different parties are involved, including family members. International, national, and local development agencies and actors should collaborate to understand the complex mechanisms of trafficking and to push their agenda towards developing laws and policies that identify and address the root cause and serve the needs and interests of victims/survivors, taking into account their gender, age, and class.

Gender gaps in economic opportunities and earnings have negatively impacted women's economic empowerment. While women are engaged in low-paying and often unpaid work, men take up paid and more remunerative work. With an increase in male migration, there is an increase in the number of female-headed households, mainly in rural areas. Female household heads are facing challenges in learning and developing new skills to take on remunerative economic activities amid other household responsibilities, and this could burden them on multiple levels. There is an opportunity for local, national, and international development agencies and actors to collaborate and design economic empowerment initiatives that will consider women's work burden as well as their financial needs, (self-)employment interests, skills, and capacities.

The links among gender, climate change, and disaster resilience in FSM is under-researched and there is little knowledge available. Development agencies and actors should collaborate to design and implement a rigorous research study to understand the links and identify potential gender gaps that could be addressed through better-informed programming. This research study should amplify women's and girls' voices at national and local levels and reflect the diversity in women's experiences of climate change and disaster impacts, their knowledge and understanding, their capacity and vulnerability, etc., by taking an intersectional approach. Additionally, the development community at both national and local levels should push for climate change and disaster risk reduction policies to include contextual gender assessment/analysis and gender action plans as critical parts of policy design and implementation, with the active participation of women and girls in decision making at national and local levels. This will make the policies more gender-responsive.

In terms of participation in national and local politics and leadership opportunities, women lag behind men in FSM. Although women-led associations are taking leadership roles in pushing forward the gender equality agenda and providing support to local women facing GBV, they have limited knowledge, skills, and resources to do so. While international, national, and local development agencies and actors should focus on involving women-led associations and local women leaders in sustainable development programmes, policymaking, and social work, they should also provide support towards developing the capacity and skills of women leaders. It is also important to ensure that national and local women leaders have equal access to public resources (e.g. information and funds) as well as an enabling environment where they can exercise their leadership and actively participate in national and local politics to influence decisions. There is also a need for advocacy and awareness-raising in communities about the importance of women's leadership, with the presentation of successful women leaders and politicians as role models.

There is limited availability of gender-disaggregated data and information on sector-specific issues. Most of what is available is outdated. There is also low capacity for gender-disaggregated data collection and management among different sectoral departments in each state, with no gender expert or even a focal point. Gender mainstreaming capacity is limited, as is funding and support for addressing gender issues concerning women, men, girls, and boys. International development agencies should collaborate with the national government and with sectoral departments in Pohnpei and other states to provide capacity-building support (e.g. training on gender mainstreaming and gender-disaggregated data collection and management) tailored to the needs of government officials in relevant sectoral departments.

Moreover, there is low capacity to address policy gaps among staff in the Gender Unit of the Department of Health and Social Affairs. The current FSM gender policy expired in 2023. Development agencies and actors should provide support to the Gender Unit to develop and implement a new gender policy—not only funding support but also technical support, appointing technical experts to provide adequate support and advice. There is also an opportunity to provide technical support for the development of the forthcoming Gender Equality Framework and toward addressing CEDAW recommendations.

Furthermore, since workplace policies have not integrated gender concerns in either the public or the private sectors, development agencies and actors should collaborate with both the public and private spheres to develop gender-responsive workplace policies. They should also communicate with the government on the importance and benefits of ratifying ILO conventions.

References

CEDAW (Committee on the Elimination of Discrimination against Women) (2017) CEDAW/C/FSM/CO/1-3, 9 March 2017: concluding observations on the combined initial to third periodic reports of the Federated States of Micronesia. CEDAW, New York

GCF (Green Climate Fund) (2019) Climate change adaptation solutions for local authorities in the Federated States of Micronesia. GCF, Incheon

Inter-Parliamentary Union (2022) Women in parliament 2022. Inter-Parliamentary Union, Geneva

IOM (International Organization for Migration) (2018) Assessing the effect of natural disasters on the health and safety of women and girls in the FSM. IOM, Geneva

Mcleod E, Arora-Johnsson S, Masuda YJ, Bruton-Adams M, Emaurois CO, Gorong B, Hudlow CJ, James R, Kuhlken H, Masike-Liri B, Musrasrik-Carl E, Otzelberger A, Relang K, Reyuw BM, Sigrah B, Stinnett C, Tellei J, Whitford L (2018) Raising the voices of Pacific island women to inform climate adaptation policies. Mar Policy 93:175–185

SPC Pacific Women (2013) Micronesia household income and expenditure survey 2013–2014. SPC, Suva

UNFPA (United Nations Population Fund) (2014) Federated States of Micronesia family health and safety study 2014: a prevalence study on violence against women. UNFPA, Palikir

US Department of State (2023) 2013 trafficking in persons report: Micronesia, Federated States of. US Department of State, Washington, DC

Chapter 3
Training the I-Kiribati to Care for 'Older Australians': A Model for Labour Mobility, Recruitment, and Sustainability

Valentine Hazelman, Sandy O'Brien, Marieta Tekabu, Bannau Tiiata, and Jason Flello

Abstract The challenges faced by small island populations over vast areas of the world's largest ocean are quite similar—socioeconomic, environmental, geographic, and political. Resources vary between countries and are challenged by issues such as environmental degradation, harsh climate, poor governance, poverty, gender inequality, and unsatisfactory health outcomes. Furthermore, "brain drain" migration affects capacity-building while contributing to a decline in population. Because of limited production bases, and the relative weakness of most economies in the region, aid from donors such as Australia and New Zealand remains an essential part of economic development. Labour mobility programmes represent a growing opportunity for more Pacific islanders to seek skilled work abroad and enhance their lives. The aged care sector has seen an exponential increase in demand. Aged care is gaining momentum as the next "golden opportunity" to access skilling and employment outside of Kiribati. This can be observed in Kiribati, a group of 33 coral atolls in the Pacific Ocean, straddling the equator, halfway between Hawaii and Australia. This chapter discusses an aged care training programme in Kiribati, the issues underpinning its start-up, integration into recognized training at the Kiribati Institute of Technology, a model for recruiting and training I-Kiribati workers for labour mobility opportunities in Australia, issues of quality, and how to embed long-term sustainability.

V. Hazelman (✉) · S. O'Brien · M. Tekabu · B. Tiiata · J. Flello
Kiribati Institute of Technology, Betio, Kiribati
e-mail: valentine.hazelman@kit.edu.ki

S. O'Brien
e-mail: sandy.obrien@kit.edu.ki

E. Monaco and M. Abe (eds.), *Sustainable Development Across Pacific Islands*,
https://doi.org/10.1007/978-981-97-3629-4_3

3.1 Introduction

The Pacific islands have long been characterized by large migration flows. Thousands of Pacific islanders have permanently resettled in the Pacific Rim, and sizeable Pacific diasporas are found in Australia, New Zealand, and the United States (ILO 2019). The challenges faced by small island populations over vast areas of the world's largest ocean are quite similar—socioeconomic, environmental, geographic, and political. Resources vary between countries and are challenged by issues such as environmental degradation, harsh climate, poor governance, poverty, gender inequality, and unsatisfactory health outcomes. Furthermore, "brain drain" migration affects capacity-building while contributing to a decline in population. Because of limited production bases, and the relative weakness of most economies in the region, aid from donors such as Australia (via the Department of Foreign Affairs and Trade, DFAT) and New Zealand (via the Ministry of Foreign Affairs and Trade, MFAT), for example, remains an essential part of economic development.

Economically, labour mobility programmes represent a growing opportunity for more Pacific islanders to seek skilled work abroad and enhance their lives. The aged care sector continues to see an exponential increase in demand. Aged care is gaining momentum as a "golden opportunity" to access skilling and employment outside of Kiribati. This can be observed in Kiribati, a group of 33 coral atolls in the Pacific Ocean, straddling the equator halfway between Hawaii and Australia. Kiribati is a member of the Pacific Community, the Commonwealth of Nations, the International Monetary Fund (IMF), the World Bank, and the Organisation of African, Caribbean and Pacific States (OACPS), and became a full member of the United Nations in 1999 (RNZ 2021). Officially the Republic of Kiribati, it is an island country in the Micronesia subregion of Oceania in the central Pacific Ocean. Formerly the Gilbert Islands, Kiribati achieved complete independence in 1979. A 2020 estimate put its population at over 119,000. More than half of the population lives on the Tarawa Atoll. Kiribati (pronounced kɪrɪˈbæs/Kiribass) has a total land area of 811 km^2, spread over 3,441,810 km^2 of ocean (IMF 2011).

This chapter discusses an aged care training programme in Kiribati, the issues underpinning its start-up, integration into recognized training at the Kiribati Institute of Technology (KIT), a model for recruiting and training I-Kiribati workers for labour mobility opportunities in Australia, issues of quality, and how to embed long-term sustainability. An overview of KIT is presented in the next section to contextualize the development of aged care training and the imperative of labour mobility in the region.

3.2 The Kiribati Institute of Technology (KIT)

KIT is a technical and vocational education and training (TVET) institute offering in-demand awards and short courses for trade and non-trade industries since 1970. Training offered by KIT aims to enhance employment opportunities domestically and internationally through accredited and non-accredited courses. KIT is government owned, as a division of the Ministry of Employment and Human Resource (MEHR), working in partnership with the Marine Training Centre (MTC).

Each year, KIT enrols over 250 students at the two main campuses in Betio in the capital, Tarawa, and Kiritimati Island, with over 400 students participating in accredited study each term. There may be up to 500 more who engage in short and customized courses and programmes annually. Betio campus, considered the central campus, houses most of the teaching facilities and schools (business, general studies, and applied technology). The Kiritimati Island campus offers bridging, vocational preparation, English, and business programmes. Up until the end of 2023, the Bikenibeu campus housed the School of Nursing and Health Science; this school has since moved to the Ministry of Health and Medical Services (MHMS). KIT is accredited with the Educational Quality and Assessment Program (EQAP) and has subcontracting agreements in place with Australian registered training organizations (RTOs) to award international qualifications through the KIT Developmental Recognition of Prior Learning (RPL) model (KIT 2023).

3.3 The Kiribati-Australia Skills for Employment Partnership (KASfEP)

The Australian government-funded Kiribati-Australia Skills for Employment Partnership (KASfEP), now in its final phase and third iteration, supports KIT and is managed through the MEHR. Australia (via DFAT) has had a long and enduring partnership with the MEHR in supporting KIT. Other donors, such as the New Zealand government (via MFAT), have also contributed to the development of the MEHR and KIT.

Since 2011, KIT has developed into a regionally recognized vocational education and training provider with Australian aid-funded assistance in areas such as skilled workforce development, labour mobility, infrastructure development, policy reform, and employment sector strengthening. KASfEP is an important investment in the development cooperation partnership between the governments of Australia and Kiribati and contributes towards the goals and objectives of the national development plan, *Kiribati 20-year vision 2016–2036* (KV20).

Among the development cooperation activities, the government of Australia:

- supports the government of Kiribati to increase sustainable employment opportunities for I-Kiribati through improving the coordination and management of the national skills and employment sector;

- enhances the profile of KIT as a training centre of excellence for the delivery of quality-assured, demand-driven skills training;
- supports KIT to deliver internationally recognized qualifications through flexible training and assessment approaches, including RPL programmes with Australian TVET providers;
- delivers an innovative youth engagement strategy for disengaged and unemployed youth to re-enter education through the Bridging Programme;
- facilitates pathways to further education and employment opportunities for KIT graduates with regional institutions, labour mobility programmes, and local industry;
- supports the mobilization of I-Kiribati overseas workers through KIT's Employment Support Services Unit, with pre-departure training and reintegration support;
- maintains strong working relationships with local industry, government ministries, and multilateral organizations to support people-to-people links between Kiribati and Australia;
- promotes gender equality and women's empowerment through programmes that support women in skills training and non-traditional trades and a Memorandum of Understanding partnership with Kiribati Women and Children Support Centre;
- provides disability support services through technology and employment training initiatives to overcome barriers for disabled people in gaining skills and accessing employment opportunities;
- supports sustainable environmental policy and climate action initiatives at KIT, including campus-based renewable energy solutions, climate mitigation and adaptation skills training, and waste reduction education (DFAT 2015).

3.4 Labour Mobility (Migration) and the South Pacific

Simply explained, labour mobility is the movement of people from one place to another, within the territory of a country or across borders, for the purpose of employment (ECSWPR 2023). Labour mobility is a significant and dynamic phenomenon in the South Pacific region, characterized by the movement of people from Pacific island nations to other countries in the region, primarily Australia and New Zealand, in search of employment opportunities. The historical context of labour mobility in the South Pacific may be rooted in the colonial and postcolonial periods. During colonization, Pacific islanders were often recruited to work on plantations and in other industries in the countries of their colonizers. This historical movement of labour created lasting ties between Pacific island nations and their former colonial powers, arguably laying the foundation for modern labour mobility or migration programmes. Labour mobility has brought substantial benefits to Pacific island countries (PICs), including employment, remittances that support households and services provided in communities, increased education, and skills development. Remittances to ten PICs (Fiji, Kiribati, Marshall Islands, Palau, Papua New Guinea, Samoa, Solomon Islands,

Tonga, Tuvalu, and Vanuatu) in 2018 amounted to approximately $689 million, with Fiji receiving the largest sum, followed by Tonga and Samoa. The Pacific island countries have also been characterized as MIRAB (migration, remittances, aid, and bureaucracy) states (ILO 2019).

According to the ILO (2019), seasonal labour migration opportunities for Pacific island countries have emerged in the last 10 years. The New Zealand Recognised Seasonal Employer (RSE) scheme was established in 2007. Australia's Seasonal Worker Program (SWP) was established in 2012 following a pilot that commenced in 2008. These schemes were designed to fill seasonal labour shortages in the horticulture and viticulture industries. Other industries, such as agriculture and accommodation, were later added to the SWP. In the 2017/18 season, a total of 9673 Pacific islanders arrived in New Zealand on an RSE visa, and 8457 SWP visas were granted by Australia to workers from PICs. The RSE, which is open to nine Pacific Island countries, was capped at 12,850 workers at the time, while the SWP was opened to all Pacific island countries and was uncapped in 2015. The number of SWP participating workers has rapidly grown with reforms. The RSE and SWP have become major labour mobility avenues for Pacific island countries. Vanuatu, Tonga, and Samoa were the major beneficiaries, followed by fewer opportunities for Papua New Guinea, Solomon Islands, Kiribati, and Tuvalu. This has gradually changed.

A. **Concerns surrounding labour mobility**

While the benefits of labour mobility have been visible and well documented, it is important to note the concerns and issues arising out of such schemes. A 2023 World Bank report on Pacific labour mobility stated that concerns arise about the pressures of workers being away from their families for extended periods, incidences of worker exploitation in host countries, and the loss of skilled labour from exporting countries. There have been documented cases (RNZ 2018; Stringer 2016) of worker exploitation, such as workers being subjected to underpayment (non-payment in some cases) and unverified pay deductions; denial of toilet breaks; verbal and physical abuse by employers and "gang-masters"; overcrowded accommodation and unreasonable above-market rate charges for accommodation and transport; racism and discrimination at work; and employer non-compliance with pre-departure and on-arrival briefing requirements.

A Pacific mobility research project by the World Bank in 2022 (Petrou et al. 2022) presented the negative social effects of labour mobility, such as a greater shift towards purchased food instead of traditional home-cooked meals when disposable income increased; increased substance abuse reported among men; and some female workers being targeted by gossip upon return home.

3.5 I-Kiribati Workers and the Labour Schemes

According to Burnett (2022), for many I-Kiribati citizens, employment opportunities are extremely limited and employment in labour mobility schemes will mean earning a significantly larger income than is possible through opportunities available at home. Approximately 500 of the 2000 students who graduate from Kiribati's secondary schools each year are employed locally, and an additional 400 pursue post-secondary study. The National Youth Policy of the government of Kiribati, 2011, states that 1100 graduates are left without training or work possibilities, while the National Statistics Office (2019) reported that as of 2015, Kiribati's overall unemployment rate was 41.3%. Local institutions contribute to skilling I-Kiribati; for example, qualified fishers and seafarers are trained at the MTC, and KIT trains tradespeople and students in business disciplines accredited to Australian qualifications. Applications for seasonal work still greatly exceed the number of available positions despite the fact that only 2.5% of Kiribati's workforce is employed by the SWP and RSE schemes. This statistic is pre-pandemic: the numbers may have since recovered or surpassed previous reporting.

A. **The PALM scheme**

Officially taking effect in April 2022, the Pacific Australia Labour Mobility (PALM) scheme allows eligible Australian businesses to hire workers from nine Pacific islands and Timor-Leste when there are not enough local workers available. The scheme helps to fill labour gaps in rural and regional Australia and nationally in agriculture and selected agriculture-related food product manufacturing sectors by offering employers access to a pool of reliable, productive workers. It also allows workers to develop their skills and send income home while working. Once approved to recruit under the PALM scheme, employers can access two cohorts of workers—short-term workers (up to nine months) and long-term workers (between one and four years). PALM scheme employers in the agriculture sector can be based anywhere in Australia, but in all other sectors they must be based in a regional or rural location (Love 2023). The PALM scheme is managed by DFAT and the Department of Employment and Workplace Relations (DEWR) with the support of the Pacific Labour Facility (PLF).

The Australian government is committed to further expanding and enhancing the PALM scheme in line with Australian and Pacific aspirations. It will strengthen the PALM scheme so that it continues to deliver for employers and for workers and their families and communities, including by:

- strengthening the government's oversight of the scheme to enhance conditions and better protect and support workers to improve their experience in Australia;
- responsibly growing the scheme and better supporting employers and participating countries by:
  - providing additional resources to DEWR to increase the government's PALM scheme regional footprint, to better support PALM scheme employers across Australia, including small growers

  - increasing resources for participating countries to mobilize more workers, to ensure that countries with aspirations to grow their participation in the scheme can do so

- supporting more than 1000 PALM scheme workers to attain formal qualifications over four years;
- increasing support to make it easier for PALM scheme workers to access their superannuation savings when they return home;
- providing access to Medicare for an initial 200 families who will participate in the PALM scheme family accompaniment pilot (Medicare is a national scheme providing Australians and some overseas visitors with free or subsidized health services; Services Australia 2023).

In February 2023, the Australian government reached a major milestone—six months ahead of schedule—with more than 35,000 PALM scheme workers now in Australia. These reforms expand the scheme responsibly so that it can continue to meet unskilled, low-skilled, and semi-skilled labour shortages, especially in regional Australia. These reforms build on those announced in October 2022 and ongoing efforts to bring together the SWP and Pacific Labour Scheme (PLS) into a more flexible and efficient PALM scheme (DFAT 2022).

2 The Aged Care Expansion (ACE) programme

In response to the encouraging reception from the pilots and ongoing demand, the Australian government has committed to expanding the number of funded aged care training places for PALM participants. The Aged Care Expansion (ACE) programme is designed to support both large and small aged care providers to secure qualified, long-term care workers from the Pacific and Timor-Leste. The intent is to partner with aged care approved employers (AEs) to deliver at least 500 new trained workers in 2023. Workers will complete their Certificate III in Individual Support (Ageing) and have the right to work with the same AEs for up to four years. AEs must commit to paying PALM workers the same as other workers in the same role (pay parity). Workers must receive a minimum of 30 h of paid work per week for the duration of their studies, increasing to full-time contracts on attainment of their Certificate III qualification (PALM 2023a). These certificate qualifications are based on the Australian Qualifications Framework (AQF), which incorporates regulated qualifications from each education and training sector. The AQF consists of ten levels from certificates (level 1) to doctoral degrees (level 10) (AQF 2013).

Through the ACE programme, AEs can apply for funding that covers the costs of the Certificate III training for workers. In applying for ACE funding, an AE is expected to work with an RTO to develop a comprehensive and integrated training programme that supports the learning, working, and welfare needs of workers throughout their qualification. A key requirement is that workers are supported to manage the challenges they will face living and working in a new country while undertaking a training programme. To ensure strong workforce protection, employers are required to invite the Fair Work Ombudsman (FWO) and relevant union representatives to the workers' arrival briefing. The FWO, under the Australian government, promotes harmonious, productive, cooperative, and compliant workplace relations in Australia and outlines the responsibilities set by the Fair Work Act (Fair Work Ombudsman 2024). ACE builds on the lessons learned from the pilots and encourages innovation in the development and delivery of ACE training programmes, including training models that include both offshore and onshore elements (PALM 2023a).

3.6 Aged Care Training at KIT

To support the increasing demand for labour mobility opportunities and address a key component of KASfEP outputs (KF 2022), the Aged Care Programme at KIT was implemented in 2022. In its fledgling stage, it has seen 116 I-Kiribati nationals leave for Australia in 2023 in four cohorts, with nearly 6000 online registrations under consideration for future cohorts. The recruitment of a long-term advisor who specializes in aged care was a key catalyst in getting the programme off the ground with agility. Before this, KIT offered sporadic short courses in aged care that ran for about seven weeks. The programme is still in development in terms of offering a full qualification at the Certificate III level. For now, a hybrid/blended training model is in place. Hybrid or blended training/learning combines traditional face-to-face classroom instruction with online learning (EDUCAUSE 2024). The next section further explains how this hybrid training works, in country and then abroad.

A. **The current model**

At the start of 2022, an online registration process via Google Forms was developed to capture public interest in the programme. As long as registered parties were fit, healthy, 21 years of age and over, and with a clean police record, they could apply. The form continues to be open as long as there is demand among aged care recruitment agencies, in Australia to begin with. The form requests the following: full name; date of birth; gender; email address; phone contact; current residence (if on the outer islands, they must indicate where); highest level of English; highest qualification, and the area of their qualification if applicable; employment status, their job, and where they work if currently employed; if they have ever engaged in the areas of social work, community, services, hospitality, caregiving, or similar areas and what type of work they engaged in; if they have ever volunteered within the community or cared for elderly family members; and other information to support their registration. Registrations are shortlisted on average every two to three months for a language, literacy, and numeracy (LLN) test before acceptance into the programme is approved. The LLN test follows a blended format in three segments:

1. Online test (50 min);
2. Paper-based test (30 min);
3. One-on-one interview (5 min).

To date, the acceptance rate into the programme following shortlisting and testing is approximately 77% (see Table 3.1).

Table 3.1 Acceptance rate into the KIT aged care programme

Cohort	Number shortlisted for LLN test	Number accepted into programme	Acceptance rate (%)	Number in class	Start of class
1	–	30*	–	30	March 2023
2	60	40	67	40	May 2023
3	60	46	77	40	May 2023
4	59	40	68	33	August 2023
5	52	40	77	39	September 2023
6	49	47	96	43	January 2024

Note * selection made prior to current model was implemented from Cohort 2 onwards

Following acceptance into the programme, students are briefed about the expectations, which primarily focuses on the fact that it is a 12-week full-time programme. Despite the acceptance number, some do not make it to the class for various reasons (often personal) that prevent them from starting. Those who are in full-time employment are advised to withdraw due to the intensive format of the programme. A session with students and their families is also organized to dispel any apprehensions or fears they may have about the programme and eventual mobilization to Australia.

In negotiation with a prominent aged care recruitment agency and RTO, five units of the full Certificate III in Individual Support are offered on-island at KIT, with the remaining ten units to be undertaken while in employment in Australia. Delivery of the five units occurs face-to-face, and online using the Moodle learning management system (cloud-based). Because of the unconventional approach of this model, enrolments in the programme do not follow the typical entry process for KIT. To date, two cohorts have completed the full qualification while working in Australia (HealthX 2023). Before leaving Kiribati, students accumulate their evidence for RPL assessment, including assessments (required competence) from the five units and additional evidence such as revised CVs; community engagements; certification of participation in activities such as Elder Abuse Awareness Day, LGBTQI awareness month, and additional workshops; references from care provided in the community; and certificates from prior study. A Moodle portal acts as a repository for the evidence that can be externally accessed by an RTO to assess RPL.

2 The model moving forward

Running in tandem with the current model for aged care training at KIT is the development of the full qualification, projected to be rolled out in 2024. The assessment and teaching materials for the programme have already been acquired from an Australian resource centre, and a course developer is currently working with subject matter experts on implementing the units online. The programme is projected to be blended, comprising face-to-face classroom instruction and online assessment. When the full qualification is finally developed and accredited, it is anticipated that enrolments will follow normal KIT processes, with possible quota-based intake to provide the most effective teacher-to-student ratio and teaching resources. Specialized teaching materials and equipment are currently being procured and set up in two temporary campus locations while the main Betio campus undergoes further infrastructural development under MFAT funding. Instead of the current split delivery of the programme onshore and offshore, it is envisioned that when the full programme is up and running at KIT, students will leave Kiribati for employment fully qualified.

3.7 Embedding Long-Term Sustainability and the Future

Migration, both permanent and temporary, is an important source of employment and income for Pacific islanders. It has facilitated higher levels of consumption and standards of living than would otherwise have been possible, in light of the geographical impediments to economic growth faced in the region (Doan et al. 2023). For aged care training for labour mobility in Kiribati, it is essential that sustainability is a permanent focus, in the areas of ensuring quality in recruitment and training, consideration for family, and community education and pastoral care, as well as close collaboration between all parties involved in the process of labour mobility. This may be the way forward.

A. **Focus on quality**

The focus for both KIT and the MEHR has been to ensure that when participants arrive in Australia to take up roles in the aged care sector as support workers, they stand out from those from the other countries competing for employment opportunities. At the commencement of this project, the MEHR and KIT agreed that no one should leave Kiribati through the PALM scheme without appropriate training or refresher training, to maintain a reputation of quality.

To assist in maintaining this reputation, supplementary to the units of competency delivered in class, students are taught additional skills and knowledge vital for relevance to the industry. The focus is on ensuring that the I-Kiribati have a strong understanding of infection control within the industry, documentation requirements, the importance of person-centred care for clients, the holistic care needs of clients, the signs of elder abuse, and showing compassion and kindness.

2 **Caring for the elderly within Kiribati**

KIT has always maintained that the aged care programmes delivered in Kiribati should not be focused solely on labour mobility. KIT and the MEHR feel they have an ethical obligation to ensure the older generation in Kiribati too are provided with the support and care they deserve. Due to the ageing population and labour mobility opportunities taken up by family members, skilled aged care workers are needed to support the older generation left behind.

The development of a Certificate II in Community Care qualification that will be accredited through EQAP is on the horizon. This qualification is being developed as an entry-level programme for community workers and will be contextualized to Kiribati, ensuring that it has a firm focus on the cultural needs of local clients. Graduates of this qualification will have a clear understanding of both the disability and the aged care sector within Kiribati and the importance of teamwork and communication. They will be able to demonstrate professionalism, follow infection control procedures within the community, participate in safe work practices, recognize signs consistent with dementia, meet basic personal support needs for clients, and work with families and carers to provide person-centred care to those in need. Successful completion of this programme can open doors to entry positions within the community, such as working as a companion, a housekeeper, or a care worker. It will provide a pathway to further education, including level III community and aged care qualifications, and can significantly enhance the expertise of participants and the level of holistic care provided within the community.

3 Giving back to the community

Future plans for aged care in Kiribati include embedding the needs of the older community and disabled people firmly within KIT programmes. Kiribati has no aged care facilities; traditionally, the I-Kiribati live in extended families and older family members are cared for at home. During the delivery of the current KIT programme, trainers and students include older community members in an 'elderly day' celebration that is a mirror of the care and support provided in a traditional respite centre (in Australia and New Zealand). It has been a success with community members and an opportunity for students to use their new skills and knowledge to support their own family members to participate in the day.

KIT would like to establish the first respite centre in Kiribati. Respite has many benefits, including:

- an opportunity for carers to take a break from looking after an older family member;
- an opportunity for a recharge, while being at peace knowing your family member is well taken care of;
- an opportunity for older community members to participate in a regular support group with local friends;
- a centre for sharing cultural traditions with younger community members;
- reducing isolation for some participants;
- a regular day out for participants to look forward to that includes specifically designed programmes for participants;
- a work placement opportunity for KIT students completing aged care training;
- an employment opportunity for returning workers working in aged care;
- strong community involvement in the delivery of aged care training in Kiribati.

4 Support for family

As previously stated, the social impacts of labour mobility can be taxing on family units, especially those family members left behind in Kiribati while the sole breadwinner is abroad for work for extended periods—up to four years for work such as that obtained through the ACE programme. While a new family accompaniment policy (PALM 2023b) is set to be trialled by a few countries to allow more family members to join their loved ones abroad, other avenues may be looked into to assist those who prefer to stay in Kiribati. The Australian government is committed to allowing PALM scheme workers on long-term placements of between one and four years to bring their families to Australia, with the agreement of their employer. This policy aims to address the social impacts of long periods of family separation and build deeper connections with the Pacific and Timor-Leste family. In terms of family members who prefer to stay behind, community-based activities and initiatives could be enhanced to engage them, whether that be environmental preservation activities, short upskilling courses, or agricultural assistance to encourage more organic, healthier lifestyles. Further, digital, information, and financial (entrepreneurship) literacy skills should be embedded in community programmes as essential, foundational skills. Digital and financial literacy (DFL) are critical areas for promoting financial inclusion in the Pacific region. With its current low levels of DFL and the increase in the adoption of digital financial services, there is a need to equip Pacific islanders with the proper digital and financial management skills (Pacific E-Commerce Initiative 2023).

5 **Data and reporting**

Further collaboration is encouraged between stakeholders in aged care training and labour mobility in Kiribati, particularly the institutions that deliver aged care training and the units that send labour. This collaboration requires consistent communication and regular reporting, which means prioritizing data, transparency, and learning. Regular satisfaction surveys of workers and employers should be undertaken, and the data should be made publicly available and supported by the establishment or enhancement of a centralized worker and family contact database.

3.8 Conclusion

Aged care training for labour mobility does not appear to be slowing down any time soon and as opportunities open up for more I-Kiribati, so will issues relating to livelihoods, family units, capacity-building, and resilience to the onslaught of developments that lie ahead. The future of labour mobility in Kiribati is likely to be influenced by factors such as changing migration policies in destination countries, efforts to address climate change, and the development of the Kiribati economy. To harness the potential of labour mobility, the government and international organizations may consider protecting migrant workers by implementing stronger legal protections for I-Kiribati workers abroad to safeguard their rights and wellbeing; diversifying the economy by investing in domestic industries to create job opportunities and reduce dependency on remittances; and working on climate change adaptation and mitigation strategies to protect Kiribati's environment and resources, with the interests of the I-Kiribati people paramount.

References

AQF (Australian Qualifications Framework) (2013) About [Online]. Available at: www.aqf.edu.au/framework/australian-qualifications-framework. Accessed 13 Feb 2024

Burnett R (2022) Kiribati: Pacific labour mobility schemes in the COVID-19 context. DAWN discussion paper 42. DAWN (Development Alternatives with Women for a New Era), Suva [Online]. Available at: https://dawnnet.org/wp-content/uploads/2022/05/DAWN-DP_42_-Pacific-Labour-Mobility-Schemes-in-the-COVID-19-Context-2.pdf. Accessed 22 Sept 2023

DFAT (Department of Foreign Affairs and Trade) (2015) Kiribati skills for employment program (SfEP) Investment design document (IDD) [Online]. Available at: www.dfat.gov.au/sites/default/files/kiribati-skills-for-employment-design-doc-2015.pdf. Accessed 22 Sept 2023

DFAT (2022) Pacific labour mobility [Online]. Available at: www.dfat.gov.au/geo/pacific/engagement/pacific-labour-mobility. Accessed 22 Sept 2023

Doan D, Dornan M, Doyle J, Petrou K (2023) Migration and labour mobility from Pacific island countries. Background paper for world development report 2023: migrants, refugees, and societies. World Bank, Washington, DC [Online]. Available at: https://thedocs.worldbank.org/en/doc/511bd7fb799a3379242b5c151b2a14d5-0050062023/original/WDR-Pacific-Islands-case-study-FORMATTED.pdf. Accessed 30 Oct 2023

ECSWPR (European Centre for Social Welfare Policy and Research) (2023) Labour mobility [Online]. Available at: www.euro.centre.org/domains/labour-mobility. Accessed 30 Oct 2023

EDUCAUSE (2024) Hybrid learning [Online]. Available at: https://library.educause.edu/topics/teaching-and-learning/hybrid-learning. Accessed 12 Feb 2024

Fair Work Ombudsman (2024) About us [Online]. Available at: www.fairwork.gov.au/about-us. Accessed 12 Feb 2024

HealthX (2023) Aged care today: securing trained aged care workers from Kiribati a win-win [Online]. Available at: https://healthx.com.au/latestnews/securing-trained-aged-care-workers-from-kiribati-a-win-win. Accessed 23 Oct 2023

ILO (International Labour Organization) (2019) Labour mobility in Pacific island countries. ILO Office for Pacific Island Countries, Suva [Online]. Available at: www.ilo.org/wcmsp5/groups/public/-asia/-ro-bangkok/-ilo-suva/documents/publication/wcms_712549.pdf. Accessed 21 Sept 2023

IMF (International Monetary Fund) (2011) 'Kiribati: 2011 Article IV consultation-staff report, informational annexes, debt sustainability analysis, public information notice on the Executive Board discussion, and statement by the Executive Director for Kiribati'. Country Report 11/113. IMF, Washington, DC. Available at: www.imf.org/en/Publications/CR/Issues/2016/12/31/Kiribati-2011-Article-IV-Consultation-Staff-Report-Informational-Annexes-Debt-Sustainability-24871. Accessed 21 Sept 2023

KF (Kiribati Facility) (2022) 'KASfEP workplan', Annex 1 to the Kiribati facility skills for employment partnership annual plan. Scope Global (unpublished)

KIT (Kiribati Institute of Technology) (2023) About KIT [Online]. Available at: https://kit.edu.ki/about-kit. Accessed 29 Nov 2023

Love S (2023) 'The Pacific labour mobility scheme: a quick guide', Research Paper Series 2023–24. Parliament of Australia, Department of Parliamentary Services, Canberra [Online]. Available at: https://parlinfo.aph.gov.au/parlInfo/download/library/prspub/9368852/upload_binary/9368852.pdf;fileType=application%2Fpdf. Accessed 12 Feb 2024

National Statistics Office (2019) Unemployment rate 1990–2015 [Online]. Available at: www.mfed.gov.ki/our-work/national-statistics-office. Accessed 12 Feb 2024

Pacific E-Commerce Initiative (2023) 'About the project', digital and financial literacy survey in seven Pacific island countries. Pacific Islands Forum Secretariat, Suva [Online]. Available at: https://pacificecommerce.org/pei-project/conducting-digital-and-financial-literacy-suvey-in-7-pacific-islands/#:~:text=Digital%20and%20Financial%20Literacy%20(DFL,digital%20and%20financial%20management%20skills. Accessed 14 Feb 2024

PALM (2023a) Aged care expansion program: information for approved employers' (V2). Australian Government, Canberra [Online]. Available at: www.palmscheme.gov.au/sites/default/files/2023-02/EOI%20attachment%20A%20-%20ACE%20information%20for%20approved%20employers.pdf. Accessed 24 Jan 2024

PALM (2023b) Family accompaniment: information for workers [Online]. Available at: www.palmscheme.gov.au/sites/default/files/2023-05/Family%20accompaniment%20frequently%20asked%20questions.pdf. Accessed 24 Jan 2024

Petrou K, Casabonne U, Doan D, Dornan M (2022) The gendered and social impacts of labour mobility in the Pacific. Presentation at the Australasian Aid Conference, 30 November [Online]. Available at: https://devpolicy.org/2022-Australasian-AID-Conference/presentations/Social-gendered-impacts-labour-mobility_KPetrou-et-al.pdf. Accessed 24 Jan 2024

RNZ (Radio New Zealand) (2018) Exploitation of kiwifruit workers is rife—union [Online]. Available at: www.rnz.co.nz/news/business/357040/exploitation-of-kiwifruit-workers-is-rife-union. Accessed 24 Jan 2024

RNZ (2021) Five Micronesian countries leave Pacific Islands Forum [Online]. Available at: www.rnz.co.nz/international/pacific-news/436039/five-micronesian-countries-leave-pacific-islands-forum. Accessed 21 Sept 2023

Services Australia (2023) About medicare [Online]. Available at: www.servicesaustralia.gov.au/about-medicare?context=60092. Accessed 13 Feb 2024

Stringer C (2016) Worker exploitation in New Zealand: a troubling landscape. Paper prepared for the human trafficking research coalition. University of Auckland Business School, Auckland [Online]. Available at: https://img.scoop.co.nz/media/pdfs/1612/Worker_Exploitation_in_New_Zealand_Stringer.pdf. Accessed 24 Jan 2024

World Bank (2023) Pacific labour mobility: the benefits, concerns and opportunities. World Bank, Washington, DC [Online]. Available at: https://thedocs.worldbank.org/en/doc/25ab899fb64f18a4162a71fa45981be0-0070012023/pacific-labor-mobility-the-benefits-concerns-and-opportunities. Accessed 24 Jan 2024

Chapter 4
The Negative Secondary Impacts of Climate Change on Pacific Islanders' Mental Health

Nikisha Smith

Abstract Climate change is recognized as one of the most serious global crises, creating worldwide health threats, including to mental health. Among the areas most affected by climate change are the Pacific Small Island Developing States (SIDS), particularly atoll nations, which have been internationally recognized as "sinking islands". Atolls nations Kiribati, Marshall Islands, and Tuvalu, are facing extreme socio-cultural challenges as they experience sea level rise and shrinking land mass. The mental health concerns resulting from the socio-cultural impacts of climate change have not been fully researched at the community level, leaving gaps in policy planning and adaptation strategies. In particular, forced migration raises many concerns over sovereignty, statehood, and national and cultural identity, creating an intrinsically complicated scenario for both migrants and host countries. This chapter will analyse the multiple ways in which the impending threat of climate change can impact individual and community mental health through: (i) first-hand experience of more severe and frequent climate-related disasters; (ii) "solastalgic" feelings of sadness when reflecting on the changing environment; and (iii) eco-anxiety over future outcomes. These intertwining mental health impacts should be considered in future decision-making when preparing for climate change mitigation.

4.1 Introduction

This chapter will explore negative mental health impacts as a secondary effect of climate change, particularly for societies contemplating climate migration, thus uprooting their systems and culture. It will further review the gaps that exist in measuring the cost of non-economic loss, such as loss of identity, sovereignty, and traditional governing systems, while also identifying the lack of non-Western perspectives and culturally appropriate services for understanding and providing

N. Smith (✉)
United Nations Multi-Country Office for Micronesia, Kolonia, Micronesia
e-mail: nikisha.smith@un.org; nikisha.smith2@gmail.com

Charles Darwin University, Darwin, Australia

E. Monaco and M. Abe (eds.), *Sustainable Development Across Pacific Islands*,
https://doi.org/10.1007/978-981-97-3629-4_4

support to deal with different forms of climate-related mental health concerns. Focusing on experiences in the Republic of Kiribati, the Republic of the Marshall Islands, and Tuvalu, the chapter will explore mental health impacts from the perspective of first-hand accounts of climate-related incidents, nostalgic feelings of loss, and eco-anxiety. It is important to note that although there are commonalities among Pacific people's experiences, there are disadvantages in treating them as one homogeneous group, as experiences may vary between Pacific individuals and cultures (Oakley-Browne et al. 2008).

4.2 Literature Review: Background Information

This section provides background on the prevalence of climate-related hazards in the Pacific region. It identifies the shared challenges and disparities encountered by Pacific atoll nations, whilst recognizing they are the most vulnerable to climate-related disasters. The section then discusses different concepts of mental health, including Western and non-Western perspectives and precolonial ideas of spiritual wellbeing which is deeply rooted in connection to land. This ideology: connection to land, mental health, and spiritual wellbeing will form the basis for an understanding of how mental health is impacted by climate change.

A. **Climate change**

Climate change is one of the most serious global crises and creates worldwide health, economic, social, and physical threats (Coffey et al. 2021). Natural hazards such as cyclones, earthquakes, tsunamis, droughts, and flooding are becoming more severe and more frequent (Costi 2020). Rising sea temperatures are increasing water acidity, affecting coral and marine microorganisms, while sea level rises and changing currents affect marine biodiversity (Costi 2020). Sea levels have the potential to rise by more than one metre if the global temperature exceeds 2 °C above pre-industrial temperatures, causing uninhabitability and displacement, particularly for atoll nations where the average elevation is approximately one metre above sea level (Costi 2020; WorldAtlas 2023a).

Climate-related disasters have been the leading cause of internal displacement since 2009, forcibly displacing 20 million people per year (Oxfam 2019). Climate change does not affect countries equally: communities in countries with lower socioeconomic status, including Small Island Developing States (SIDS), are 150 times more likely to be displaced due to extreme weather events than European communities (Oxfam 2019). Since 1970, people living in the Asia–Pacific region have been five times more likely to be affected by natural disasters than those who live elsewhere (ESCAP 2017). The Economic and Social Commission for Asia and the Pacific (ESCAP 2017) predicts that 40% of the global economic losses associated with climate-change-related disasters will occur in the Asia–Pacific region. The Pacific is experiencing sea level rises at a rate two to three times the global average (UNDP

2023). The remoteness of island nations increases the risk of both slow- and sudden-onset events (Costi 2020; UNDP 2023). This includes issues associated with sea level rises, such as storm surges, king tides, and salinization (Campbell 2022). This increasing exposure to frequent and severe weather events, rising sea levels, and warming sea temperatures indirectly affects communities, by impacting food security and clean water sources and increases the risk of vector-borne diseases such as dengue fever, as well as forcing people to contemplate the future habitability of their nations (Hashim and Hashim 2016; Straits Times 2022).

B. **Atoll nations**

Atoll islands are among the island nations most vulnerable to climate change. They consist of a thin ring-shaped strip of islands where the land is close to sea level (WorldAtlas 2023a). For example, the Marshall Islands' height above sea level averages approximately one metre with the highest point at 10 m above sea level, while Tuvalu's highest point is only 4.5 m above sea level. At its narrowest, the country is just 20 m in width (Fainu 2023; Rudiak-Gould 2013; The Pacific Project 2021). The narrow and low composition of the atoll nations makes them more vulnerable to hazards such as cyclones, tropical storms, tsunamis, and droughts (Allen 2004). Atolls are vulnerable to climate change because of rising sea levels, coastal erosion receding shorelines, and salination, impacting food, water, and energy security (Campbell 2022; Yates 2022). Naturally, fresh drinking water is scarce in the atoll nations as there are no lakes or rivers and rainwater is infrequent during the dry season. Ocean acidification and coral bleaching affect catchments of fish, and salination affects crop and water sources, making the islands increasingly uninhabitable (Rudiak-Gould 2013). Climate change has multilayered compound impacts, meaning that an initial event causes secondary or cascading risks with a more widespread effect than initially anticipated (Costi 2020; Eiser et al. 2012). Secondary risks including salination, extreme weather, temperature changes, and long-term drought heavily impact local food security, threatening habitats and generating reliance on imported, expensive, nutrient-poor food (Fainu 2023). Because of this, atoll nations are having to consider relocating their populations as livelihoods are affected and physical land disintegrates (Roy 2019).

C. **Mental health**

The World Health Organization (WHO 2022) defines mental health as "a state of mental well-being that enables people to cope with the stressors of life", which "underpins our individual and collective abilities to make decisions, build relationships and shape the world we live in". It identifies mental wellbeing as a human right and as "crucial to personal, community and socio-economic development" (WHO 2022). Whether a person experiences positive or negative mental health and wellbeing is linked to how they see the world and their emotional engagement within it, and how this impacts their daily lives (MacDonald 2006). There is no universal understanding of the intricate differences between mental health, mental illness, and mental well-being, and the terms can mean different things to different people depending on their cultural discourse (MacDonald 2006). To people from the Pacific, mental illness can be considered a disconnect between one's mind, body, and spirit, or a breakage in one's bond with land, kinship, and spirituality (Samu and Suaalii-Sauni 2009). People from the Pacific recognize the importance of strong cultural identities in supporting their mental health through connection, family relationships, traditions, and spirituality (LeVa 2014). Collectivist cultures like those of the Pacific understand their identity and wellbeing as intrinsically interconnected with community and family values as they share an interdependent social identity (Haluza-DeLay 2014; Lavell et al. 2012; Ward et al. 2001). Changing physical environment can disrupt these ties, causing detrimental mental health impacts. Negative mental health in the form of psychological distress can impact all aspects of daily life. At times, psychological distress can manifest into different types of disorders, including mood disorders, anxiety disorders, substance abuse, and psychosocial and stress-related or stress-induced disorders (Oakley-Browne et al. 2008; Smith 2022). There are higher rates of psychotic disorders such as schizophrenia and paranoia among Pacific peoples who have migrated to other countries. In New Zealand, for example, these disorders disproportionately affect Pacific people, who are referred to emergency inpatient care for schizophrenia, paranoia, and acute psychotic disorders at a higher rate than non-Pacific people (66% compared with 39% respectively) (Mila-Schaaf and Hudson 2009). However, the primary research on mental health is from the point of view of Western interpretations, with limited information from the Pacific cultural context. Mental health is addressed differently in different cultures because of taboos or beliefs, often influenced by religious values and spiritual connections (MacDonald 2006). Yet, colonization forced Western systems and ideologies into the position of dominant discourses, shaping global understandings of mental health (Mila-Schaaf and Hudson 2009). As a result, Christianity accounts for approximately 95% of religious beliefs in Marshall Islands and Tuvalu and 96% in Kiribati (Central Statistics Division of the Government of Tuvalu 2017; Kiribati National Statistics Office 2022; WorldAtlas 2023b). Christianity therefore shares an influence on concepts of mental health and wellbeing, alongside traditional faith, medicines, and practices.

D. **Pacific cultural and spiritual connections to the land**

An individual's identity, health, and wellbeing are dependent on family connections, heritage, and roles and responsibilities. These are entwined with the importance of kin relationships, traditional healers, and traditional medicines that are found in the natural environment (Samu 2009). To deny spirituality or culture is to deny identity in both the personal and the collective sense (Passmore et al. 2023). Traditional ecological knowledge (TEK) is a form of knowledge uniquely specific to land. In this conception, the relationship between people and the environment is interdependent (Spencer et al. 2020). The land holds specific spiritual connection to ancestors whose spirits continue to protect and live through the land, and specific cultural practices continue to connect people with their ancestors (Spencer et al. 2020). A study by the University of the South Pacific (Nunn et al. 2016) identified that 86% of Pacific islanders consider their welfare to be intrinsically linked with nature. Further, 89% of participants felt deeply interconnected with the inherent historical archives that live through the land as Pacific knowledge is passed down orally and through artifacts—contrasting with the dominant Western practice of archiving information by documenting it (Neale and Kelly 2020; Nunn et al. 2016). Loss of land is therefore more than just physical loss: it affects the foundations of individual and collective identities and threatens peoples' sense of belonging and communities' cultural survival (Parry et al. 2007). Mental health and the related support systems are predominately understood from Western perspectives. There is little research specializing in mental health perceptions from a non-Western perspective different spiritual views towards mental health, spirituality and services in scope with traditional practices as identified in *Te Rau Hinengaro*—the New Zealand Mental Health Survey. *Te Rau Hinengaro* found that Pacific people reportedly experience psychological distress 1.5 times more frequently than non-Pacific people but seek to access available support systems at a much lower rate (Ministry of Health 2016). Only a quarter of Pacific people who report experiencing psychological distress access mental health services and receive a diagnosis (Mila-Schaaf and Hudson 2009). Of those with a diagnosis, only 25% went on to receive further treatment, compared with 58% of non-Pacific people with a similar diagnosis (Oakley-Browne et al. 2008). This stark contrast highlights the gaps in mental health services and support for Pacific people. This disparity has been linked to mixed feelings that Pacific islanders in New Zealand have regarding their identity, sense of belonging, and connection to culture, as they experience "identity tension" in trying to negotiate a sense of belonging to both cultures (Manuela and Sibley 2014). Research on second-generation Pacific people in New Zealand indicates that people who feel accepted by their ethnic group were 50% less likely to have suicidal ideation and 70% less likely to attempt suicide compared with people who felt that they were not accepted (Mila-Schaaf 2010). Additionally, New Zealand-born Pacific islanders were twice as likely to have a mental health disorder compared with those who migrated as adults (Oakley-Browne et al. 2008). Pacific people of multi-ethnic backgrounds internalize negative stereotypes associated with their Pacific identities, or social isolation, confusion, and exclusion as a result of not feeling that they belong to the culture of their host country or to their Pacific heritage (Ataera-Minster and Trowland 2018; Keddell 2006; Manuela and Sibley 2014). There are different perceptions of illness and treatment for Pacific people based on their combined belief systems. Mediating the relationship between these practices can provide culturally safe spaces and appropriate support systems. Some methods for this include indigenous treatments and practices (such as *kava* ceremonies) to support and promote individual wellbeing (Mila-Schaaf and Hudson 2009). Negative stigma and cultural perceptions of mental health can impact people accessing services (Ataera-Minster and Trowland 2018). According to results from the 2015 New Zealand Mental Health Monitor, stigma and negative attitudes around mental health and people with mental health disorders are more prevalent within Pacific communities (Deverick et al. 2017). Terms with derogatory connotations such as "crazy" are commonly used within Pacific communities, and strong Christian influence has led people with mental illnesses to believe they are cursed (Ataera-Minster and Trowland 2018; Samu and Suaalii-Sauni 2009). The limited nature of culturally appropriate support systems also contributes to lack of engagement in mental health support systems among Pacific people.

4.3 Conceptual Framework

According to Böhm (2003), there are three ways that climate change can affect mental health:

1. Experiencing extreme weather events caused by climate change can cause a secondary impact of direct stress and lead to mental illnesses, post-traumatic stress syndrome (PTSD), obsessive–compulsive disorder (OCD), and depression, as well as coping mechanisms such as alcoholism.
2. It can engender a feeling of "solastalgia"—the nostalgic sense of loss as people observe gradual environmental changes. This is especially apparent for people from communities that have a strong attachment to their environment, particularly indigenous peoples.
3. Contemplating and hearing of the future impacts of climate change and the feeling of fear and hopelessness can result in "eco-anxiety" (Coffey et al. 2021). Additionally, losing national identity, sovereignty, and statehood as a result of relocation and emigration causes feelings of despair, anger, and confusion. This can result in a fracturing of the connection to traditional practices and cultural and spiritual links with place, and a loss of identity.

4.4 Country Cases

Looking at each of the atoll nations, Kiribati, Marshall Islands, and Tuvalu, this section will cross-reference Bohm's theory on the impacts of climate change and identify the loss of identity through climate migration.

A. **Experiencing extreme weather events**

Surviving regular and severe climate-related disasters generates severe stress and emotional trauma responses which have been linked to feelings of shock, anxiety, survivor guilt, denial, depression, and PTSD (Babbel 2010; Gibson et al. 2020). The occurrence of more extreme disasters increases the likelihood of PTSD: up to 40% of people can experience PTSD post-disaster, with lower socioeconomic groups particularly affected (Galea et al. 2005; Samuels 2019). Rising sea levels, king tides, flooding, salinization, droughts, cyclones, and tsunamis continue to cause instability for Pacific island nations. As climate-related disasters increase in severity and frequency, it can be assumed that psychological concerns such as PTSD will also be on the rise. It is also important to note that religion—in the form of both traditional beliefs and modern Christianity—significantly influences these nations. Climate deniers may believe that their ancestors are looking out for them as they are always protected by the traditional god. Some trust in "god's will", god's promise to Noah that a flood would never destroy the earth (Rudiak-Gould 2013; Siose 2017). Others believe that climate change has always been the norm as climates have always changed over time thus they deny climate change as factual because it is based on estimates and patterns that have limitations (Morton 2020). This causes confusion among citizens as they are unsure what to believe from the contrasting information.

The three-year drought (since November 2021) in Kiribati has put significant strain on local water resources; groundwater has become unreliable as king tides and rising sea levels increase salinization (UNICEF 2022). Lack of water availability results in deepening ground wells, resulting in brackish drinking water. Water and food insecurity causes great stress for families, particularly women, who rely on access to water for cooking, cleaning, and hygiene purposes. Rising sea levels have caused inundation in some of the outer islands of Kiribati. For example, in 2010, inundation and extreme weather events left the the village of Tebunginako on the island of Abaiang uninhabitable, only dead coconut trees remaining where the village used to be (Reed 2010). This has forced I-Kiribati to migrate to the main island strip of Kiribati, Tarawa, adding to congestion, overcrowding, and increased stress on its inhabitants. Some residents have nowhere else to go and have resigned themselves to the regular flooding resulting from high tides, forced to tuck their belongings into their thatched roofs as water washes through their houses (Weiss 2015). There are mixed opinions as to whether this is due to poor infrastructural planning or climate change. Some I-Kiribati have identified that they are more stressed about the immediate impacts of climate change than the future impacts because of how it impacts their daily lives. Flooding increases vector-borne diseases, impacts roads and telecommunications networks, and causes the deterioration of freshwater sources, while prolonged droughts impact hygiene practices, access to clean drinking water, and food security (Morton 2020).

In 2024, large, powerful waves inundated the Roi Namur islet in Marshall Islands. The ocean waves caused serious damage to infrastructure and an army base as they swept swiftly over the island, and 80 people had to be evacuated (Jacobo et al. 2024; Reliefweb 2024). In 2016, Marshall Islands was declared in a state of emergency due to prolonged drought; as of March 2024, extreme drought and inundation had reportedly affected almost 4000 people in the north and western Marshall Islands, seriously affecting water security in 18 atoll islands (Milman 2016; Rippey and Heim 2024). Such circumstances add to the compound effects of climate change, impacting the physical and psychological health of people who live in or are from Pacific SIDS as the mental health impacts are greater for those already encountering multiple sources of hardship (Berry et al. 2010; Dodman et al. 2022). The sense of helplessness has led some Marshallese to deny climate change as a threat (Rudiak-Gould 2013).

Tuvalu is vulnerable to storm surges, sea level rises, and flooding. Coastal inundation and drought impact groundwater, which is relied on for drinking, cleaning, and cooking. In 2021, this groundwater reached its lowest point ever. The 2011 drought amplified the spreading of disease and infection, as hygiene and sanitation practices and handwashing were significantly affected (Reliefweb 2021). Tuvaluans identify the spring tides of 2024 as the worst ever, and flooding is expected to increase through February and March. This is also due to the impact of El Niño, where warming temperatures impact ocean currents and fish migration patterns and increase the incidence of unpredictable disasters such as droughts, floods, and cyclones (National Geographic n.d.). Water thus encroaches on Tuvalu from the sides and from underground, evoking sadness as the land and beaches disappear (ABC Pacific 2024). In 2015 the country was hit by Cyclone Pam, which caused severe damage to 30% of homes in the capital. It was again affected just five years later in 2020, by Cyclone Tina, which again caused significant damage in the capital city (Tima 2023).

B. **Solastalgia**

The term "solastalgia" was coined to describe the negative emotions experienced at the loss of livelihood and environment as it once was. It is a sense of loss for what is no longer there, and Pacific communities are prone to it as their island landscapes change at a rapid rate. At a practical level, traditional food crops such as certain species of taro cannot be grown any more as a result of salination, and this also has the effect of changing cultural practices and clan linkages associated with these crops. Additionally, land is very valuable because of its scarcity and is traditionally passed down through family lineage, thus representing a person's value and status. Family burial plots are located on kin territory so that ancestors can watch over their descendants. Therefore, among the non-economic losses of climate change and the resultant human migration is the loss of status. Mobility shifts the land–person relationship, invoking emotions linked with identity loss, anxiety, stress, sadness, and nostalgia (Yates et al. 2023). It disrupts the culture, language, governance, and social structures that are retained through physical presence in the homeland (Smith 2013).

I-Kiribati who used to live in the village of Tebunginako on Abaiang reminisce about how their village looked, the trees, churches, maneabas (traditional meeting house), and beaches where they played which are no longer there. Sixty-three-year-old Toroua Beree talks about leaving Tebunginako after the life was taken from the land. He explains that the life is gone because the coconut, banana, and babai trees have died, taking away the people's food security (Bowers 2017). An entire community is now empty and deserted (Reed 2010). I-Kiribati describe the feelings of loss as they relocate to the densely populated Tarawa, where high levels of congestion place strain on limited resources such as fresh water supply, sanitation, and food (Bowers 2017).

In the Marshall Islands, the symbolic loss of familiar surroundings produces feelings of despair and helplessness (Kasl 1972). Mourning practices have emerged in which people host funerals for their islands, to mark the "grave" of their generational home (Jetñil-Kijiner 2022). To commemorate their ties to their land, Marshallese people have started to name their children after their family's generational land which is no longer habitable (Jetñil-Kijiner 2022). In five years, Ellekan, an islet in Marshall Islands previously abundant with coconut and pandanus trees, has completely diminished to nothing more than a sandbar. Marshallese have already had a funeral for the island similar in style to a Western wake while the memory of the islet remains among them, and this points to the fact that people struggle to explain the loss of an island in the same way as they struggle to come to terms with the loss for a person (Jetñil-Kijiner 2022). As sea levels rise, buried remains are being washed up, causing deep sadness for Pacific islanders who hold their ancestors in great honour and dignity (Komai 2015). In contrast to typical Western practice regarding grave sites, ancestors are buried on family land; these sites are highly regarded, and it is not easy to just relocate them. Where they have had to be moved, the Marshallese have reburied their ancestors in above-ground graves in hopes that they will ultimately be able to return them to their original resting place.

As the Marshallese national anthem identifies, "I love the islands where I was born, the surroundings, the paths, the gatherings I will never leave because it is my true home and my inheritance forever. It is best that I die there." (Rudiak-Gould 2013, p. 107). This emphasizes deep connections to land as a key connection to identity and sense of belonging.

A case study by Gibson et al. (2020) identifies that Tuvaluans feel psychological distress as a result of present climate change events as well as the abstract future climate change threats to their low-lying atoll island nation. Seventy-five per cent of participants said that this was impairing their daily life and experienced "profound sadness over the observed environmental impacts such as losing their home, erosion and effect on food security" (Gibson et al. 2020, p. 4). The loss of the land can create feelings of resentment, distress, and fear as people visually witness the shrinking of their islands (Yates 2022). Aselu (2015, pp. 83–84) indicates that cultural and spiritual values and beliefs are core to the Tuvaluan concept of wellbeing, encapsulated in the terms "olaga tokagamalie" and "olaga lei". "Olaga tokagmalie" refers to the vitality of the land, family, and community through traditional values, practices, and beliefs. "Olaga lei" refers to the needs of the people and the resources that make them feel happy and satisfied. Compound losses as a result of climate change affect both olaga tokagmalie and olaga lei, including loss of locational security (land loss), livelihood (food and water security), and habitat (increase in diseases or hazardous environment). Alternatively, when culture is practised, it strengthens Pacific islanders' capacity for resilience and overall health (Bateteba 2015; Campbell 2022; Spencer 2020).

C. Contemplating the future (eco-anxiety)

Sea levels have been rising at an average rate of 3.4 mm per year since 1992, and scientists predict that Tuvalu will be uninhabitable by 2100 as 95% of the land mass will be underwater (Fainu 2023; Habib 2015; National Ocean Service n.d.). The feelings of fear, loss, and hopelessness due to such extreme climate-change-related prospects is termed "eco-anxiety" or "climate anxiety" (Coffey et al. 2021; Stanley et al. 2021). Eco-anxiety is generated in multiple ways, including from hearing about climate change, contemplating the future implications of climate change, and experiencing the physical health impacts of climate change (Gibson et al. 2020). Similarly, "ecological grief" and "environmental distress" refer to the sorrow felt when reflecting on the past or anticipating future loss in one's home environment and can lead to depression, insomnia, eating disorders, and obsessive thoughts (Coffey et al. 2021; Higginbotham et al. 2006; Saving Tuvalu Global Campaign 2021). Gibson et al. (2020) identify that witnessing the impacts of climate change causes the same amount of psychological distress as contemplating the impacts of it. In a 2016 study of over 1000 Pacific islander students, 65% of respondents were extremely worried about climate change and 99% saw it as a threat to them and their future (Nunn et al. 2016). Additionally, WHO identifies forced displacement and the growing climate crisis as contributing factors in mental health risks (WHO 2022).

Future generations of I-Kiribati are worried about where they will go and what they will do if their islands succumb to climate change—whether they will have to leave the only land and life they know (Bowers 2017). They cannot help but feel despair as they try and stay optimistic about the future and prepare for whatever comes next. Former president Anote Tong wanted to migrate with dignity and purchased 23 km^2 of land on Vanua Levu island in Fiji as a plan B (Pala 2021). This was intended to alleviate the stress and anxiety associated with contemplating the future impacts of climate change. However, some people, particularly the older generation, say they will go down with the islands rather than leave their ancestorial homeland, and therefore the current focus has shifted to climate adaptation (Yates 2022; The Pacific Project 2021). I-Kiribati say that those who have migrated overseas for economic or educational opportunities still wish to return to the homeland, as it is deeply rooted in their identity. They want to stay in their ancestral homes to preserve their connection to identity, culture, lifestyle, and traditions, and to maintain their legacy for future generations. There is fear that out-migration will result in migrants losing their identity as they are forced to assimilate into the identity of their host country (Reuters 2022; Straits Times 2022).

Leaders in Marshall Islands have discussed changing the location of their capital city due to rising sea levels, commenting "imagine changing the location of your capital city due to climate change, as if we're just moving houses" (Jetñil-Kijiner 2022, p. 1). They have labelled this the worst-case scenario as they plan for detrimental impacts, as it would change customary land laws, cultural stories, and connections that are ingrained in the environment around them (Jetñil-Kijiner 2022). Migration and relocation shift relations with land and culture, causing fear and concern over the loss of traditions (Coffey et al. 2021). Additionally, climate change puts further strain on existing environmental concerns around nuclear testing (Wheeler et al. 2020). Marshallese must consider the impact of rising sea levels on the "Runit Dome" which was constructed between 1977 and 1980 to contain the radioactive waste from the US detonation of 67 atmospheric and nuclear bombs in Marshall Islands (Breese 2023). The 18-inch-thick concrete dome on Runit Island, Enewetak atoll, encapsules 3.1 million cubic feet of hazardous radioactive waste. As sea levels rise and the dome ages, there is heightened risk that toxic waste will leak and infiltrate the sea water and surrounding atolls. This would retraumatise the Marshallese population who are still seeking reparations for the irreparable damage done by the nuclear and atmospheric testing that occurred from 1946 to 1958 which left many of their islands forever toxic to humans (AIM Band 2024; Breese 2023). This leakage, would also pose a significant health threat to Marshallese who are settled in nearby atolls (including those resettled in southern Enewetak atoll).

Tuvalu has been described both locally and internationally as "sinking", while its inhabitants have been referred as "endangered", thus heightening emotional anxiety while exposing Tuvaluans as the helpless "poster child" for climate change's negative impacts (Gibson et al. 2020). The constant awareness of this status heightens communal distress, as Tuvaluans are among the first to have to contemplate future sovereignty and identity in the face of the destruction of their habitat by climate change (Reuters 2022). There is increasing global awareness of "sinking islands", but this very increase risks generating apathy or a "bystander effect" in higher-ground countries. Countries not witnessing first-hand the devastating consequences of global warming in their daily lives are less likely to accept the evidence, or on the other hand they may see the problem as too big to resolve (Morton 2020). Personalizing climate change is important, to encourage people to engage psychologically and undertake meaningful personal action (Morton 2020). Tuvaluans say that the fear of an uncertain future is comparable to any other fear, such as being afraid of the dark or of heights, that could affect their daily functioning. This state of fear additionally causes economic, social, and cultural changes, driving a cycle of distress and disorder (Gibson et al. 2020).

D. **Future relocation**

Relocation has been identified as an option to deal with various climate change impacts in the Pacific. This is regarded as the last resort while countries focus on adaptation to maintain collective identity, culture, and sovereignty. Migration can be proactive or reactive, which has impacts on the people who leave and those who stay behind. Personal choice is key in determining the outcomes of relocation. Family reunification, labour and education pathways enable migrants to access different skill sets and economic opportunities to remit money back to homelands, however, as noted above, those who have migrated overseas for economic or educational opportunities still want to return to the homeland at some point as it is deeply rooted in identity (IPCC 2007 p.736). The aspiration and opportunities of seeking a different life are tempered by knowing that the possibility of returning to one's ancestral land is uncertain (Yates et al. 2023).

However, forced displacement due to habitation and infrastructure loss increases the negative outcomes for those involved (Burson and Bedford 2013). For the island nations, removal from home is removal from identity, severing the connection to the past and future (Simich et al. 2010). Previously valued social roles, status, knowledge, and cultural practices are specific to the native environment. Prospective removal from this generates fear of disconnect for future generations (Heidi et al. 2011). WHO (2023, p. 131) identifies that forced migration usually creates negative effects on social wellbeing, and an increased risk of mental disorders including PTSD, suicidal ideation, anxiety, depression, psychosis, and substance abuse. Additionally, the New Zealand government has identified that there are no government support programmes supported by either host or home government for the relocation or resettling of climate refugees (Yates et al. 2023). Gaps in the system in terms of language, culture, and identity contribute heavily to stress, confusion, and helplessness. Due to this lack of support, I-Kiribati, Marshallese, and Tuvaluans who migrate are vulnerable to cycles of entrenched poverty and negative health outcomes. The struggle to maintain traditional identity and practices is exacerbated as migrants are dispersed sporadically throughout the host nation. If they do not migrate to a communal place with similar systems, they are at risk of assimilating into a new one, developing feelings of loss or identity tension, stuck between two cultures (Manuela and Sibley 2014; Yates et al. 2023). Assimilation to another country's governance systems can take a particular toll on people from nations that have previously sought independence from colonizers, as climate migrants become second-class citizens (or aliens) in another person's country (Campbell 2022; Rudiak-Gould 2013). The countries have adopted survival plans for domestic climate adaptation and internal relocation if needed, as it is still unclear how it would be possible to preserve cultural identities in a situation of resettlement elsewhere (Editor 2023; Jetñil-Kijiner 2022).

Furthermore, identity crisis is exacerbated by limited knowledge of the displaced nation among people in host countries. In some instances, employers in New Zealand do not recognize I-Kiribati nationality, impacting migrants' ability to obtain employment, which in turn is one of their visa requirements and can also affect their ability to receive government financial support (Yates et al. 2022). The risk of becoming an illegal immigrant, in a state of limbo without permanent residency status, adds to feelings of despair and confusion (Heidi et al. 2011). Citizens of host countries New Zealand and Australia have limited understanding of climate migration, fuelled by generalized information in the media, potentially contributing to negative attitudes towards climate migrants (Yates et al. 2023). Large-scale migration is causing cultural shifts: New Zealand's 2018 census identified that the country was hosting 3225 I-Kiribati and 4653 Tuvaluans, while the 2020 census found approximately 47,300 Marshallese people living in the US. These numbers are expected to continue to increase rapidly (Yates et al. 2023; United States Census Bureau n.d.).

Under international law, specifically the Montevideo Convention on the Rights and Duties of States (1933), state sovereignty is the recognized legitimate governing of a geographical territory with a permanent population that can engage in diplomatic relations (Habib 2015). This challenges whether countries continue to exist if climate change impacts their ability to remain above sea level: if a territory is no longer inhabitable, this leads to the discontinuation of national identity and international decision-making representation and governance (Costi 2020; The Economist 2023). This raises uncertainties around citizenship, governance, and the right to self-determination as well as concerns about retaining national maritime boundaries that will continue to bring in revenue through fishing licences.

Approximately one-third of the Marshallese population have migrated to the US, primarily Hawaii, Arkansas, and Washington. In contrast to I-Kiribati and Tuvaluans who rely on specific labour or education visa opportunities, Marshallese can migrate freely to work, live, or study without a visa through the Compact of Free Associations (CoFA) agreement (Heslin 2019). This has allowed Marshallese to migrate to locations with larger Marshallese populations, creating Marshallese communities across the US. These pockets can retain elements of their cultural traditions, language, and Marshallese celebrations which are widely accepted in the areas they reside. There are, however, still some challenges in terms of adapting to the different habitat. This affects older and younger generations differently, but both identify challenges in the form of the culture shock they experience and the different systems they are not accustomed to (Wheeler et al. 2020). Marshallese who have moved to Hawaii have identified that the similar environment reminds them of their home, whereas those in Arkansas and Washington have had to adapt to a different environment, causing changes to some customs and traditions, such as fishing, handicraft making, and traditional foods. Flights to and from the islands can be costly and time-consuming, making return visits difficult, and causing further disconnect for those who have emigrated (Heslin 2019). Many young people plan to return once they have completed their education to contribute to their society there (Rust 2019).

For many, climate change is viewed as a distant issue, and there is therefore little empathy around notions of climate justice and responsibility towards the Pacific (Yates et al. 2023). According to Costi (2020), with reference to historical examples of "exiled" communities, statehood can be maintained if a homogeneous group relocates together and maintains their shared ethnicity, dialect, past, and culture. But Ambassador Aunese Simati, Tuvalu's Permanent Representative to the United Nations, has said "we can't be called Tuvaluans if we live in another country", and without retaining sovereignty many feel they will also forfeit their identity, leaving everything they know (Komai 2015; Moana Blue Pacific 2022). Tuvalu, predicted to be uninhabitable by 2050, is optimising ways to prepare for this worst-case scenario. The Tuvaluan Minister for Climate Justice, Communication, and Foreign Affairs, Honerable Simon Kofe, has stated the need for islanders to find their own strategies to deal with what they are experiencing as they witness the imminent disappearance of their islands (Moana Blue Pacific 2022, and that they could not wait for the world to react. The "Future Now Project", a move to make Tuvalu the first digital nation, is developing initiatives to recreate the nation virtually as climate change threatens its physical presence (Fainu 2023). This solution is aimed at protecting sovereignty, statehood, land, and culture for the next generations (Moana Blue Pacific 2022). Transferring governance and consular services to the cloud would enable the country to continue self-rule and allow Tuvaluans to interact with each other in a virtual dimension (Fainu 2023).

In Tuvalu's Climate change policy, Goal 7 focuses on two ways to safeguard Tuvaluans in the case that the land becomes uninhabitable: "guaranteeing the security of the people of Tuvalu from the impacts of climate change" by securing an exclusive economic zone (EEZ) to ensure land and maritime zones are preserved when the land is no longer visible (Te kaniva 2012); and "maintaining national sovereignty despite climate change impacts" to protect the identity of Tuvaluans after resettling in another country (Smith and McNamara 2015). Tuvalu is working with legal experts on options to retain sovereignty and statehood (Te kaniva 2012), for example by applying for a declaration of the nation as a cultural and national heritage site through UNESCO (Komai 2022), as well as creating a digital record of the country's cultural traditions, dances, and songs along with interviews to be retained in the metaverse so that Tuvalu's heritage can be preserved forever and its citizens connected wherever they are in the world (Komai 2022).

Since Tuvaluans are migrating individually through bilateral migration agreements rather than as a collective nation, there are further constraints to how they might retain their statehood, culture, and identity. They identify feeling a strong sense of disconnection from their homeland as well as betrayal to their homeland and their people (Fainu 2023). Relocating independently dismantles their community, connections, traditional practices, and way of life (Fainu 2023). Tuvaluans residing in New Zealand express struggles with the drastic contrast in lifestyle, values, and practices living in a capitalist society. One-fifth of the Tuvaluan population have migrated to New Zealand, but they struggle to adapt to the high reliance on money for survival (Trehaan 2023). Navigating new systems on their own puts people at higher risk of falling through the gaps. Tuvalu is very resourceful and self-sufficient. People survive on the land as a community with their family, but now, climate migrants must confront new challenges including discrimination in housing, health, education, and employment systems (Yates 2022). This will affect future generations, entrenching them in cycles of poverty—something that would not occur in the Tuvaluan culture context, with the values of “olaga fakafenua” (communal living systems), “kaitasi” (shared responsibility), and “fale-pili” (being a good neighbour) which are learned by all (Fainu 2023). Involuntary relocation can also create changes to diet and livelihoods, resulting in negative health consequences. For Pacific people, this can involve the loss of daily sustenance practices such as fishing or collecting local fruit (pandanus, breadfruit, taro, coconuts, and bananas), significantly changing a persons’ dietary and physical habits (Kasl 1972).[1]

Rituals and traditions of family and land commitments are understood differently in homelands compared with host countries. Traditionally, weddings are celebrated for a week in Kiribati and funerals have long periods of mourning; in Australia and New Zealand, by contrast, work commitments have formal processes to take work leave and breaks are on “palagi” time (Fainu 2023). In Kiribati, there are specific celebrations for a woman’s first menstruation, marriage, and funeral rituals which require specific preparation work, but this time cannot be afforded in other countries. Marshallese women try to return to the islands after childbirth for the “ka kūrae”, a traditional postpartum bath that can last up to three months and requires special herbs, flowers, and other plants only found in the Marshall Islands. Again, such cultural practices cannot easily be maintained after migration.

[1] Climate refugees are not protected under the 1951 UN Refugee Convention; thus, the Tuvalu government has collaborated with the Green Climate Fund and the United Nations Development Programme (UNDP) to develop “Te Lafiga o Tuvalu”, a long-term national adaptation strategy focused on adaptation and land reclamation (Fainu 2023; UNDP 2023).

4.5 Policy Implications and Limitations

This section will focus on the inequalities smaller countries face in seeking to "climate-proof" themselves in climate adaptation. It identifies the existing global strategies to cope with climate change and gaps in support to cope with non-economic loss. It also identifies the limitations of this chapter.

A. **Policy implications**

Although awareness of climate change impacts on health have increased, the mental health implications have been neglected (Hayes et al. 2018). This is a particular concern as the psychological trauma resulting from climate-related disasters has been found to be 40 times greater in scale than the physical impacts (Links 2017). Mental health in general is under-studied and under-resourced on a global scale even without the added influence of—and difficulty of identifying and quantifying—climate-related psychological distress (Hayes et al. 2018).

Climate-related impacts are inherently unfair in a globalised world. Unequal power dynamics exist in the distribution of resources for climate-proofing, generating significant cycles of vulnerability. Low-emitting countries, such as the SIDS, account for less than 0.03% of greenhouse gas emissions but are the prime receptors of their effects. They also do not have the financial means to climate-proof themselves (Eiser et al. 2012; Salem 2020). This creates further constraints on atoll nations' autonomy and ability to adapt and respond to uncertainty or function in the face of multiple hazards (Bahadur et al. 2016; Dodman et al. 2022; Jigyasu et al. 2013; Lavell et al. 2012). This unfair dynamic promotes heavy reliance on foreign aid, generating a burden of debt and, in turn, creating more stress on vulnerable nations, impacting their autonomy to make dignified climate-related decisions (Needham 2022; Roy 2019; Stallard 2022). Such lack of control can contribute to feelings of anger, frustration, and disempowerment (Salem 2020). Feelings of frustration are heard in the statement by the Pacific Island Forum Secretary General, Henry Puna: "imagine if you were to consider leaving all that you've known, all that you have been, all that you are now, and all that you hope to be. All because of somebody else's failures" (Moana Blue Pacific 2022). Puna alludes to the unfair, disproportionate impact of climate change between countries. This highlights the inequalities, that smaller nations have against larger emitters in the face of climate change (Allen 2004; Gibson et al. 2020; Paton et al. 2013; Steinbach 2022). Feelings of powerlessness, despair, hopelessness, and moral distress can have fundamental impacts in terms of poorer psychological functioning, which may take the form of eco-anxiety and eco-paralysis (inability to act due to emotional distress) as individuals feel unable to contribute to effective action to mitigate the risks (Hayes et al. 2018). Additionally, disaster preparedness strategies are designed by countries that receive only 25% of disaster impacts and are adapted to affected countries (Gibson et al. 2020). They therefore fail to capture country-specific information on cultural ideals of wellbeing, spiritual and psychological preparedness, and existing traditional knowledge in order to generate culturally appropriate solutions (Haluza-DeLay 2014; Nunn et al. 2016; Paton et al. 2013).

The Loss and Damage Fund was endorsed at the COP27 in 2022 and operationalized at COP28 in 2023 as a global mechanism for a more equitable approach to climate mitigation, acknowledging that vulnerable countries have higher risks of climate-related loss and damage even though they are the lowest contributors (UNEP n.d.). The Loss and Damage Fund is divided under the two categories of *economic loss and damage*, which can be quantified as infrastructure or financial loss, and *non-economic loss and damage*, which is harder to quantify, often taking the form of irreversible damage to culture and societal structures (UNEP n.d.). The Fund relies on ongoing financial commitments from developed countries, made according to an honour system. It is yet to be demonstrated how this simplistic solution addresses the intrinsically complex issue of non-economic losses such as social, cultural, and community deterioration, and loss of statehood and livelihood for those at risk of climate migration as well as the "unseen impacts" of climate change in the form of mental health consequences (Bhandari et al. 2023; Hayes et al. 2018; Stallard 2022; Campbell 2022).

B. **Limitations**

Academic studies on climate change in Kiribati, the Marshall Islands, and Tuvalu are readily available; however, studies on mental health impacts are very limited and none focus on mental health deterioration as a result of experiencing: (i) climate-related disasters; (ii) solastalgia; (iii) eco-anxiety; and/or (iv) relocation and migration. Tuvalu is the only country of the three for which published studies exist that focus on mental health impacts related to climate change, but these are still limited.

Quantifying non-economic loss remains challengingly complex as cultural identities shift. Most studies have been delivered from a Western perspective and exclude methods of meaning-making through traditional knowledge, shared orally through emotionally connected poems, storytelling, speeches, song, dance, and arts (including tattooing). Further field studies, qualitative interviews, and engagement with traditional practices should be undertaken in order that policymakers can better understand the mental health impacts of climate change-related disasters.

4.6 Conclusion

The disproportionate negative mental health outcomes experienced by Pacific people living in foreign countries such as Australia, New Zealand, and the United States demonstrate the lack of studies and support systems available in relation to the complex impacts of climate-related psychological distress. Accurate information on Pacific peoples' mental health is necessary in order for evidence-based, culturally appropriate climate preparedness initiatives and response policies to be developed, including appropriate climate migration plans. Researchers, mental health practitioners, and policymakers should emphasise the importance of psychological preparedness and non-economic loss and damage in disaster risk reduction and adaptation plans (Gibson et al. 2020; Paton et al. 2015).

As atolls become more uninhabitable as food crops are unable to be grown and drinking water and land become scarce, people are more likely to migrate (Campbell 2022; Fainu 2023). As migration increases, further research is required to create culturally engaged policies that recognize the different spiritual beliefs and mental health concerns for Pacific people as they adapt to new structures and habitats different from those of their ancestorial homelands. Providing effective mental health solutions for climate migrants requires a synergy of Pacific indigenous knowledges and Western models in a "negotiated space", applying culturally recognized diagnosis and treatments, and an all-sector global response is required for global ownership and shared responsibility for climate change (Costi 2020; Mila-Schaaf 2010; Moana Blue Pacific 2022).

References

ABC Pacific (2024) Tuvalu residents are fighting for their home in the face of worsening tides and climate change [Online]. Available at: www.abc.net.au/pacific/programs/nesia-daily/kato-ewekia/103483948. Accessed 5 Apr 2024

AIM (Al in Majel) Band (2024) Marshall Islands' 70th nuclear victims remembrance day [Video]. Youtube, 1 March [Online]. Available at: www.youtube.com/watch?v=X9G9rIYCY68. Accessed 1 April 2024

Allen L (2004) Will Tuvalu disappear beneath the sea? Smithsonian Magazine, August [Online]. Available at: www.smithsonianmag.com/science-nature/will-tuvalu-disappear-beneath-the-sea-180940704. Accessed 20 Nov 2023

Aselu B (2015) A Tuvaluan concept of well-being: reflection on national planning-Te Kakeega II. Doctoral dissertation, Auckland University of Technology

Ataera-Minster J, Trowland H (2018) Te kaveinga: mental health and wellbeing of Pacific peoples. Results from the New Zealand mental health monitor & health and lifestyles survey. Health Promotion Agency, Wellington

Babbel A (2010) The trauma that arises from natural disasters. Psychology Today, 21 April [Online]. Available at: www.psychologytoday.com/us/blog/somatic-psychology/201004/the-trauma-arises-natural-disasters#:~:text=Key%20points%201%20The%20most%20immediate%20reaction%20to,more%20than%20one%20month%20should%20seek%20professional%20help. Accessed 1 April 2024

Bahadur A, Tanner T, Pichon F (2016) Enhancing urban climate change resilience: seven entry points for action. Asian Development Bank, Mandaluyong City

Bateteba A (2015) A Tuvaluan concept of well-being: reflection on national planning: te kakeega II. Master's thesis, Auckland University of Technology. Available at: https://openrepository.aut.ac.nz/bitstream/handle/10292/9199/AseluB.pdf?sequence=1&isAllowed=y. Accessed 15 Feb 2024

Berry HL, Bowen K, Kjellstrom T (2010) Climate change and mental health: a causal pathways framework. Int J Public Health 55(2):123–132

Bhandari P, Warszawksi N, Javadi-Abhari N, Simonetti M, Lechat T, Biermann A (2023) 3 questions on loss and damage funding to tackle before COP28 [Online]. Available at: www.wri.org/insights/loss-and-damage-funding-questions-transitional-committee. Accessed 20 Nov 2023

Böhm G (2003) Emotional reactions to environmental risks: consequentialist versus ethical evaluation. J Environ Psychol 23(2):199–212

Bowers M (2017) Waiting for the tide to turn: Kiribati's fight for survival. Guardian, 23 October [Online]. Available at: www.theguardian.com/world/2017/oct/23/waiting-for-the-tide-to-turn-kiribatis-fight-for-survival. Accessed 31 Mar 2024

Breese A (2023) The story of Runit Dome, the concrete 'tomb' in the Marshall Islands that's filled with deadly nuclear waste [Online]. Available at: https://allthatsinteresting.com/runit-dome. Accessed 31 Mar 2024

Burson B, Bedford R (2013) Clusters and hubs: toward a regional architecture for voluntary adaptive migration in the Pacific. Technical Paper. The Nansen Initiative, Geneva

Campbell JR (2022) Climate change, population mobility and relocation in Oceania. Policy Brief 132. Toda Peace Institute, Tokyo

Central Statistics Division of the Government of Tuvalu (2017) Population and housing census 2017 [Online]. Pacific Data Hub. Available at: https://microdata.pacificdata.org/index.php/catalog/269/data-dictionary/F10?file_name=SPC_TUV_2017_PHC_Person_v01. Accessed 1 April 2024

Coffey Y, Bhullar N, Durkin J, Islam M, Usher K (2021) Understanding eco-anxiety: a systematic scoping review of current literature and identified knowledge gaps. J Clim Health 3:100047

Costi A (2020) In the eye of the storm: reflections from the Second Pacific climate change conference. Secretariat of the Pacific Regional Environment Programme (SPREP), Apia

Deverick Z, Russell L, Hudson S (2017) Attitudes of adults towards people with experience of mental distress: results from the 2015 New Zealand mental health monitor. Health Promotion Agency, Wellington

Dodman D, Hayward B, Pelling M, Castan Broto V, Chow W, Chu E, Dawson R, Khirfan L, McPhearson T, Prakash A, Zheng Y, Ziervogel G (2022) Cities, settlements and key infrastructure. In: Pörtner H-O, Roberts DC, Tignor M, Poloczanska ES, Mintenbeck K, Alegría A, Craig M, Langsdorf S, Löschke S, Möller V, Okem A, Rama B (eds) Climate change 2022: impacts, adaptation and vulnerability. Cambridge and New York, pp 907–1040

Editor (2023) Climate crisis: New Zealand urged to make it easier for people moving from sinking islands. Pacific News Service, 18 October [Online]. Available at: https://pina.com.fj/2023/10/18/climate-crisis-new-zealand-urged-to-make-it-easier-for-people-moving-from-sinking-islands. Accessed 1 April 2024

Eiser JR, Bostrom A, Burton I, Johnston DM, McClure J, Paton D, van der Pligt J, White MP (2012) Risk interpretation and action: a conceptual framework for responses to natural hazards. Int J Disaster Risk Reduction 1:5–16

ESCAP (2017) Leave no one behind: disaster resilience for sustainable development. Asia-Pacific disaster report 2017. ESCAP, Bangkok

Fainu K (2023) Facing extinction, Tuvalu considers the digital clone of a country. Guardian, 27 June [Online]. Available at: www.theguardian.com/world/2023/jun/27/tuvalu-climate-crisis-rising-sea-levels-pacific-island-nation-country-digital-clone. Accessed 23 Nov 2023

Galea S, Nandi A, Vlahov D (2005) The epidemiology of post-traumatic stress disorder after disasters. Epidemiol Rev 27(1):78–91

Gibson KE, Barnett J, Haslam N, Kaplan I (2020) The mental health impacts of climate change: findings from a Pacific Island atoll nation. J Anxiety Disord 73:102237

Habib B (2015) Climate change and the re-imagination of state sovereignty [Online]. Available at: www.e-ir.info/2015/11/08/climate-change-and-the-re-imagination-of-state-sovereignty. Accessed 23 Nov 2023

Haluza-DeLay R (2014) Religion and climate change: varieties in viewpoints and practices. Wiley Interdiscip Rev: Clim Change 5(2):261–279

Hashim JH, Hashim Z (2016) Climate change, extreme weather events, and human health implications in the Asia Pacific region. Asia Pacific J Public Health 28(2_suppl):8S–14S

Hayes K, Blashki G, Wiseman J, Burke S, Reifels L (2018) Climate change and mental health: risks, impacts and priority actions. Int J Mental Health Syst 12, article 28

Heidi B, Miller AB, Baldwin H, Abdi S (2011) New directions in refugee youth mental health services: overcoming barriers to engagement. J Child Adolesc Trauma 4:69–85

Heslin A (2019) Climate migration and cultural preservation: the case of the Marshallese diaspora. In: Mechler R, Bouwer L, Schinko T, Surminski S, Linnerooth-Bayer J (eds) Loss and damage from climate change: concepts, methods and policy options. Springer, Cham, pp 383–391

Higginbotham N, Connor L, Albrecht G, Freeman S, Agho K (2006) Validation of an environmental distress scale. EcoHealth 3(4):245–254

IPCC (2007) Climate change 2007: impacts, sdaptation and vulnerability. Contribution of working group II to the fourth assessment report of the intergovernmental panel on climate change. In: Parry ML, Canziani OF, Palutikof JP, van der Linden PJ and Hanson CE (eds) Cambridge university press, Cambridge, UK, pp 976

Jacobo J, Manzo D, Peck D (2024) Extreme wave in Marshall Islands highlights dangers of climate change, experts say. ABC News, 23 January [Online]. Available at: https://abcnews.go.com/amp/International/extreme-waves-marshall-islands-highlights-dangers-climate-change/story?id=106598347. Accessed 29 Feb 2024

Jetñil-Kijiner K (2022) How do we mourn an island? Where do we mark its grave? Guardian, 1 November [Online]. Available at: www.theguardian.com/world/2022/nov/02/how-do-we-mourn-an-island-where-do-we-mark-its-grave. Accessed 29 Feb 2024

Jigyasu R, Murthy M, Boccardi G, Marrion C, Douglas D, King J, Osihn M (2013) Heritage and resilience: issues and opportunities for reducing disaster risks. Northumbria University, Newcastle upon Tyne

Kasl SV (1972) Physical and mental health effects of involuntary relocation and institutionalization on the elderly: a review. Am J Public Health 62(3):377–384

Keddell E (2006) Pavlova and pineapple pie: selected identity influences on Samoan-Pakeha people in Aotearoa/New Zealand. Kōtuitui: New Zealand J Soc Sci Online 1(1):45–63

Kiribati National Statistics Office (2022) Kiribati census atlas. Pacific Community, Noumea [Online]. Available at: nso.gov.ki/wp-admin/admin-ajax.php?juwpfisadmin=false&action=wpfd&task=file.download&wpfd_category_id=117&wpfd_file_id=2022&token=&preview=1. Accessed 30 Mar 2024

Komai M (2015) Tuvalu and Kiribati have different policies on relocation. The Pacific Islands News Association, 19 March [Online]. Available at: https://reliefweb.int/report/tuvalu/tuvalu-and-kiribati-have-different-policies-relocation. Accessed 20 Nov 2023

Lavell A, Oppenheimer M, Diop C, Hess J, Lempert R, Li J, Muir-Wood R, Myeong S (2012) Climate change: new dimensions in disaster risk, exposure, vulnerability, and resilience. In: Field CB, Barros V, Stocker TF, Qin D, Dokken DJ, Ebi KL, Mastrandrea MD, Mach KJ, Plattner G-K, Allen SK, Tignor M, Midgley PM (eds) Managing the risks of extreme events and disasters to advance climate change adaptation: special report of the Intergovernmental Panel on Climate Change. Cambridge University Press, Cambridge and New York, pp 25–64

Le Va (2014) Preventing suicide for Pasifika: top 5 tactics [Online]. Available at: www.leva.co.nz/wp-content/uploads/2014/03/PreventingSuicideForPasifika-Top5_Tactics-web.pdf. Accessed 20 Nov 2023

Links J (2017) Predicting community resilience and recovery after a disaster [Online]. Available at: https://blogs.cdc.gov/publichealthmatters/2017/08/predicting-community-resilience-and-recovery-after-a-disaster. Accessed 31 Mar 2024

MacDonald G (2006) What is mental health. In: Cattan M, Tilford S (eds) Mental health promotion: a lifespan approach. Open University Press, Maidenhead, Berks, pp 8–32

Manuela S, Sibley CG (2014) Why do Pacific people with multiple ethnic affiliations have poorer subjective wellbeing? Negative ingroup affect mediates the identity tension effect. Soc Indicators Res 115:319–336

Mila-Schaaf K (2010) Polycultural capital and the Pasifika second generation: negotiating identities in diasporic spaces. PhD Thesis, Massey University

Mila-Schaaf K, Hudson M (2009) The interface between cultural understandings: negotiating new spaces for Pacific mental health. Pac Health Dialog 15(1):113–119

Milman O (2016) Obama declares disaster as Marshall Islands suffers worst-ever drought. Guardian, 18 April [Online]. Available at: https://amp.theguardian.com/world/2016/apr/28/obama-marshall-islands-drought. Accessed 15 Feb 2024

Ministry of Health (2016) Annual update of key results 2015/16: New Zealand Health Survey, Ministry of Health, Wellington

Moana Blue Pacific (2022) Promoting regional human security responses to climate-related mobility in SIDS: progress and challenges [Online]. Available at: https://us02web.zoom.us/w/86288651408?tk=PnjIjhXcWM24SZ-LdNgPSUCUQQTwPeFFOo5HHcNk_LI.DQMAAAAUFzRUkBZyWXRKX2RZX1J4ZVFDMXJ2Z0pWTS1BAAAAAAAAAAAAAAAAAAAAAAAAAAAA&uuid=WN_7B-VfJpVT0yJt67yvvpp9A. Accessed 23 Nov 2023

Morton J (2020) The biggest story ever. In: Costi A, Renwick J (eds) In the eye of the storm: reflections from the second Pacific climate change conference. Secretariat of the Pacific Regional Environment Programme (SPREP), Apia, pp 167–189

Neale M, Kelly L (2020) First knowledges songlines: the power and promise. Thames & Hudson Australia, Melbourne

Needham K (2022) Tuvalu, sinking in the pacific, fears becoming a superpower "pawn". Reuters, 13 May [Online]. Available at: www.usnews.com/news/world/articles/2022-05-13/tuvalu-sinking-in-the-pacific-fears-becoming-a-superpower-pawn. Accessed 31 Mar 2024

Nunn PD, Mulgrew K, Scott-Parker B, Hine DW, Marks AD, Mahar D, Maebuta J (2016) Spirituality and attitudes towards nature in the Pacific Islands: insights for enabling climate-change adaptation. Clim Change 136(3):477–493. https://doi.org/10.1007/s10584-016-1646-9

Oakley-Browne MA, Wells JE, Scott KM (2008) Te Rau Hinengaro: the New Zealand Mental Health Survey. In: Kessler RC, Ustun TB (eds) The WHO World Mental Health Surveys: global perspectives on the epidemiology of mental disorders. Cambridge University Press, Cambridge, pp 486–508

Oxfam (2019) Climate fuelled disasters number one driver of internal displacement globally forcing more than 20 million people a year from their homes [Online]. www.oxfam.org/en/press-releases/forced-from-home-eng#:~:text=Published%3A%202nd%20December%202019%20Climate%20fuelled%20disasters%20were,-%20to%20leave%20their%20homes%2C%20said%20Oxfam%20today. Accessed 9 Mar 2024

Pala C (2021) Kiribati's president's plans to raise islands in fight against sea-level rise. Guardian, 10 August [Online]. Available at: www.theguardian.com/world/2020/aug/10/kiribatis-presidents-plans-to-raise-islands-in-fight-against-sea-level-rise. Accessed 29 Jan 2024

Parry M, Canziani O, Palutikof J, van der Linden P, Hanson C (eds) (2007) Climate change 2007: impacts, adaptation and vulnerability. Contribution of working group II to the fourth assessment report of the intergovernmental panel on climate change. Cambridge University Press, Cambridge and New York

Passmore HA, Lutz PK, Howell AJ (2023) Eco-anxiety: a cascade of fundamental existential anxieties. J Constr Psychol 36(2):138–153

Paton D, Okada N, Sagala S (2013) Understanding preparedness for natural hazards: a cross-cultural comparison. IDRiM J 3(1):18–35

Paton D, Jang LJ, Irons M (2015) Building capacity to adapt to the consequences of disaster: linking disaster recovery and disaster risk reduction. In: Brown D (ed) Capacity building: planning, programs and prospects. Nova Science Publishers, Hauppauge, NY, pp 85–114

Reed B (2010) A Kiribati village slowly succumbs to the sea around it [Online]. Available at: www.npr.org/sections/thetwo-way/2010/12/01/131708517/a-kiribati-village-slowly-succumbs-to-the-sea-around-it. Accessed 31 Mar 2023

Reliefweb (2021) Tuvalu: drought—Aug 2021 [Online]. Available at: https://reliefweb.int/disaster/dr-2021-000120-tuv. Accessed 28 Feb 2024

Reliefweb (2024) Marshall Islands: storm surge—Jan 2024 [Online]. Available at: https://reliefweb.int/disaster/ss-2024-000006-mhl. Accessed 29 Feb 2024

Reuters (2022) Tuvalu seeks to retain statehood if it sinks completely as sea levels rise. Guardian, 11 November [Online]. Available at: www.theguardian.com/world/2021/nov/11/tuvalu-seeks-to-retain-statehood-if-it-sinks-completely-as-sea-levels-rise. Accessed 25 Nov 2023

Rippey B, Heim R (2024) National drought summary [Online]. Available at: https://droughtmonitor.unl.edu/services/data/summary/html/usdm_summary_20240326.html. Accessed 31 Mar 2023

Roy EA (2019) One day we'll disappear: Tuvalu's sinking islands. Guardian, 16 May [Online]. Available at: www.theguardian.com/global-development/2019/may/16/one-day-disappear-tuvalu-sinking-islands-rising-seas-climate-change. Accessed 23 Nov 2023

Rudiak-Gould P (2013) Climate change and tradition in a small island state: the rising tide. Routledge, London

Rust S (2019) They came here after the U.S. irradiated their islands. Now they face an uncertain future. Los Angeles Times, 31 December. Available at: www.latimes.com/world-nation/story/2019-12-31/marshall-islands-uncertain-future-us-marshallese-spokane. Accessed 1 April 2024

Salem S (2020) Climate change and the sinking island states in the Pacific [Online]. Available at: www.e-ir.info/2020/01/09/climate-change-and-the-sinking-island-states-in-the-pacific. Accessed 20 Nov 2023

Samu KS, Suaalii-Sauni T (2009) Exploring the "cultural" in cultural competencies in Pacific mental health. Pac Health Dialog 15(1):120–130

Samuels M (2019) After natural disaster, economic help reduces PTSD [Online]. Available at: www.bu.edu/sph/news/articles/2019/after-natural-disaster-economic-help-reduces-ptsd/#:~:text=The%20researchers%20saw%20a%20nearly%20two-%20to%20six-fold,study%20author%20Gregory%20Cohen%2C%20statistical%20analyst%20in%20epidemiology. Accessed 20 Jan 2024

Saving Tuvalu Global Campaign (@savingtuvalu) (2021) Climate anxiety [Online]. Available at: www.instagram.com/p/CRzGOyrh_O0/?igsh=MWRnazJjNzU1NzdzZA%3D%3D. Accessed 28 Feb 2024

Simich L, Este D, Hamilton H (2010) Meanings of home and mental well-being among Sudanese refugees in Canada. Ethn Health 15(2):199–212

Siose L (2017) Community perception on migration as an adaptation strategy to the impact of climate change in Tuvalu: the case of communities in Tuvalu and migrated communities in New Zealand. PhD Thesis, University of the South Pacific

Smith R (2013) Should they stay or should they go? A discourse analysis of factors influencing relocation decisions among the outer islands of Tuvalu and Kiribati. J New Zealand Pacific Stud 1(1):23–39

Smith J (2022) List of mental health conditions (psychological disorders) [Online]. Available at: https://psychcentral.com/conditions/conditions-index. Accessed 20 Feb 2024

Smith R, McNamara KE (2015) Future migrations from Tuvalu and Kiribati: exploring government, civil society and donor perceptions. Climate Dev 7(1):47–59

Spencer MS, Fentress T, Touch A, Hernandez J (2020) Environmental justice, Indigenous knowledge systems, and native Hawaiians and other Pacific islanders. Hum Biol 92(1):45–57

Stallard E (2022) What is loss and damage and will rich nations pay for climate change? BBC News, 21 November [Online]. Available at: www.bbc.com/news/science-environment-63478446?at_campaign=KARANGA&at_medium=RSS. Accessed 20 Oct 2023

Stanley S, Hogg T, Leviston Z, Walker I (2021) From anger to action: differential impacts of eco-anxiety, eco-depression, and eco-anger on climate action and wellbeing. J Clim Change Health 1:100003

Steinbach D, Bahadur A, Shakya C, Thazin Aung M, Burton C, Gallagher C, Mbewe S, Greene S, Regmi B, Granderson A, Ramkissoon C, Kostka W, Andon L, Greenstone-Alefaio T, Dolcemascolo G, Gupta S, Tewary A, Lopez M, Barnes J, Mirza A, Bodrud-Doza M, Akhter F, Rozario S, Reyes C (2022) The good climate finance guide for investing in locally led adaptation. IIED, London [Online]. Available at: www.iied.org/21231iied. Accessed 20 Oct 2023

Straits Times (2022) As tiny Tuvalu sinks, its prime minister fights to save the archipelago's identity. Straits Times, 22 September [Online]. Available at: www.straitstimes.com/world/united-states/as-tiny-tuvalu-sinks-pm-fights-to-save-the-archipelagos-identity. Accessed 27 Feb 2024

Te kaniva (2012) Tuvalu climate change policy. Ministry of Foreign Affairs, Trade, Tourism, Environment and Labour, Funafuti [Online]. Available at: https://reliefweb.int/report/tuvalu/te-kaniva-tuvalu-national-climate-change-policy-2012-2021. Accessed 20 Nov 2023

The Economist (2023) Tuvalu plans for its own disappearance. The Economist, 12 October [Online]. Available at: www.economist.com/asia/2023/10/12/tuvalu-plans-for-its-own-disappearance. Accessed 29 Jan 2024

The Pacific Project (2021) Tuvalu seeks to retain statehood if it sinks completely as sea levels rise. Guardian, 11 November [Online]. Available at: www.theguardian.com/world/2021/nov/11/tuvalu-seeks-to-retain-statehood-if-it-sinks-completely-as-sea-levels-rise. Accessed 31 Mar 2024

Tima S (2023) Coastal inundation in Tuvalu [Online]. Available at: https://storymaps.arcgis.com/stories/1175821480b74fe2bfeeadb50b3cf493. Accessed 19 Jan 2024

Trehaan A (2023) Tuvalu, world's fourth smallest country, faces rising sea level threat. NewsBytes, 27 July [Online]. Available at: www.newsbytesapp.com/news/lifestyle/tuvalu-to-disappear-soon-here-s-why/story. Accessed 19 Jan 2024

UNDP (United Nations Development Programme) (2023) Notes from Tuvalu: leading the way in adapting to sea-level rise [Online]. Available at: www.undp.org/blog/notes-tuvalu-leading-way-adapting-sea-level-rise. Accessed 23 Nov 2023

UNEP (n.d.) About loss and damage [Online]. Available at: www.unep.org/topics/climate-action/loss-and-damage/about-loss-and-damage#:~:text=Non-economic%20loss%20and%20damage%20refers%20to%20negative%20impacts,These%20tends%20to%20be%20more%20irreparable%20and%20irreversible. Accessed 31 Mar 2024

UNICEF (2022) Humanitarian situation report no. 1 on drought in Kiribati and Tuvalu. Pacific Islands Multi-Country Office, Suva [Online]. Available at: www.unicef.org/media/125171/file/Pacific-Islands-Humanitarian-SitRep-No.1-Drought-in-Kiribati-and-Tuvalu-August-2022.pdf. Accessed 14 Mar 2024

United States Census Bureau (n.d.) Decennial census: total population [Online]. Available at: https://data.census.gov/table/DECENNIALDDHCA2020.T01001?t=3901. Accessed 31 Mar 2024

Ward C, Bochner S, Furnham A (2001) The psychology of culture shock. Routledge, London

Weiss KR (2015) Kiribati's dilemma: before we drown we may die of thirst. Scientific American, 28 October [Online]. Available at: www.scientificamerican.com/article/kiribati-s-dilemma-before-we-drown-we-may-die-of-thirst. Accessed 15 Mar 2024

Wheeler BL, Fitzpatrick J, Van Der Geest K, Burkett M (2020) Marshallese migration: comparative well-being in U.S. destination states [Online]. Available at: https://collections.unu.edu/eserv/UNU:7781/Well-BeingBrief_2020_META.pdf. Accessed 5 April 2024

WHO (2022) Mental health [Online]. Available at: www.who.int/news-room/fact-sheets/detail/mental-health-strengthening-our-response. Accessed 1 April 2024

WHO (2023) Mental health of refugees and migrants: risk and protective factors and access to care. WHO, Geneva

WorldAtlas (2023a) Coastal and oceanic landforms: what is an atoll? [Online]. Available at: www.worldatlas.com/articles/coastal-and-oceanic-landforms-what-is-an-atoll.html. Accessed 23 Oct 2023

WorldAtlas (2023b) The major religions practised in Tuvalu [Online]. Available at: www.worldatlas.com/articles/the-major-religions-practised-in-tuvalu.html. Accessed 23 Oct 2023

Yates O (2022) Stories of neighbours and navigators: perceptions and implications of climate mobility from Tuvalu and Kiribati to Aotearoa New Zealand. Doctoral Thesis, University of Auckland

Yates O, Manuela S, Groot S, Neef A (2023) Neighbours and navigators: preparing for climate mobility from Tuvalu and Kiribati to Aotearoa. The University of Auckland, Auckland

Part II
Prosperity

Chapter 5
Revisiting Development Models for the Pacific Island Countries and Territories: "BlueEARTH" for a Prosperous and Sustainable Future

Masato Abe and Nick Freeman

Abstract As numerous Pacific island countries and territories (PICTs) achieved independence, scholars and development agencies advocated pursuing many development models. Those development models span a relatively diverse range of elements intended to generate the desired improvement in national incomes and help the countries attain the next level of socioeconomic development. A small island government can formulate development strategies and policies based on these models to substantially transform itself from a near-non-existent, nascent, or ailing economy towards an economic structure that offers improved growth prospects. This chapter presents the challenges that PICTs commonly face and briefly describes conventional economic development models, such as industrial policies, and the more recent burgeoning of global value chains and digitalization. It then assesses various small island development models proposed since the mid-1980s. The chapter ends by proposing a new development direction for PICTs, designated "BlueEARTH", that the authors would contend is more sustainable, offers greater resilience, and mainstreams climate change and environmental protection issues.

This study was prepared under Jaap Van Hierden's direction and Kay Schwendinger's coordination. Miri Asano provided substantive input to the manuscript. Naoyuki Yoshino and Sharon Sakuma provided helpful insights to enhance the quality of the study. Hesborn Kisambo and Amy Aiken provided thorough administrative services. Section 3 of this chapter takes information primarily from the first author's earlier work with Jaewon Kim and Sheikh Morshed Jahan (Abe et al. 2023).

M. Abe (✉)
United Nations Multi-Country Office for Micronesia, Kolonia, Federated States of Micronesia
e-mail: abem@un.org

N. Freeman
Lafayette, California, United States
e-mail: njfreeman@fastmessaging.com

E. Monaco and M. Abe (eds.), *Sustainable Development Across Pacific Islands*,
https://doi.org/10.1007/978-981-97-3629-4_5

5.1 Introduction

Small island development models consist of a wide range of elements that seek to structurally guide a small island economy towards the next level of development. A small island government can formulate development strategies and policies based on a single model or a combination of multiple models, intended to substantially transform the state of its near-non-existent, nascent, or ailing economy towards a socioeconomic structure that offers better growth prospects. For the Pacific island countries and territories (PICTs), which have each faced various development challenges since their independence in the second half of the last century, such an approach is the key to enabling autonomy over their sustainable socioeconomic development.

This chapter profiles the challenges that PICTs commonly face and then briefly describes conventional economic development models, such as industrial policies, and the more recent burgeoning of global value chains and digitalization. It then assesses various small island development models that scholars and development agencies have proposed since the mid-1980s. It concludes by proposing a new development direction for PICTs that the authors would contend is more sustainable, offers greater resilience, and mainstreams issues of climate change and environmental protection.

5.2 The Pacific Island Countries and Territories

The PICTs, which comprise 14 Small Island Developing States (SIDS)[1]—see Fig. 5.1—have a cumulative population of slightly less than 2.5 million people: less than 0.03% of the global population (World Bank 2023). However, they possess enormous territories cumulatively spanning 15% of the world's surface. While the specific profiles of the 14 PICTs vary considerably, they also share some common denominators, including relative remoteness, limited landmass, small population, the modest size of their economies, and high exposure and vulnerability to external environmental and economic shocks (ESCAP 2022). They have also typically depended on marine resources, tourism, inward remittances, development partner assistance, and high levels of imported food and other commodities, albeit to varying degrees (Tisdell 2016).

Notwithstanding their large offshore territories, the PICTs possess a narrow resource base and host small domestic markets, which deprives them of benefits stemming from economies of scale (although they significantly contribute to a few niche global food supply chains, such as tuna and copra).[2] They face a combination

[1] The United Nations categorizes the SIDS globally as comprising 57 member states and associate members (United Nations, no date).

[2] Although almost no cereals are grown in the PICTs, wheat-based foods and rice play a significant role in the diets of their citizens, substituting for traditional staple foods like taro, breadfruit, and cassava.

Fig. 5.1 Pacific island countries and territories. *Source* Reproduced from United Nations in the Pacific (2022)

of being far from export markets and import resources and low and sometimes irregular international traffic volumes of many essential inputs (UNCTAD 2022b). This, in turn, translates into high energy, infrastructure, transportation, and communication costs (particularly on a per capita basis). Moreover, most of the PICTs rely on exporting a few primary commodities and attracting inbound tourists, making them highly vulnerable to external economic shocks, and lack the resilience that comes from having a more diverse array of income sources. As a cumulative result, there are limited opportunities for private sector development in the PICTs, and they tend to experience pronounced volatility in their economic growth patterns (ESCAP 2022). This partly explains why PICTs suffer from a vicious cycle of low productivity and sparse investment. All these characteristics act as further structural impediments to the countries' long-term development.

The PICTs face numerous other challenges, such as elevated rates of non-communicable diseases (NCDs), vulnerable food systems, inadequate education opportunities, and the perils posed by climate change (e.g., erratic and extreme weather-related events and sea level rise), all of which impact adversely on livelihood prospects (ESCAP 2022). The impact of the COVID-19 pandemic (from 2020 to 2023)—and various policy measures implemented to restrict its spread—were pronounced for all PICTs, leading to a near total economic paralysis for the region and far-reaching ramifications for food security (FAO and WFP 2022).

5.3 Industrial Policies

Before profiling the PICT-focused development models, this section briefly discusses conventional industrial policies, which consist of a wide range of measures that seek to structurally guide an economy towards its next level of socioeconomic development.[3] A state can adopt such policies to transform an underdeveloped economy towards a more productive structure that offers better prospects for economic growth. For latecomer or marginalized economies like the PICTs, industrial policies provide fundamental guidance towards their sustainable economic development, although they cannot postulate solutions to all challenges that the PICTs typically face (cf. Bertram and Watters 1985). The question is not whether there should be industrial policies in place but instead to what extent and in what manner such policies should be implemented to achieve optimal outcomes (Abe et al. 2023).

Within this context, on the one hand, governments need to incentivize private-sector-led economic growth and national competitiveness, while on the other hand, they need to address market failures and negative externalities associated with such a growth strategy (Abe et al. 2015). Likewise, governments need to provide a conducive enabling environment for all market actors—large or small, home-grown or foreign—according to the specific needs of the sector and the development challenges of the country (Abe et al. 2023). Table 5.1 summarizes six broad approaches found in industrial policies: (i) horizontal policy; (ii) selective policy; (iii) matrix policy; (iv) cluster policy; (v) global value chain policy; and (vi) digitalization.

5.3.1 *Horizontal Policy*

A horizontal or indiscriminate industrial policy approach entails a broad policy stance, whereby the state indiscriminately offers general support throughout the economy, providing measures that regulate industries and enterprises (Warwick 2013). With this type of policymaking, the state's role involves creating conducive conditions for industrial growth and efficiency, thus attracting investment and enabling the healthy evolution of market players. Horizontal industrial policy hinges on the notion that a homogeneous approach has spillover benefits regarding ancillary aspects such as workforce attributes, market imperfections, and research and development (R&D) (Jacquemin 1983). In its broadest understanding, this type of policy involves the framework of all enterprises, instituting the removal of administrative barriers, the proper rule of law, and good governance (Adams and Klein 1983). Horizontal policy typically includes the provision of subsidized credit to small- and medium-sized enterprises (SMEs), labour training and wage subsidies, infrastructure in economic zones or industrial areas, state support to industrial research and education, incentivization of R&D, protection of intellectual property rights, and, more recently, competition-oriented policies (Rodrik 2004). Though they are applied

[3] This section is based primarily on Abe, Kim, and Jahan (2023).

Table 5.1 Industrial policies

Approach	Study	Definition
Horizontal	OECD (1975)	Policies concerned with promoting industrial growth and efficiency
Selective	Evenett (2003)	Policies attempting to alter the structure of production in favour of sectors that are expected to offer better prospects for economic growth (a.k.a. "picking winners")
Matrix	European Commission (2002)	Policies bringing together the horizontal and the selective approaches and considering the specific needs and characteristics of individual sectors
Cluster	Porter (2000)	Policies aimed at removing obstacles, relaxing constraints, and eliminating inefficiencies that impede productivity and innovation in an industrial cluster
Global value chain	Gereffi and Sturgeon (2013)	Policies targeting specialized niches in global value chains rather than the facilitation of fully vertically integrated domestic value chains
Digitalization	Kim et al. (2019)	Policies fostering development in an economy where data flows are ubiquitous and a profound transformation takes place towards forging hyper-connectivity among the government, enterprises, civil society, systems, and machines, principally through ICT infrastructure and digital networks

Note Abe et al. (2023) provide detailed discussions on this topic
Source Authors' construction based on sources listed

neutrally, horizontal policies are likely to have different impacts on different sectors or may even be implemented in a targeted manner to achieve a nation's economic or industrial goals (Abe et al. 2021; Warwick 2013).

5.3.2 Selective Policy

In practice, however, industrial policy is rarely purely horizontal. Selective, or sector-specific, industrial policy targets specific sectors and industrial activities, tailoring regulations and interventions to harness, among other things, increased productivity, capacity-building, and sectoral restructuring (Chang 2006). A need is felt to supplement a broad regulatory approach with measures that address the specific requirements of certain sectors (Tyson and Zysman 1983). In some PICTs, selective policies may be adopted to address the needs of a sector deemed to be lagging or to have untapped potential, such as the agriculture, aquaculture, and tourism industries. Thus, "selective policy" is not a term that can be understood only to indicate horizontal measures but also includes other sectoral and ancillary or vertical policies. Selective industrial policy measures include export subsidies or import tariffs where differential rates are offered based on the level of productivity, temporary financial assistance, and diversion of credit to specific sectors (Abe et al. 2023). Industrial policies within the import substitution industrialization (ISI) framework are regarded as examples of selective approaches, which are adopted extensively by economies in the early stages of industrialization—such as the PICTs—to establish domestic production capacity instead of relying on imports (Krugman and Obstfeld 1991). Another form of selective policy is the choosing of national champions or the development of large domestic enterprises to eliminate foreign competition (Lin and Chang 2009).

5.3.3 Matrix Policy

Matrix industrial policy is a policy framework that entails a combination of horizontal and selective industrial policies. It has been proposed by numerous countries, focusing on coordinative initiatives between centralized policies and more sector-specific policies, as contemporary approaches to industrial policy have become more difficult to characterize as singularly horizontal or vertical (Johnson 1984). This type of multifaceted policy approach has been termed the "matrix approach" (Aiginger and Sieber 2005). As those policy measures originally designed to be horizontal have de facto vertical effects, the dividing lines between "horizontal" and "vertical" policies have become increasingly blurred (Abe et al. 2023). Growing recognition that the traditional horizontal/vertical dichotomy often does not reflect the complexity of economic systems has led to the notion that industrial policy can be better portrayed as a two-dimensional matrix.

5.3.4 Cluster Policy

The propensity of interrelated enterprises and associated institutions to operate in spatial proximity is called "clustering" (Porter 2000). Such agglomerations of associated enterprises or industries tend to have a competitive advantage and observable benefits, compared with stand-alone set-ups. Firms in a cluster may gain competitive advantages from their proximity to specialized suppliers, distributors, and customers; pools of skilled workforce; and easy and fast transfers of information and technology (UNIDO 2004). Particularly in the case of SMEs, clusters offer opportunities to overcome obstacles and constraints associated with size, networks, resources, and costs (Baptista and Swann 1998; Ellison et al. 2010). However, "the purely top-down approach to cluster creation should be exercised with caution", because "the formation of clusters takes time and needs an ecosystem based on market forces" (Zeng 2011, p. 7). Governmental policy and support are then best implemented to facilitate the development of clusters rather than to facilitate their inception, as a policy stance that aims to create groups of industries from scratch is costly and risky and may have a counterproductive impact (Warwick 2013). Conditions permitting, industrial areas or special economic zones (SEZs) can be formed from these clusters to promote further industrial growth.

5.3.5 Global Value Chain Policy

A global value chain (GVC) refers to the "full range of cross-border, value-added business activities that are required to bring a product or service from conception, [through to] design, sourcing raw materials, and intermediate inputs stages, to production, marketing, distribution and supplying the final consumer" (Abe et al. 2012, p. 173). While traditional approaches to industrial policies take into account international challenges and opportunities, targeting foreign supplies and markets is generally a consequence of these policy approaches rather than a principal concern. Given the significant interdependence of neighbouring economies, industrial policies that focus on international or regional markets should be an essential component of policy portfolios. Thus, industrial policies that focus on "internationalization" by leveraging GVCs have become of paramount importance (Milberg et al. 2014). GVC-oriented industrial policy requires the identification of international business linkages and the positions of lead firms within the overall value chain. A GVC policy must address the issue of "industrial upgrading",[4] to enhance the competitiveness and global presence of firms through the enhancement of the producer or service provider's capabilities. This means that the producer or service provider enhances its capacity and capability over time and thereby takes on more complex, higher-value-added functions within a GVC in incremental steps. The role of governments in designing industrial policies that promote foreign direct investment (FDI) inflows and the adoption of digitalization is another critical factor enabling local entities' greater integration into GVCs (OECD 2015).

5.3.6 Digitalization Policy

The advent of technology-driven digitalization has transformed global economies into more-integrated but increasingly complex systems or structures. This emerging trend has brought dynamic changes in various industries through advanced ICT infrastructure, artificial intelligence (AI), machine learning (ML), smart factories, digitally controlled logistics, and skilled labour (Kim et al. 2019). It has also elevated the importance of the services sector as a key component of the economy. The

---

[4] A typical industrial upgrading pattern could be described as a process by which economies and their respective corporate sectors develop their activities from primarily assembly activities to more sophisticated own-equipment manufacturing and, ultimately, own-brand manufacturing. See Gereffi (1999) for further details.

impacts of digitalization on manufacturing can be illustrated through the concept of "Industry 4.0".[5] With this wave of technological advancement, countries aim to establish an industrial ecosystem wherein every value chain process and function is connected to and interacts through digital networks (Kim et al. 2019). Digitalization presents potentially massive opportunities for the PICTs, disadvantaged by geographical constraints such as remoteness, diffusion, and small size, to overcome those challenges through quick, seamless, and efficient information and communication networks. Many of the frictions and transaction costs of conventional business activity are being unpicked by digitalization trends across a range of "tech" sectors and so-called "disruptive" ventures. However, a considerable gap exists in the degree of digital uptake among the PICTs, as well as between citizens and firms. One crucial issue is the varying degrees of internet connectivity among the PICTs; for example, some (e.g., Kiribati, Nauru, Palau, Tokelau, and Tuvalu) still do not have submarine internet cable connections. Further assessment is needed of the PICTs' digital readiness and of critical success factors in digitalization.

5.4 Pacific Development Models

Over the years, scholars and development agencies have proposed numerous development models to overcome the challenges the PICTs have faced (Tisdell 2016). Earlier, some strategies aimed to enhance the PICTs' self-sufficiency (e.g., securing external funds or earning adequate incomes to sustain livelihoods and develop the provision of modern infrastructure), as they are too small to capture economies of scale in their domestic markets (Baldacchino 2006). Others have suggested diversifying the PICTs' revenue sources to enhance their long-term sustainability (e.g., fisheries and tourism incomes and private sector activities and investment). More

[5] Industry 4.0, or the fourth industrial revolution, is a strategic initiative pioneered by the German government in a bid to integrate industrial manufacturing with ever-evolving innovative digital or ICT applications (McKinsey 2016). This initiative has subsequently stretched well beyond Germany, changing the manufacturing landscape throughout economies, sectors, clusters, and GVCs. It refers to an industrial ecosystem where manufacturing and distributing processes and functions are connected and interact with digital networks (Soori et al. 2023). This new wave of manufacturing is based on digitalized factories that can enhance speed, flexibility, and efficient resource allocation. Industry 4.0 has also been driven by the exponential increase of data flows and connectivity and by digitally supported human–machine interactions (McKinsey 2016). One of the core principles of Industry 4.0 rests on integrating players within GVCs, whereby closely linked players, such as lead suppliers, distributors, and service providers, can achieve greater transparency, flexibility, and efficiency by working as one entity. The stages of GVCs are digitally connected through ICT and logistics infrastructures, and GVC players can exchange key business and technical information on product development and production systems. SMEs are also among the primary target audiences of Industry 4.0, as they are expected to face challenges in absorbing fast-changing new industrial processes through automation or digitalization. Industry 4.0 is expected to offer unprecedented opportunities for SMEs by exhibiting highly efficient business models with reduced production costs, and improved capacity to respond more adeptly to ever-changing market requirements (GTAI 2014).

recently, models have pivoted to address sustainability issues (e.g., dealing with climate change impacts and maintaining maritime ecosystems), broadly congruent with implementing the SDGs (UNCTAD 2022a).

5.4.1 Scholastic Models

Perhaps the most oft-recounted model is the so-called MIRAB, proposed in the 1980s, which has four main components: migration (MI), remittance (R), foreign aid (A), and public bureaucracy (B) (Tisdell 2016). The MIRAB model proposes two distinct revenue sources. The first depends on foreign aid inflows, used mainly to fund the government bureaucracy, leading to a local multiplier effect on incomes and employment. The second revenue source involves remittances from emigrés to kin remaining at home, again leading to a multiplier effect. However, "import leakage" from these effects is typically high, so the multiplier effect may not be as potent as desired.[6] In the mid-1990s, the TOURAB (tourism, remittance, aid, and bureaucracy) model focused on inbound tourism-oriented activities for revenues, supplemented by aid and remittance inflows (Guthunz and von Krosigh 1996). On the other hand, the FFAB (fund, fish royalty, aid, and bureaucracy) model, fundamentally following the MIRAB concept, emphasizes the importance of a sovereign wealth fund and the fisheries sector for national revenue generation (Kazama 2002). There are also the ROT (remittance, official development assistance/ODA, and tourism), SITE (small island tourism economies), and PROFIT (people, resources, overseas management, finance, and transport) models (Kakazu 2019; Tisdell 2016)—all of them to a greater or lesser extent proposed based on the groundwork of the MIRAB. There have also been attempts to generate economic revenues from providing offshore services, such as offshore private banking, international vessel registration, digital residency, and so on.[7] Table 5.2 summarizes these development models for PICTs.

5.4.2 International Agencies' Models

Moving to multilateral development agencies, the United Nations Conference on Trade and Development (UNCTAD) broadly categorizes development strategies for SIDS, which include all the PICTs, in terms of (i) agriculture-led development, (ii)

[6] "Import leakage" refers to the phenomenon by which inflows of funding do not, as intended, get reinvested in domestic production and the development of local supply, but rather get used to underwrite greater imports, resulting in the funding inflows becoming outflows, with relatively little domestic capture.

[7] Refer to various Article IV Staff Reports at IMF (no date).

Table 5.2 Taxonomy of development models for PICTs

Models	Key elements	Income sources	Enablers	Studies
MIRAB	[MI]gration [R]emittance [A]id [B]ureaucracy	International remittances and foreign aid	Migration and public bureaucracy	Bertram and Watters (1985, 1986)
TOURAB	[TOU]rism [R]emittance [A]id [B]ureacracy	Tourist receipts, international remittances, and foreign aid	Tourism specialization, dynamic private sector, migration, and public bureaucracy	Guthunz and von Krosigh (1996)
FFAB	[F]und [F]ish royalty [A]id [B]ureacracy	Sovereign wealth fund, fishing licence, and foreign aid	International financial market, marine resources, public bureaucracy	Kazama (2002)
ROT	[R]emittance [O]DA [T]ourism	International remittances, foreign aid, and tourist receipts	Migration, public bureaucracy, tourism	Kakazu (2019)
SITEs	[S]mall (warm-water) [I]sland [T]ourist [E]conomies	Tourist receipts	Tourism specialization and FDI	McElroy (2006), Oberst and McElroy (2007)
PROFIT	[P]eople (migration) [R]esources [O]verseas management (diplomacy) [FI]nance [T]ransport	Various	Enabling domestic policy framework, dynamic private sector, and strategic diversification	Baldacchino (2006)

Source Authors' construction based on sources listed

manufacturing-led industrialization, (iii) extraction-led development, (iv) service-led development, and (v) the "blue economy" (UNCTAD 2022a).[8] The organization argues that SIDS can follow one or more development strategies that best fit with their own specific geographic and demographic endowment structures. Figure 5.2 depicts an overview of these development strategies among SIDS.

Based on comparative advantage theory, the International Monetary Fund (IMF) has proposed a PICT development strategy as depicted in the "Pacific Pyramid" (Fig. 5.3) (Chen et al. 2014). The strategy implies the PICTs' comparative advantage in their trade patterns and performance, intrinsically linked to their small size and remoteness. The PICTs lack economies of scale and exhibit high-cost structures, significantly disadvantaging some sectors, such as manufacturing. The pyramid

[8] UNCTAD (2022a) does not elaborate on the concept of the blue economy.

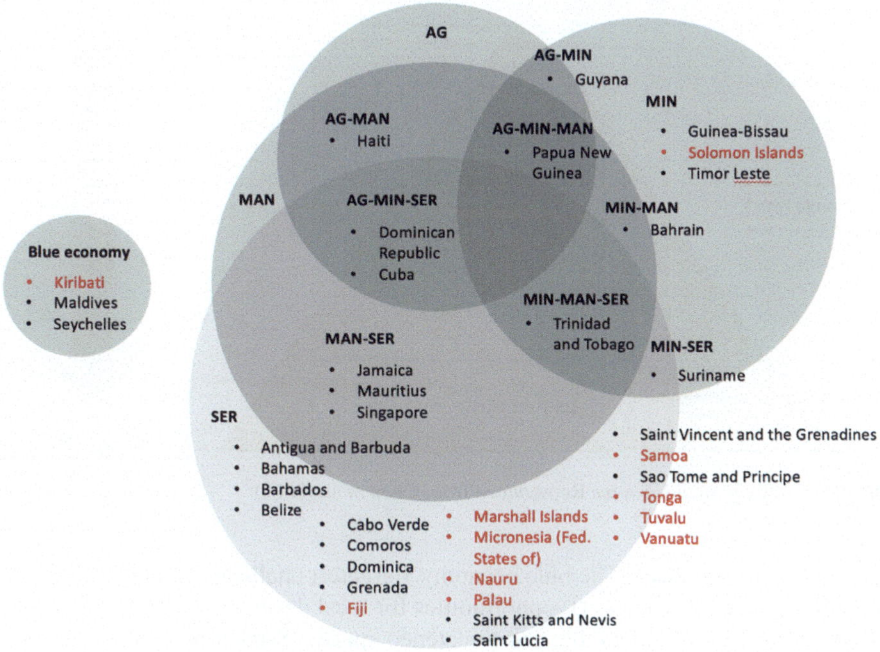

Fig. 5.2 Development strategies for SIDS. *Notes* AG = natural resource-led strategy, agriculture variant; MAN = manufacturing-led industrialization; MIN = natural resource-led strategy, minerals variant; SER = service-led development; countries in red are PICTs. *Source* Authors' illustration based on UNCTAD (2022a)

suggests that a descending degree of comparative advantage exists, from the (non-tourism) "services" sector to the "natural resources" sector (e.g., minerals, hydrocarbons, fisheries, and forestry). The PICTs enjoy a strong comparative advantage in the tourism sector due to factors such as tropical climate, sandy beaches, pristine waters, and distinctive cultures. Agriculture ranks third in the pyramid, where land and water resources are relatively abundant with a tropical climate. However, distance to major markets and high transportation costs considerably lessen this advantage.

5.4.3 The Blue Economy

The "blue economy" is a development concept that aims to achieve socioeconomic progress simultaneously with ocean environmental protection and sustainable maritime resource extraction (Srinivasan et al. 2022). It potentially spans fisheries, eco-tourism, ocean transport, aquaculture (i.e., seafood farming), seabed extractive activities, marine biotechnology, and bioprospecting. It is a relatively new term and broadly adopts the "green economy" concept in the maritime context (see The

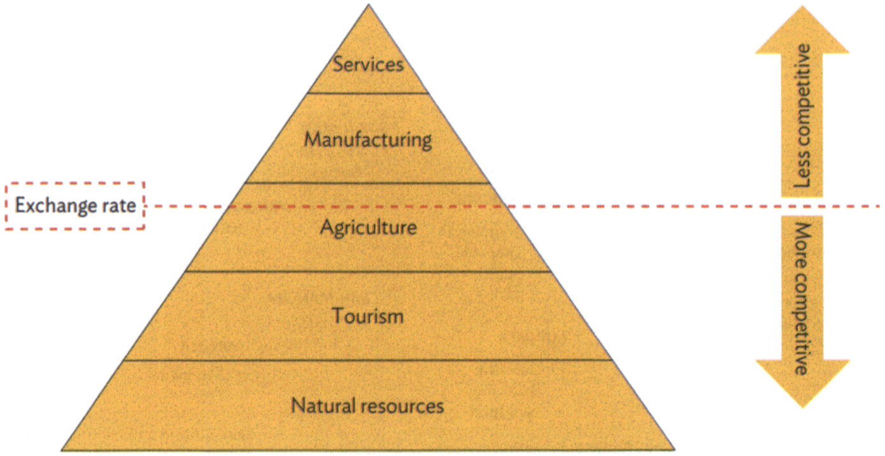

Fig. 5.3 Pacific pyramid. *Source* Reproduced from Chen et al. (2014)

Blue Economy, no date). The blue economy's greatest challenge is reconciling two competing interests, namely (i) opportunities for local development and growth and (ii) the protection of vulnerable and threatened spaces (Srinivasan et al. 2022; Lee et al. 2020).

In recent years, numerous PICT governments and agencies have been increasingly dedicated to promoting the blue economy and implementing various proactive policies and programmes (PIFS 2022). They aim to realize their development aspirations by enhancing outputs from their vast ocean territories and projected resources. As a significant step in such a trajectory, the *2050 strategy for the Blue Pacific continent* was endorsed by 18 countries and territories at the Pacific Islands Forum (PIF) in 2022.[9] The strategy consists of seven themes:

1. Strong political leadership and Pacific regionalism;
2. Resource mobilization and economic development;
3. Climate change;
4. Oceans and the natural environment;
5. People-centred development;
6. Technology and connectivity;
7. Peace and security.

The strategy is intended to guide how the countries of the Pacific navigate various challenges confronting the region (including the impacts of climate change, slow economic growth, poor health and education outcomes, and significant ocean- and land-based environmental degradation), while also leveraging their collective

[9] The 18 countries and territories are Australia, Cook Islands, Federated States of Micronesia (FSM), Fiji, French Polynesia, Kiribati, Nauru, New Caledonia, New Zealand, Niue, Palau, Papua New Guinea, Marshall Islands, Samoa, Solomon Islands, Tonga, Tuvalu, and Vanuatu (PIFS 2022).

strengths (including local cultures and traditions, demographic dividends, and significant island and ocean resources). The ocean and its resources are critical for the PICTs, accounting for the substantial economic value to be derived from marine and coastal products and services, including fisheries, tourism, carbon storage, floating towns and deep-sea mining (Lister and Muk-Pavic 2015; Rouatu et al. 2017; Singh 2021). Other initiatives might usefully include offshore renewable energy; decarbonized shipping and climate-resilient ports; adopting circular economy principles in production, processing and services; and sustainable marine food production and processing.

5.4.4 The PICTs' Development Status

As described above, numerous development models have been proposed for the PICTs. However, any one strategy or model is unlikely to effectively cover the specific needs of all countries, due to their diversified and distinct characteristics. Policymakers may need to combine strategies and policy options from different models, congruent with the specificities of their own country, while continuously searching for new and innovative development approaches to suit the PICTs under changing conditions. Table 5.3 provides a statistical overview of the PICTs' positions regarding the development models summarized above. The table illustrates the diversified profiles of the development of the PICTs, which further supports the above notion.

5.5 The "BlueEARTH" Model

While navigating a way through increasing geo-strategic competition in the Pacific, predominantly between China and the United States and its allies, the PICTs have also faced various challenges and conundrums, spanning (but not limited to) education, healthcare, food, labour, migration, infrastructure, finance, trade and investment, tourism, climate change, natural disasters, gender, and youth. To a greater or lesser extent, all of these issues stem from one crucial dilemma—that is: the PICTs have come to depend significantly on inflows of foreign capital and knowledge, while at the same time steadily ceding their own valuable domestic assets (whether they be capital, human, tangible, or intangible in form) to others (notably Australia, China, Japan, New Zealand, the United States, and other neighbouring countries such as those in South East Asia). The provenance of this vicious cycle can largely be found in the countries' histories of colonial subjugation and stunted sovereign development, as well as their geopolitical setting. A culture of dependency has both inhabited and inhibited the ability of most PICTs to identify and execute development strategies that would allow them to break this cycle. And the postcolonial (arguably neocolonial)

Table 5.3 A statistical overview of PICT's comparative development status

Country	**Population** 2022 data, except Niue: 2019, Cook Island: 2020, Tokelau: 2019	**Migration stock (% of population)** Indicates what percentage of the population is represented by migrants who entered (immigrant) and left (emigrant) the country (2020 data)		**GDP** $ million		**GNI/capita** Atlas method $		**Remittance (%)** % of GDP		**Aid (%)** % of government budget		**Bureaucracy** Shows how many times greater than GDP the national budget is: the higher the number is, the larger the private sector is		**Tourism** Shows how many times greater the number of tourists per year than the country's population		**Composition of GDP by sector of origin (%)**				**EEZ size** Square km	**Tuna fisheries** Catch in national waters, $million, 2021 data
		Immigrant	Emigrant		Year		Year		Year		Year		Year		Year	Agriculture	Industry	Services	Year		
Papua New Guinea	10,142,619	0.35	0.68	30,633	2022	2730	2022	0.01	2022	12.64	2019	4.82	2019	0.00	2021	22.1	42.9	35	2017	2,396,575	791
Fiji	929,766	1.91	15.20	4943	2022	5270	2022	9.28	2022	12.79	2020	2.96	2020	0.03	2021	13.5	17.4	69.1	2017	1,281,703	31
Solomon Islands	724,273	1.39	0.63	1595	2022	2220	2022	5.09	2022	41.69	2019	3.02	2019	0.00	2021	34.3	7.6	58.1	2017	1,596,464	212
Vanuatu	326,740	0.67	3.33	984	2022	3560	2022	15.25	2022	36.79	2019	2.64	2019	0.07	2020	27.3	11.8	60.8	2017	827,626	10
Samoa	222,382	3.08	53.23	832	2022	3630	2022	33.63	2022	63.41	2020	3.30	2020	0.01	2021	10.4	23.6	66.0	2017	131,535	5
Kiribati	131,232	2.23	12.56	223	2022	3280	2022	6.72	2022	37.63	2017	0.92	2017	0.01	2020	23.0	7.0	70.0	2016	3,437,132	534
FSM	114,164	2.76	13.45	427	2022	4130	2022	5.46	2022	74.58	2012	1.70	2012	0.16	2019	26.3	18.9	54.8	2013	2,992,415	212
Tonga	106,858	1.53	43.61	469	2021	4930	2021	46.22	2021	55.08	2019	2.61	2019	0.09	2020	19.9	20.3	59.8	2017	664,751	9
Marshall Islands	41,569	2.98	11.00	280	2022	7920	2022	10.73	2022	43.12	2019	1.52	2019	0.02	2020	4.4	9.9	85.7	2013	1,992,022	128
Palau	18,055	31.82	92.15	218	2021	12,790	2021	1.17	2021	20.62	2019	2.30	2019	1.00	2020	3.0	19.0	78.0	2016	604,253	4
Nauru	12,668	43.69	14.71	151	2022	17,870	2022	4.99	2018	17.88	2020	0.79	2020			6.1	33.0	60.8	2009	308,506	225
Tuvalu	11,312	2.11	35.66	60	2022	7210	2022	4.14	2022	41.45	2019	0.62	2019	0.09	2020	24.5	5.6	70.0	2012	751,672	119
Cook Islands	8574	13.53	103.41							1.14	2016			2.92	2020	5.1	12.7	82.1	2010	1,960,027	24
Niue	2000	18.41	292.29											6.18	2017	23.5	26.9	49.5	2003	316,584	91
Tokelau	1647									62.74	2017					N/A	N/A	N/A		319,049	13

Note Papua New Guinea is included as a comparison
Source Authors' construction based on World Bank (2023), OECD (2021), CIA (2024), ADB (2023), and FAO (no date)

stances of far greater economic powers have made it even harder for the PICTs to chart their own course.

Put simply, money flowing into the PICTs or generated within the islands can either contribute to domestic value creation or be lost through outflows. To foster sustainable economic growth, it is crucial for a proportion of funds to remain within the PICTs and for assets to be developed, thereby enabling local reinvestment and catalysing a development cycle. This chapter contends that the PICTs should aim to prioritize the value-creation process within their borders, which will effectively reduce or even halt an excessive outflow of assets and underwrite investments and reinvestments domestically. For instance, significant money is spent on imported goods and foods. While certain food products, like rice and wheat, may not be producible within the islands, there are opportunities to locally produce other goods or seek equivalent substitutes, which are usually better in nutritional value and at preventing NCDs (such as diabetes), simultaneously reducing healthcare costs. Furthermore, imported goods—such as (but not limited to) cars, motorcycles, furniture, and canned foods and drinks—increase the amount of waste at the end of GVCs. The PICTs urgently need to pursue circular economy practices, such as adopting recycling, reusing, reproducing, and dumping more environmentally soundly. Presently, locally caught tuna is also exported without processing, leading to low prices and reduced income for the local economy.

To retain a greater proportion of funds within the islands, it is crucial to develop a self-reliant domestic workforce capable of fulfilling demanding jobs across various fields. This requires sufficient education and healthcare services to be provided to citizens and foreign workers in necessary and specialized fields, so that the money they earn can circulate within the domestic economy. The lack of a conducive business environment in the PICTs also discourages domestic and foreign inbound investments. Another significant outflow of money stems from investments made overseas rather than that money being reinvested within local boundaries to foster sustainable, inclusive, and resilient development.[10] Human assets have shown the same trend, with out-migration becoming a popular option for many Pacific islanders, for various reasons (e.g., work, study, military service, family, illness), whether under the Compact of Free Association agreements with the United States or overseas temporary and seasonal work arrangements with Australia and New Zealand (Bedford 2014).

This chapter contends that the PICTs should focus on retaining capital within the country as much as possible, ostensibly by emphasizing domestic value-creation processes, reducing outflows where feasible, and reinvesting funds in the domestic market. This approach will contribute to greater socioeconomic growth and resilience. This strategy implies three critical policy implications:

1. The PICTs should focus on investment in domestic value creation (e.g., industries, education, environmental protection, climate change adaptation) and healthcare

[10] For example, Nauru made a series of poorly informed foreign investments that resulted in significant losses. This helped to take the island state from one of the most affluent countries in the world (on a per capita basis) to one of the poorest.

and waste management, to safeguard against the negative impacts of imported foods and goods.

2. The PICTs should seek to discourage value outflows through various "leaking" channels (e.g., imported goods, foods, and fuels, migration, low-value-added exports, outward FDI and loan repayments), by implementing relevant counter-measures (e.g., through laws and regulations, taxes and duties, incentives, contracts, institutional capacity-building, and human resource development).
3. Each PICT should develop a comprehensive, bespoke package of policies, comprising the above two policy streams, in a carefully designed mix so that the islands can enhance their interventions' effectiveness and efficiency while reducing any potential cancelling-out effect. Care needs to be taken to ensure that, in pursuing the two policy streams, no measures executed in support of one policy stream serve to undermine the other policy stream. For example, domestic investments targeted towards households and businesses may be constrained by over-zealous import restrictions, reducing the availability of essential foods and goods and increasing living costs. A marked rise in inflation would also imperil the willingness of firms and individuals alike to pursue investment activity, as an adverse macroeconomic backdrop heightens the perceived risks of committing finite capital.

In partnership with various stakeholders, including other islands, bilateral donors, multilateral development banks (MBDs), international financial institutions (IFIs), and others (e.g., civil society organizations and the private sector), the PICTs should develop and implement a holistic development framework intended to comprehensively break out of the vicious cycle they have encountered and strengthen their socioeconomic fundamentals. Such a strategy would aim to develop and maintain the domestic value-creation systems within the PICTs' own borders while encouraging international cooperation with other countries and entities. The aim should be to bring about greater economic resilience and attain a more environmentally sustainable growth trajectory.

In this context, we propose a new development model for consideration by the PICTs, potentially adaptable to other SIDS globally, which we call "BlueEARTH". The term denotes a (Blue) economy, (E)ducation, (A)id, (R)emittances, (T)ourism, and (H)ealth. The model builds on some of the critical concepts and components of previous SIDS development models, such as MIRAB, TOURAB, SHIFT, and PROFIT, but expands them to cover other crucial issues and challenges that PICTs currently have to contend with, as briefly depicted earlier in this chapter. The aim of the BlueEARTH approach is to break the vicious cycle of the past and pivot towards a more virtuous cycle for the future (Table 5.4).

Part of the model's merit is in identifying multiple revenue sources for the PICTs, namely fisheries, foreign development assistance, international remittances, and blue ocean tourism. This diversification of income streams allows for greater resilience against exogenous shocks, such as the recent global pandemic. In addition, consideration should be given to innovative resources for the future, such as

Table 5.4 The BlueEARTH development model for PICTs

Model	Key elements	Principal income sources	Policy components
BlueEARTH	(Blue) Economy (E)ducation Development Foreign (A)id (R)emittance Inflows Inbound (T)ourism (H)ealth	Fisheries and aquaculture earnings; foreign development assistance (both technical and financial); inward remittances; blue ocean tourism revenues	Improving education and healthcare; nurturing a more dynamic and robust private sector (using both domestic and foreign investment); mainstreaming environmental and biodiversity protection; adopting the circular economy approach; greater international engagement and cooperation; institutional capacity-building in support for improved governance; leveraging advances in digitalization

Source Authors' construction

blue carbon credits, and the careful pursuit of deep-sea rare mineral extraction.[11] The model also identifies the key policy components: improved education and healthcare, a more dynamic private sector, environmental preservation, the adoption of a circular economy, greater international cooperation, improvements in governance, and advances derived from new "unlocks" created by digitalization. This framework can provide the basis for national and international development cooperation among various stakeholders and development partners, as elaborated in this chapter. Mainstreaming environment protection and biodiversity in the pursuit of a robust domestic blue economy also offers the prospect of genuine sustainability.

Partnerships with bilateral development partners (such as Australia, China, Japan, New Zealand, the United States, and the European Union), regional and international organizations (such as ESCAP, the PIF and the Pacific Community/SPC), MDBs (such as the Asian Development Bank/ADB and the World Bank), and IFIs can all help in leveraging much-needed financial and non-financial (i.e., technical) inputs and hopefully would generate positive impacts. Harnessing the financial and technical capacities of these institutions and their considerable prior experience is highly recommended. Within the Pacific, partnering with other PICTs to develop joint approaches to regional socioeconomic and environmental issues of mutual concern

[11] The topic of deep-sea mining is controversial, due largely to questions and concerns around the potential for considerable adverse environmental and biodiversity impacts. This chapter does not take a position on this debate other than to counsel for a cautious, incremental approach to any interventions in this field and a willingness to halt them if the adverse impacts (or risks) become apparent. See Schiffman (2023); Ocean14 Capital (2023); Planet Tracker (2023).

would also be beneficial, sharing and leveraging resources, avoiding the unnecessary duplication of effort, and ensuring that the wheel is not reinvented. Sharing best practices and lessons learned and pursuing innovative approaches to economic development and climate change challenges all help to enhance, rather than divert, domestic institutional capacity. Further, bilateral and multilateral agreements with neighbouring island countries can help to create and strengthen trade and investment ties, to build momentum, and, hopefully, to attain critical mass.

5.6 Conclusion

Discourses around socioeconomic development policy have always generated vigorous debate, and sometimes even heated controversy. These discourses have ranged from fundamental questions on their necessity to questions about which specific approach, or what cocktail of multiple approaches, is optimal for a specific country and at a particular stage of development. Clear answers often seem elusive. Tangible and positive impacts can seem inconsistent. Unintended and deleterious consequences are not uncommon. New solutions come and go. The alchemy of development policy remains both alluring and yet frustratingly evasive. The creation of different development models for the PICTs serves as tangible evidence of this.

In this context, any new policy prescription in the field of socioeconomic development needs to be offered with considerable humility and a recognition that care must be taken in its pursuit. It is in this spirit that we wish to suggest that integrating blue economy principles into the PICTs' development strategy—i.e., adopting the BlueEARTH approach—has the potential to contribute significantly to the islands' sustainable growth prospects. It seeks to build on earlier Pacific development models and hopefully add some critical missing components to the development approach. Only by implementing this approach will we discover if it can bring about the desired impacts.

References

Abe M, Troilo M, Juneja JS, Narain S (2012) Policy guidebook for SME development in Asia and the Pacific. The United Nations, Bangkok

Abe M, Troilo M, Batsaikhan O (2015) Financing small and medium enterprises in Asia and the Pacific. J Entrepreneurship Public Policy 4(1):2–32

Abe M, Freeman N, Troilo M (2021) Rethinking MSME finance in Asia and the Pacific: a post-crisis policy agenda. United Nations, Bangkok

Abe M, Kim J, Jahan SM (2023) Global value chain-oriented industrialization: policies revisited. Int J Bus Manag Res 11(3):71–80

Adams G, Klein LR (1983) Industrial policies for growth and competitiveness. Lexington Books, Lanham

ADB (Asian Development Bank) (2023) Key indicators for Asia and the Pacific 2023. ADB, Mandaluyong City

Aiginger K, Sieber S (2005) The matrix approach to industrial policy. Int Rev Appl Econ 20(5):573–601

Baldacchino G (2006) Managing the hinterland beyond: two ideal-type strategies of economic development for small island territories. Asia Pac Viewp 47(1):45–60

Baptista R, Swann P (1998) Do firms in clusters innovate more? Res Policy 27:525–540

Bedford R (2014) Population mobility in the Pacific region in the 21st century: trends and prospects. In: Paper presented at the 17th Biennial conference of the Australian population association, Hobart, 3–5 December 2014

Bertram IG, Watters RF (1985) The MIRAB economy in South Pacific microstates. Pac Viewpoint 26(3):497–519

Bertram IG, Watters RF (1986) The MIRAB process: earlier analyses in context. Pac Viewpoint 27(1):47–59

Chang HJ (2006) Industrial policy in East Asia: lessons for Europe. EIB Papers 11(2):106–132

Chen H, Rauqeuqe L, Singh SR, Wu Y, Yang Y (2014) Pacific island countries: in search of a trade strategy. In: IMF working paper WP/14/158. International Monetary Fund (IMF), Washington, DC

CIA (2024) The world factbook [Online]. Available at www.cia.gov/the-world-factbook. Accessed 16 Jan 2024

Ellison G, Glaeser EL, Kerr WR (2010) What causes industry agglomeration? Evidence from coagglomeration patterns. Am Econ Rev 100:1195–1213

ESCAP (United Nations Economic and Social Commission for Asia and the Pacific) (2022) Asia-Pacific countries with special needs development report 2022: financing a sustainable recovery from COVID-19 and beyond. United Nations, Bangkok

European Commission (2002) Industrial policy in an enlarged Europe. In: COM, 714, 11 December

Evenett S (2003) Study on issues related to a possible multilateral framework on competition policy. World Trade Organization, Geneva

FAO (Food and Agriculture Organization) (no date) FishStatJ database [Online]. Available at www.fao.org/fishery/en/collection/capture. Accessed 16 Jan 2024

FAO and WFP (World Food Programme) (2022) Pacific island countries: impact of rising costs of food, feed, fuel, fertilizer and finance. In: Bulletin, 1(November). FAO and WFP, Suva

Gereffi G (1999) International trade and industrial upgrading in the apparel commodity chain. J Int Econ 48(1):37–70

Gereffi G, Sturgeon T (2013) Global value chain-oriented industrial policy: the role of emerging economies. In: Elms DK, Low P (eds) Global value chains in a changing world. World Trade Organization (WTO) Secretariat, Geneva, pp 329–360

GTAI (German Trade and Investment) (2014) Industrie 4.0: smart manufacturing for the future. GTAI, Berlin

Guthunz U, von Krosigh F (1996) Tourism development in small island states: from "MIRAB" to "'TOURAB." In: Briguglio L, Archer B, Jafari J, Wall G, Harrison D, Filho WL (eds) Sustainable tourism in islands and small states: issues and policies. Pinter, London, pp 18–35

IMF (International Monetary Fund) (no date) IMF Article IV staff reports [Online]. Available at www.imf.org/en/Publications/SPROLLs/Article-iv-staff-reports#sort=%40imfdate%20descending. Accessed 6 Jan 2024

Jacquemin A (1983) Industrial policies and the community. In: Coffey P, Nijhoff M (eds) Main economic policy areas of the EEC. Springer, Dordrecht, pp 27–58

Johnson C (1984) The idea of industrial policy. In: Johnson C (ed) The industrial policy debate. Institute for Contemporary Studies, San Francisco, pp 3–26

Kakazu H (2019) Nissology. Kokin Publishing, Tokyo

Kazama K (2002) Against class differentiation: the rise and fall of small businesses in southern Kiribati. In: Shiota M (ed) Islands and class: modernity and inequality in the Pacific. Institute of Developing Economies, Chiba, pp 101–150

Kim J, Abe M, Valente F (2019) Impacts of the digital economy on manufacturing in emerging Asia. Asian J Innovation Policy 8(1):1–30

Krugman P, Obstfeld M (1991) International economics: theory and policy. Pearson-Addison Wesley, Boston

Lee K, Noh J, Khim JS (2020) The blue economy and the United Nations' sustainable development goals: challenges and opportunities. Environ Int 137:105528

Lin J, Chang H (2009) Should industrial policy in developing countries conform to comparative advantage or defy it? DPR Debate. Dev Policy Rev 27(5)

Lister N, Muk-Pavic E (2015) Sustainable artificial island concept for the Republic of Kiribati. Ocean Eng 98(1):78–87

McElroy JL (2006) Small island economies across the life cycle. Asia Pac Viewp 47(1):61–77

McKinsey (2016) Industry 4.0 at McKinsey's model factories: get ready for the disruptive wave [Online]. Available at https://docplayer.net/33468267-Industry-4-0-at-mckinsey-s-model-factories-get-ready-for-the-disruptive-wave.html. Accessed 14 Jan 2024

Milberg W, Jiang X, Gereffi G (2014) Industrial policy in the era of vertically specialized industrialization. In: Salazar-Xirinachs J, Nübler I, Kozul-Wright R (eds) Transforming economies: making industrial policy work for growth, jobs and development. ILO and UNCTAD, Geneva, pp 151–178

Oberst A, McElroy JL (2007) Contrasting socio-economic and demographic profiles of two, small island, economic species: MIRAB versus PROFIT/SITE. Island Stud J 2(2):163–176

Ocean14 Capital (2023) Deep-sea mining: into the unknown, Blog, 8 July [Online]. Available at https://ocean14capital.com/2023/08/07/deep-sea-mining-into-the-unknown. Accessed 6 Jan 2024

OECD (Organisation for Economic Co-operation and Development) (1975) Objectives and instruments of industrial policy: a comparative study. OECD, Paris

OECD (2015) Trade policy implications of global value chains. OECD, Paris

OECD (2021) Aid (ODA) disbursements to countries and regions (DAC2a) [Online]. Available at https://stats.oecd.org/Index.aspx?DatasetCode=TABLE2A. Accessed 16 Jan 2024

PIFS (Pacific Islands Forum Secretariat) (2022) 2050 strategy for the blue Pacific continent. PIFS, Suva

Planet Tracker (2023) The sky high cost of deep sea mining. Planet Tracker, London

Porter M (2000) Location, competition, and economic development: local clusters in a global economy. Econ Dev Q 14(1)

Rodrik D (2004) Industrial policy for the twenty-first century. In: Paper prepared for UNIDO

Rouatu I, Leport G, Pascal N, Wendt H, Abeta R, Brander L, Fernandes L, Seidl A, Salcone J (2017) National marine ecosystem service valuation: Kiribati. MACBIO (GIZ/IUCN/SPREP), Suva

Schiffman R (2023) Can we mine the world's deep ocean without destroying it? Yale Environ 360, 15 June

Singh PA (2021) What are the next steps for the International Seabed Authority after the invocation of the "two-year rule"? Int J Mar Coast Law 37(1):152–165

Soori M, Arezoo B, Dastres R (2023) Internet of things for smart factories in industry 4.0: a review. Internet Things Cyber-Phys Syst 3:192–204

Srinivasan M, Kaullysing D, Bhagooli R, Pratt S (2022) Marine tourism and the blue economy: perspectives from the Mascarene and Pacific islands. In: Urban ER, Ittekot V (eds) Blue economy. Springer, Singapore, pp 153–189

The Blue Economy (no date) The blue economy: the blue economy does not recycle, it regenerates! [Online]. Available at www.theblueeconomy.org/en/the-blue-economy. Accessed 6 Jan 2024

Tisdell CA (2016) Models of the international economic dependence of Pacific microstates: a critical review with important implications for international policies and relations. J Self Gov Manag Econ 4(2):7–27

Tyson L, Zysman J (1983) American industry in international competition: government policies and corporate strategies. Cornell University Press, Ithaca

UNCTAD (United Nations Conference on Trade and Development) (2022a) 'Note by the UNCTAD secretariat, TD/B/C.II/EM.6/2', at the expert meeting on revisiting development strategies for small island developing states in the post-pandemic competitive landscape, trade and development board, investment, enterprise and development commission, United Nations, Geneva, 24 October

UNCTAD (2022b) Review of maritime transport 2022: navigating stormy waters. United Nations, Geneva

UNIDO (United Nations Industrial Development Organization) (2004) Industrial clusters and poverty reduction: towards a methodology for poverty and social impact assessment of cluster development initiatives. UNIDO, Vienna

United Nations (no date) List of SIDS [Online]. Available at www.un.org/ohrlls/content/list-sids. Accessed 6 Jan 2024

United Nations in the Pacific (2022) United Nations Pacific sustainable development cooperation framework 2023–2027. United Nations, Suva, Kolonia, and Apia

Warwick K (2013) 'Beyond industrial policy: emerging issues and new trends', OECD science, technology and industry policy papers 2. OECD, Paris

World Bank (2023) DataBank: world development indicators [Online]. Available at https://databank.worldbank.org. Accessed 6 Jan 2024

Zeng DZ (2011) How do special economic zones and industrial clusters drive China's rapid development? World Bank, Washington, DC

Chapter 6
Migration, Digitalization, and Sustainable Development Across Pacific Islands

Adrian J. Bailey and Jialing Zou

Abstract This chapter explores the opportunities, experiences, and prospects of digitalization in transforming the relationship between migration and sustainable development across Pacific Island countries and territories. We consider how digitalization, understood as integrating digital data and technologies into daily life, is transforming the migration–development nexus framework beyond the earlier migration, remittances, aid, and bureaucracy model to enable enhanced information exchange, digital remitting, digital economy, digital residence, and the digital management of migration. Across Pacific islands, realizing the potential for sustainable development means considering digital access, utilization and datafication, stakeholder coordination, and the fragmentation of knowledge.

6.1 Introduction

Migration can influence development positively. International migration policy orthodoxy—enshrined in the migration–development nexus (MDN)—claims that, properly coordinated and managed, migrant labour, migrant remittances, and migrant skills can offer mutual benefits for countries of both origin and destination (De Haas 2010). Recently, migration has been posited as a way to accelerate progress towards meeting the delayed 2030 Agenda for Sustainable Development (IOM 2023). As policy takes stock of the digital strategies deployed by migrants during the COVID-19 pandemic, digitalization (the integration of digital data and technologies into daily life) is regarded as offering opportunities to further leverage migration for development (McAuliffe and Triandafyllidou 2021; Kikkawa et al. 2021).

A. J. Bailey (✉)
Beijing Normal University–Hong Kong Baptist University United International College, Zhuhai, China
e-mail: bailey@uic.edu.cn

J. Zou
Guangdong University of Foreign Studies, Guangzhou, China

E. Monaco and M. Abe (eds.), *Sustainable Development Across Pacific Islands*,
https://doi.org/10.1007/978-981-97-3629-4_6

Understanding if and how digitalization can connect migration with sustainable development is an urgent matter across Pacific Island countries and territories (PICTs). While the MDN framework has been influential since the 1980s, when the migration, remittances, and aid bureaucracy (MIRAB) model argued that PICTs could supplement trade-led development by promoting remitting, progress on the SDG (Sustainable Development Goals) Agenda remains limited. As of 2023, 75% of the 2030 SDG targets were not expected to be met on time, and at the Agenda's midpoint, only 14% progress had been achieved (United Nations ESCAP 2022, 2023). Moreover, in a region being profoundly reshaped by climate and environmental change, digitally enabled and managed migration is thought to offer a viable mitigation strategy (IOM 2019; Vince 2022). In this context, the broad aim of our chapter is to explore the opportunities, experiences, and prospects of digitalization in transforming the relationship between migration and sustainable development across PICTs.

To understand these opportunities, experiences, and prospects, the chapter asks: how is migration practised and how are its consequences understood? How is policy identifying and reorienting to the opportunities of digitalization? What are the current experiences and challenges of leveraging digitalization to link migration with sustainable development across PICTs? The argument unfolds across five sections. Following the introduction, Sect. 6.2 briefly introduces the diversity of migration practices and reviews scholarship on the reciprocal relationship between migration and social reproduction across PICTs. Section 6.3 identifies trends in MDN policy and summarizes the potential opportunities of a digital MDN. Section 6.4 takes stock of existing experiences of digitalization and an emerging digital MDN across PICTs and identifies four pinch points that collectively shape future prospects. The concluding Sect. 6.5 aligns our argument with extant scholarship and calls for a broader rethinking of migration and development. To ground the discussion, we review evidence from PICTs as exemplars of Small Island Developing States (SIDS) located within the region defined by the United Nations as Oceania.

6.2 Migration and Social Reproduction

Oceania and its islands have long been cross-cut by human lives and journeys (Crocombe 2007; Lee and Tupai Francis 2009). Most journeys are classified as examples of so-called "voluntary" migration, including those responding to economic, educational, family, and cultural factors. However, forced migration, referring to mobility arising from situations of coercion or the lack of viable alternatives, continues to blight the region. For example, more than 60,000 people were relocated as indentured labourers to Australia in the 1900s (so-called "blackbirds"; Petrou and Connell 2022). During the Japanese occupation of Nauru between 1942 and 1945, much of the island's indigenous population was forced to leave. After the Second World War, the population of Banaba Island was relocated to Rabi Island (Fiji) due to environmental damage associated with phosphate mining in the former. The United

States resettled populations in its newly acquired Trust Territory of Marshall Islands between 1946 and 1958 due to nuclear weapon testing. Modern-day slavery, trafficking, forced labour, sexual exploitation, including of minors, and child domestic servitude are still recognized as urgent policy issues (UNODC 2023). Climate change is regarded as a growing source of forced migration requiring novel international responses. In a recent and significant move, the United Nations High Commissioner for Refugees held that:

> People seeking international protection in the context of the adverse effects of climate change or disasters may have valid claims for refugee status. They may have a well-founded fear of persecution under Article 1A(2) of the 1951 Convention, or be compelled to seek protection outside their own country owing to events seriously disturbing public order under Article I(2) of the 1969 OAU [Organization of African Unity] Convention and Conclusion III(3) of the 1984 Cartagena Declaration. In addition, there may be grounds for international protection under general international human rights law, i.e. non-refoulement obligations, including the right to life. (UNHCR 2020, p. 11)

Across Oceania, migrants comprised 22% of the population in 2020, representing the largest share of migrants in any United Nations global region. Considering the subregions of Micronesia, Melanesia, and Polynesia as points of origin (i.e., excluding migrants from Australia and New Zealand), emigration grew from 375,176 in 2000 to 565,281 in 2020 (UNDESA 2020, Table 2). There is substantial variation in emigration among these subregions. In 2020, 258,262 emigrants left Polynesia, 256,021 emigrants left Melanesia, and 50,998 emigrants left Micronesia. Most emigrants moved to Australia or New Zealand (319,996, or 56.6% of all emigration), the United States or Canada (156,994, or 27.8% of all emigration), or within and between the three subregions (69,783, or 12.3% of all emigration) (UNDESA 2020). Again referring to 2020, 36% of emigrants from Kiribati moved to New Zealand, 18% to Fiji and Australia, and six per cent to Marshall Islands; 39% of emigrants from FSM moved to the United States, 50% to the US Territory of Guam, and five per cent to the US Territory of the Commonwealth of Northern Mariana Islands (CNMI); 63% of Nauruans who emigrated did so to Kiribati and 32% to Australia (Capal 2020; Orozco and Porteret 2020; Porteret 2020). These patterns suggest a significant trans-Pacific diaspora, with overseas migrants and their descendants often outnumbering on-island populations: for example, there are 12 times more Niueans in New Zealand than living on Niue. That relatively few emigrate to Asian destination countries may reflect non-economic factors including destination immigration policy and the historical roles of the English language and Christian religion in channelling migration (Crocombe 2007).

Scholarship acknowledges an intimate relationship between migration and social reproduction across PICTs. Here we introduce six aspects of this relationship. First, the direction, type, and ongoing consequences of migration are framed and mediated by legal status. Compacts of Free Association (CoFAs) were signed between the United States and RMI (1986), FSM (1986), and Palau (1994). These enable the former to station and operate armed forces on island territories and grant islanders legal status to enter, remain, and work in the United States, with some access to welfare benefits, including Medicaid. However, McElfish et al. (2015) describe how welfare reform in 1996 greatly restricted access to support and benefits at the federal level while state financial conditions further limited support available to PICT migrants. Diaz (2012) argues that such de facto delivery of CoFAs perpetuates the dependency of islanders living in the United States and has "changed the structure of Micronesian life forever" (Diaz 2012, p. 46). Legal status also mediates how emigrants participate in seasonal worker schemes (Petrou and Connell 2022). Up to one in four or five Tongans, Samoans, and ni-Vanuatans have found employment at least once through seasonal worker schemes in Australia and New Zealand. The Australian Seasonal Worker Programme (SWP) has enabled residents of nine PICTs to work seasonally or, with employer sponsorship, for up to four years. Petrou and Connell characterize the SWP as "asymmetrical, ephemeral, and occasionally exploitative" (2022, p. 449). New Zealand's Recognised Seasonal Employer (RSE) scheme enables horticulture or viticulture employers to recruit up to 14,000 workers for a season. Since 2018, the Pacific Labor Scheme has given semi-skilled migrants from ten PICTs the opportunity to work in Australia for up to three years.

Second, emigration also reflects, and may perpetuate, experiences of "truncated choices" and "poverty of opportunity" reported in everyday life (Petrou and Connell 2022, p. 416; ADB 2023). Geographical isolation, limited resources, dis-economies of scale, and heightened vulnerability to natural disasters and climate change prompt both emigration (United Nations ESCAP 2023) and more localized mobility, as Latai-Niusulu et al. (2023) describe among those displaced by floods in Samoa who relocated to nearby family homes. Truncated opportunities may also explain why few emigrants from FSM anticipate any permanent return, with migrants citing poor economic conditions in their place of origin (Orozco and Porteret 2020). Nurses and skilled healthcare workers returning to Niue and Cook Islands have reported a feeling of gradual deskilling, lack of professional development opportunities, nepotism, and experiences of passive resistance to their work practices from existing workers (Connell 2009, p. 149). Some returnees cite the relative lack of opportunity as a reason to not remain but re-migrate and practise a more "circular" mobility strategy (Lee 2009, p. 49). Emigration and circulation of skilled workers can contribute to "brain drain" and reproduce disadvantage.

Third, migration is a structural aspect of the social reproduction of institutions such as families and religious communities (Campbell and Warrick 2014). Motives for migration often take heed of family and faith norms and relations alongside or sometimes contra to purely economic calculations. Families have been described as "transnational entities" and "kin corporations" that enable and strategize migration and residence practices to contribute to their social reproduction (Marcus 1981; Bertram and Watters 1985). Religious institutions and beliefs influence migration strategies through service obligations and attitudes about environmental risks (Campbell and Warrick 2014).

Fourth, the reciprocal relationships between migration and social reproduction are further entwined in economic and cultural connections with land and place (Yates et al. 2023). Customary land, its access, and its meanings mediate livelihood, identity, and community. Latai-Niusulu et al. (2023) describe how Samoans ascribe multiple meanings to place that encompass the economic (kin-mediated access to land and resources), the social (community values, family land, ancestral orientation and connection), and the cultural (national identity). As their obligations, activities, and resources are known to be territorially separated, Samoans understand emigration, return migration, and circulation as necessary aspects of social reproduction. Thus, Macpherson and Macpherson (2009) highlight how Samoan return migration practices contribute to social reproduction through, for example, delivering service to family (*tautau*), seeking cultural authenticity by reconnecting with older members of the Samoan community, seeking to transform Samoan society and its institutions, and a kind of exploration seeking to reconnect to the places featured in kin narratives. Similarly, Tongans have stated that they returned to help Tonga and to better learn the culture, with many overseas Tongans maintaining homes on the island to facilitate extended visits which often last more than a year (Lee 2009). The power of land and place in social reproduction can lead to active strategies to not migrate, as practised by island residents of Nauru who objected to emigration in the 1950s and 1960s despite being faced with the environmental destruction of their land caused by phosphate mining. Their objection to dispersion continued a decade later when the offer of relocation to a portion of the Australian territory of Curtis Island was made subject to their accepting Australian citizenship (Tabucanon and Opeskin 2011).

Fifth, the close association between migration and social reproduction manifests in material and symbolic ways as exchanges of economic and social remittances between migrants, their families, and their island communities. Remitting is often understood as an exchange of resources "necessary but not sufficient" for ongoing social reproduction (Connell and Brown 2005). In FSM, 40% of all households receive remittances, often channelling them into basic needs such as food, shelter, and education. Social remittances enable migrants to maintain customs, express cultural values, and meet obligations to family, such as the Samoan practice of *fa'alavelave* for weddings, funerals, and chiefly title ceremonies (Lee and Francis 2009). Economic and social remittances complement each other to support the reproduction of island life (Le Dé and Jackson-Becerra 2021). In the case of Timor-Leste, remittances from migrants employed in the Australian SWP have been used to strengthen livelihoods, invest in businesses, and consolidate social and cultural capital in ways that can improve social and economic resilience (Wu et al. 2023). Contrary to economic theory, but consistent with their role in social reproduction, remittances are durable, including during and after such shocks as recession and pandemic. That said, the balance of economic and social remitting varies between PICTs. Economic remittances comprise as much as 41% of GDP in Tonga but less than one per cent of GDP in Nauru (KNOMAD 2023).

Sixth, as an intimate aspect of social reproduction, migration both follows from and anticipates moments and episodes of disruption, crisis, and shock. Environmental degradation, typhoons, coups, pandemics including COVID-19, and climate change have all triggered short-term adaptive responses that are nested within longer-term strategies of social reproduction (Tabucanon and Opeskin 2011; Yates et al. 2023). That is, while disruption and crisis does precipitate changing migration and remitting strategies, these strategies tend to reinforce rather than redirect social reproduction priorities (McAuliffe and Triandafyllidou 2021, p. 123; Latai-Niusulu et al. 2023). Le

Dé and Jackson-Becerra (2021) document how migrant remitting increased following Cyclones Ofa and Val (1990, 1991), the coup in Fiji in 2000, and the 2009 tsunami that impacted Samoa. While Samoans working in New Zealand's RSE scheme during the COVID-19 pandemic diverted potential remittances to cover their own living costs in the short term, these migrants quickly resumed remitting, with the volume of economic remittances sent to Samoa between May and September of 2020 some 19% higher than that of remittances sent during the (pre-COVID 19) year before. Remitters explain that "love for the family" led to anticipatory practices and "we don't think about ourselves but for our *aiga* [family] and we want to make sure they have the funds for their church donation and also to help out with maintaining our home and land" (Le Dé and Jackson-Becerra 2021, p. 7).

In summary, long-standing and diverse experiences of voluntary and forced migration are understood in the context of a close, reciprocal, and unfolding relationship between migration and social reproduction across PICTs. Over centuries, diverse human journeys reflect a volatile and sometimes exploitative external context of colonial, imperial, and neoliberal relations while representing investments in the integrity of social reproduction. However, while islanders may understand migration as an embedded and embodied aspect of social reproduction and meaning making, the complex and sometimes paradoxical nature of their migration realities stands in some contrast to the more essentialist tropes that run through international policy linking migration with development, as introduced in the next section.

6.3 Towards a Digital Migration–Development Nexus

This section uses the figure of the migration–development nexus (MDN) to introduce and trace broad trends in policy linking migration with development (De Haas 2010). The MDN gained currency as a policy framework in the 1980s. It balanced neoclassical economic ideas that emphasized emigration as a rational response to unemployment which could enable economic growth with dependency theory insights that brain drain and exploitation could, left unchecked and unregulated, create structural cycles of inequality. Across PICTs, the MDN unsettled the prevailing policy pathway of trade- and export-oriented growth leading to development. New Zealand economists counter-argued that official development assistance (ODA), an inflow of economic remittances from migrants, and governmental activity and regulation could provide an alternative basis for growth (Bertram and Watters 1985). In short, the so-called migration remittances and aid bureaucracy (MIRAB) model explicitly linked development with migrant remittances.

The MDN framework broadened during the early 2000s, reflecting a wider context of increased securitization and politicization of migration (Bailey 2010, p. 376). Policy was oriented towards not just emigrants but also circular, diasporic, and transnational migrants, and it embraced economic and social remitting. There was increased emphasis on migration management and coordination among local, national, and international stakeholders, with the underlying concept of human security acknowledging linked geopolitical, economic, ecological, and climate security risks. Following the global recession of 2007/08, the MDN framework increasingly emphasized sustainable development. The 2030 Agenda for Sustainable Development announced in 2015 promoted "safe and orderly migration" as a tool for reducing inequality (Target 10.7). The 2018 Global Compact for Safe, Orderly and Regular Migration (GCM) coincided with the positioning of the International Organization for Migration (IOM) as "the United Nations migration agency" and lent greater institutional prominence to migration in sustainable development agendas.

A number of PICTs developed policy with reference to this MDN framework. The 2015 Kiribati National Labour Migration Policy recognized that I-Kiribatis should have more opportunities for dignified migration, to address both the lack of jobs and the possible need for later climate-related relocation from the island. Kiribati's Development Plan 2016–19 explicitly promoted economic remitting and introduced predeparture training to assist migrants (Porteret 2020). The 2005–25 Nauru National Sustainable Development Strategy, which initially called for increased job opportunities for migrants locally and regionally, was revised in 2009 to focus more explicitly on the receipt of migrant financial remittances (Capal 2020). FSM's 2004 Strategic Development Plan also identified the positive role of remittances in boosting social security, an aspiration later enlarged with the opening of an IOM Migrant Resource Centre in 2013 (Orozco and Porteret 2020). The IOM became the lead partner in the 2019 multi-agency Pacific Climate Change Migration and Human Security Programme (IOM 2019). This three-year initiative sought to increase the capacity of PICTs such as Kiribati and Marshall Islands to coordinate "safe labour migration" as a strategy for sustainable development and climate adaptation, and to increase research on the human security framing of the MDN. Elsewhere, the Pacific Islands Forum (PIF) and the Pacific Immigration Development Committee also contributed to the coordination of migration management across the region. In common with other SIDS, a few PICTs introduced formal diaspora engagement policies.

The midpoint anniversary of the 2030 Agenda in 2023 occasioned stakeholder introspection and reflection on the speed of progress, with the IOM noting:

> none of today's challenges, from climate change to conflict, can be tackled effectively without considering human mobility. While migrants are often among the furthest left behind, they simultaneously push forward development, well-being and growth for people and planet. Human mobility is already a force for progress that the international community must leverage to help reach the SDGs. Well-managed human mobility is key to achieving the 2030 Agenda. (IOM 2023, p. 1)

Within this latest orientation to sustainable development is a recognition of the significance of digitalization. Digitalization is a process which transforms modes of production, distribution, and consumption and patterns of social organization and reproduction (Brynjolfsson and McAfee 2011). In September 2023, the United Nations Development Programme's (UNDP) SDG Digital Acceleration Agenda proposed 34 digital solutions (two per SDG) to get SDG progress back on track (UNDP 2023). Concerning the MDN framework, the IOM recommends adding digital "leverage" points to, for example, open safe pathways for migrants through enhanced cooperation; remove barriers to the productive participation of migrants; reduce the costs of remitting; weave mobility into development, urban, and climate planning agendas; and enable migrants to contribute to sustainable development. Furthermore, by reducing the "digital access gap migrants can become better integrated and able to realize their goals of entrepreneurship and so contribute innovative and green practices" (IOM 2023, p. 32).

The emergence of what may be characterized as a "digital MDN" (DMDN) also coincided with COVID-19 pandemic conditions. For McAuliffe and Triandafyllidou (2021, p. 6), a "deep digitalization of an already digitalizing world will be one of the most significant long-term effects of COVID-19". Pandemic conditions led to the successful use of digital strategies by migrants to negotiate the challenges they and their families faced in everyday life within the parameters of longer-term social reproduction. For example, awareness and use have increased of digital remitting channels and instances of value and norm transfers through virtually mediated social remitting (Galstyan and Galstyan 2021; United Nations ESCAP 2022; Wu et al. 2023). Migration processes are becoming increasingly shaped by the digital mediation of management tools and systems (including diaspora engagement and the use of big data and analytics); the application of artificial intelligence (AI) to manage and enhance migrant safety and public health; the use by migrants and their communities of ICT and digital platforms for work, study, and communication; and the threat of disinformation about migration and greater prejudice against migrants (McAuliffe and Triandafyllidou 2021, p. 184).

In summary, the MDN framework has evolved from emphasizing migrant- and remittance-led growth to consider the potential impact of digitalization on sustainable development. Scholarship on an emerging DMDN suggests a number of pathways through which digitalization may connect migration with sustainable development. First, offering migrants greater, more immediate, more reliable, and more economical access to information can improve awareness of job opportunities, rights and protections, integration and reintegration support, skill development, financial resources, and the transnational and epistemic activities of other migrants (Kikkawa et al. 2021). Second, the financial, material, and symbolic exchanges that drive sustainable development can be cheaper, faster, and more traceable and reliable when digitally mediated, including as digital remitting and blockchain systems of distribution. Third, by using and co-creating digital solutions, migrants become change agents for long-term digital transformation. Their participation in digital economy, digital society, and digital governance widens the participation of their families and communities too, and it goes beyond the transformation of livelihoods to influence the symbols and metaphors used in communication, strategies for building and reproducing identity and community, positioning in (and sometimes exclusion from) society, and the existential meanings of (geographical) territorial separation. Fourth, the digital restructuring of labour markets creates opportunities for regions and nations to attract new workers and residents. Fifth, an expanding arsenal of tools, systems, and practices exploit digital technologies to increase the effectiveness of support, regulation, and management of migrants and migration. For example, digitalization improves the modelling of the direct and indirect health and morbidity risks of climate change

(Cauchi et al. 2019) and the accuracy of predictive models of migration (Guan et al. 2022).

6.4 Experiences and Prospects

This section considers the prospects of digitalization in aligning migration with the sustainable development of PICTs by first briefly taking stock of early trends in digitalization and DMDN across the region.

6.4.1 Experiences

There is growing international evidence that digitalization is reshaping migrant practices and, as a consequence, transforming patterns of social reproduction (for example, Crush and Tawodzera 2023). PICT-origin migrants are no strangers to digital transformation, notably through transnational practice (including remitting) which has been enabled by access to ICT since the 1970s (Lee and Tupai Francis 2009). During COVID-19, digital migration and remitting intensified. Migrants and migrant families used digitally mediated strategies both to meet immediate needs and to contribute to social reproduction. For example, migrants in the Samoan diaspora used Facetime, Messenger, Skype, and Zoom to enhance communication. They used online shopping and service platforms to remit material items such as food, building materials, and appliances (Enari and Rangiwai 2021). Certain aspects of funerals—stories, chants, oratory—were transacted through images and videos shared on Facebook. Enari and Rangiwai (2021, p. 349) conclude that “despite modernity, a global pandemic and death, these groups still remain interconnected. Through digital innovation, physical distance is no longer a barrier that stops family members from paying their last respects to the deceased.” Enari and Faleolo (2020) describe Samoans and Tongans living in Brisbane during COVID-19 as more than resilient in practising a “purposed creativity” via engagements mediated through the digital places of social media. Elsewhere, businesses based in New Zealand developed blockchain vouchers to enable those migrant family members remaining in countries of origin to shop close to home for essential items (Le Dé and Jackson-Becerra 2021).

Concurrently, PICT governments are actively engaging with digitalization in ways that directly and indirectly reflect an emerging DMDN (United Nations Micronesia 2023). Some adopt explicit digital strategies, such as Kiribati’s *Development Plan 2016–19*, the *Digital Federated States of Micronesia Environmental and Social Management Plan* (2019), and the Nauru *National Broadband Plan and Nauru ICT Strategy*. PICTs have worked and are working with external partners—including the Asian Development Bank (ADB), the World Bank, United Nations, Australia, Japan, and China—to actualize digital projects. For example, China signed a memorandum of understanding with Nauru in 2017 that established the private firm Acclinks as the island's full-service telecom operator. Governments in both migrant origin and destination countries, along with international organizations, recognize the importance of digital remitting (Renn et al. 2021). The Samoan government has activated a Diaspora Unit that it had earlier established to help those overseas to channel humanitarian assistance, support kin, and meet religious and cultural obligations and responsibilities (Le Dé and Jackson-Becerra 2021). New Zealand has lowered some transaction fees to help "stretch" migrants' remitting dollars. Beyond the DMDN, and concerning investments in their wider digital economies, Kiribati, FSM, Marshall Islands, and Nauru worked with "Digital Champions" from the Pacific Tourism Organisation in 2023 to position the region as a premier tourist destination in the digital realm.

Digitalization is also changing the way that governments define and manage the legal status of migrants, including residency provisions. For example, Malta introduced a Nomad Residence Permit in 2021 which offers year-long residency for "digital nomads" working remotely and recognizes the potential multiplier effects of such migration for local growth in the form of entrepreneurship, service provision, tax base, and domestic in-migration (see Reichenberger 2018). Digital nomad visas have become available in some traditional destinations for PICT migrants, including Australia and Singapore. E-residency programmes enable participants to pursue business opportunities (for example, company registration) and circumvent regulations governing access to online resources, including cryptocurrency exchange markets, by presenting a valid "Know Your Customer" token. Globally, an estimated 100,000 people from 179 countries were classified as e-residents in 2022 (Etradeforall 2023). E-residence programmes have been initiated in Estonia (2014), Azerbaijan (2018), Lithuania (2021), and, among PICTs, Palau (2021).

6.4.2 Prospects

A series of pinch points influence how widely and how rapidly the potential of digitalization can be realized for sustainable development across PICTs. Here we identify four interconnected issues: digital access; utilization and datafication; stakeholder coordination; and fragmentation.

6.4.2.1 Digital Access

First, PICTs lag globally on measures of digital access and participation (IOM 2023). In 2000, consistent with socioeconomic and geographical position and limited resources, less than one in four PICT households used home internet (Spennemann 2004). The International Telecommunication Union (ITU 2023) suggests that in 2023, internet use across the wider Asia–Pacific region was the second-lowest among six global regions, with a six-percentage-point gender disparity. Considerable variation exists in the internet penetration rate (internet users per head of population), with 2023 values ranging from 36.1% (Solomon Islands), to 40.4% (FSM), 54.2%

(RMI), 78.3% (Samoa), 83.9% (Nauru), and 87.7% (Fiji; Datareportal 2023). While there is no specific data on the digital position of PICT emigrants overseas, there is no reason to suspect that the general pattern of emigrants experiencing a digital gap would not equally apply (IOM 2023).

Improving digital access means overcoming challenges of geographical isolation, some legacy reliance on expensive satellite provision, and the lack of submarine internet connections (for example, to Kiribati and Nauru; United Nations ESCAP 2022). Thus, Kiritimati limits bandwidth to five megabytes, supplied at high unit cost owing to the use of geostationary satellites. Both its location (2000 km east of Kiribati's most populated island, Tarawa) and its small population (6000) undermine market-based solutions for internet provision (ADB 2023). That said, investments in the region's digital infrastructure have been the subject of discussion during the past decade. These include a planned fibre-optic submarine cable extension to Palau and Kiribati (ADB 2023) and the approval of World Bank support in 2020 to better connect FSM (2020), Marshall Islands (2021), and Tarawa (2022) to the East Micronesia Cable system (World Bank 2020). In 2023, the United Nations' Joint SDG Fund began coordinating digital investments across Micronesia through seven organizations, namely the ITU, the Food and Agriculture Organization (FAO), the International Labour Organization (ILO), the United Nations Office for Project Services (UNOPS), the United Nations Educational, Scientific and Cultural Organization (UNESCO), the United Nations Children's Fund (UNICEF), and the United Nations Office on Drugs and Crime (UNODC) (United Nations Micronesia 2023; UNESCO 2023). Areas of investment include e-health, e-agriculture, and e-commerce (FAO); digital skills training utilizing the Smart Villages and Smart Islands model (ITU); the formulation of national employment policies targeting job creation in the digital economy and promoting digital entrepreneurship (ILO); digital governance and inclusivity in education (UNESCO); and maritime surveillance (UNODC).

6.4.2.2 Utilization and Datafication

Second, variations in digital data availability, coverage, storage, and transfer influence the adoption and successful utilization of digital technologies. For example, limited digital infrastructure and digital platforms contribute to the costs of remitting to PICTs being among the highest globally (Hahm et al. 2021). Concerning migration management, gaps in existing data undermine, for example, the accurate and timely identification of visitors versus returnees, the intensity and nature of remitting, and trafficking activities (UNODC 2023). Improved analyses are needed to ascertain how digitalization will impact on temporary work programmes such as PALM and RSE, where it is unclear if employment opportunities for unskilled workers will follow existing global trends in the substitution of labour by capital or be reversed, as demographic ageing and labour shortages boosts demand for key workers.

Beyond the accurate and timely provision and exchange of data lie wider technological, social, and ethical tasks of data verification, harmonization, storage, access, and purposing (Kikkawa et al. 2021, pp. 92–93; McAuliffe and Triandafyllidou

2021). For example, constructing migration management databases involves new interactions between unfamiliar stakeholders and new constructs through which to exploit digital insights. One of these constructs embedded in the Visa Information System is "migrant traceability", with Glouftsios and Scheel (2021) warning of its potential to perform—and limit—disembodied migrant identities. Another unintended consequence of digital data exchange requiring oversight is the opening of new digital channels for irregular migration. Moreover, the rapid exchange of sometimes unverified digital content between anti-immigrant groups can fuel prejudice against migrants (Leurs and Smets 2018). While datafication concerns are not exclusive to PICTs, the region's capacity to be proactive requires further internal and external coordination (United Nations ESCAP 2022).

6.4.2.3 Stakeholder Coordination

Therefore, third, improving digital access and linking digital migration with development requires close stakeholder coordination. Concerning sustainable development, coordination is needed to help offset the costs of short-term economic headwinds. For example, Renn et al. (2021) argue that achieving ecological sustainability through decarbonization, dematerialization, and re-naturalization means overcoming short-term increases in energy consumption associated with the spread and use of digital technologies. Similarly, circular economies often entail complex logistical arrangements that impose increased energy expenditures. Some digital economies generate considerable "electronic waste" through practices of obsolescence and irreparability.

The increased scope of stakeholders and their agendas across the DMDN deepens the complexity of coordination (Castles 2009). For Leurs and Smets (2018), finding common ground means considering the diverse digitally mediated practices of a range of DMDN stakeholders:

- migrants and "left-behind" family members using digital communication and consumption trends to secure long-term social reproduction, shape business decisions and entrepreneurship, and self-represent;
- government and non-governmental actors at all levels participating to varying degrees in the digital management and control of migration;
- businesses introducing digital products and platforms, including digital remitting, services, and digital employment opportunities for migrants;
- social and print media producing, collating, and circulating discourses, representations, and misinformation about migration and migrants;
- netizens and activists producing and policing diverse and sometimes politically motivated narratives and ideologies about migration and migrants;
- academics and experts producing, consuming, and critiquing information, knowledge, and ideology surrounding the DMDN;
- artists and cultural workers reimagining and extending the channels and platforms through which visualization, symbols, and meanings circulate across the DMDN.

Furthermore, challenges of coordination and finding common ground are complicated by the geographical and geopolitical realities faced by PICTs. For Micronesian states, digital coordination has, to date, involved working with larger or more powerful partners, raising additional questions of ownership, control, and influence (Spennemann 2004). Finding common ground means grappling with issues and agendas that are technological (for example, interoperability, linguistic), economic (for example, who pays, how, and when), institutional (for example, IOM is not one of the seven United Nations agencies part of the region's joint digital investment initiative), and geopolitical (for example, mediating across "the US approach of commercialization and the Chinese approach of governmental oversight"; Renn et al. 2021, p. 23).

6.4.2.4 Fragmentation

Fourth, coordination and finding common ground requires avoiding what Castles (2009, p. 462) refers to as the "fragmentation of knowledge". While underpinning MDN research has been criticized for using static, binary, and hierarchical classifications (including "temporary migration", "return migration", "circulation migration", "transnational migration", "voluntary/forced migration", "insider/outsider": see Chapman 1991; Connell and Brown 2005; Lee 2009; Le Dé and Jackson-Becerra 2021), migrants and migrant families experience and understand ambivalence, ambiguity, and paradox across the unfolding relationship between migration and social reproduction, not least in its territorial separation of obligations, activities, and resources; long-distance acquisition of skills and resources; often extended separations from dependent and remaining families (Connell 2009, p. 158); and complexity of strategy (Chapman 1991). Digitalization may offer new possibilities for avoiding such fragmentation. A digital domain inspires fresh epistemologies, as it takes shape not as a borderless or abstract electronic space but a as hybrid of the geographical and virtual that bridges real island places; embodied actors; national-, regional-, and international-level institutions; and virtual worlds. For Brynjolfsson and McAfee (2011), such digitally mediated everyday life is inherently associated with emergence and creativity and can be approached through concepts including relationality, hybridity, and motility.

A growing number of authors suggest that indigenous practices of metaphor, such as journeying, narration, storytelling, singing, and performance, can be mobilized to overcome fragmentation and build new understandings for the digital domain (see, for example, Vaioleti 2006; Timon and Kaunda 2019; Yates et al. 2023). For Kupferberg (2021), a metaphorical re-articulation of categories such as belonging, place, and community affords connections that are intergenerational and intercultural and lays the ground for coordination based on trust and dignity rather than risk and division. Indigenous practices might help migrants and their families to reclaim agency (Cauchi et al. 2019) and unsettle discourses of climate change that paint islanders as "helpless victims without choices" (Campbell and Warrick 2014). Indeed, when local knowledge is accented, policy can be successful. For example, in their work on the blending of indigenous and non-indigenous food production by the Live and Learn Project in Temwaiku, South Tarawa, Cauchi et al. (2019, p. 6) found that "when traditional knowledge is valued and communities are involved as active participants, not as mere one-time consultants in order to 'tick boxes', projects can be remarkably successful". Moreover, the use of indigenous concepts and symbols may better fit with the human security ethos of the MDN.

Island knowledge and its digital practices can thus scaffold meaning-laden and meaning-creating connections and exchanges. From this, the monetarization of existing migrant practices may sustain improvements in wellbeing. Valorization of the meanings of (say) the apparently banal act of online shopping can build trust and sow the seeds for a larger scale blockchain-based platform which reduces the costs of economic and material remitting, creating scope to divert "savings" into a mutual fund for collective insurance and small-scale investments—themselves perhaps attracting matched crowd funding from diaspora members. That said, the digital domain is not without its structural inequalities, dependencies, and exploitation: a progressive DMDN needs open, critical, and ethical leadership.

6.5 Summary and Conclusion

Realizing the digital prospects of enhancing the role of migration in the sustainable development of PICTs means addressing uneven digital access, utilization and datafication, coordination, and fragmentation. Our arguments align with those of scholars who recognize the significance of migration as an aspect of social reproduction and highlight how indigenous metaphorical practice can offer inspiration for productive cooperation. We subscribe to Chapman's view that "more attention should be paid to the dynamism of time, culture, and local environment interacting with the social processes of island movement … to incorporating the ambiguity and paradox that lie at the heart of island behavior, especially as imbedded within local conceptions of the movement of people" (1991, p. 263). We also concur with Yates et al. (2023), who stress fresh co-creative approaches to sustainable development:

> expanding defective immigration frameworks could repeat the mistakes of exploitative colonial relocations … magnifying the power imbalances which marginalise frontline communities while compounding climate-related precarity. Alternatively, states, regional actors and Pacific communities can circumvent obstacles to well-being by co-planning for mobility. In this, Pacific knowledge systems can guide the development of culturally-specific, whole-of-community protection. (Yates et al. 2023, p. 939)

Renn et al. (2021, p. 27) similarly call for "more space for co-creative discourses that promote sustainable development in the digital world".

While the rapid and uneven emergence of digital practices makes our argument necessarily preliminary, we close with the (repeated) call to expand the horizons of how migration and development are thought about. The digital mediation of migration, migration and development policy, and social reproduction means that the connections between people, land, and institutions are at once geographical and virtual ties. As the digital becomes an increasingly prevalent mode and praxis for connection and belonging, strictly territorial and bounded definitions of migration and development are exceeded, with fresh possibilities for (re)linking migration with human and non-human wellbeing. This may resist what the IOM calls the simplification, stigmatization, and politicization of migration and clear the road for "a fundamental shift in migration-related narratives" (IOM 2023).

References

ADB (Asian Development Bank) (2023) Sector assessment (summary): information and communication technology [Online]. Available at www.adb.org/sites/default/files/linked-documents/50348-001-ssa.pdf. Accessed 12 Oct 2023

Bailey AJ (2010) Population geographies, gender, and the migration–development nexus. Prog Hum Geogr 34(3):375–386

Bertram IG, Watters RF (1985) The MIRAB economy in South Pacific microstates. Pac Viewpoint 26(3):497–519

Brynjolfsson E, McAfee A (2011) Race against the machine: how the digital revolution is accelerating innovation, driving productivity, and irreversibly transforming employment and the economy. Digital Frontier Press, Lexington

Campbell J, Warrick O (2014) Climate change and migration issues in the Pacific. United Nations Economic and Social Commission for Asia and the Pacific, Suva

Capal J (2020) Diaspora engagement mapping: Nauru [Online]. Available at https://diasporafordevelopment.eu. Accessed 4 Oct 2023

Castles S (2009) Development and migration or migration and development: what comes first? Asian Pac Migr J 18(4):441–471

Cauchi JP, Correa-Velez I, Bambrick H (2019) Climate change, food security and health in Kiribati: a narrative review of the literature. Glob Health Action 12(1):1603683

Chapman M (1991) Pacific island movement and socioeconomic change: metaphors of misunderstanding. Popul Dev Rev 17(2):263–292

Connell J (2009) Bittersweet home? Return migration and health work in Polynesia. In: Conway D, Potter RB (eds) Return migration of the next generations. Ashgate, Farnham, pp 139–160

Connell J, Brown RP (2005) Remittances in the Pacific: an overview. Asian Development Bank, Manila

Crocombe R (2007) Asia in the Pacific islands: replacing the West. University of the South Pacific IPS Publications, Suva

Crush J, Tawodzera G (2023) Digital disruptions in the South Africa–Zimbabwe remittance corridor during COVID-19. Migration and Development [Online]. Available at https://doi.org/10.1177/21632324231205996. Accessed 29 Jan 2024

Datareportal (2023) Global social media statistics [Online]. Available at https://datareportal.com/social-media-users. Accessed 29 Jan 2024

De Haas H (2010) Migration and development: a theoretical perspective. Int Migr Rev 44(1):227–264

Diaz KK (2012) The compact of free association (COFA): a history of failures [Online]. Available at https://scholarspace.manoa.hawaii.edu/server/api/core/bitstreams/a0e512d7-02d5-419d-9623-3f184dfa1839/content. Accessed 19 Jan 2024

Enari D, Faleolo R (2020) Pasifika collective well-being during the COVID-19 crisis: Samoans and Tongans in Brisbane. J Indigenous Soc Dev 9(3):110–126

Enari D, Rangiwai BW (2021) Digital innovation and funeral practices: Māori and Samoan perspectives during the COVID-19 pandemic. AlterNative Int J Indigenous Peoples 17(2):346–351

Etradeforall (2023) Palau: digital residency [Online]. Available at https://etradeforall.org/news/e-%E2%81%A0residency-of-estonia-vs-palau-digital-residency. Accessed 5 Oct 2023
Galstyan N, Galstyan M (2021) Social remittances during COVID-19: on the "new normality" negotiated by transnational families. Comp Migr Stud 9(1):51–63
Glouftsios G, Scheel S (2021) An inquiry into the digitisation of border and migration management: performativity, contestation and heterogeneous engineering. Third World Q 42(1):123–140
Guan Q, Raymer J, Pietsch J (2022) Estimating international migration flows for Pacific Island countries: a research brief. Popul Res Policy Rev 41(5):1917–1930
Hahm H, Subhanij T, Almeida R (2021) Finteching remittances in paradise: a path to sustainable development. Asia Pac Policy Stud 8(3):435–453
IOM (International Organization for Migration) (2019) Enhancing protection and empowerment of migrants and communities affected by climate change and disasters in the Pacific region [Online]. Available at https://environmentalmigration.iom.int/pccmhs-enhancing-protection-and-empowerment-migrants-and-communities-affected-climate-change-and-disasters-pacific-region. Accessed 9 Oct 2023
IOM (2023) Leveraging human mobility to rescue the 2030 Agenda [Online]. Available at www.iom.int/sites/g/files/tmzbdl486/files/2023-09/iom-flagship-report-leveraging-human-mobility-to-rescue.pdf. Accessed 10 Oct 2023
ITU (International Telecommunication Union) (2023) Measuring digital development: facts and figures. ITU, Geneva
Kikkawa A, Justo CJ, Sirivunnabood P (2021) Migtech: how technology is reshaping labor mobility and the landscape of international migration. In ADB Institute, Organisation for Economic Co-operation and Development, and International Labour Organization (eds) Labor migration in Asia: impacts of the COVID-19 crisis and the post-pandemic future. ADB, Tokyo, pp 60–102
KNOMAD (Global Knowledge Partnership on Migration and Development) (2023) Remittances [Online]. Available at www.knomad.org/data/remittances. Accessed 10 Oct 2023
Kupferberg JS (2021) Migration and dignity: relocation and adaptation in the face of climate change displacement in the Pacific—a human rights perspective. Int J Hum Rights 25(1):1–26
Latai-Niusulu A, Tsujita M, Neef A (2023) Climate micro-mobilities as adaptation practice in the Pacific: the case of Samoa. Philos Trans R Soc B 378(1889):20220392
Le Dé L, Jackson-Becerra FJ (2021) COVID-19 and transnational remittances in Samoa: maintaining family ties in the face of crisis. In: Campbell Y, Connell J (eds) COVID in the Islands: a comparative perspective on the Caribbean and the Pacific. Palgrave Macmillan, Singapore, pp 279–297
Lee H (2009) The ambivalence of return: second-generation Tongan returnees. In: Conway D, Potter RB (eds) Return migration of the next generations. Ashgate, Farnham, pp 41–58
Lee H, Tupai Francis S (eds) (2009) Migration and transnationalism: Pacific perspectives. ANU Press, Canberra
Leurs K, Smets K (2018) Five questions for digital migration studies: learning from digital connectivity and forced migration in (to) Europe. Social Media+ Soc 4(1) [Online]. Available at https://doi.org/10.1177/2056305118764425. Accessed 22 Aug 2023
Macpherson C, Macpherson L (2009) "It was not quite what I had expected": some Samoan returnees' experiences of Samoa. In: Conway D, Potter RB (eds) Return migration of the next generations. Ashgate, Farnham, pp 19–40
Marcus GE (1981) Power on the extreme periphery: the perspective of Tongan elites in the modern world system. Pac Viewpoint 26:242–262
McAuliffe M, Triandafyllidou A (eds) (2021) World migration report 2022. IOM, Geneva
McElfish PA, Hallgren E, Yamada S (2015) Effect of US health policies on health care access for Marshallese migrants. Am J Public Health 105(4):637–643
Orozco M, Porteret A (2020) Diaspora engagement mapping: Federated States of Micronesia [Online]. Available at https://diasporafordevelopment.eu. Accessed 4 Oct 2023
Petrou K, Connell J (2022) Pacific islands guestworkers in Australia: the new blackbirds? Springer Nature, Singapore

Porteret A (2020) Diaspora engagement mapping: Kiribati [Online]. Available at https://diasporafordevelopment.eu. Accessed 4 Oct 2023

Reichenberger I (2018) Digital nomads: a quest for holistic freedom in work and leisure. Ann Leisure Res 21(3):364–380

Renn O, Beier G, Schweizer PJ (2021) The opportunities and risks of digitalisation for sustainable development: a systemic perspective. GAIA Ecol Perspect Sci Soc 30(1):23–28

Spennemann DH (2004) Digital divides in the Pacific islands. IT Soc 1(7):46–65

Tabucanon GM, Opeskin B (2011) The resettlement of Nauruans in Australia: an early case of failed environmental migration. J Pac Hist 46(2):121–140

Timon T, Kaunda C (2019) "I stand in the middle of the ocean": the emerging coconut theology of climate change in Kiribati. Pharos J Theol 100 [Online]. Available at www.pharosjot.com/uploads/7/1/6/3/7163688/article_34_vol_100_2019_south_korea.pdf. Accessed 27 Oct 2023

UNDESA (United Nations Department of Economic and Social Affairs, Population Division) (2020) International migrant stock 2020 [Online]. Available at https://www.un.org/development/desa/pd/content/international-migrant-stock. Accessed 27 2024

UNDP (United Nations Development Programme) (2023) SDG digital acceleration agenda [Online]. Available at www.undp.org/publications/sdg-digital-acceleration-agenda. Accessed 27 Oct 2023

UNESCO (United Nations Educational, Scientific and Cultural Organization) (2023) Digital transformation in Micronesia [Online]. Available at https://core.unesco.org/en/project/263RAS1001. Accessed 4 Oct 2023

UNHCR (United Nations High Commissioner for Refugees) (2020) Legal considerations regarding claims for international protection made in the context of the adverse effects of climate change and disasters [Online]. Available at https://www.refworld.org/docid/5f75f2734.html. Accessed 19 Jan 2024

United Nations ESCAP (Economic and Social Commission for Asia and the Pacific) (2022) Report of the sixth pacific forum on sustainable development. United Nations ESCAP, Bangkok

United Nations ESCAP (2023) Asia and the Pacific SDG progress report: championing sustainability despite adversities. United Nations ESCAP, Bangkok

United Nations Micronesia (2023) UN agencies and Micronesian governments unite to accelerate SDGs through digital transformation [Online]. Available at https://micronesia.un.org/en/239356-un-agencies-and-micronesian-governments-unite-accelerate-sdgs-through-digital-transformation. Accessed 4 Oct 2023

UNODC (United Nations Office on Drugs and Crime) (2023) Regional report on the existing capacities to measure trafficking in persons in the Pacific islands [Online]. Available at www.unodc.org/roseap/uploads/documents/Publications/2023/UNODC_RegionalReport_PacificIslands_2023.pdf. Accessed 26 Oct 2023

Vaioleti TM (2006) Talanoa research methodology: a developing position on Pacific research. Waikato J Educ 12:21–34

Vince G (2022) Nomad century: how to survive the climate upheaval. Penguin, London

World Bank (2020) Digital Federated States of Micronesia project [Online]. Available at https://projects.worldbank.org/en/projects-operations/project-detail/P170718. Accessed 4 Oct 2023

Wu A, Neilson J, Connell J (2023) Remittances and social capital: livelihood strategies of Timorese workers participating in the Australian Seasonal Worker Programme. Third World Q 44(1):96–114

Yates OE, Groot S, Manuela S, Neef A (2023) "There's so much more to that sinking island!": restorying migration from Kiribati and Tuvalu to Aotearoa New Zealand. J Community Psychol 51(3):924–944

Chapter 7
Blue Ocean Tourism: The Evolution of Friendship Islands in the Pacific

Masato Abe and Luisa Pischulti

Abstract Blue ocean tourism has been one of the most critical industries for sustainable socioeconomic development in the Pacific, while the Pacific island countries and territories commonly face severe geographical and resource constraints driven by their small domestic markets and isolation from global markets. This chapter explores the development of blue ocean tourism through collaboration among "friendship islands" in the Pacific. Friendship islands adopt the concepts of sister cities and other related terms (e.g., border, partner, and twin cities). This study applies the case study approach, specifically choosing three pairs of Pacific friendship islands (or cities): (i) Nadi and Suva in Fiji; (ii) Samoa and American Samoa; and (iii) Palau and the Yap State of Federated States of Micronesia. The three case studies highlight the opportunities and challenges of friendship islands in promoting blue ocean tourism and its sustainable development.

7.1 Introduction

The Pacific constitutes the world's largest ocean expanse, with thousands of small islands. The Pacific island countries and territories (PICTs) comprise 14 small island states, namely Cook Islands, Kiribati, Fiji, Federated States of Micronesia, Marshall Islands, Nauru, Niue, Palau, Samoa, Solomon Islands, Tokelau, Tonga, Tuvalu, and Vanuatu. They claim a combined land area of about 520,000 square kilometres—slightly more than the size of Thailand. However, their combined exclusive economic zones (EEZs) cover 16.8 million square kilometres—more than the land area of the Russian Federation (CIA 2023). Most PICTs are archipelagos consisting of numerous inhabited and uninhabited islands, with Nauru and Niue being the only PICTs comprising a single island. The region had a total population of over 2.5

M. Abe (✉)
United Nations Multi-Country Office for Micronesia, Kolonia, Federated States of Micronesia
e-mail: abem@un.org

L. Pischulti
Waseda University, Tokyo, Japan

E. Monaco and M. Abe (eds.), *Sustainable Development Across Pacific Islands*,
https://doi.org/10.1007/978-981-97-3629-4_7

million inhabitants in 2021, with Fiji the largest (924,610) and Niue the smallest (approximately 2000) (CIA 2023; World Bank 2023).

The PICTs persistently face cost disadvantages in producing goods and providing services due to their remoteness from substantial markets and the need for an economy of scale. They rely heavily on foreign resources, such as capital, labour, and supplies, for their domestic activities, while often facing external impacts instantly and significantly despite their physical isolation (United Nations ESCAP 2022). These issues have caused the PICTs' deficiencies in exporting and consequent trade imbalances. The divide between the main and the outer islands is another key issue among the PCITs, as the main islands and capitals always offer more opportunities than outer islands (United Nations ESCAP 2022). They are also characterized as vulnerable to the impacts of climate change, including rising sea levels, beach erosion, saltwater intrusion, susceptibility to natural disasters, and fragile ecosystems (Perkins and Krause 2018). The PICTs' capacities and resources to respond to these issues are significantly limited, and this will strongly influence the long-term viability of the islands' populations, societies, and cultures.

In addition to the traditional fisheries and agriculture sectors, tourism has become one of the most important industries in the PICTs. The sector generates considerable income and employment while attracting scarce foreign currency for the PICTs (Tisdell 2016). Before the COVID-19 pandemic, their tourism sector grew continuously as they typically offered excellent maritime tourist attractions and distinct arts and culture in the Pacific (Cheer et al. 2018). In the recovery phase of the post-pandemic period, as travel restrictions began to ease, bold policy interventions could be implemented to boost the tourism industry and accelerate economic recovery in the Pacific.

A significant challenge for the PICTs is to turn the focus of its tourism sector to blue ocean tourism to enhance its sustainability in the face of weakened demand, natural ecosystem degradation, and climate change threats. Specific strategic actions may include developing comprehensive tourism plans, linking infrastructure development to tourism promotion, improving air transportation linkages, nurturing the "Pacific brands", and promoting a regional tourist destination collectively (Cheer et al. 2018; Everett et al. 2018). In this vein, the small island states, consisting of cities and provinces, may wish to implement their collective actions by formulating several clusters, or friendship islands, in the Pacific. Such a strategy could provide an operational basis on which to manage the sector's development plans, mobilizing multiple funds and resources and articulating expected benefits for both primary and secondary tourist destinations among friendship islands.

Against this background, this chapter proposes the concept of friendship islands as one that can play an essential role in joint tourism promotion in the PICTs.[1] Friendship cities observed in the Pacific have contributed to the PICTs' transformation of their tourism industries into blue ocean tourism, even if they are still in the nascent stage. The chapter focuses on assessing the phenomenon of friendship islands by studying

[1] The authors appreciate Sorami Ikoma's valuable research assistance. Sharon Sakuma provided valuable comments on the chapter.

three cases: (i) Nadi and Suva in Fiji; (ii) Samoa and American Samoa; and (iii) Palau and the Yap State of Federated States of Micronesia. The three case studies will consider policy implications by assessing the opportunities and challenges of the friendship islands phenomenon as a component of Pacific blue ocean tourism.

7.2 Friendship Islands and Their Practices in Joint Tourism Promotion

The concept of friendship islands adopts the broad content of concepts such as "sister cities" and other similar terms (e.g., "border", "partner", and "twin cities"), as well as displaying some unique aspects (Massoni and Abe 2022). Sister cities involve city-to-city twinning and are developed based on citizen diplomacy and para-diplomacy (Rahayu 2021; Yamin and Utami 2016). They can function domestically and internationally, although cross-border partnerships are more common (e.g., bi-national and international boundary cities) (Massoni and Abe 2022). The concept of sister cities also suggests diversified, long-term partnerships according to official agreements between two communities in two countries (SCI 2019). The term "network" is also frequently used to describe the phenomenon, including intercity cooperation networks (Liu and Hu 2018; Mahyuni and Syahrin 2021).

Table 7.1 summarizes the literature on sister cities and other similar concepts in Asia and the Pacific. It depicts that they are a relatively new phenomenon in the region, while the development of sister and twin cities has been a common feature in North America and Europe for many years (Massoni and Abe 2022; SCI 2019).[2] The literature covers various scientific fields, such as law, economics, international relations, public administration, and environmental studies, suggesting that sister cities are a multifaceted phenomenon. The concept of sister cities can also apply to varied subnational actors, such as provinces, prefectures, districts, towns, and villages, located adjacently or at a distance from each other.

Based on the literature review, this paper defines friendship islands as "small island states' affiliations based on multifold relationships". This simplified definition provides a practical operational basis for the study while covering rich conceptual dimensions, broad geopolitical issues, various stakeholder engagements, and different institutional settings.[3]

The literature review also highlights several determinants of prosperous friendship islands. First, sustainable friendship islands must be developed based on cultural and human ties and mutual socioeconomic benefits, such as shared histories, languages, education, and sectoral complementarities (Cremer et al. 2001; Intasi et al. 2012). Second, in addition policy and regulatory support from the federal government,

[2] These US and European cities led the sister cities movement particularly as part of peacebuilding efforts in the post-World War II period (Cross 2010).

[3] On the other hand, Sister Cities International (SCI 2019, p. 6) defines friendship cities more formally as something "initiated by a partnership agreement between two cities".

Table 7.1 The literature on sister cities in Asia and the Pacific

Study	Concept	Definition	Country/region	Scientific field
Cremer et al. (2001)	Sister cities, twin cities	City-to-city affiliations across the globe based on multifold entrepreneurial relationships	New Zealand/various	Economics; sociology
Cross (2010)	Sister cities	Relationships built on cultural understanding and peace through citizen diplomacy	New Zealand/various	Public administration
Gooding et al. (2015)	Friendship cities, sister cities	International relationships based on cooperative arrangements and activities	Australia/various	Public administration
Intasi et al. (2012)	Border cities, sister cities, tourist cities, twin cities	International city twinning	Lao People's Democratic Republic/Thailand	International relations
Kitkuakul (2021)	Allies' cities, friendship cities, partner cities, sister cities, twin cities	A broad-based, long-term partnership between two communities in two countries based on a formal agreement	Thailand/various	Public administration
Liu and Hu (2018)	Friendship cities, intercity corporate networks, sister cities and provinces	Inter-province and city twinning	China/various	Economics
Lyndi and Iqbal (2018)	City partnership and cooperation, sister cities	A long-term, cooperative relationship between two cities in different countries through which cultural, educational, business, and technical exchanges take place	Indonesia/Uzbekistan	Law

(continued)

Table 7.1 (continued)

Study	Concept	Definition	Country/region	Scientific field
Mahyuni and Syahrin (2021)	Cross-country city partners, intercity government cooperation networks, sister cities	A form of cooperation that involves cities in one country with cities in other countries to increase the sense of fraternity between them and provide benefits to them	Indonesia/various	International relations; public administration
Massoni and Abe (2022)	Bi-national cities, border crossing cities, companion cities, double cities, friendship cities, international boundary cities, neighbouring cities, partner cities, sister cities, trans-frontier metropolia, twin cities	Adjacent townships of different nations that develop with varying degrees of parallelism, often sprouting up across rivers and linked by international bridges	Lao People's Democratic Republic/Thailand	Regional cooperation
Ogawa (2012)	Friendship and cross-cultural partnerships, intercity networks, sister cities, town twinning	A "device", "repertoire", and "model" that could be tailored and used by all different kinds of municipalities in various contexts with diverse aims	Japan/the United States	Environmental studies; international relations
O'Toole (2000, 2001)	City-to-city affiliations, sister cities	To increase international understanding and foster peace by furthering international communication and exchange at the person-to-person level	Australia/Japan/others	International relations; public administration
Pang et al. (2022)	City-to-city ties, friendship cities, sister cities, twin cities	A stable diplomatic relationship between international subnational entities, such as provinces, districts, states, and prefectural cities, to promote city development	China/South East Asia	Economics

(continued)

Table 7.1 (continued)

Study	Concept	Definition	Country/region	Scientific field
Putri and Elvianti (2021)	Sister cities	A form of cooperation involving cities as urban areas	Indonesia/South Africa	International relations
Rahayu (2021)	Sister cities, twin cities	A collaboration that is included in the category of para-diplomacy	Indonesia/Bosnia and Herzegovina	International relations
Rochman and Hudalah (2020)	Partner cities, sister cities	A long-term relationship between two or more communities in at least two countries, fostered through exchange of technology, resources, and knowledge	Indonesia/various	Public administration
Saylan (2019)	Friendship cities, sister cities	A broad-based, long-term partnership between two communities in two countries	Turkey/various	Regional cooperation
Sitinjak et al. (2014)	Sister cities, twin cities	Intercity cooperation and bonds which are formally agreed upon	Indonesia/various	Public administration
Yamin and Utami (2016)	Sister cities	A type of para-diplomacy where local government and administrations play a significant role in foreign relations	Indonesia/Thailand	International relations
Zhang et al. (2019)	Adjacent cities, border cities	For leisure, entertainment, health, business, visits to relatives and/or friends, religion, social events, or shopping	China/various	Regional cooperation

Note The table covers only tourism-related literature
Source Authors' compilation based on stated sources

subnational governments must actively lead the relationship-building, which requires commitment, an institutional framework, leadership, knowledge and skills, and resources (Cross 2010; Kitkuakul 2021; Lyndi and Iqbal 2018; Massoni and Abe 2022; Rochman and Hudalah 2020). Third, citizen diplomacy and associated joint actions must be enhanced by cultivating awareness and involvement at the grassroots community level (Gooding et al. 2015; Mahyuni and Syahrin 2021; O'Toole 2001). Fourth, friendship islands must jointly preserve the environment, ethnic arts and culture, and historical assets and legacy to enhance their value through proper planning and investment while increasing risk resiliency (Ogawa 2012; Sitinjak et al. 2014; Zhang et al. 2019).

Tourism commonly serves as a pillar sector in friendship islands' collaboration. Friendship islands benefit from collective actions, establishing and strengthening commercial relations through tourism based on a mutual appreciation of their diverse cultures and endowments. Their physical assets, cultural diversity, local resources, and institutional and grassroots relationships encourage joint tourism promotion to enhance tourist flows, generate income, and create jobs (Yamin and Utami 2016; Zhang et al. 2019). In this context, investments are needed in urban planning, accommodation, transportation, and other tourism facilities (Saylan 2019; Putri and Elvianti 2021). One promotional strategy the literature proposes is "cultural and heritage tourism", which raises local cultural and heritage awareness and creates a platform from which to promote tourism through cultural, historical, and environmental preservation on both friendship islands (Ogawa 2012).

7.3 Blue Ocean Tourism in the Pacific

This section presents the concepts and practices of blue ocean tourism in the Pacific. It touches on four critical aspects: (i) the blue economy; (ii) the tourism industry in the Pacific; (iii) blue ocean tourism; and (iv) tourism promotional initiatives.

The "blue economy" aims to achieve socioeconomic progress simultaneously with environmental protection and sustainable resource extraction (Srinivasan et al. 2022). It is a relatively new notion that adopts the core concept of the "green economy" into the maritime context.[4] Although the blue economy has yet to be fully conceptualized, it is widely accepted as "the sustainable use of ocean resources for economic growth, improved livelihoods, and jobs while preserving the health of ocean ecosystem" (World Bank 2017, p. 6). Fisheries, maritime transport, climate change adaptation, renewable energy, waste management, and tourism are the main components and activities of the blue economy (World Bank 2017, p. 6).

The Pacific region faces substantial challenges in establishing a blue economy, while at the same time the impacts of climate change and non-sustainable ocean exploitation increase the region's vulnerability (PIFS 2022). Here, the greatest challenge is to reconcile two competing interests: (i) opportunities for local development and growth; and (ii) protection of vulnerable and threatened spaces (Lee et al. 2020; Srinivasan et al. 2022). In recent years, many PICT governments and agencies have

---

[4] A green economy is "driven by public and private investment into ... economic activities, infrastructure and assets that allow reduced carbon emissions and pollution, enhanced energy and resource efficiency, and prevention of the loss of biodiversity and ecosystem services" (UNEP 2023).

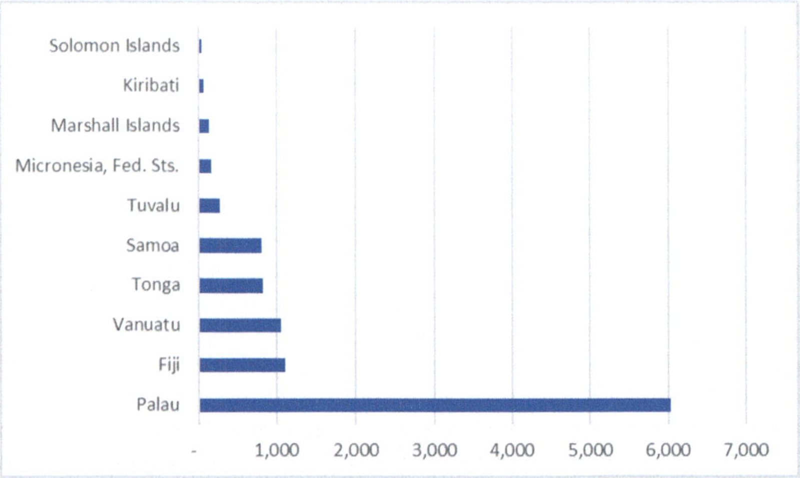

Fig. 7.1 Pre-pandemic tourist arrivals in the PICTs (per 1000 citizens, three-year average, 2017–19). *Note* The figure excludes Cook Islands, Nauru, Niue, and Tokelau because of lack of data. *Source* Authors' illustration based on World Bank (2023)

increasingly committed to promoting the blue economy by implementing various proactive policies and programmes (Keen et al. 2018).

The global tourism industry had grown continuously before the COVID-19 pandemic (Wolf et al. 2021). In 2019, tourism accounted for 10.3% of global GDP (UNWTO 2019). This upward trend was also noticeable specifically in Asia and the Pacific, and especially in the PICTs, which had emerged as popular hubs for all types of tourists in the preceding decades (Srinivasan et al. 2022). The region, home to numerous maritime nations and coastal communities, is particularly attractive for seaside holidays as the islands offer exceptional beaches and diverse water activities to their visitors (Srinivasan et al. 2022). As a result, the tourism sector has recently constituted one of the most important sources of income in the PICTs, employing many people living in the region (Everett et al. 2018).[5]

Figure 7.1 presents the trends of international tourist arrivals in the PICTs before the COVID-19 pandemic. While Palau attracts the largest number of tourists compared with its population size, the small island states in the South Pacific (i.e., Fiji, Vanuatu, Tonga, Samoa, and Tuvalu) receive far more tourists than their North Pacific counterparts (i.e., Federated States of Micronesia, Marshall Islands, and Kiribati).

The discourse about blue ocean tourism has recently gained more attention as a driver of climate change adaptation and mitigation (Wolf et al. 2021). In this chapter, blue ocean tourism is considered an emerging strategy to promote income generation and job creation by strengthening a small island's tourism industry and responding

[5] The tourism sector in the Pacific, comprising such Pacific small island states as American Samoa, Federated States of Micronesia, Fiji, Samoa, and Palau as well as Australia and New Zealand, had an average total contribution to GDP of 20.8% in 2017 (Tonazzini et al. 2019).

to declining environmental conditions. Massive environmental challenges are seen today and continue to increase, and the oceans and life underwater are not spared from these developments. While contributing only a tiny fraction to worldwide greenhouse gas (GHG) emissions, the PICTs are among the countries most affected by climate change (Althor et al. 2016). Rising sea levels, declining coral reefs, and endangered fish species, along with more frequent extreme weather events such as cyclones and droughts, result from a heating planet and destructive activities (He and Silliman 2019). It is particularly true that the tourism sector and its related activities pose considerable environmental stress. For instance, due to its high energy consumption, the sector significantly contributes to global carbon dioxide (CO_2) emissions (Wolf et al. 2021). Hence, integrating sustainability into tourism development policies is a fundamental step towards developing a profitable and long-lasting tourism industry in the Pacific (Bhattacharya and Dash 2021).

Despite the region's challenges, there is a growing commitment to promoting blue ocean tourism. In 2021, the South Pacific Tourism Organisation (SPTO 2021) launched a framework which outlines the vision, policies, and actions necessary to transform tourism into a more sustainable industry—i.e. to implement blue ocean tourism—without compromising profits for Pacific communities. The Coral Triangle Initiative, a collaboration among six Asia–Pacific developing countries, aims to promote the conservation of coral reefs, among other things, by suggesting blue ocean tourism practices that protect marine biodiversity (CTI-CFF 2021). Furthermore, there are numerous national initiatives, such as the introduction of the Pristine Paradise Environmental Fee in Palau, which every international tourist must pay upon entry to the country (Palau Customs 2018). The *Samoa tourism sector plan 2022/23–2026/27* was recently launched with the goal of achieving more resilient and sustainable green growth within the tourism sector of Samoa. Key activities include increasing accessibility and providing education and training to support community needs (Government of Samoa 2022). With the introduction of the *Vanuatu sustainable tourism strategy 2021–2025*, the Pacific island's government is seeking to recover from the COVID-19 pandemic's impacts on tourism. Through sustainable tourism certification, agritourism diversification, and niche tourism promotion, the strategy puts a strong emphasis on environmentally friendly solutions (Vanuatu Department of Tourism 2021). The following section assesses the role of friendship islands in tourism and how it can contribute to realizing blue ocean tourism.

7.4 Case Studies

This section presents three case studies that illustrate the development of friendship islands in the Pacific as a vehicle for promoting blue ocean tourism. It specifically reviews the modalities of collaborations between three pairs of friendship islands (and cities): (i) Suva and Nadi; (ii) Samoa and American Samoa; and (iii) Palau and the Yap State of Federated States of Micronesia. On the one hand, the three studies present the historical background, present status, and challenges and opportunities of the three collaborations. On the other hand, they highlight diverse opportunities involved in friendship islands' blue ocean tourism industry.

7.4.1 Suva and Nadi

Suva and Nadi are among the most populated cities of Fiji, both located on the coast of Viti Levu, the principal island. Suva, the island state's capital since colonial times[6] and located on the east side of Viti Levu, is the larger, with around 93,000 inhabitants in 2017, accounting for one-third of the entire population of Fiji (Fiji Bureau of Statistics 2017). Due to its key institutions and infrastructure, Suva is considered Fiji's political and commercial centre. It is also the site of prominent educational institutions, such as the main campus of the University of the South Pacific, the Fiji School of Medicine, and the Pacific Theological College. Furthermore, Suva hosts various regional organizations, such as the headquarters of the Pacific Islands Forum and the regional office of the Secretariat of the Pacific Community.

Nadi is located on the western side of Viti Levu, 115 km away from Suva. According to the 2017 consensus, around 70,000 people live in the conurbation, making it the third-largest city in Fiji. While Suva serves as Fiji's administration hub, Nadi is a popular travel destination, providing a vast range of tourism-related activities and attractions. Together with Denarau, a small resort island, the area hosts around 42% of all tourists visiting Fiji. The city has a significant concentration of accommodation, ranging from high-end to backpacker hostels, and is home to extensive convention facilities and Fiji's biggest international airport, adding considerable advantage to the city (Republic of Fiji 2021).

Although Suva and Nadi are officially not considered sister or friendship cities, their collaboration features characteristics of friendship cities through their administrative, functional, and commercial complementarity. With the aim of boosting Fiji's economy and fostering development in the region, these two major cities have evolved to collaborate in several ways. One pillar of their cooperation is trade and commerce, particularly in the context of the tourism industry. Much of the tourism infrastructure in Nadi, including hotels, resorts, restaurants, and retail shops, relies on goods and services provided by businesses based in the capital, Suva. As the commercial centre, Suva can distribute goods and services throughout Fiji to provinces with limited infrastructure. Regarding education in Fiji, the Fiji National University and the University of the South Pacific have campuses in both Nadi and Suva. Close cooperation between the campuses and colleges enhances access to quality higher education across both cities and provides trained personnel to the two cities' tourism sector.

To improve accessibility between the two cities, the government has announced the construction of a freeway between Suva and Nadi. The project, costing 1.4 billion Fijian dollars, is expected to commence in 2025 and be completed in six years (Kumar

[6] Fiji became independent in 1970.

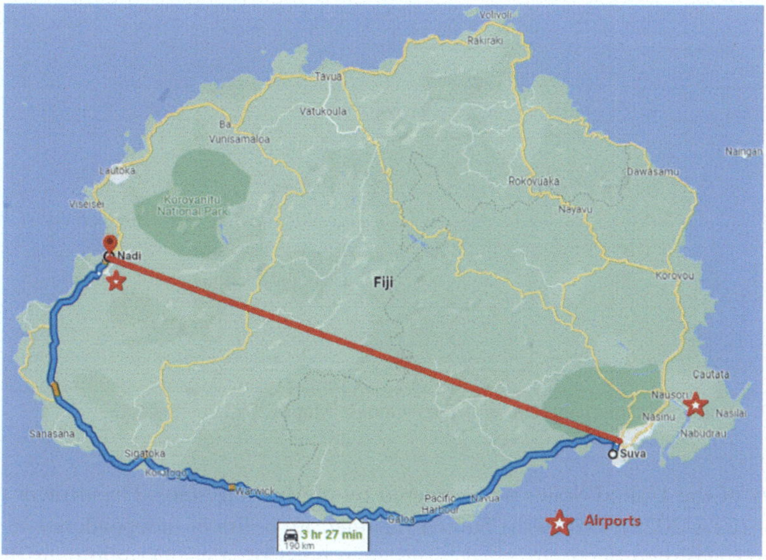

Fig. 7.2 The present Suva–Nadi coastal route and the planned freeway. *Source* Google Maps/ Kumar (2022)

2022). The government has offered assurance that the project will benefit Fiji by creating jobs, enhancing access to services, and reducing traffic in the current circle link roads (Fig. 7.2). Moreover, the authorities plan to build the road to climate-resilient standards. The new freeway is expected to decrease travel time between Suva and Nadi from over three hours to one hour.

As Fiji relies very much on the tourism sector as a significant employer and source of income, the promotion of Suva and Nadi as friendship cities as part of presenting them as attractive travel destinations has a high priority for all stakeholders. The Fijian government is currently working on improving visitor information on Fiji's tourist attractions and intends to develop visitor guides aligned to Fijian brands to boost the growth of special-interest tourism. These guides will be advertised in both cities, Suva and Nadi, allowing tourists to access information about the respective attractions and advantages in both locations (Republic of Fiji 2021).

7.4.2 Samoa and American Samoa

Samoa, formerly called Western Samoa, and American Samoa are archipelagos in the South Pacific that share maritime borders (Fig. 7.3). Due to colonial disputes, the island groups were divided into spheres of influence at the end of the nineteenth century. The western part of Samoa was assigned to Germany, while the United States gained control over the eastern part. Today, American Samoa is an unincorporated

Fig. 7.3 Samoa and American Samoa. *Source* Google Maps (2023)

territory of the United States administered by the United States Department of the Interior (CIA 2023). (Western) Samoa regained its political independence in 1962 and has since then been governed by its own head of state. Despite their distinct administration, the two Samoan island states share a common cultural heritage and language (Keesing 1934). This historical connection and their short distance from each other undoubtedly incentivize them to collaborate in many areas.[7] Hence, Samoa and American Samoa naturally make friendship islands.

"Atoa o Samoa" is a vital part of Samoan culture and tradition and refers to gatherings of Samoan chiefs and other important community members in which decisions are reached concerning the Samoan population. Today, these Atoa o Samoa meetings are held twice a year between Samoa and American Samoa. During the talks of October 2022, a memorandum of understanding (MoU) was signed recognizing the two nations' significant and enduring relations founded on shared history, language, and culture. To enhance sustainable development, this MoU includes objectives in the areas of trade, health, education, infrastructure, agriculture, and tourism, among others. The two governments agreed to establish a permanent committee to oversee the processes of these initiatives, signalling their commitment to collaboration projects (Government of Samoa and Government of American Samoa 2022).

Both Samoa and American Samoa attract thousands of tourists annually, mainly visiting friends and relatives (United Nations 2021; Yamamoto 2009). Samoa's economy relies heavily on visitors, with American Samoa, only a 30–40-min flight away, being the third-largest source of incoming tourists, after New Zealand and Australia.[8] In 2019, nearly 15,000 people (approximately one-third of American

[7] American Samoa is one of Samoa's four largest remittance source markets, following the United States, New Zealand, and Australia, accounting for approximately five per cent of total gross private remittance inflow (Central Bank of Samoa 2021).

[8] Samoa also operates regular ferry services to American Samoa (a journey of 80 kms from Apia).

Samoa's population) travelled from the United States territory to Samoa and injected approximately $31 million into its economy (STA 2023).[9]

Despite their political boundaries, the two island states are strongly committed to working closely together to maintain friendly relations and enhance overall prosperity through blue ocean tourism promotion. To strengthen their tourism sectors jointly they have worked on some pertinent issues, including (i) the "Two Samoas" strategy; (ii) subregional cooperation; (iii) digital connectivity; and (iv) the "Discover Beautiful Sales Mission".

In 2011, the two island states adopted the *Strategic plan for the Two Samoas Environmental Collaboration: an archipelago-wide approach to management and conservation* (Government of Samoa and Government of American Samoa 2011). This joint strategic development plan has served as a guide for funding and investment opportunities directed at the conversation of the countries' fragile ecosystems. One of the plan's main goals, "build[ing] a regional partnership between the two Samoas for improved archipelago-wide environmental management", recognizes their interconnectedness and demonstrates their commitment to cooperation and joint actions to strengthen their blue ocean tourism (Government of Samoa and Government of American Samoa 2011, p. 8).

Both Samoa and American Samoa are members of the Polynesian Leaders Group (PLG). This subregional governmental cooperation group is a collaboration of independent countries and territories in Polynesia that addresses social and economic issues. Since the MoU of the PLG was signed in 2011, the four member countries and eight territories have worked closely together for a more prosperous future for the Polynesian people and to preserve the subregion's identity. Sustainable economic prosperity and democratic values are the core of the group. Key areas of cooperation range from education, culture, and language to environmental conservation, agriculture, and fishery, all of which play an essential role in promoting blue ocean tourism (Feagaimaali'I 2021).

Another vital area of collaboration between the two archipelagos is telecommunication, a critical part of the infrastructure for the tourism industry (e.g. for information dissemination and online air ticket and tour booking). In December 2022, Samoa's Ministry of Communication and Information Technology and the American Samoa Telecommunication Authority signed an MoU to boost digital transformation for both parties, in turn enhancing commercial communications and tourist flows between the two island states (MCIT and ASTCA 2022). The programme outlined in the MoU includes the aims of sharing resources and promoting joint efforts in various areas. For instance, deploying a submarine cable between the two Samoan states is a key goal of the collaboration. On the one hand, this project will benefit American Samoa by increasing the capacity of the main submarine cable that connects the United States mainland with American Samoa, which has promoted economic development through telecommunication-related business, such as call centres. On the other hand,

[9] See Yamamoto (2009) on travellers visiting friends and relatives in Samoa. This trend is partially attributed to the large gap in economic development. While American Samoa had a GDP per capita of $15,743 in 2021, Samoa's figure was only $3857 in the same year (World Bank 2023).

Samoa will be equipped with increased and higher-quality communication capacity while decreasing service costs and improving digital services (MCIT and ASTCA 2022). Such activities improve telecommunication linkage while enhancing mutual economic development and promoting blue ocean tourism.

Finally, to boost the tourism industry, which was severely impacted by the COVID-19 pandemic, the Samoa Tourism Authority (STA) launched the "Discover Beautiful Sales Mission" initiative at the end of 2022 (STA 2022). Together with a group of hoteliers and tour operators, the STA travelled to American Samoa to promote Samoa as a destination and the country's products and services. As stated by the STA, the initiative was part of Samoa's efforts to re-engage with American Samoa at all levels, including government, business, and community, and to increase Samoan brand awareness (STA 2022).

Based on historical, cultural, and geographical ties, Samoa and American Samoa have shown a strong relationship and cooperation in attracting Samoan tourists between the two friendship islands. However, more joint actions for blue ocean tourism, including marketing research and developing the mix of products and services, would significantly increase tourism flows from other international markets.[10] One crucial step that could further enhance their development is a revision of the *Strategic plan for the Two Samoas environmental collaboration* tailored to today's challenges and threats. An intensified joint commitment to environmental protection will benefit a sustainable tourism sector.

7.4.3 Palau and the Yap State of Federated States of Micronesia

Palau is in the North Pacific, 800 km south-east of the Philippines and 800 km north of Papua New Guinea (Fig. 7.4). It has a land mass of 450 square kilometres, making it the sixteenth-smallest country in the world, with 1500 km of coastline and a population of around 20,000 (CIA 2023). It is an archipelago comprising six island groups totalling more than 340 islands of varying topography, from the high, mountainous main island of Babeldaob to low, coral islands, often fringed by extensive barrier reefs. The town of Koror, on Koror Island, which served as the country's capital from independence in 1994–2006, is the largest settlement in Palau, with over 11,000 residents (CIA 2023). This comprises more than 70% of Palau's population, resulting in issues of overcrowding and water insecurity. Until 1994 Palau was a Pacific Trust Territory of the United States, and bilateral relations continue under a Compact of Free Association (CoFA), through which the United States provides financial assistance and defence to Palau in exchange for the right to maintain a military presence (US Department of Health and Human Services 2023). As a result of the uninhibited access that Palauan citizens have to the United States, granted by the CoFA provisions, around 7000 Palauans reside in the United States.

[10] This opportunity will be also facilitated by more-regular air service and ferry connections.

The standard of living in Palau is among the highest in the Pacific, with relatively well-established health and education services. The World Bank (2023) classifies it as an upper-middle-income country. Palau's economy has performed well in recent years, despite a temporary economic slowdown during the COVID-19 pandemic, but is nonetheless reliant on development assistance (from the US Compact and Trust Fund), external grants, foreign direct investment (FDI), and imported food.

Yap is one of four member states, along with Chuuk, Pohnpei, and Kosrae, of Federated States of Micronesia (FSM). It consists of a cluster of four high islands and 14 atolls and small islands distributed over 400,000 square kilometres and located midway between Guam and Palau. Yap is one of the six districts of the former Trust Territory of the Pacific Islands (TTPI), administered by the United States under the trusteeship of the United Nations after World War II and presently under the CoFA (US Department of Health and Human Services 2023). Thus, Yap shares a similar historical background to Palau. Yap provides virtually all governmental and economic activities within the state, equipped with administration offices, commercial banks, a hospital, a two-year college, and an international airport. According to the census in 2010, Yap's population is 11,377 (Government of FSM, undated).

Palau has been one of the most tourism-driven economies in the Pacific (see Fig. 7.1). Its tourism industry generates most of the country's income and labour, producing over 80% of the nation's GPD and accounting for nearly two-thirds of its workforce (Medel 2020). The success of tourism can be explained by the country's reputation as one of the best destinations in the world for diving, the rise of air connections, diversified travellers, and the nation's proximity to Guam, the region's leading tourist destination (Medel 2020). However, the rapid expansion of tourism, mainly from China, before the pandemic, increased the demands on the country's fragile environment while amplifying saturation and capacity overload problems for the small island nation.[11] The sector was also among the hardest hit by the adverse impacts of the COVID-19 pandemic, albeit temporarily, with the economy contracting by over 20% in 2020/21 (IMF 2021). Yap provides tourists with a similar package to Palau, including an attractive maritime environment, distinct culture and social life, and WWII and other historical sites. Travellers to Yap are predominantly from North America (PSDI 2021).

Despite their distinct cultures and traditions, Palau (specifically its Koror State) and Yap continue to be connected through historical and political ties and even familial relationships in their traditional systems.[12] These ties present a good opportunity for cultural and heritage tourism. Palau and Yap have jointly explored attracting tourists through historical tours focusing on stone money and its inter-island trade. During the pre-modern era, people in Yap travelled to Palau to carve out thousands of giant circular-shaped coins, often called "stone money" (Fig. 7.5). Stone money was made from limestone and brought from Palau to Yap by sailing boats, more than 400 km away (Glumac and Fitzpatrick 2020). They were (or even are) essential

[11] This issue appeared visibly during a surge of Chinese tourist flows in 2017 and 2018.

[12] Traditional leaders in Koror, where Yapese chiefs quarried stone money, have strong friendships—even familial relationships—with Yap.

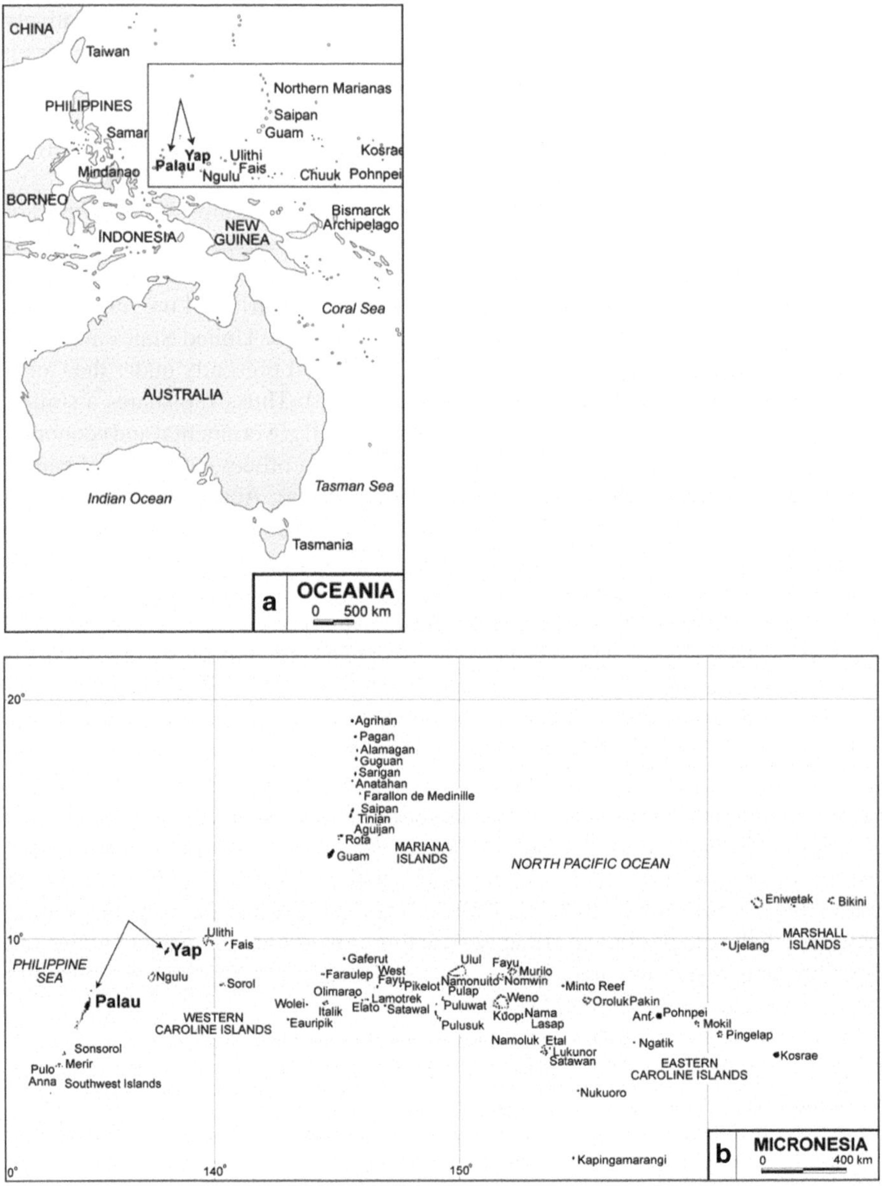

Fig. 7.4 Location of Palau and Yap in Oceania (**a**) and Micronesia (**b**). *Source* Glumac and Fitzpatrick (2020)

Fig. 7.5 Stone money on Yap. *Source* Glumac and Fitzpatrick (2020)

exchange valuables, symbolizing Yap's cultural tradition. Since Yap lacks limestone terrain, its islanders had to travel to the neighbouring islands, i.e., Palau and the Commonwealth of the Northern Mariana Islands (CNMI) (Glumac and Fitzpatrick 2020). Tours of the stone money trade from Palau to Yap could complement Palau's already-saturating diving destinations while fostering Yap's much-needed tourism industry.

Palau and Yap are connected by a local airline at a reasonable cost; however, it operates only weekly, with limited capacity and routes (Yap Visitors Bureau 2023). While Palau provides a variety of accommodations, Yaps can offer only limited capacity, with moderate to basic quality (PSDI 2021).[13] On the other hand, Yap is connected by a submarine internet cable, while the donor agencies (Australia, Japan, and the United States) are currently still working for such a connection from Guam to Palau (Goodman and Wayland 2022). Telecommunication linkage has become crucial for the success of the tourism industry.

Both Palau and Yap rely heavily on their rich biodiversity and natural habitats to generate income and prosperity. To minimize the risk of overexploitation of the environment, both territories have launched guidelines and policies with far-reaching measures. Palau's *Responsible tourism policy framework* is a national policy with a cross-sectoral approach. With its six targets to be accomplished in five years between 2017 and 2021, Palau has committed itself to achieving sustainable and responsible tourism. Contributors to the framework recognized the threat to Palau's environment posed by the increased number of tourist arrivals in recent years. Therefore,

[13] In this vein, Chinese investment has recently increased in Yap's tourism industry. One example is a planned and long-waiting major resort hotel development in Colonia, the capital of the Yap State (Morris 2017).

the primary focus is on shifting the current tourism profile from a low-end, mass-market, package-travel model to a niche, high-value tourism model. Critical targets for accomplishing this goal include responsible visitor management, sustainable product development, and community-driven tourism planning and decision-making (Bureau of Tourism and Ministry of Natural Resources, Environment and Tourism 2016).

The *Yap biodiversity strategy and action plan* (YBSAP) is a comprehensive framework first introduced in 2004 and updated in 2019. It aims to protect Yap's environment by incorporating tangible objectives and actions, acknowledging that the Yap State's culture, economy, and lives depend on its rich biodiversity. Several of the objectives include consulting with other Pacific nations, including Palau. For instance, by seeking advice from more experienced Palauan agencies, Yap is endeavouring to address the issue of invasive species more effectively. Yap is also implementing a stormwater management system that was developed in Palau (FSM 2019). These examples demonstrate Yap's eagerness to collaborate with Palau as a nation that has experienced similar challenges and offers great learning potential. Further amplifying this collaboration in the future can result in valuable opportunities, especially against the background that an intact environment is indispensable for a flourishing blue ocean tourism sector in this region.

The case of Palau and Yap highlights the need for diversification within the tourism sector (IMF 2021). Upgrading supporting infrastructure (e.g., transport and internet connectivity and quality accommodation) and cooperation for cultural and heritage tourism will provide a new opportunity for the friendship islands' blue ocean tourism.

7.5 Policy Implications

The three case studies considered above suggest implications for policymakers, practitioners, and researchers. First, this chapter has proposed a new concept of friendship islands based on sister cities and similar concepts found particularly in the Western world. Pacific governments, whose capacity is limited due to their islands' geographical constraints, such as small size, remoteness, and lack of resources, may take it to complement their present policy mix.

Second, given their nature, the friendship islands concept can be well suited to promoting blue ocean tourism, mainly through facilitating collaboration and joint actions between neighbouring island states. As mentioned above, such small island states share similar constraints and challenges, so they can easily find a way to cooperate over their development strategies, including promoting blue ocean tourism.

Third, friendship islands require multidimensional collaboration, which manifests in various relationships between the islands: federal among multi-stakeholders: provincial, city, and district governments; the private sector; and civil society organizations. Collaboration for jointly designed and developed infrastructure and public services is particularly needed.

Fourth, cultural and historical linkages could be used to promote collaboration in blue ocean tourism between friendship islands. Such linkages are commonly observed in the Pacific, even while each entity maintains its distinct legacy.

7.6 Conclusions

This chapter has proposed the concept of friendship islands based on sister cities and related phenomena. The friendship islands concept implies adopting and implementing various policies to promote blue ocean tourism, the most pertinent industry for the future of island nations in the Pacific. The Pacific friendship islands could strengthen inter-island collaboration by designing and implementing joint actions in the tourism sector. The concept is particularly powerful in addressing infrastructure-sharing, functional complementarity, cultural and heritage tourism promotion, and communication enhancement.

This study, however, has some limitations. First, it has studied only three Pacific cases. Second, more vigorous qualitative studies are required, interviewing multiple stakeholders such as governments, the private sector, civil society organizations, and international donor agencies. Future studies need to be undertaken to address these limitations and to better understand the phenomenon and its practical implications.

References

Althor G, Watson JEM, Fuller RA (2016) Global mismatch between greenhouse gas emissions and the burden of climate change. Sci Rep 6:20281

Bhattacharya P, Dash AK (2021) Determinants of blue economy in Asia-Pacific island countries: a study of tourism and fisheries sectors. Ocean Coast Manag 211:105774

Bureau of Tourism and Ministry of Natural Resources, Environment and Tourism (2016) Palau responsible tourism policy framework: ensuring a pristine paradise. Palau for everyone, 2017–2021. Republic of Palau, Ngerulmud.

Central Bank of Samoa (2021) Visitor earnings and remittances statistics. Central Bank of Samoa, Apia

Cheer JM, Pratt S, Tolkach D, Bailey A, Taumoepeau S, Movono A (2018) Tourism in Pacific island countries: a status quo round-up. Asia Pac Policy Stud 5:442–461

CIA (Central Intelligence Agency) (2023) World factbook [online]. Available at www.cia.gov/the-world-factbook. Accessed 15 Apr 2023

Cremer RD, De Bruin A, Dupuis A (2001) International sister-cities: bridging the global–local divide. Am J Econ Sociol 60(1):377–401

Cross B (2010) Sister cities and economic development: a New Zealand perspective. Transylvanian Rev Adm Sci 30E:104–117

CTI-CFF (Coral Triangle Initiative of Coral Reefs, Fisheries and Food Security) (2021) Annual report 2020. CTI-FCC Regional Secretariat, Manado

Everett H, Simpson D, Wayne S (2018) 'Tourism as a driver of growth in the Pacific: a pathway to growth and prosperity for Pacific Island countries', Issues in Pacific Development 2. Asian Development Bank, Manila

Feagaimaali'I J (2021) Polynesian leaders group in virtual meet. SamoaObserver, 27 January [online]. Available at www.samoaobserver.ws/category/samoa/78126. Accessed 28 Mar 2023
Fiji Bureau of Statistics (2017) Fiji population and housing census: administrative report. Available at www.statsfiji.gov.fj. Accessed 18 Mar 2023
FSM (2019) Yap biodiversity strategy and action plan 2018–2023 [online]. Available at https://fsm-data.sprep.org/system/files/Yap%20BSAP%20-%2026Oct18%20-%20Governor%20Signature%201_8_19.pdf. Accessed 15 Apr 2023
Glumac B, Fitzpatrick SM (2020) Yapese stone money: local marble as a potential inspiration for producing limestone exchange valuables in Palau, Micronesia. In: Cooney G, Gilhooly B, Kelly N, Mallía-Guest S (eds) Cultures of stone: an interdisciplinary approach to the materiality of stone. Sidestone Press, Leiden, pp 65–78
Gooding A, Gibbs M, Woods R, Pillora S, Smith R (2015) Sister cities and international alliances. Australian Centre of Excellence for Local Government, Sydney
Goodman MP, Wayland M (2022) Securing Asia's subsea network: U.S. interests and strategic options. CSIS Briefs, April. Center for Strategic & International Studies (CSIS), Washington, DC
Government of FSM (undated). Summary analysis of key indicators from the FSM 2010 census of population and housing. FSM Office of Statistics, Palikir, Pohnpei
Government of Samoa (2022) Samoa tourism sector plan 2022/2023—2026/2027. Government of Samoa, Apia
Government of Samoa and Government of American Samoa (2011) Strategic plan for the Two Samoas Environmental Collaboration: an archipelago-wide approach to management and conservation. As adopted at the Two Samoas Environmental Collaboration Meeting, Apia, Samoa, 7–8 November
Government of Samoa and Government of American Samoa (2022) Memorandum of understanding between the government of the independent state of Samoa and the government of the territory of American Samoa on development co-operation. 14 October
He Q, Silliman BR (2019) Climate change, human impacts, and coastal ecosystems in the Anthropocene. Curr Biol Rev 29:R1021–R1035
IMF (International Monetary Fund) (2021) Republic of Palau: staff report for the 2021 Article IV Consultation. IMF, Washington, DC
Intasi W, Jaiborisudhi W, Kaewkumkong A, Changklang C (2012) Mukdahan–Suvannakhet sister cities: the study of cultural factors that affect the appropriateness of the sister city relationship-building policy between border towns in the Mekong sub-region. Int J East Asian Stud 17(2):50–65
Keen MR, Schwarz A-M, Wini-Simeon L (2018) Towards defining the blue economy: practical lessons from Pacific ocean governance. Mar Policy 88:333–341
Keesing FM (1934) Modern Samoa: its government and changing life. G. Allen & Unwin Ltd., London
Kitkuakul P (2021) A study on the implementation of sister city relationship policy by Thai provincial governments. Dissertation submitted in partial fulfilment of the requirements for the degree of Doctor of Philosophy (Development Administration), School of Public Administration National Institute of Development Administration, Bangkok
Kumar R (2022) Construction on Suva to Nadi free-way to begin in 2025 and Nadi to Lautoka bypass in 2024. Fijivillage, 28 October [online]. Available at www.fijivillage.com/feature/Construction-on-Suva-to-Nadi-free-way-to-begin-in-2025-and-Nadi-to-Lautoka-bypass-in-2024-x85r4f. Accessed 15 Apr 2023
Lee K-H, Noh J, Khim JS (2020) The blue economy and the United Nations' sustainable development goals: challenges and opportunities. Environ Int 137:105528
Liu X, Hu X (2018) Are "sister cities" from "sister provinces"? An exploratory study of sister city relations (SCRs) in China. Netw Spat Econ 18(3):473–491

Lyndi IF, Iqbal MP (2018) City partnership (sister city) between Banda Ache (the Republic of Indonesia) and Samarqand (the Republic of Uzbekistan) on trade and industry in Banda Ache. JIM Bidang Hukum Kenegaraan 2(2):383–393
Mahyuni M, Syahrin MN (2021) Sister city cooperation model in wetland environmental governance: case study in Banjarmasin, south of Kalimantan. Int J Politic Pub Policy Environ Issues 1(2):115–125
Massoni H, Abe M (2022) Fostering cross-border twin cities in the Greater Mekong Subregion. J Mekong Soc 18(1):125–153
MCIT (Samoa Ministry of Communication and Information Technology), ASTCA (American Samoa Telecommunications Authority) (2022) Telecom MOU signing between Samoa and American Samoa. A joint press release
Medel IL (2020) The Palau legacy pledge: a case study of advertising, tourism, and the protection of the environment. Westminster Pap Commun Cult 15(2):178–190
Morris D (2017) A remote Pacific island faces up to China: can Yap Island both protect its unique heritage and capitalize on Chinese investment?' The Diplomat, 26 June
Ogawa A (2012) Sister city as a preservation strategy. MSc thesis, Graduate School of Architecture, Planning, and Preservation, Columbia University, New York
O'Toole K (2000) From mates to markets: Australian sister city type relationships. Policy Organ Soc 19(1):43–64
O'Toole K (2001) Kokusaika and internationalisation: Australian and Japanese sister city type relationships. Aust J Int Aff 55(3):403–419
Palau Customs (2018) Public notice: Palau Pristine Paradise Environmental Fee (PPEF) [online]. Available at www.palaucustoms.org/files/common_unit_id/c8672894-ba61-43f7-b6c4-6a69acbd1b61/PUBLIC%20NOTICE.pdf. Accessed 15 Apr 2023
Pang F, Tang J, Xie H (2022) Investigating whether connecting people can promote subnational economic development: evidence from China–ASEAN friendship cities. Int Stud Econ 17:499–530
Perkins RM, Krause SM (2018) Adapting to climate change impacts in Yap State, Federated States of Micronesia: the importance of environmental conditions and intangible cultural heritage. Island Stud J 13(1):1–14
PIFS (Pacific Islands Forum Secretariat) (2022) 2050 strategy for the Blue Pacific Continent/Pacific Islands Forum Secretariat. PIFS, Suva
PSDI (Pacific Private Sector Development Initiative) (2021) Federated States of Micronesia, Pacific tourism sector snapshot, November 2021. PSDI, Sydney
Putri IGAMDK, Elvianti W (2021) Affecting factors of sister city cooperation between Denpasar government and Mossel Bay government in 2019. Indonesian J Int Relat 5(2):264–291
Rahayu FD (2021) Sister city cooperation (twin cities) between Magelang city and Brcko district (Hubungan kerjasama sister city (kota kembar) antara kota Magelang dan distrik Brcko). Available at www.researchgate.net/publication/357151423_Sister_City_Cooperation_Twin_Cities_Between_Magelang_City_and_Brcko_District_Hubungan_Kerjasama_Sister_City_Kota_Kembar_Antara_Kota_Magelang_Dan_Distrik_Brcko. Accessed 29 Nov 2023
Republic of Fiji (2021) Fijian tourism 2021. Available at https://site2.mcttt.gov.fj/wp-content/uploads/2022/05/FT2021.pdf. Accessed 15 Apr 2023
Rochman GP, Hudalah D (2020) How does leadership factors spur the success of sister city cooperation? J Phys: Conf Ser 1469:012032
Saylan U (2019) Sister cities and tourism: the case of Turkey. Stud Interdisc Econ Bus 2:185–193
SCI (Sister Cities International) (2019) 2019 membership directory. SCI, Washington, DC
Sitinjak E, Sagala S, Rianawati E (2014) Opportunity for sister city application to support resilience city. In: Working paper 8, May. Resilience Development Initiative, Bandung
SPTO (2021) The Pacific 2030 sustainable tourism policy framework. SPTO, Suva
Srinivasan M, Kaullysing D, Bhagooli R, Pratt S (2022) Marine tourism and the blue economy: perspectives from the Mascarene and Pacific islands. In: Urban Jr ER, Ittekot V (eds) Blue economy: an ocean science perspective. Springer, Singapore, pp 153–189

STA (Samoa Tourism Authority) (2022) Discover beautiful sales mission to American Samoa [online]. Available at www.samoatourism.org/articles/424/discover-beautiful-sales-mission-to-american-samoa. Accessed 29 Nov 2023
STA (2023) Samoa Tourism Authority: corporate website [online]. Available at www.samoatourism.org. Accessed 29 Nov 2023
Tisdell CA (2016) Models of the international economic dependence of Pacific microstates: a critical review with important implications for international policies and relations. J Self Gov Manag Econ 4(2):7–27
Tonazzini D, Fosse J, Morales E, González A, Klarwein S, Moukaddem K, Louveau O (2019) Blue tourism: towards a sustainable coastal and maritime tourism in world marine regions. eco-union, Barcelona
UNEP (United Nations Environment Programme) (2023) Green economy [online]. Available at www.unep.org/regions/asia-and-pacific/regional-initiatives/supporting-resource-efficiency/green-economy. Accessed 15 April 2023
United Nations (2021) Special Committee on the situation with regard to the Implementation of the Declaration on the Granting of Independence to Colonial Countries and Peoples: American Samoa. A/AC.109/2021/1. General Assembly, 11 March
United Nations ESCAP (Economic and Social Commission for Asia and the Pacific) (2022) Advancing Pacific priorities 2022. Subregional Office for the Pacific, United Nations ESCAP, Suva
United Nations in the Pacific (2023) United Nations Pacific sustainable development cooperation framework 2023–2027. United Nations, Apia, Kolonia and Suva
UNWTO (World Tourism Organization) (2019) Tourism highlights: 2019 edition. UNWTO, Madrid
US Department of Health and Human Services (2023) Overview of the state—Federated States of Micronesia—2021 [Online]. Available at https://mchb.tvisdata.hrsa.gov/Narratives/Overview/4cb122c1-e9f3-4e3d-908f-820b070e0577. Accessed 29 Nov 2023
Vanuatu Department of Tourism (2021) Vanuatu sustainable tourism strategy 2021–2025. Department of Tourism, Port Vila
Wolf F, Filho WL, Singh P, Scherle N, Reiser D, Telesford J, Milković IB, Havea PH, Li C, Surroop D, Kavaleva M (2021) Influences of climate change on tourism development in small Pacific island states. Sustainability 13:4223
World Bank (2017) The potential of the blue economy: increasing long-term benefits of the sustainable use of marine resources for Small Island Developing States and coastal least developed countries. World Bank, Washington, DC
World Bank (2023) GDP per capita (current US$): Samoa and American Samoa [online]. Available at https://data.worldbank.org. Accessed 23 Apr 2023
Yamamoto M (2009) Migration and tourism development in Samoa. People Cult Oceania 24:51–66
Yamin M, Utani AT (2016) Towards sister city cooperation between Cilacap and Mueang Chonburi district. In: Proceedings of the 2016 International Conference on Public Management (ICPM 2016), Kunming, China, 15–17 July, pp 402–405
Yap Visitors Bureau (2023) Visit Yap [online]. Available at www.visityap.com. Accessed 15 Apr 2023
Zhang S, Zhong L, Ju H, Wang Y (2019) Land border tourism resources in China: spatial patterns and tourism management. Sustainability 11(1):236

Chapter 8
Small Island Sustainability: A Comparative Analysis of Bali and Palau Islands

Tan Farlynda

Abstract The quest for sustainable development has become a paramount global concern, and small islands serve as microcosms of this endeavour, exemplifying the delicate balance between environmental preservation and socioeconomic progress. This study presents a comparative analysis of two islands, Bali and Palau, that have garnered international attention for their unique approaches to sustainability. Focusing on Sustainable Development Goal 12, "responsible consumption and production", this research aims to uncover the strategies employed by these islands in achieving sustainable practices while implementing a circular economy. Through an in-depth examination of policies, initiatives, and community engagement, the study reveals the multifaceted efforts undertaken by Bali and Palau. Both islands showcase commendable dedication to responsible consumption, incorporating eco-friendly practices in sectors such as tourism, agriculture, and waste management. It highlights successful approaches, identifies areas for improvement, and emphasizes the importance of local engagement. The study offers actionable recommendations for policymakers, businesses, and communities seeking to establish a circular economy in an island state that balances ecological integrity with social and economic wellbeing.

Sab Faro contributed to this chapter by coordinating between the author and the editor.

T. Farlynda (✉)
Murdoch University, Murdoch, Australia
e-mail: sabfaro@sabfarocollectives.com

E. Monaco and M. Abe (eds.), *Sustainable Development Across Pacific Islands*,
https://doi.org/10.1007/978-981-97-3629-4_8

8.1 Introduction

8.1.1 Background and Significance of Sustainable Development for Small Islands

The idea of sustainable development has become extremely important in a time of rapidly increasing urbanization and globalization and urgent environmental issues. By 2050, it is expected that there will be nine billion people on the planet, most of them living in quickly expanding cities. The increased demand for food, energy, and resources as a result of this urbanization trend puts significant strain on the environment, and raises concerns about the viability of our present development paths. As it attempts to achieve a healthy balance between economic growth, social progress, and environmental preservation, sustainable development has become crucial (Zhong et al. 2023).

Researchers have long been drawn to small islands because of their special qualities; scientist Edward O. Wilson has observed that small islands provide natural laboratories for biodiversity and evolution (Whittaker et al. 2017). However, invasive species and environmental changes can make islands more susceptible to habitat degradation and loss of biodiversity and can increase vulnerability to extreme events, and this has prompted academics such as Jared Diamond to focus on their fragility (McAnany and Yoffee 2009). Island communities, despite the difficulties they face, show resilience by adjusting to their scarce resources. Along with dealing with a variety of difficulties, small island states have come under scrutiny due to worries about their long-term sustainability, including problems with the environment, society, and the economy (Gowdy 2005). These remote landmasses, encircled by the vastness of the oceans, provide a pristine canvas for the investigation of sustainable development ideas. Islands must deal with the same global concerns as larger continents within their limited bounds, but frequently with more severe repercussions and with fewer resources at their disposal. As a result, the inventions and techniques that come from these isolated areas can teach the rest of the world some important lessons.

8.1.2 Rationale for the Study

This study focuses on two islands globally celebrated for their achievements in sustainability: Bali and Palau. Despite their distinct geographical and cultural contexts, both islands exhibit a similarly strong commitment to embracing sustainable practices and the principles of a circular economy. This dedication aligns seamlessly with United Nations Sustainable Development Goal 12, which emphasizes responsible production and consumption. The objective underscores the importance of waste reduction, efficiency, environmentally friendly consumption patterns, and sustainable resource management, all of which are integral to the sustainability initiatives of islands.

By offering a comparative examination of the methods and policies adopted by two countries and highlighting some of the major difficulties and opportunities they have been confronted with, this research makes a contribution to the field of sustainable development in small island nations. The chapter also identifies a number of possible areas for further investigation, including the contribution of traditional knowledge and cultural heritage to sustainable development and the possibilities for inter-regional cooperation and knowledge exchange among small island states.

8.1.3 Research Questions and Objectives

8.1.3.1 Research Questions

- How can Bali and Palau incorporate the principles of responsible consumption and production, particularly in tourism, agriculture, and waste management?
- What are the fundamental similarities and differences between the approaches of Bali and Palau to attaining sustainable development?
- What challenges have Bali and Palau faced in their efforts to achieve sustainable development, and how have they overcome these challenges to ensure the long-term viability and success of their strategies?
- How might the experiences of Bali and Palau help other islands and regions to build a circular economy that balances environmental sustainability with socioeconomic progress?

8.1.3.2 Research Objectives

The goal of this study was to perform a comparative examination of approaches to sustainable development in Bali and Palau, with a focus on responsible consumption and production, and to present actionable recommendations for establishing a circular economy.

8.1.4 Methodology

This study examined the sustainable development efforts of Bali and Palau using a comparative analysis methodology. A qualitative method was used in the research design to ensure thorough knowledge of plans for achieving responsible consumption and production on small islands and to inform the adoption of circular economy principles.

8.1.4.1 Data Collection

Qualitative field studies were undertaken in Bali and Palau to explore changes in island sustainability as a result of tourism, agriculture, and waste management. Both islands exemplify impactful sustainability initiatives, emphasizing tourism, waste reduction, and agricultural practices. This study was intended to analyse how key stakeholders perceive tourism, agriculture, and waste management by applying a qualitative approach, thereby offering a contribution to the existing literature on island sustainability.

8.1.4.2 Interviews

The study used semi-structured interviews to capture key perspectives of stakeholders on tourism, waste management, and agricultural development. The (eight) interview questions were prepared to investigate, understand, and appreciate local perspectives and attitudes in order to collect more detailed data.

8.1.4.3 Sampling

Strategic sampling was used to select interviewees based on objectives of the research. The primary goal was to identify native Balinese and Palauan people who had been impacted by increased tourism, waste mismanagement, and agricultural product damage on the islands. Twelve interviews were acquired from Bali and Palau, and the dataset was deemed to be saturated. Table 8.1 shows a summary of the interviews. The results of the interviews were not generalized to the entire population of Bali and Palau, but they can be viewed as rich data on the selected interviewees.

8.1.4.4 Comparative Analysis

Utilizing comparative analysis, the researchers aimed to identify themes in the collected data, facilitating a quick comparison between Bali and Palau (Nowell et al. 2017). To a large extent, Bali and Palau were selected for this comparative analysis of island sustainability because of their disparities in environmental, economic, cultural, and governance aspects. These distinctions can provide essential insights into best practices for sustainable development not only for the two islands studied but for other small island nations and regions confronted with similar issues (Hakim et al. 2009). Comparative analysis of the data, represented on colour-coded Post-It notes, revealed six major themes: waste management strategies and challenges, tourism strategies and challenges, and sustainable agriculture strategies and challenges.

Table 8.1 Strategies, challenges, and issues for the sustainability of waste management, agriculture, and tourism in Bali and Palau

Island	Participants	Sector	Strategies	Challenges	Issues
Bali	2	Waste management	Better waste-to-energy infrastructure; comprehensive e-waste recycling programmes	Insufficient waste collection services; limited public awareness and participation in waste separation	No funding to improve infrastructure for waste management and to conduct awareness programmes related to sustainable waste management
	2	Agriculture	Revert to traditional farming methods such as heritage farming practices; royal spices are trying to persuade farmers to switch from growing rice to high-value crops, particularly vanilla; compost to create soil full of microbes and multitudes of different micro-organisms, for which no genetically modified organisms (GMOs) are needed	Intermediaries and brokers; disruption to ecology caused by President Suharto's inception of rice self-sufficiency policy in 1971	Farmers using pesticides; intermediaries; lack of awareness; lack of educational initiatives; govt pressure to grow commercial rice; slugs causing crop damage

(continued)

Table 8.1 (continued)

Island	Participants	Sector	Strategies	Challenges	Issues
	2	Tourism	Promoting eco-friendly accommodation, responsible wildlife tourism, waste reduction initiatives, cultural preservation, and community-based tourism; development of the Special Economic Zone (KEK) Kura-Kura Bali in Serangan, for luxury international-class tourism activities: includes an integrated marina area, a centre for excellence for education, a tech park, and a lifestyle wellness centre	Over-tourism; environmental degradation; cultural commodification; need for better waste management and infrastructure to support responsible tourism	Waste management problems; strains on local resources; cultural exploitation; need for stronger regulations to curb uncontrolled development; regulations to curb growth in numbers of illegal workers; collaborating with Bali Regional Police to coordinate the resolution of issues such as immigration with the Foreigner Supervision Team (Tim PORA), the State Intelligence Agency Foreigner Monitoring Team (Tim POA), Bali Regional Police within their jurisdiction, and the regional police in accordance with their authority

(continued)

Table 8.1 (continued)

Island	Participants	Sector	Strategies	Challenges	Issues
Palau	2	Waste management	Reducing plastic use; promoting recycling and composting; implementing waste separation at source	Limited landfill space; difficulties in recycling due to island's remote location; impact of marine litter on pristine coastal areas	Limited landfill space; inadequate recycling infrastructure; marine pollution from plastic waste affecting the country's pristine coastal areas
	2	Agriculture	Organic farming practices; traditional crop rotation; rainwater harvesting; promotion of indigenous crop varieties	Limited arable land; water scarcity; invasive species; impacts of climate change on crop yields	Limited arable land; water scarcity; pest and disease management; need to adapt to climate change impacts; preserving traditional farming knowledge while integrating modern practices
	2	Tourism	Implementing marine conservation and eco-tourism practices; promoting responsible visitor behaviour; regulating tourist numbers to protect fragile marine ecosystem	Need for effective waste management; balancing tourism with environmental conservation; addressing pressure on coral reefs and marine ecosystem	Over-tourism; environmental degradation; cultural preservation; need for responsible waste management and sustainable practices

Source Author's construction based on survey participants' responses

8.1.4.5 Abductive Process

An abductive procedure was employed, driven by a combination of inductive and deductive approaches. The inductive process involved generating themes from the data without relying on a pre-existing theoretical framework. Unlike in traditional coding, the emphasis was on uncovering emergent themes rather than fitting data into predefined codes. The theoretical framework underwent revisions after interview data was collected. The researchers continually moved between the collected data and the theoretical framework, employing an ongoing inductive process to enhance the understanding necessary to address the aim of this study (Nowell et al. 2017).

8.1.4.6 Method Reflection

A qualitative approach was employed to gain a better understanding of perceptions of tourism, agriculture, and waste management sustainability from residents. Connections were made with several sectors in Bali and Palau in order to obtain this data by conducting online and face-to-face interviews while overcoming cultural obstacles. A comparative design can sometimes prompt researchers to look for differences in empirical material rather than using an open approach, although achieving equivalence between variables, methodologies, and samples employed can be difficult. Semi-structured interviews are ideal for achieving an open approach because there are only a few interview questions, allowing the conversation to flow naturally.

8.1.4.7 Trustworthiness and Transparency

The qualitative investigation prioritized transparency towards participants about the aims of the study. The research process, data acquisition, analysis, and interpretation of interviewee responses were presented in depth to participants. While acknowledging the subjectivity inherent in qualitative methods, effort was made to frame interview questions neutrally to elicit impartial responses.

8.2 Conceptual Framework

8.2.1 Sustainable Development Goals and Their Relevance to Island Sustainability

Small islands play a significant role in global ecological and socioeconomic storylines despite making up only a small portion of the surface of the earth. Because of their innate vulnerability, island ecosystems are at risk from a variety of threats, including the effects of climate change, a lack of resources, and pressures from development and tourism (Spalding et al. 2007). Sustainable development prioritizes people over the exclusive focus on GDP seen in the twentieth-century paradigm. The introduction of the Human Development Index (HDI) by the United Nations Development Programme (UNDP) in 1990 marked a shift towards a multidimensional understanding of development, integrating wealth, education, and health measures (Bach and Morgan 2020). The HDI served as a precursor to the Sustainable Development Goals (SDGs), emphasizing "people first" and "leaving no one behind". Unfortunately, the post-Cold War era and globalization gave rise to a new world order that facilitated productive relocations from developed to developing countries, driven by cost reduction and profit maximization motives. In the context of SDG 12 on decoupling economic growth from unsustainable resource use, a case study involving tourism-driven economic growth in Palau highlighted challenges posed by the pandemic, which led to a significant stagnation in visitor arrivals compared with pre-pandemic levels (Simonova 2019). Tourism in Palau, particularly visitors from Japan (compared with visitors from other countries), remained below five per cent of pre-pandemic levels in July 2022, leading to a substantial 26.1 per cent economic contraction in the 2021/22 period (Rahman et al. 2021).

8.2.2 Previous Research and Studies on Sustainability Efforts in Bali and Palau

8.2.2.1 Sustainability Efforts and Projects in Bali

The Green School in Bali is an internationally recognized educational institution that focuses on environmental institutions and sustainability. It is well known for its one-of-a-kind bamboo building as well as its dedication to educating pupils about sustainability, conservation, and environmental care (Iwan and Rao 2017). Bali has been researching and adopting sustainable tourism practices for several decades, with increased emphasis in the twenty-first century in response to concerns about over-tourism and environmental deterioration. International travellers and organizations committed to sustainable tourism have taken notice of eco-friendly accommodations, responsible tour operators, and community-based tourist initiatives (Astawa et al. 2019). Bamboo has increasingly been used in construction and architecture in Bali. One example is its use in Bio Arc architecture. The bamboo-based work of this enterprise, developed by a Spanish architect, has won accolades for its eco-friendliness and promised as a model for sustainable construction (Liua et al. 2022). Ubud, the cultural and tourism centre of Bali, has focused on environmental and sustainability measures such as waste and green space management programmes and has attempted to promote ecologically friendly practices among local enterprises (Koski-Karell 2019). For example, the use of disposable shopping bags has been regulated to encourage the reduction of plastic consumption (Agustina and Aprinica 2021).

8.2.2.2 Sustainability Efforts and Projects in Palau

Palau is well known for having established the Palau National Marine Sanctuary, one of the world's largest marine sanctuaries. The country made a large chunk of its exclusive economic zone (EEZ) off limits to commercial fishing in 2015, conserving the marine environment and encouraging biodiversity (Burgwyn 2021). The government of Palau was among the first to create a shark sanctuary, prohibiting all commercial shark fishing within its borders. This initiative to safeguard shark populations and marine biodiversity has been hailed as a model for marine conservation around the world (Vianna et al. 2012). Palau has actively encouraged sustainable tourist practices such as ethical diving and snorkelling tours, environmentally friendly lodgings, and cultural preservation. Engaging in global conservation efforts, Palau signed the Our Ocean 2017 declaration at the 4th Our Ocean conference held in Malta in October 2017, emphasizing a commitment to sustainably managing oceans (Unger et al. 2017). Despite increased tourist arrivals, peaking at 160,000 in 2018 against a population of 21,685 (July 2020), dedicated initiatives aimed at aligning natural resources with economic development, such as the 2013 Palau Responsible Travel campaign and the Palau National Marine Sanctuary, have fallen short of anticipated impacts (Chan 2018).

8.2.3 Circular Economy Practices and Their Application in Island Contexts

Bali has actively promoted waste reduction through innovative recycling programmes and upcycling initiatives, and has transformed waste materials into products such as furniture and ornaments (Ain et al. 2021). Sustainable agricultural practices, including organic farming and farmer cooperatives, have contributed to soil health and support local farmers (Sriartha et al. 2021). The tourism sector has integrated circular principles, emphasizing sustainable accommodation, farm-to-table dining, and eco-friendly transportation. Bali has explored waste-to-energy initiatives to convert non-recyclable waste into electricity, aligning with its commitment to minimize waste, conserve resources, and promote sustainable development (United Nations ESCAP and iBAN 2021).

Palau has actively reduced waste and increasing recycling rates. Efforts include an increase in separation of recyclables from general waste and the development of recycling centres. The country has implemented efforts to limit single-use plastics, including a ban on plastic bags and restrictions on use of plastic straws and foam containers. To encourage sustainable seafood production, sustainable fishing practices, such as size and bag limitations, have been enforced (Global Sustainable Tourism Council and Destination Stewardship Centre 2021). To reduce reliance on fossil fuels and promote clean energy options, the island has researched renewable energy sources such as solar power and wind energy. Efforts to support local agriculture, such as traditional agricultural practices and community gardens, have helped to increase food security and minimize the demand for imported items. Palau has been exploring waste-to-energy projects that can convert non-recyclable waste into energy, addressing waste management and energy generation simultaneously. The island has collaborated with international organizations and partners to further develop circular economy initiatives and leverage best practices from around the world.

8.3 Sustainable Development in Bali

8.3.1 Environmental and Socioeconomic Context

Bali boasts a unique environmental and socioeconomic context shaped by its tropical climate, rich biodiversity, and cultural heritage. The island has faced many challenges related to rapid tourism-driven development, resulting in issues such as waste management challenges and water scarcity. Traditional Balinese practices, deeply rooted in Hindu culture, has contributed to the resilience of the island (Tohari et al. 2021). Sustainable agriculture initiatives, such as organic farming and traditional rice cultivation, are gaining prominence. Collaborative efforts between the government, local communities, and international organizations have played a vital role in shaping the sustainability agenda of Bali.

8.3.2 Policies and Initiatives for Responsible Production and Consumption

There are several policies and initiatives for responsible production and consumption in Bali, seeking to protect the environment, support local farmers, and ensure food security. For example, the government and non-governmental organizations (NGOs) have provided training and support to farmers to help them to adopt sustainable crop practices, such as crop rotation, integrated pest management, and the use of organic fertilizers to reduce the environmental impact of farming (Tchedry 2020). In addition, various certification programmes, such as Fair Trade and Organic certifications, are available to the farmers of Bali. These certifications provide market access and premiums for sustainable and ethical farming practices (Campera et al. 2021).

8.3.3 Circular Economy Practices in the Tourism Industry

Many hotels and resorts have adopted circular economy practices by investing in energy-efficient infrastructure, water-saving technologies, and waste reduction measures. Some hotels and resorts use recycled or locally sourced building materials for construction and renovations to reduce the environmental impact of construction and promote circularity. The introduction of electric scooters and bicycles for rent is reducing reliance on fossil fuels, and car-pooling and ride-sharing services are also being encouraged in order to minimize traffic congestion and pollution. Some accommodations and tour operators in Bali seek green certifications to prove their commitment to circular economy principles. Certifications such as EarthCheck and Travelife help tourists to identify businesses that prioritize sustainability (Felkers 2015).

8.3.4 *Eco-friendly Agriculture and Waste Management Efforts*

Agroforestry practices have been encouraged in Bali to promote tree planting and sustainable land use, in order to provide farmers with additional sources of income from timber, fruits, and other products (Purwestri et al. 2022). The waste issue in Bali had become so pronounced that it was declared a "garbage emergency" in 2017. This crisis prompted local authorities, businesses, and communities to take action. Waste-to-energy projects were initiated to convert non-recyclable waste into electricity, to help reduce the volume of waste going into landfill sites and provide a source of renewable energy (Schlehe and Yulianto 2020). Recycling and waste-to-energy projects have helped Bali to conserve valuable resources, reduce the strain on landfill sites, and promote resource efficiency.

8.4 Sustainable Development in Palau

8.4.1 *Environmental and Socioeconomic Context*

With more than 340 islands and islets, Palau is a small island nation in the western Pacific Ocean, characterized by coral reefs, lagoons, and thick forests. The three main sectors of the economy of Palau are agriculture, tourism, and fishing, with tourism accounting for the majority of the nation's GDP (Friedlander et al. 2017). The political and legal system of Palau is that of a presidential representative democratic republic, with a constitution that recognizes the importance of environmental protection and sustainable development. Palau has implemented several policies and regulations to promote sustainability, including the Palau National Marine Sanctuary, which protects 80% of Palau's EEZ from commercial fishing and other extractive activities (Jaiteh et al. 2021). The culture and society of the island is deeply connected to the environment, with traditional practices and values emphasizing respect for nature and the importance of sustainability. For example, central to Palauan culture is the concept of bul, which means respect for nature and the environment. The traditional leaders of Palau, known as chiefs, play an important role in environmental management and conservation efforts (Pollack 2018).

8.4.2 *Policies and Initiatives for Responsible Production and Consumption*

Palau has implemented regulations governing land use to ensure sustainable agricultural practices. Zoning policies allowed areas to be designated for agriculture while preserving ecologically sensitive zones. Policies addressing responsible water use and management have been crucial for sustainable agriculture. During interviews it was revealed that agroforestry practices have been encouraged in Palau which integrate trees and crops to enhance biodiversity, improve soil quality, and provide additional income streams.

8.4.3 Circular Economy Practices in the Tourism Industry

Palau has implemented robust waste reduction and recycling programmes within hotels, resorts, and tourist facilities and has adopted circular design principles in the construction and maintenance of tourist facilities to ensure the longevity and recyclability of products and infrastructure. Moreover, education programmes have been conducted for tourists on the importance of responsible and sustainable tourism, to encourage them to participate in eco-friendly activities and support local conservation initiatives. Sustainable transportation has been promoted for tourists on the island in the form of electric vehicles, bicycles, or walking tours. Hotels and restaurants in Palau source their food locally to support the local economy and reduce the carbon footprint associated with transporting food from other regions. Palau has also adopted recognized certifications and standards for sustainable tourism, to provide assurance to tourists and to foster accountability within the industry (United Nations 2019).

8.4.4 Eco-friendly Agriculture and Waste Management Efforts

Palau has made a strong commitment to sustainable development, as evidenced by its efforts to manage waste and encourage a circular economy, in light of its remote location and environmental sensitivity. It has implemented waste reduction strategies and has established recycling programmes for materials such as paper, glass, plastic, and metal. Waste-to-energy initiatives have been explored, through which non-recyclable waste has been used to generate energy, and innovative technologies have been adopted to convert waste into a valuable resource. Public awareness campaigns have been conducted in Palau to educate residents and tourists on responsible waste disposal and to encourage waste segregation at source to facilitate recycling. Furthermore, Palau has adopted circular economy principles to minimize waste through reuse, recycling, and resource efficiency and to encourage sustainable product design and packaging.

8.5 Comparative Analysis

Both renowned tourist destinations, Bali and Palau display some similarities in their efforts to address environmental and socioeconomic challenges linked to tourism dependence. Both regions rely heavily on tourism for economic growth, leading to the need to implement sustainable practices to balance development and environmental preservation. Cultural traditions, such as Bali's subak system and Palau's community-based conservation, contribute to sustainable living. Waste management is a shared challenge, with initiatives for reduction, recycling, and proper disposal in both regions. However, despite commonalities, differences arise due to geographical and economic distinctions. Palau faces unique challenges as a small island nation, while Bali benefits from a larger land area and more diversified economy. Government policies and international partnerships vary, impacting the effectiveness of sustainability. Bali excels in sustainable agriculture and cultural preservation, while Palau emphasizes marine conservation and climate resilience. Challenges persist in waste management for Bali and climate change vulnerability for Palau. Both destinations grapple with the delicate balance between tourism-driven economic growth and preserving natural and cultural heritage, in turn highlighting the global need for sustainable development.

8.5.1 Similarities and Differences Between Bali and Palau in Sustainable Development Efforts

Bali and Palau, despite differing cultural and geographical contexts, share strategies for sustainable development. Both prioritize community involvement, integrate cultural preservation into modern efforts, and emphasize responsible tourism practices. To address tourism-related waste management challenges, they have implemented reduction and recycling programmes. Sustainable agriculture, renewable energy adoption, and education are common focuses, promoting food security, environmental preservation, and awareness. Collaboration with international partners enhances the effectiveness of their initiatives, highlighting a holistic approach to achieving a balance between economic growth, environmental conservation, and community wellbeing in these unique regions. The "Cash for Trash" programme, which incentivizes residents to collect and recycle plastic waste, has been successful in reducing the amount of plastic waste in both Palau and Bali, promoting sustainable waste management practices.

8.5.1.1 Eco-tourism

Some divergence between the two islands in sustainability approaches was evident in their respective initiatives. While Bali has introduced a new policy of charging tourists a tax as an incentive for sustainable practices, Palau has implemented the Palau Pledge, wherein visitors commit to environmentally responsible behaviour during their stay (United Nations 2019). Tax policy in Bali addresses sustainability at the macroeconomic level, influencing businesses and industry practices. The tax serves as a financial incentive for businesses to adopt sustainable practices. Businesses that align with sustainable principles not only contribute to conservation efforts but also gain potential financial advantages. This economic model aims to integrate sustainability into the broader tourism industry, fostering a self-sustaining cycle of responsible practices. On the other hand, the Palau Pledge focuses on individual responsibility. By requiring visitors to commit to environmentally friendly actions, the initiative seeks to create a sense of personal accountability. Palau has also initiated the Ol'au Palau initiative: with the help of the Ol'au Palau website, travellers can determine the total carbon footprint of their trip, taking into account their ground transportation, flights, hotel, food, and activities. They can then participate in conservation initiatives to offset their carbon footprint. By preserving and rehabilitating coastal ecosystems, which serve as organic storm barriers and blue carbon sinks, these projects will lower emissions and increase climate resilience (EDO 2022).

8.5.1.2 Sustainable Agriculture and Community Engagement

Both Bali and Palau have implemented programmes to support local farmers and promote sustainable agriculture practices. For example, many hotels and restaurants in Bali and Palau source their food locally, which supports the local economy and reduces the carbon footprint associated with transporting food from other regions. Both Bali and Palau have emphasized community engagement, achieved through grassroots initiatives and partnerships with stakeholders in sustainability programmes such as river clean-ups.

8.5.2 Factors Influencing Successful Implementation and Challenges Faced

The success of sustainable practices in both Bali and Palau depend on a combination of cultural, environmental, and economic factors. Both regions boast rich cultural heritage, fostering a deep connection between local communities and their natural surroundings. Traditional practices, such as subak system of Palau and community-based conservation efforts in Palau, contribute to a shared ethos of environmental stewardship. However, the implementation of sustainable practices has not been without challenges. In Bali, rapid urbanization and tourism development have posed threats to traditional agriculture. Balancing the economic benefits of tourism with environmental preservation has remained a complex task, and waste management is a significant challenge in both regions due to increasing tourist numbers.

Climate change vulnerability in Palau, particularly in the context of rising sea levels, adds a layer of complexity to sustainability efforts. Furthermore, the economic resources of Palau are comparatively limited, impacting the scale and scope of sustainable development initiatives. Both Bali and Palau are confronted with the need to navigate a delicate equilibrium between economic development and environmental conservation. Successful sustainable practices are contingent on addressing these challenges through innovative solutions, community engagement, and strategic partnerships. Continuous adaptation and collaboration at local, national, and international levels are essential to overcome obstacles and ensure the long-term success of sustainable practices in these island nations.

8.6 Implications and Lessons Learned

The comparative analysis of sustainability efforts in Bali and Palau offers insights for other small island nations. Integrating cultural practices is crucial, with both regions emphasizing the significance of preserving and incorporating local cultures into sustainability plans. Community engagement, balancing tourism and conservation, efficient waste management, renewable energy adoption, and climate change resilience emerge as key lessons. Small island nations can replicate these approaches to ensure sustainable development, emphasizing community participation, responsible tourism practices, waste reduction, and building adaptive capacities for climate resilience.

8.6.1 Key Insights from the Comparative Analysis

The comparative analysis yields key insights and findings that underscore the intricate interplay between cultural, environmental, and economic factors in the pursuit of sustainable development. Both regions emphasize the integral role of cultural integration, leveraging traditional practices as a robust foundation for environmental stewardship. The success of sustainability initiatives is intricately tied to active community engagement, emphasizing the importance of local ownership and alignment with community values. Balancing tourism and conservation emerges as a common challenge, prompting the adoption of responsible tourism practices to harmonize economic benefits with environmental preservation. Waste management is a shared concern exacerbated by tourism, driving the implementation of effective waste reduction and recycling strategies. Both Bali and Palau recognize the imperative of adopting renewable energy to mitigate environmental impact, particularly through initiatives such as solar power projects. Engagement with international partners underscores the collaborative nature of sustainable development, showcasing the significance of external expertise, funding, and support. Moreover, the vulnerability to climate change of Palau in particular highlights the paramount importance of building resilience, with both regions acknowledging the need for climate-resilient strategies. In synthesis, Bali and Palau offer a holistic blueprint for sustainable development, navigating challenges through cultural preservation, community involvement, responsible tourism, waste management, renewable energy, collaboration, and climate resilience. These insights provide valuable lessons applicable to other regions, especially small island nations, striving to achieve a harmonious balance between economic growth and environmental conservation.

8.6.2 Identifying Best Practices for Sustainable Development in Islands

Sustainable development in Bali and Palau necessitates a comprehensive approach, encompassing environmental conservation, social equity, and economic viability. In Bali, the preservation of cultural and natural heritage is paramount, with an emphasis on responsible tourism practices and sustainable agriculture. Palau, known for its marine biodiversity, should prioritize sustainable fisheries management and marine conservation, including strict regulations and community engagement. Both islands can benefit from investing in renewable energy sources to reduce reliance on fossil fuels. Collaboration among government bodies, NGOs, and the private sector is vital for the effective implementation and enforcement of sustainable development practices.

8.6.3 Lessons for Other Small Island Nations

The experiences of Bali and Palau offer invaluable lessons for similar island contexts grappling with the complex challenge of sustainable development. First, the integration of cultural practices into sustainability initiatives emerges as a cornerstone, emphasizing the significance of leveraging traditional wisdom and values to establish a strong foundation for environmental stewardship. Second, the active engagement of local communities is crucial; fostering a sense of ownership and aligning initiatives with community needs ensures the sustainability of projects. Third, the delicate balance between tourism and conservation is evident, emphasizing the need for responsible tourism practices that mitigate environmental impact while supporting economic growth. Waste management strategies, particularly in the face of escalating tourism, provide critical insights into effective waste reduction and recycling programmes. The adoption of renewable energy, as demonstrated by initiatives such as solar power projects, showcases a commitment to cleaner and more sustainable energy sources. Collaborating with international partners proves instrumental, allowing for the exchange of expertise and resources. Lastly, the vulnerability of Palau to climate change underscores the imperative of building resilience, offering a crucial lesson for similar island contexts facing climate-related challenges. In essence, the experiences of Bali and Palau provide a comprehensive guide for navigating the complexities of sustainable development in island contexts, emphasizing the need for cultural integration, community engagement, responsible tourism, waste management, renewable energy adoption, international collaboration, and climate resilience.

8.7 Recommendations

To promote circular economy practices and sustainable development on islands, policymakers should implement supportive regulatory frameworks, incentives for businesses adopting circular models, and educational programmes to inform and engage communities. Prioritizing the development of local circular economies through support for small and medium-sized enterprises (SMEs) and fostering public–private partnerships are crucial steps. Additionally, fostering innovation, integrating circular principles into urban planning, and engaging communities directly in decision-making processes are essential components. This multifaceted approach, combining policy measures, economic incentives, community engagement, and technological innovation, is fundamental to fostering circular economies that contribute to island sustainability.

8.7.1 Policy Recommendations for Promoting Circular Economy and Responsible Consumption

To promote circular economy practices and responsible consumption in Bali and Palau, policymakers should implement specific and tailored policy recommendations. First, adopting extended producer responsibility (EPR) policies can incentivize producers to take responsibility for the entire lifecycle of their products. This includes designing products for recyclability, establishing take-back systems, and promoting eco-friendly packaging. Furthermore, introducing legislation to regulate single-use plastics, such as bans on certain items and the promotion of reusable alternatives, can significantly reduce plastic waste.

Incentivizing businesses to embrace circular business models is crucial. Providing tax breaks or financial incentives for companies adopting circular practices, such as recycling and reusing materials, can encourage the private sector to align with sustainable principles. Policymakers should also facilitate the development of local circular economy businesses, particularly in recycling and upcycling, by offering support programmes and creating a conducive regulatory environment.

Educational campaigns aimed at locals and tourists are essential to fostering responsible consumption habits. Implementing public awareness programmes can inform residents and visitors about the environmental impact of their choices, encouraging practices such as waste reduction, recycling, and supporting local, sustainable products. Additionally, policymakers can collaborate with the tourism industry to promote eco-friendly tourism practices, including guidelines for accommodations to reduce their environmental footprint.

Establishing waste separation and recycling infrastructure is critical for effective circular waste management. Policymakers should invest in waste collection systems that promote segregation at the source and ensure efficient recycling facilities. Furthermore, implementing deposit return systems for beverage containers can incentivize recycling and reduce littering.

In summary, a comprehensive policy approach should encompass regulations on single-use plastics, support for circular business models, educational campaigns, and the development of robust waste management infrastructure. Collectively, these measures can contribute to the promotion of circular economy practices and responsible consumption, aligning with the SDGs.

8.7.2 Strategies for Enhancing Community Engagement and Participation

A multifaceted approach is necessary to strengthen community engagement in sustainable development initiatives on islands such as Bali and Palau. Regular community workshops and training sessions will equip locals with useful information, and online forums and meetings that facilitate interactive decision-making offer opportunities for active involvement. Funding for regional sustainability projects and the inclusion of cultural components in programmes help to match projects with regional values. A more all-encompassing approach to community engagement includes engaging youth, organizing skill-building workshops, and starting communication campaigns. Combining educational, financial, and cultural components, this dynamic and inclusive framework promotes shared responsibility and active involvement in forming sustainable goals.

8.7.3 *Practical Suggestions for Policymakers, Businesses, and Communities*

Crafting tailored policies for countries like Bali and Palau should be a paramount concern for policymakers, considering the distinctive economic, cultural, and environmental context. Achieving relevance and acceptance necessitates active collaboration with local communities throughout the policy formulation process. Policymakers can leverage innovative approaches, such as incorporating journalism into policy strategies in the digital age, to drive sustainability transformations. Recognizing the value of NGO incentive programmes and offering grants, tax breaks, or monetary incentives to individuals and businesses can stimulate the adoption of sustainable practices. Establishing a platform for community decision-making, including grassroots engagement, technological initiatives, and online forums, is vital to encouraging resident involvement in shaping sustainable development projects. Additionally, integrating sustainability education into regional school curricula and allocating funds for educational initiatives equips community members with the knowledge and skills essential for embracing sustainable living practices.

Consumers should be informed about sustainable practices that can be implemented by businesses and that they can implement themselves. Regulations are needed that support EPR, waste reduction goals, and the concepts of the circular economy. Thorough waste management systems should be put in place that prioritize recycling and waste reduction. Funding research and development will help to promote innovation and circular design. Tax breaks and green procurement regulations should be established for companies that implement environmentally friendly practices. Cooperation should be encouraged between industry associations and stakeholders and, through consumer education, responsible consumption should be promoted. SMEs need support as they make the switch to sustainable practices; this should include setting up systems for tracking progress and reporting. Finally, it is imperative to customize these suggestions to the unique circumstances of other nations besides Bali and Palau themselves.

8.8 Conclusion

Best practices for sustainable development on islands have been identified by a comparative analysis of the two islands of Bali and Palau, which have different approaches to the concept of sustainable development. These practices include eco-friendly agriculture, waste management, tourism, and responsible consumption and production. The study also emphasizes how crucial community involvement and engagement are to efforts towards sustainable development.

This study emphasizes how important it is to have a circular economy, and how economic growth should be separated from the use of unsustainable resources. In an effort to balance social and economic wellbeing with ecological integrity, it promotes the creation of a circular economy on the islands.

8.9 Summary of Findings

The comparative analysis of Bali and Palau reveals that both islands have implemented circular economy practices and sustainable tourism initiatives to promote responsible consumption and production. The study highlights the importance of local engagement and community input in achieving the SDGs. The research provides valuable insights into the similarities and differences between Bali and Palau in their pursuit of circular economy practices, identifies successful approaches, and emphasizes the importance of balancing ecological integrity with social and economic wellbeing. The study offers actionable recommendations for policymakers, businesses, and communities seeking to establish a circular economy on islands. Overall, the research contributes to the field of island sustainability by providing a holistic blueprint for sustainable development that can be applied to other regions, especially small island nations.

8.9.1 Contributions to the Field of Island Sustainability

A comprehensive blueprint for sustainable development that other regions, especially small island nations, can use in their pursuit of sustainable development, is one of the study's many valuable contributions to the field of island sustainability. The information and conclusions can support comparative studies between islands, policymaking, and decision-making initiatives.

8.9.2 Limitations of the Study and Suggestions for Future Research

8.9.2.1 Limitations

Although this study offers insights into sustainable island development, it is important to acknowledge some limitations that might have affected the breadth and depth of our analysis.

The data extraction from Palau was particularly challenging, and cooperation is one of the main restrictions. A further constraint stemming from the intricacy of obtaining official tourism data was the duration required to obtain official tourism data from Bali. Due to in-person interviews with farmers who speak different languages, language was another obstacle.

8.9.2.2 Challenges

Small island nations like Palau often face constraints due to limited arable land, making sustainable agriculture challenging. High dependence on food imports may pose challenges to achieving self-sufficiency in food production, which is often a goal of sustainable agriculture. The unique environmental challenges of island nations, including sea level rise and extreme weather events, can pose significant difficulties in adopting sustainable agriculture. Farmers may also face barriers to adopting sustainable practices due to limited awareness, education, or access to resources.

8.9.2.3 Suggestions

Improved Data Collaboration with Stakeholders

Future research should focus on enhancing collaboration and data-sharing in Palau to overcome the challenges faced in data extraction. Strengthening partnerships with local stakeholders and utilizing alternative data collection methods could be explored.

Efficient Data Collection Strategies in Bali

Addressing the time constraints in obtaining data from Bali requires the development of more efficient data collection strategies. Leveraging technology, engaging with local authorities, and exploring publicly available datasets could expedite the process. Incentives were also given to the farmers for data collection.

Language Access in Farmer Interviews

To overcome language barriers in farmer interviews, future research should consider utilizing local interpreters and technology for multilingual data collection. This approach can ensure accurate representation of diverse perspectives within the farming community.

Promotion of Island-Focused Research

More island-focused research initiatives should be encouraged and supported, in order to build a comprehensive understanding of sustainable development, particularly in the context of responsible delivery of the SDGs. This could involve establishing research networks and collaborations between academic institutions, local communities, and relevant organizations.

Innovative Data Sources

Satellite or crowd-sourced data should be utilized to supplement traditional data collection methods.

References

Agustina A, Aprinica NPI (2021) The effect of regulations on using disposable plastic in community and tourism behaviors in Denpasar, Bali. J Bus Hospital Tourism 7(1):33–38

Ain KQ, Nasri MA, Alamsyah MN, Pratama MDR, Kurniawan T (2021) Collaborative governance in managing plastic waste in Bali. IOP Conf Ser Earth Environ Sci 905(1):012115

Astawa IN, Budiasa IW, Suastika K (2019) Sustainable tourism development in Bali: a review. J Environ Manage 232:563–574

Bach M, Morgan MS (2020) Measuring difference? The United Nations' shift from progress to poverty. Hist Polit Econ 52(3):539–560

Burgwyn H (2021) Identifying community leaders. In: Sanoff H, Cohn S (eds) EDRA 1: proceedings of the 1st annual environmental design research association conference. Routledge, London

Campera M, Budiadi B, Adinda E, Ahmad N, Balestri M, Hedger K, Imron MA, Manson S, Nijman V, Nekaris KAI (2021) Fostering a wildlife-friendly program for sustainable coffee farming: the case of small-holder farmers in Indonesia. Land 10(2):121

Chan N (2018) "Large ocean states": sovereignty, small islands, and marine protected areas in global oceans governance. Global Gov Rev Multilateralism Int Organiz 24(4):537–555

EDO (Environmental Defenders Office) (2022) A roadmap for climate reform. EDO, Sydney

Felkers I (2015) Planet, people, prosperity in Finnish and Dutch mass tour operators' customer communications. Thesis, Haaga-Helia University of Applied Sciences

Friedlander AM, Golbuu Y, Ballesteros E, Caselle JE, Gouezo M, Olsudong D, Sala E (2017) Size, age, and habitat determine effectiveness of Palau's marine protected areas. PLoS ONE 12(3):e0174787

Global Sustainable Tourism Council and Destination Stewardship Center (2021) Destination stewardship report: summer 2021. Destination Stewardship Center

Gowdy J (2005) Sustainability and collapse: what can economics bring to the debate? Glob Environ Chang 15(3):181–183

Hakim L, Kusumawati R, Santosa I (2009) Island sustainability: challenges and opportunities for Bali and Palau. J Environ Manage 90(8):2548–2560

Iwan R, Rao P (2017) The Green School Bali: a model for sustainable education. In: Leal Filho W, Brandli L, Castro P, Newman J (eds) Handbook of theory and practice of sustainable development in higher education. Springer, Cham

Jaiteh V, Peatman T, Lindfield S, Gilman E, Nicol S (2021) Bycatch estimates from a Pacific tuna longline fishery provide a baseline for understanding the long-term benefits of a large, blue water marine sanctuary. Front Mar Sci 8

Koski-Karell NS (2019) Integrated sustainable waste management in tourism markets: the case of Bali. Indian J Publ Adm 65(3):646–660

Liua K, Jayaramana D, Shib Y, Harriesc K, Yangb J, Jina W, Shid Y, Wua J, Jacomea P, Trujilloe D (2022) Bamboo: a very sustainable construction material. Sustain Struct 2(1):000015

McAnany PA, Yoffee N (eds) (2009) Questioning collapse: human resilience, ecological vulnerability, and the aftermath of empire. Cambridge University Press, Cambridge

Nowell LS, Norris JM, White DE, Moules NJ (2017) Thematic analysis: striving to meet the trustworthiness criteria. Int J Qual Methods 16(1)

Pollack A (2018) Bridging the gap: the nexus of tradition, tourism and collaborative marine management in the Republic of Palau. Ph.D. dissertation, University of Hawai'i at Manoa

Purwestri RC, Lusiana B, Wirawan NN, Fahmi I, Habibie IY, Sane M, Hochmalová M, Fetriyuna F, Hájek M, Handayani D (2022) Agricultural contribution to the nutritional status of children: a comparative study of annual crop, agroforestry, and mixed-farming type in Buol, Indonesia. Food Energy Secur 11(1):e338

Rahman MK, Gazi MAI, Bhuiyan MA, Rahaman MA (2021) Effect of COVID-19 pandemic on tourist travel risk and management perceptions. PLoS ONE 16(9):e0256486

Schlehe J, Yulianto VI (2020) An anthropology of waste: morality and social mobilisation in Java. Indonesia Malay World 48(140):40–59

Simonova MD (2019) Beyond GDP: measuring what counts for economic and social performance. MGIMO Re Int Relat 12(5):172–180

Spalding MD, Fox HE, Allen GR, Davidson N, Ferdaña ZA, Finlayson C, Halpern BS, Jorge MA, Lombana A, Lourie SA, Martin KD, McManus E, Molnar J, Recchia CA, Robertson J (2007) Marine ecoregions of the world: a bioregionalization of coastal and shelf areas. Bioscience 57(7):573–583

Sriartha IP, Diatmika IPG, Putra PYP (2021) Farmers' responses to the adoption of organic rice farming in Buleleng Regency, Bali. In: Proceedings of the 3rd international conference on law, social sciences, and education (ICLSSE 2021), 9 September 2021, Singaraja, Bali, Indonesia

Tchedry V (2020) Transition of agroecology in Bali, Indonesia. MA paper, Swedish University of Agricultural Sciences (SLU)

Tohari A, Raya M, Fuad K (2021) The meaning of religious moderation on the resilience of Muslim minority in Balinese Hindus. J Contemp Islam Muslim Soc 5(1):77–103

Unger S, Müller A, Rochette J, Schmidt S, Shackeroff J, Wright G (2017) Achieving the sustainable development goal for the oceans. IASS Policy Brief 1/2017. IASS (Institute for Advanced Sustainability Studies), Potsdam

United Nations (2019) Sungai Watch is an environmental organization on a mission to stop plastic from going into the ocean [Online]. Available at https://sungai.watch/pages/about-us. Accessed 23 Jan 2024

United Nations ESCAP (Economic and Social Commission for Asia and the Pacific) and iBAN (Inclusive Business Action Network) (2021) Towards a roadmap for inclusive business in wellness tourism in Indonesia. United Nations ESCAP, Bangkok

Vianna GM, Meekan MG, Pannell DJ, Marsh SP, Meeuwig JJ (2012) Socio-economic value and community benefits from shark-diving tourism in Palau: a sustainable use of reef shark populations. Biol Cons 145(1):267–277

Whittaker RJ, Fernández-Palacios JM, Matthews TJ, Borregaard MK, Triantis KA (2017) Island biogeography: taking the long view of nature's laboratories. Science 357(6354): eaam8326

Zhong C, Guo H, Swan I, Gao P, Yao Q, Li H (2023) Evaluating trends, profits, and risks of global cities in recent urban expansion for advancing sustainable development. Habitat Int 138:102869

Chapter 9
Building Resilient Infrastructure in Pacific Small Island Developing States

Scott M. Hook

Abstract There has been a renewal of interest among development partners in directly supporting infrastructure development in the Pacific. This reflects an approach of using infrastructure policy as a more tangible form of development assistance to enable sustainable development. Hence, this is an opportune time to discuss the value for money in developing resilient infrastructure to meet the developmental needs of Pacific people and their economies, and the interaction of infrastructure with the increasing pressure being faced in terms of climate and disaster risks, in the context of national policy, regional initiatives such as the 2050 Strategy for the Blue Pacific, and post-COVID-19 global strategies to promote resilience to climate and disaster risk. The chapter highlights the economic importance of incorporating climate and disaster resilience into infrastructure design, procurement, and maintenance to enable sustainable development in Pacific island countries (enabling a focus on Small Island Developing States). The chapter is part of ongoing research into infrastructure in the Pacific and the importance of incorporating climate and disaster risks into development plans that support green development pathways.

9.1 Introduction

Hook (2021a) highlights that Small Island Developing States (SIDS) are a heterogeneous group of countries and territories, with diverse characteristics. They exhibit large variations in terms of population size and density, geographical spread, and relative development progress, and they include some of the world's smallest, most remote, and geographically dispersed countries.

Despite the differences, Hook (2021a) identifies that one common aspect they face is that the threats of natural hazards and human-made disasters can substantially reverse economic and development gains. For example, according to a post-disaster needs assessment, Cyclone Pam destroyed over 60% of Vanuatu's GDP in 2015 (Esler 2016). Decades of development gains can be wiped out in a few hours.

S. M. Hook (✉)
Principal Economist, Economics, Policy and Ideas, Brisbane, Australia
e-mail: scottmhook@gmail.com

E. Monaco and M. Abe (eds.), *Sustainable Development Across Pacific Islands*,
https://doi.org/10.1007/978-981-97-3629-4_9

Infrastructure[1] is a critical enabler of growth and development. But is enough being invested in it to understand and manage risk? It appears from recent papers by the ADB (2022), Adeoti et al (2020), and Forum Economic Minister Meeting (FEMM) (Pacific Islands Forum 2023) that the availability and quality of infrastructure in many SIDS, especially in the Pacific, is often considered to be poor, with low standards, poor quality materials, and insufficient funding for maintenance (PRIF 2013).

Another key aspect is that financing is difficult to obtain, whether for planning, procurement, operation, or maintaining infrastructure. The global finance architecture that SIDS confront is complex (UK Government 2021; Pacific Islands Forum Secretariat 2013), and Hook (2021a) identifies that it often involves lengthy application processes that are particularly challenging for counties with limited capacity. When a hazard turns into a disaster, there is an additional burden of dealing with a national emergency, which also means that there are limited timelines in which to respond in a coordinated and comprehensive way. The challenges have been particularly highlighted through the impact of COVID-19, as many SIDS struggled to cope given their high dependency on and narrow economic base in sectors exposed to external risks and climate change (such as tourism, agriculture, and fisheries), meaning that their export earnings are easily affected by a supply-side shock.[2]

Preventing and managing adverse events of all kinds and building resilience, including to the impacts of climate change and disasters, are real and present challenges for SIDS. Without adequate funding, sound governance, and clear planning and policy, SIDS cannot adopt a risk-informed approach to development or invest in reducing climate and disaster risks and building resilience to future shocks. The fiscal space for investing in ex ante risk reduction and prevention is further constrained by humanitarian needs and pressures to respond effectively and to build back better in a risk-informed manner post-disaster. Consequently, they can become caught in a cycle of inadequate disaster response, recovery, and reconstruction coupled with the challenges of macroeconomic destabilization, debt problems, and weaker growth, thereby increasing levels of risk across social, economic, and environmental systems. Many SIDS already face debt distress, and this cycle will only weaken future development outcomes and aspirations to meet the Sustainable Development Goals (SDGs). Hence, building resilience provides a way to front-load the challenge of reducing the costs of the effects of disasters and climate change. This chapter discusses the link between resilience and development though considering the value of building

[1] "Infrastructure" is defined in the widest sense, to include buildings, energy, ICT (information and communications technology), social infrastructure (such as hospitals, schools, and community buildings), solid waste, transport, water, and wastewater.

[2] Hook (2021a) reported that a 2017 ADB report estimates the Pacific's infrastructure investment needs are around $42 billion in the period 2015–30: that is, an annual average investment of $2.8 billion or roughly 8.2% of the GDP of Pacific Developing Member Countries (PDMCs). The report also outlines that infrastructure investment needs for the PDMCs increase to $46 billion from 2015–30 when accounting for the impact of climate change—equivalent to around $3.1 billion in investment annually (on average) or 9.1% of PDMCs' GDP.

resilient infrastructure. Approaches to resilience-centred planning provide an opportunity to foster better policy integration. In the sections that follow, the chapter will:

- discuss the definition of resilience in the context of infrastructure development;
- review relevant national and regional economic policies for Fiji (see Box 9.1) and the Pacific (through the *Framework for resilient development in the Pacific*) on building resilience and minimizing climate and disaster risks;
- examine how the government, private sector, development partners, and disaster risk reduction and climate change communities of practice can benefit from a robust economic assessment of improved resilience (see next section);
- consider some lessons and principles on how resilience might best be reflected in future projects and studies that seek to build sustainable development in the Pacific.

9.2 How Climate and Disaster Risks Affect Infrastructure

In the Pacific, infrastructure provides critical social and economic services required to meet the developmental needs of the people and the economy. Given that infrastructure investments have an economic life expectancy of 30 years or more, it is important to note that infrastructure is sensitive both to the climatic conditions prevailing during its construction and to the climate variations over decades of use; these aspects need to be planned for in the design phase and incorporated into the maintenance and operation of the infrastructure (Rahiman 2019).

Climate-fuelled disasters are damaging roads, railways, power networks, and other vital infrastructure worldwide to the tune of hundreds of billions of dollars per year, urging better planning for more turbulent weather and rising seas as the planet warms. The scale of the problem is huge: the Coalition for Disaster Resilient Infrastructure (CDRI) estimates that disasters alone are causing average losses of $732–845 billion each year to infrastructure and buildings, equal to 14% of growth in global GDP in 2022.

Infrastructure also provides the means for contributions to climate change by generating greenhouse gas emissions from its direct operations, the materials used in its construction, and the activities it enables. For example, transport emissions have increased more than 60% since 1990, accounting for around one-fifth of total emissions in 2019. The infrastructure built today can lock in future emissions, especially without a plan to convert it to zero-emissions technology later. New infrastructure must also function in a warmer, drier climate and be resilient to more extreme weather. These changes affect infrastructure's performance under extreme conditions, and the demand for it. Changing operating conditions may require changes to the location, design, construction, operation, maintenance, and upgrade of infrastructure, and in some cases reassessing assets' continued viability. The infrastructure decisions made now will affect climate change response in coming decades and constrain future choices.

9.3 Defining Resilience (of What and for Whom?)

The resilience of systems is vital to all communities in the Pacific. Infrastructure as a system has to be resilient to ensure that communities can continue to trade and can gain access to basic services in light of disruptions. The concept of resilience (Hook 2021b) offers an opportunity to break down the silos of climate change adaptation, disaster risk reduction, and sustainable development within the SIDS development agenda and allow a focus on a common, cross-cutting, and coherent outcome.

A. **Resilience: one name, many different actions**

Sudmeier-Rieux (2014) highlights that the difficulty in discussing, describing, and operationalizing resilience is that it has numerous different meanings and is expected to accomplish many different policy objectives for which it was not really intended (Béné et al. 2014). It has been popularized in ecology, economics, child psychology, and engineering. Limiting ourselves to what is relevant in the development field, some of the key points arising from existing discussions are as follows:

- The Resilience Alliance (cited in Wahl 2017), an international network of researchers and practitioners focused on understanding the complex dynamics of change in socio-ecological systems (which includes integrated systems of people and the natural environment), defines resilience as "the capacity of an ecosystem to tolerate disturbance without collapsing into a qualitatively different state that is controlled by a different set of processes". In addition, systems can move into new (better or worse) states; this is referred to as "transformability" (Sudmeier-Rieux 2014).
- In systems science and economics, resilience is "the ability of a system to withstand a major disruption within acceptable degradation parameters and to recover within an acceptable time and composite costs and risks" (Haimes 2009). In these discussions, other characteristics of resilience include robustness, redundancy, resourcefulness, and rapidity (Bruneau et al. 2003).
- In regard to disaster risk reduction and climate change adaptation for infrastructure, resilience primarily refers to the ability of a human system (such as infrastructure) to respond and recover from shocks or stress. According to Cutter et al. (2008, identified in Hook 2021b), it includes those inherent conditions that allow the system to absorb impacts and cope with an event, as well as post-event adaptive processes that facilitate the ability of the system to reorganize, change, and learn in response to the event. The following is a range of definitions used by various agencies in the field.
- The *Framework for resilient development in the Pacific* (FRDP) uses the United Nations Office for Disaster Risk Reduction (UNISDR 2009, p. 24) defines resilience as "the ability of a system, community or society exposed to hazards to resist, absorb, accommodate to and recover from the effects of a hazard in a timely and efficient manner, including through the preservation and restoration of its essential basic structures and functions" (Pacific Islands Forum 2016), but there is a further adjoining comment not included in the FRDP: "the resilience of

a community in respect to potential hazard events is determined by the degree to which the community has the necessary resources and is capable of organizing itself both prior to and during times of need" (UNISDR 2009, p. 24).

- The Intergovernmental Panel on Climate Change (IPCC) defines resilience as the ability to "absorb disturbances while retaining the same basic structure and ways of functioning" (Pachauri and Reisinger 2007, p. 86), modifying this somewhat in 2012 to the "ability of a system and its component parts to anticipate, absorb, accommodate, or recover from the effects of a hazardous event in a timely and efficient manner" (IPCC 2012b, p. 3).[3]
- Many other organizations and groups use variations of these definitions as they seek to respond at multiple levels. Generally, resilience is about bouncing back or even going forward but not about being robust (Capano and Woo 2016). Variations of these definitions are popular but can be problematic, as they could be advocating a conceptualization of resilience which emphasizes economic efficiencies in returning to "essential basic structures" or the status quo, which is likely to continue fostering risk (noted in Sudmeier-Rieux, 2014, p. 3).[4]

According to Frontier Economics (2019), resilient infrastructure can be defined as infrastructure that is capable of:

- withstanding disruption so it can continue to operate in the face of shocks and stressors;
- adapting to changing circumstance as uncertainties are resolved, i.e., incorporating the flexibility to be modified as circumstances change (adapted from Infrastructure NSW 2018; Lloyd's of London and Arup 2017).

The value of resilience (Hook, 2021b) is that it can be useful as a unifying concept for adaptation, sustainable development, and disaster risk reduction. By putting resilience, as opposed to adaptation, at the core of infrastructure planning, sustainable development and disaster risk reduction, various actors can pursue solutions that contribute to all three global agendas. Sectoral approaches to planning that are centred on resilience provide an opportunity to foster better policy integration;—hence the extensive literature that has arisen in the last several years on building and maintaining resilient infrastructure (see Hallegatte, Rentschler, and Rozenberg 2019; OECD 2018; World Bank 2013).

There has been some active work in building resilience in the Pacific, detailed in Box 9.1.

[3] In IPCC's (2012a) AR6 glossary, the definition of resilience is "the capacity of interconnected social, economic and ecological systems to cope with a hazardous event, trend or disturbance, responding or reorganizing in ways that maintain their essential function, identity and structure. Resilience is a positive attribute when it maintains capacity for adaptation, learning and/or transformation."

[4] For example, the United Nations (2018) defines resilience is the ability of individuals, households, communities, cities, institutions, systems, and societies to prevent, resist, absorb, adapt, respond, and recover positively, efficiently, and effectively when faced with a wide range of risks, while maintaining an acceptable level of functioning and without compromising long-term prospects for sustainable development, peace and security, human rights, and wellbeing for all.

Box 9.1: Country Approaches to Resilience in the Pacific

As part of this chapter, various national strategies for Cook Islands, Fiji, and Tonga were reviewed. The use of resilience is highly contextual, and the pathways to enhancing it vary from one country to the next. As an initial observation from its use in various documents is that several definitions of resilience that are drawn from the UNDRR (formerly UNISDR) and IPCC definitions.

Cook Islands' second joint national action plan *JNAPII: are we resilient?* (2016) is designed to increase resilience to climate change and disasters. The word is used throughout the document, defined as "the ability of a system, community or society exposed to hazards to resist, absorb, accommodate and recover from the effects of a hazard in a timely and efficient manner, including through the preservation and restoration of its essential basic structures and functions" (Cook Islands 2016, p. 75).

Resilience features prominently throughout Fiji's *National climate change policy* (2018). In this document, "Resilience is understood as the ability to cope with shocks and disturbances with minimal disruption and successful return to a stable state" (Government of Fiji 2018, p. 17). The introduction of the concept of resilience building as an objective within development narratives is associated with an increased focus on the strengthening of the existing capacity, emphasis on enhancing systems, and the promotion of collaboration between actors and across disciplines. National resilience is understood through the characteristics of a nation's government, society, and environment and is often assessed through the consideration of coping capacity, adaptative capacity, and transformational capacity. Fiji also uses a definition of resilience as being woven together with economic, social, and environmental priorities. This puts resilience out in the commons for policy development and makes for stronger linkages across a variety of national policies that Fiji is progressing.

Tonga uses resilience throughout its JNAP2 (Government of the Kingdom of Tonga 2018) to identify and guide the outcomes, but there is no attempt to define "resilience" in the document.

B. **The case for system-wide resilience**

Infrastructure has a critical role in building resilience, but there is a key gap in the understanding of what this means and entails. It is part of a system that must follow the same guidance as other parts. Reflecting on the previous section poses the question of how individuals, communities, organizations, and countries (also known as systems) can build and sustain resilience. Much of the discussion on human/social resilience in these systems has been about reducing the risk of long-term detrimental impacts induced by specific adverse events (Béné et al. 2012; 2014). Some of the discrete aspects refer to:

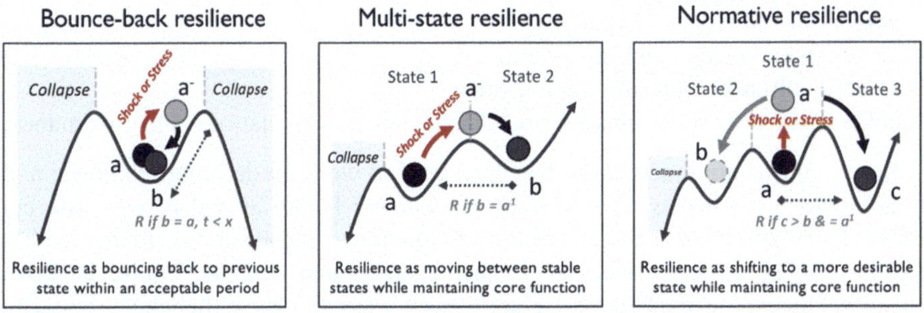

Fig. 9.1 States of resilience. *Source* reproduced with permission from Trundle (2020)

- absorptive capacity: the ability of a system to maintain its original structure and functioning by absorbing infrequent and low magnitude risks, by either anticipating or responding to a shock;
- adaptive capacity: the ability to make small adjustments to existing risk management strategies, improving a system's original structure or functioning in anticipation of future risk;
- transformative capacity: a system's ability to fundamentally change in its structure or functioning and adopt new strategies to move beyond vulnerability thresholds.

These explored are in Fig. 9.1.

In essence this conceptualization of resilience means that building resilience requires interventions that strengthen the three components to maintain the status quo (absorptive), incorporate incremental change (adaptive), and, finally, undertake structural change (transformative resilience). It also means that in their response to events, systems do not simply try to reduce the detrimental impact of these shocks; they also try to (i) minimize the costs it takes to respond and (ii) recover from these events, although this may not to be to the same position they were in prior to the shock. Resilience outcomes therefore result from trade-offs and combinations among three different dynamics depending on the intensity of shock, the costs of impact, and the costs of response (Adger et al. 2013).

The concept of climate-resilient development has become a popular way of reflecting the various elements of the absorptive, adaptive, and transformation aspects combined. The World Bank (2013, p. 4) uses the following definition: "a set of institutional arrangements, processes and instruments that help identify the risks from disasters, climate extremes, gradual and long-term climatic changes, and their associated impacts, and the design of measures to reduce, transfer and prepare for such risks". Climate- and disaster-resilient development combines development benefits with reductions in vulnerability over the short and longer term, using a development planning, multi-sectoral, and multi-stakeholder approach.

How do we build resilience into our systems? According to Béné et al. (2012), the main factors that affect resilience are:

- perceptions of risks and changes;
- access to knowledge and information;
- beliefs, culture, social rules, and norms;
- collective actions, coordination, social cohesion, power relations, and governance.

Based on this approach, there has been further work on defining resilience and transformative resilience as indicators of systemic health at and across different scales. There are, however, cases where too much persistence and resilience within systems can slow down necessary transformation and decrease future adaptive capacity. Thus, some of the literature has been about finding the right balance between resilience as persistence of the status quo and the transformative resilience that enables us to avoid collapse through innovation. Hutchins (2012), in his review of the literature, suggests that working with disruptions as an invitation to transformative change can create the exciting opportunity to turn breakdown into breakthrough.

There is common agreement that as the resilience of a system declines, the magnitude of a shock from which it cannot recover gets smaller and smaller. In general, resilience shifts attention from purely growth and efficiency to the time and resources needed for recovery and flexibility. Growth and efficiency alone can often lead infrastructure systems, businesses, and societies into fragile rigidities, exposing them to turbulent transformations (see Wahl 2017). Learning, recovery, and flexibility open eyes to novelty and new worlds of opportunity (Wahl 2017). Evidence suggests that infrastructure disruptions in the Pacific impose significant costs on low- and middle-income households and countries (such as in Fiji after Cyclone Winston in 2014), and building resilience can contribute significantly to avoiding future loses (see PRIF 2013).

C. **The platform for building resilient infrastructure in the Pacific**

Reflecting on the discussion in the previous sections, we now come to how we can support resilient infrastructure. Infrastructure investments usually involve large and irreversible investments with long asset lives, which makes consideration of resilience particularly relevant.

In a region, such as the Pacific, that faces specific weather and geological hazards (IPCC 2018) that are being affected by climate change variability, it is important to design, build, and maintain infrastructure to a standard that reflects ongoing challenges and the threat of shocks and new stresses increasing its exposure to risk. There has been some work done in the region, and as a rule of thumb it is generally accepted that one dollar of preventive measures is equal to five dollars of repairs (PRIF 2013). Therefore, as Rahiman (2019) suggests, there is a need to prioritize investment decisions for resilient infrastructure, and for a comprehensive policy framework to integrate climate resilience, improve risk assessment and information, and identify innovative financing mechanisms.

There are some relevant projects that show how resilience can be incorporated. In Kiribati, the South Tarawa Water Supply Project (STWSP) has been designed to address several of these issues. The project, co-financed by the Green Climate Fund, the ADB, the government of Kiribati, and the World Bank, involves the construction of a seawater desalination plant run on solar power. The plant will provide the more than 55,000 people of South Tarawa (around 51% of the national population) with a climate-resilient water supply, while an expanded water supply network will reduce leakages and ensure that residents have access to clean water. The project will achieve this through major water infrastructure upgrades, including a desalination plant, water supply network improvement, and a WASH (water, sanitation, and hygiene) awareness programme. The inclusion of renewable energy is also highly relevant on islands which rely largely on imported fossil fuel for energy generation.

In Nauru, ADB is developing a climate-resilient port, which includes the construction of new port infrastructure, including a wharf, a berth pocket, and a breakwater that will be resilient to forecasted increases in sea level and storm events. It will also reconstruct port buildings, the container storage, and port security facilities with buildings climate-proofed for increased storm activity. The new port, co-financed by the Green Climate Fund and the Government of Australia, will provide a much-needed lifeline for the 11,300 residents of this fragile and vulnerable island nation. In Solomon Islands, the ADB has provided financing for new bridges, stream crossings, and culverts that incorporate improvements to meet forecast increased rainfall, storm events, and cyclones, to boost East Guadalcanal's connectivity with the rest of the country, while helping 39,000 residents to better withstand the impact of climate change and more frequent natural disasters.

While resilient infrastructure development projects have been implemented in the Pacific, climate and disaster risks have further intensified recently, strongly requiring ways to plan, design, and construct more robust infrastructure. Rahiman, in a paper on building climate-resilient infrastructure (2019), highlights that current practice in building infrastructure considers only past climate patterns, which are likely to be altered due to climate change.[5] Typically, infrastructure is designed based on historic climate data; however, reflecting on ongoing work arising from the IPCC (see e.g. IPCC 2018), during its design life it could be subjected to a varying climate which may be different from past climate trends. In the Pacific, the climate is projected to change at an increasingly rapid pace, with likely alterations in long-term climatic averages and the frequency and severity of extreme weather events, all of which play an important role in the planning, design, operations, maintenance, and management of infrastructure. The lack of climate-related information for designing and adopting appropriate adaptation measures for infrastructure also poses a barrier. Further, there are often no enabling policies or institutional environment to steer the current and future course of infrastructure management to ensure the mainstreaming of climate change concerns into infrastructure development. Apart from this, Rahiman (2019) finds that the existing literature suggests that developing resilient infrastructure through climate-proofing will entail additional financial costs and is likely to be more cost-effective than rebuilding infrastructure in the wake of an event (see ADB 2022).

[5] Although matters are changing in the Pacific. In the 2023 FEMM, the PRIF presented a draft set of principles for quality infrastructure financing and development that was endorsed at the meeting.

9.4 Climate- and Disaster-Resilient Growth

Climate change and disaster risks are not the only factors influencing Pacific governments and businesses. They have also been required to operate at the centre of three major interrelated structural challenges:

1. The challenge of planning and budgeting in the face of increasing national exposure to the effects of global trends (climate change, global market volatility, and geopolitical tensions) and the national financial risks they entail (natural hazard events, climate change impacts, and their economic losses).
2. The challenge of maintaining progress against national economic and social development priorities in parallel with the additional cost implications of growing climate and disaster risk mitigation needs and priorities.
3. The resulting financial and strategic challenge of managing competing interests within resource decisions (due to increasingly complex social, economic, and environmental trade-offs).

These challenges provide a significant barrier to creating a clear policy environment. Making reductions in risk requires clarity on incentives, policies, and regulations. Reflecting on recent studies (for example: ADB 2022; Adeoti et al. 2020; PRIF 2023) on the importance of building and maintaining resilient infrastructure, the following represents a summary of thoughts on some possible lessons and principles to consider.

The adoption of standards: ISO 14090:2019 and 14091: 2021 (Adaptation to Climate Change) could be adopted and used to encourage the institutionalization of climate change knowledge into risk management frameworks which would adhere to international standards.

An enabling environment to encourage mainstreaming (such as effective governance, sound institutions, and clear regulatory environment): this should seek to encourage collaboration among experts across different stakeholders, and this needs to start early.

Mainstreaming: ensuring that each stage of the design, build, materials, maintenance, financing, and monitoring incorporates climate and disaster resilience. These considerations should be focused, targeting natural hazards which are specific and relevant to the infrastructure and location.

Improve decision-making (improved data, building of models for various weather and geological events, development of minimum standards such as in relation to materials and construction, assessment methodologies and benchmarks of performance, and capacity to use and understand the analysis): this should enable improved consistency in the assessment, identification, and options for adaptation and mitigation of emissions, and the decisions made. Similarly, the process should become continuous across the assets lifecycle and able to adapt to changing circumstances as new data is received and modelling undertaken.

Finance (that is simplified, affordable, and accessible): funding has to be proportional to the level of consideration (such as scale of asset, exposure to risk, and extent of interdependencies with other investments) and likely size of the investment.

Inclusivity (incorporating the private sector and communities through standards and legislation for public–private partnerships: how does the infrastructure support specific groups such as disabled people, older people, and women and children): accounting for all relevant costs and benefits requires extending assessments and consideration beyond the immediate beneficiary. For example, the construction of schools and community facilities can also provide shelters and places where basic supplies can be stored.

Nature-based Solutions: seeking cheaper solutions through the environment. According to the International Union for Conservation of Nature (IUCN, no date), Nature-based Solutions (NbS) are a cost-effective way to build infrastructure resilient to a changing climate while also delivering other societal benefits. They protect, sustainably manage, and restore natural and modified ecosystems that address societal challenges effectively and adaptively, simultaneously benefiting people and nature.

Limited investment in maintenance (challenging the "build-neglect-rebuild" paradigm for gifted infrastructure) and building the capacity of countries to ensure that the necessary engineering and technical skills are available.

9.5 Other Challenges Facing Infrastructure in the Pacific

Climate and disaster risks are cross-cutting issues that are critical to current and future infrastructure. These also exacerbate existing issues that have held back infrastructure development in the Pacific, including:

- limited bankable projects based on minimum cost recovery over the lifetime of the infrastructure asset; this can also include non-economic cost recovery of infrastructure, e.g., creation of infrastructure assets that have few spillover benefits for citizens (such as a road that reaches a limited number of remote households);
- issues of land acquisition (noting the innate customary linkages to land in the Pacific) and appropriate economic compensation for infrastructure development;
- legal and regulatory frameworks (including risk protection for investors) and sometimes abrupt changes to legal and regulatory frameworks: most infrastructure investment and recovery are long-term and based on continued certainty of key policies and regulations for the foreseeable future; effective regulation is also the means to improve access and distribute the benefits;
- limited interest and participation of private sector and finance;
- capacity issues within countries in dealing with multiple infrastructure projects, due to the limited resources; this can be compounded by high levels of corruption or mismanagement by bureaucracies.

9.6 Conclusion

For infrastructure, resilience should include the following key elements:

1. Resilience concerns infrastructure at all stages of its design, finance, construction, operation, and maintenance.
2. Resilience concerns the ability to manage exposure to hazards, shocks, or stresses through maintaining or transforming standards aiming at long-term prospects.
3. Resilience requires a balance between rigidity to spring back and flexibility to enable ongoing progress and development of these systems.

Resilience is a dynamic process characterized by multiple adaptive cycles interacting across a range of scales and dimensions (Brown and Westaway 2011; Craeynest, 2010; Manyena 2006). Fostering resilience by itself, however, is difficult, as is measuring it (CARRI 2017). In essence, this conceptualization means that building resilience requires interventions that strengthen the three components to maintain the status quo (absorptive), incorporate incremental change (adaptive), and, finally, undertake structural change (transformative resilience). Furthermore, the lack of climate-related information to support the design and adoption of appropriate adaptation measures for infrastructure also poses a barrier and more data and analysis is required. Further, there are often no enabling policies or institutional environment to ensure the mainstreaming of climate change concerns into infrastructure development.

It also requires that in their response to events, systems do not simply try to reduce the detrimental impact of shocks; they also try to minimize the costs of responding and recover from the events, although this may not to be to the same position as prior to the shock. Resilience outcomes therefore result from trade-offs and combinations among three different dynamics depending on the intensity of shock, the costs of impact, and the costs of response.

References

ADB (2022) Disaster resilient infrastructure: unlocking opportunities for Asia and the Pacific. ADB, Manila

Adeoti T, Fantini C, Morgan G, Thacker S, Ceppi P, Bhikhoo N, Kumar S, Crosskey S, O'Regan N (2020) Infrastructure for Small Island developing states. United Nations Office for Project Services, Copenhagen

Adger N, Adams H, Evans L, O'Neill S, Quinn T (2013) Human resilience to climate change and disasters: response from the University of Exeter (Online). Available at: https://royalsociety.org/~/media/policy/projects/resilience-climate-change/parts1-20.pdf. Accessed 15 Oct 2023

Béné C, Godfrey-Wood R, Newsham A, Davies M (2012) Resilience: new utopia or new tyranny? Reflection about the potentials and limits of the concept of resilience in relation to vulnerability reduction programmes, IDS Working Paper 405. Institute of Development Studies (IDS), Brighton

Béné C, Newsham A, Davies M, Ulrichs M, Godfrey-Wood R (2014) Review article: resilience, poverty and development. J Int Dev 26:598–623

Brown K, Westaway E (2011) Agency, capacity and resilience to environmental change: lessons from human development, well-being and disasters. Annu Rev Environ Resour 36(1):312–342

Bruneau M, Chang S, Eguchi RT, Lee GC, O'Rourke TD, Reinhorm AM, Shinouzuka M, Tierney K, Wallace WA, von Winterfeldt D (2003) A framework to quantitatively assess and enhance the seismic resilience of communities. Earthq Spectra 19(4):733–752

Capano G, Woo J (2016) Resilience and robustness in policy design: a critical appraisal. Policy Sci 50(3):399–426

CARRI (Community and Regional Resilience Institute) (2017) What is community resilience and why is it difficult to measure? (Online). Available at: https://www.nist.gov/system/files/documents/el/building_materials/resilience/NIST-April-7-2014.pdf. Accessed 1 June 2019

Cook Islands Government (2016) JNAPII: are we resilient? The Cook Islands 2nd joint national action plan. A sectoral approach to climate change and disaster risk management, 2016–2020. Government of the Cook Islands, Rarotonga

Craeynest L (2010) Loss and damage from climate change: the cost for poor people in developing countries. Johannesburg: ActionAid (Online). Available at: https://actionaid.org/sites/default/files/loss_and_damage_-_discussion_paper_by_actionaid-_nov_2010.pdf. Accessed 15 Oct 2018

Cutter S, Barnes L, Berry M, Burton C, Evans E, Tate E, Webb J (2008) A place based model for understanding community resilience to natural disasters. Glob Environ Chang 18(4):598–606

Esler S (2016) Fiji: post-disaster needs assessment. Government of Fiji, Suva

Government of Fiji (2018) Fiji national climate change policy. Available at: https://wrd.unwomen.org/practice/resources/fiji-national-climate-change-policy-2018-2030. Accessed 1 June 2022

Government of the Kingdom of Tonga (2018) Tonga: joint national action plan 2 on climate change and disaster risk management (JNAP 2) 2018–2028. Department of Climate Change, Nuku'alofa

Haimes Y (2009) On the definition of resilience in systems. Risk Anal 29(4):498–501

Hallegatte S, Rentschler J, Rozenberg J (2019) Lifelines: the resilient infrastructure opportunity. World Bank, Washington, DC

Hook SM (2021a) Disaster risk financing for small island developing states: final draft, paper drafted for UNDESA (United Nations Department of Economic and Social Affairs) (Online). Available at: https://sdgs.un.org/sites/default/files/2022-01/Disaster_Risk_Financing_forSIDS_DraftFinalReport.pdf. Accessed 15 Oct 2023

Hook SM (2021b) How can we build resilient infrastructure in the Blue Pacific? Presentation to the Australian conference of economists, 12 July (Online). Available at: http://esacentral.org.au/365/images/HookScott.pdf. Accessed 4 Mar 2024

Hutchins G (2012) The nature of business (Online). Available at: https://thenatureofbusiness.org/2012/08/23/giles-hutchins-introduces-the-nature-of-business. Accessed 11 Feb 2024

Infrastructure NSW (2018) State Infrastructure Strategy 2018–2038: building momentum. Infrastructure NSW, Sydney

IPCC (Intergovernmental Panel on Climate Change) (2012a) Annex I: glossary. In: Field CB, Barros V, Stocker TF, Qin D, Dokken DJ, Ebi KL, Mastrandrea MD, Mach KJ, Plattner G-K, Allen SK, Tignor M, Midgley, PM (eds) A special report of working groups I and II of the intergovernmental panel on climate change. Cambridge University Press, Cambridge and New York, pp 119–130

IPCC (2012b) Summary for policymakers: managing the risks of extreme events and disasters to advance climate change adaptation. In: Field CB, Barros V, Stocker TF, Qin D, Dokken DJ, Ebi KL, Mastrandrea MD, Mach KJ, Plattner G-K, Allen SK, Tignor M, Midgley PM (eds) A special report of working groups I and II of the intergovernmental panel on climate change. Cambridge University Press, Cambridge and New York, pp 1–19

IPCC (2018) Global warming of 1.5 °C (Online). Available at: https://www.ipcc.ch/sr15. Accessed 17 Apr 2019

IUCN (no date) Nature-based solutions (Online). Available at: https://www.iucn.org/our-work/nature-based-solutions. Accessed 13 May 2019

Lloyd's of London and Arup (2017) Future cities: building infrastructure resilience. Lloyd's of London, London

Manyena S (2006) The concept of resilience revisited. Disasters 30(4):434–450
OECD (Organisation for Economic Co-operation and Development) (2018) Climate resilient infrastructure: policy perspectives, Environment Policy Paper 14. OECD, Paris
Pachauri RK, Reisinger A (eds) (2007) Climate change 2007: synthesis report Online. Cambridge University Press, Cambridge. Available at: https://www.ipcc.ch/report/ar4/syr. Accessed 17 Mar 2016
Pacific Islands Forum (2016) The framework for resilient development in the Pacific (Online). Available at: https://www.forumsec.org/frdp. Accessed 13 May 2019
Pacific Islands Forum (2023) 2023 Forum economic ministers meeting (Online). Available at: https://www.forumsec.org/forum-standing-meetings/#1509852820328-025d2cef-7b10. Accessed 26 Feb 2024
Pacific Islands Forum Secretariat (2013) The Pacific climate change finance assessment framework (PCCFAF): final report (Online). Available at: https://library.sprep.org/content/pacific-climate-change-finance-assessment-framework-final-report-may-2013. Accessed 26 May 2018
PRIF (Pacific Regional Infrastructure Facility) (2013) Infrastructure maintenance in the Pacific: challenging the build-neglect-rebuild paradigm (Online). Available at: https://www.theprif.org/sites/default/files/documents/build_neglect_rebuild_revised_full_report_2014.pdf. Accessed 10 Oct 2023
PRIF (2023) PRIF Week 2023 (Online). Available at: https://www.theprif.org/prif-week-2023. Accessed 26 Feb 2024
Rahiman R (2019) Addressing critical issues for building climate resilient infrastructure, paper submitted to G20 Japan, 2019 (Online). Available at: https://www.global-solutions-initiative.org/wp-content/uploads/2022/11/t20-japan-tf3-8-critical-issues-climate-resilient-infrastructure-1.pdf. Accessed 15 Oct 2023
Resilience Alliance (2007) Assessing resilience in social-ecological systems: a workbook for scientists, version 1.1 (Online). Available at: https://library.uniteddiversity.coop/Transition_Relocalisation_Resilience/resilience_workbook_for_scientists.pdf. Accessed 18 Mar 2019
Sudmeier-Rieux KI (2014) Resilience: an emerging paradigm of danger or of hope? Disaster Prev Manag 23(1):67–80
Trundle A (2020) Resilient cities in a sea of islands: informality and climate change in the South Pacific. Cities 97:102496
UK Government (2021) 'Small Island Developing States (SIDS) and access to finance: statement and call to action', policy paper, 7 October (Online). Available at https://www.gov.uk/government/publications/small-island-developing-states-sids-and-access-to-finance-call-to-action-7-october-2021/small-island-developing-states-sids-and-access-to-finance-statement-and-call-to-action-7-october-2021. Accessed 1 June 2022
UkAid (2011) Defining disaster resilience: a DFID approach paper Online. Available at: https://www.gov.uk/government/uploads/ssytem/uploads/attachement_data/file/186874/defining-disaster-resilience-approach-paper.pdf. Accessed: 20 Dec 2017
UNISDR (2009) International strategy for disaster reduction (Online). Available at: https://www.preventionweb.net/english/professional/terminology/?pid:6&pih:2. Accessed 21 June 2019
United Nations (2018) Common guidance on helping build resilient societies, December 2018 version. United Nations, New York
Wahl D (2017) What exactly are resilience and transformative resilience? (Online). Available at: https://designforsustainability.medium.com/what-exactly-are-resilience-and-transformative-resilience-a0783595023f#:~:text=Resilience%20contributes%20to%20maintaining%20the,path%20towards%20a%20regenerative%20future. Accessed 21 June 2019
World Bank (2013) Building resilience: integrating climate and disaster risk into development. Lessons from World Bank Group experience. World Bank, Washington, DC

Part III
Planet

Chapter 10
The Fragility of the Ocean: From Coral Reef Protection to Deep-Sea Mining

M. James C. Crabbe, George R. Barker, Linda Wong, and Jinfeng Zhou

Abstract The ocean environment around Pacific island countries and territories (PICTs) is fragile, from coral reefs along the coasts to deep-ocean habitats; 30% of the world's reefs are important in the fishing and tourism sectors, with a total value estimated at nearly $36 billion. Global reef surveys during 2014–17 revealed that 80% of surveyed reefs had experienced significant coral bleaching and 35% had experienced significant coral mortality. Observations demonstrate that the widespread damage to coral reefs caused by global warming is accelerating, underscoring the threat that anthropogenic climate change poses in terms of the irreversible transformation of these essential ecosystems. But it is not only island coastal regions that face significant damage. There is also potential damage to the deep-sea (>200 m depth) areas around PICTs—where there are many gaps in our knowledge about biodiversity and ecosystems—owing to the encroaching possibility of mining for precious metals in the deep ocean. We describe an ecosystems services valuation approach to the cost–benefit analysis (CBA) of decision-making over deep-sea mining, and an economic approach to decision-making under uncertainty which supports a wait-and-see approach to allow more information to be obtained when there are high non-reversible costs at stake. We also explore relevant governing legal and financial options, such as mining trials and environmental financial assurance (EFA) bonds—as a prior condition of awarding a mining licence—to cover the costs of clean-up common in terrestrial mining. Protection of the coastal and deep-sea areas of PICTs is a major challenge that needs global cooperation.

M. J. C. Crabbe (✉) · G. R. Barker
Wolfson College, Oxford University, Oxford, UK
e-mail: james.crabbe@wolfson.ox.ac.uk

L. Wong · J. Zhou
China Biodiversity Conservation and Green Development Foundation, Beijing, China

E. Monaco and M. Abe (eds.), *Sustainable Development Across Pacific Islands*,
https://doi.org/10.1007/978-981-97-3629-4_10

10.1 Introduction

Coral reefs are important because they protect coastlines from storms and erosion, provide jobs for local communities, and offer recreation opportunities. They are also major sources of biodiversity and a vital source of food and medicines. There are at least 758 known species of Indo-Pacific corals, many of which surround the coastal areas of the Pacific island countries and territories (PICTs); the Caribbean has only 62 species.

Coral reefs throughout the world face severe challenges from a variety of anthropogenic and environmental factors, including overfishing, destructive fishing practices, coral bleaching, ocean acidification, sea level rise, algal blooms, agricultural run-off, coastal and resort development, marine pollution, increasing incidence of coral diseases, invasive species, and hurricane/cyclone damage. Two consequences of these challenges are reduced time available for the recovery of corals and reduced coral cover. Indo-Pacific reef-building corals are inherently resilient, and overall resilience remains high in some areas, although coral species are becoming at increased risk of extinction as the twenty-first century progresses (Crabbe 2019; IPCC 2018; Pandolfi et al. 2011). However, it is not just the coastal reefs that are threatened: the deep sea is under threat from mining by large industrial companies. This chapter will cover the underlying threats for reefs and the deep sea and possible ways to mitigate their fragility.

10.2 Threats to Coral Reefs

Threats to coral reefs have been increasing for many decades, owing to climate change and human practices which impact reef ecosystems.

A. **Climate change**

The most recent, and first, multi-year global "bleaching" event (spanning hundreds of kilometres or more and including PICTs) was from 2014 to 2017. Seventy-five per cent of reefs were affected by bleaching-level stress, with more than 50% of affected reef areas impacted at least twice over the period (Eakin et al. 2019; IPCC 2018), and some locations experienced almost complete coral cover loss (Skirving et al. 2019; Vargas-Ángel et al. 2019). Almost all coral reefs are very likely to have degraded from their current state by 2100, even if global warming remains at less than 2 °C above pre-industrial levels, meaning that species composition will differ and their diversity and extent will be reduced (IPCC 2018). There is limited scope for future latitudinal range extension of current reefs towards the poles (Muir et al. 2017), and severe bleaching episodes can also cause positive feedback, including impairment of larval recruitment via mortality of adult brood stock (Hughes et al. 2018; 2019).

B. **Human pressures**

Tropical coral reef biomes around PICTs are also at particular risk from localized human pressures, with 58% of coral reefs less than 30 min from the nearest human settlements (Maire et al. 2016). Localized threats to corals include over-intensive fisheries, coastal development (industry, settlement, tourism, and transportation), changes in native species dynamics, introduction of invasive species (competitors, predators, pathogens, and parasites), destructive fishing (e.g., using dynamite), chemical fishing, pollution from agriculture and industry, domestic pollution, recreation and tourism activities, and global trade (Erftemeijer et al. 2012). Macroalgae are a major competitor with corals that reduce growth, cause disease, prevent new coral recruitment, and can tip the entire ecosystem into a less diverse and less productive "algal-dominated" reef. Macroalgal levels are controlled by both bottom-up provision of nutrients and top-down herbivory by parrotfish; hence, while the immediate threat to the coral is from the algae, the ultimate threat may be sewage, fertilizer from agriculture, or overfishing of herbivorous fish (Anthony et al. 2015).

Fishing

Fishing activities can affect corals directly and indirectly. Direct threats include destructive fishing techniques using dynamite or poison that can kill corals, and trawling and net entanglement that can break colonies and disturb sediment. Indirectly, fishing affects corals by disrupting the food web and removing key ecological roles. Overfishing of parrotfish and other herbivorous fish removes top-down control of macroalgae, allowing this seaweed to overgrow and out-compete corals. Removal of predators allows the growth of urchin populations, which then predate on coral larvae as they graze the reef (McClanahan and Maina 2003).

Land use

Increased sediment and nutrient-rich run-off into the sea through catchment-level land use change can significantly affect coastal coral reef communities at local to regional scales. Run-off can cause increased turbidity, smothering, inhibited recruitment, and reduced growth of corals, as well as introducing toxic pollutants, pathogens, and competition with algae (Comeros-Raynal et al. 2021).

General use and trade

Coral is harvested and traded to supply building materials domestically, and curios, jewellery, and ornamental organisms for the aquarium industry globally. Although not considered a major threat to most species, population declines associated with trade have led to the listing and monitoring of more than 2000 species of coral globally by the Convention on International Trade in Endangered Species of Wild Fauna and Flora (CITES, 2020). Almost all of the CITES-monitored exported coral between 2007 and 2016 was recorded as either wild-sourced live (transported in water, recorded by number of pieces only) or raw coral (dead coral, base rock, and live rock, reported by kilogram), totalling 19.8 million pieces and 24 million kilograms, respectively (CITES 2020).

C. **Other issues**

These include issues where the aetiology is complex or not known in detail.

Crown-of-thorns starfish

Crown-of-thorns starfish (COTS; *Acanthaster planci*), found throughout the Indo-Pacific, including around PICTs, can undergo massive outbreaks that rapidly devastate reefs on a local and regional level, triggered through human impacts such as enhanced nutrient loads (Pratchett et al. 2014). Populations of COTS have greatly increased since the 1970s, have been known to kill large areas of coral reef habitat, and have contributed to the overall decline and destruction of reefs in PICTs (Kensington 2019; Pratchett et al. 2014).

Coral disease

Coral disease is emerging as a serious threat to coral reefs worldwide, causing large-scale reef deterioration in PICTs as elsewhere (Aeby et al. 2011; Haapkylä et al. 2013; Jacobson 2006; Weil et al. 2006; Willis et al. 2004), and may be as likely to cause mortality as bleaching in the coming decades (Maynard et al. 2015). Increased coral disease prevalence and mortality have been linked to increased thermal stress, reduced water quality and clarity, dredging-associated sedimentation, and plastic pollution (Lamb et al. 2018)—thus linking human actions with coral diseases. White syndrome has been reported in numerous locations, including PICTs, and constitutes a growing threat to coral reef ecosystems (Aeby et al. 2020; Bourne et al. 2015; Maynard et al. 2015; Miller and Richardson 2015; Sussman et al. 2008), supporting the prediction that disease levels will increase further with higher sea surface temperatures. In most instances, the disease is a symptom of escalating anthropogenic stressors such as thermal stress, increased turbidity, nutrient enrichment, and even scuba diving and tourist activities (Chen et al. 2017; Lamb et al. 2018; Pollock et al. 2014; Ruiz-Moreno et al. 2012; Sutherland et al. 2004; Vega Thurber et al. 2014), which have placed coral reefs in the PICTs at high risk of collapse.

Cyclones

Cyclones can affect reefs at latitudes of 7–25° north and south of the equator (Scoffin et al. 1992) but very rarely occur in equatorial regions (Puotinen et al. 2020). They mainly affect shallow-water corals down to a depth of around 20 m through large waves that can break or remove colonies, with branching species being most susceptible to storm damage (De'ath et al. 2012; Scoffin et al. 1992). Ecologically, the impact of cyclones is similar to that of coral bleaching, where an acute impact rapidly reduces the coral population. As with coral bleaching, the frequency of cyclones is expected to increase with climate change (Puotinen et al. 2020), meaning that the time for reefs to recover between these acute impacts is reduced, potentially preventing recovery. Storm strength is also increasing; repeated storm damage without sufficient recovery can lead to a reduction in coral species diversity, coral cover, and reef complexity and can result in a phase shift to a macroalgae- or rubble-dominated state (Vercelloni et al. 2020). The resultant physical damage to reefs leads to an increase in mobile rubble, which typically inhibits the recruitment and regrowth of corals for many years (Scoffin et al. 1992). However, counterintuitively, storms could also mitigate the effects of bleaching in some instances, by causing large-scale mixing and cooling of heated waters.

Marine litter

Marine litter is a growing problem in PICTs seeking cost-effective solutions to address the issue. Marine litter is defined as any solid material that has been deliberately discarded or unintentionally blown or washed into the ocean, with over 90% of it being plastics originating from land- and sea-based sources (SPREP 2018; UNEP, 2009). Globally, around 6.4 million tonnes of marine litter enters the oceans each year—about eight million items every day (McIlgorm et al. 2008; UNEP 2005). Based on a survey of 159 reefs in the Asia–Pacific region, the likelihood of disease increases 20-fold when corals are in contact with plastic (Lamb et al. 2018).

Marine litter threatens human health and impacts marine wildlife. Entanglement of or ingestion by wildlife is often fatal. Ingestion of microplastics by fish may also be a pathway for the transport of harmful chemicals into the food web and eventually to humans (Li et al. 2021). At the heart of the issue is the need for behavioural change and improvements to waste management to prevent plastic pollution from entering waterways. Marine litter is everyone's responsibility to reduce, reuse, and recycle.

D. **Coral conservation**

Recommended measures for conserving coral species include research on taxonomy, population, abundance and trends, ecology and habitat status, and threats and resilience to threats; restoration action; identification, establishment, and management of new protected areas; expansion of protected areas; recovery management; and disease, pathogen, and parasite management. Marine protected areas are designated areas of the ocean set aside for conservation and management purposes. Unless they are "no-take" zones, where no fish, invertebrate, or coral biomass may be removed, they can also promote sustainable use of these resources (Hall et al. 2023). Artificial propagation and techniques such as cryo-preservation of gametes may become important for conserving coral biodiversity (CBD 2010; Hoegh-Guldberg et al. 2018; IUCN 2016; UNEP-WCMC 2020). Timely access to national-level trade data for CITES analysis reports is valuable for monitoring trends (Liew et al. 2021). Many species are targeted by collectors for the aquarium trade, and fisheries management is required, e.g., through marine protected areas, quotas, size limits, etc. Consideration of the suitability of species for aquaria should also be included as part of fisheries management, and population surveys should be carried out to monitor the effects of harvesting.

10.3 Deep-Sea Mining

Deep-sea mining (DSM) is the process of retrieving mineral deposits from the ocean bed at depths of below 200 m (Crabbe 2022; Heffernan 2019). There has been interest in this since the 1970s, but this has increased significantly recently owing to the depletion of deposits from terrestrial sources of metals such as manganese (Figueiredo et al. 2021). There is demand for many seabed minerals in the manufacturing of digital equipment, including mobile phones, tablets, laptops, and batteries, as well as green technologies to mitigate climate change, including wind turbines (Childs 2018; Milinovic et al. 2021). The International Energy Agency (IEA) estimates that the world will need 19 times more nickel by 2040 to meet its decarbonization targets. Indonesia, the world's biggest nickel supplier, is bulldozing rainforests to expand mines.

DSM requires seafloor vehicles to crush and collect the material, which is then fed to the support vessel. However, there are many gaps in our knowledge about ocean bed biodiversity and ecosystems (Clark et al. 2020). The majority of proposed DSM sites are in the Pacific and directly involve the PICTs. The sites are near polymetallic nodules or active and extinct hydrothermal vents at 1400–3700 m (4600–12,100 ft) below the ocean's surface (Hein et al. 2020). The vents create globular or massive sulphide deposits which contain valuable metals such as silver, gold, copper, manganese, cobalt, and zinc (Hein et al. 2020). There is a great opportunity for recovering materials much needed for current digital technology, but the costs in terms of environmental damage could be enormous and irretrievable.

A. **Deep-ocean sediment ecosystems**

Deep-ocean sediment (DOS) ecosystems cover more than half of the earth's surface and remain one of the least-explored ecosystems on the planet. The DOS is where nutrient recycling for the healthy functioning of ocean ecosystems and carbon sequestration occur for the regulation of the earth's climate over geological timescales, and both are essential (Cordier et al. 2022). Concerted international efforts are vital to further understanding DOS system biodiversity and their ecological role in planetary biogeochemical cycles (Perrings et al., 1992; Jones et al. 2021).

Sea cucumbers, brittle stars, worms, and wispy new species related to jellyfish and coral make their home in deep-sea nodule fields. Mining vehicles will rake up fine particles in bottom waters, sucking up nodules, and operators will discharge sediment carried up in pipes back into the ocean (Fig. 10.1). Muddy water can clog the delicate mucus filters of animals such as the giant anemone (*Relicanthus* sp.) or obscure light needed by species such as the vampire squid (*Vampyroteuthis infernalis*) and the barbeled dragon fish (*Idiacanthus antrostomus*) (Orcutt et al. 2020; Vonnahme et al. 2020). DSM increases ambient noise in normally quiet pelagic environments. Anthropogenic noise is known to affect deep-sea fish species and marine mammals. Many scientists believe that seabed mining is poised to irreparably harm fragile abyssal plain habitats (Cordier et al. 2022).

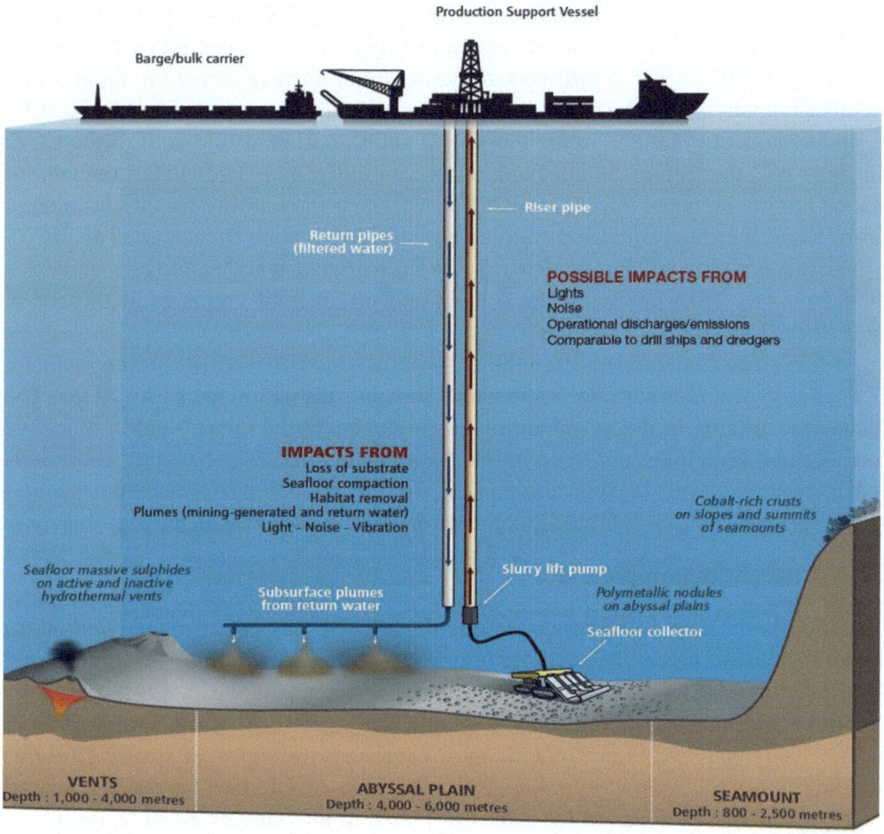

Fig. 10.1 Potential impacts of deep-sea mining. *Source* authors' adaptation of a figure taken from the Secretariat of the Pacific Community Annual Report (2013). Copyright: IUCN

B. **Management of mining activities: The International Seabed Authority**

The International Seabed Authority (ISA), an organization affiliated with the United Nations, is tasked with managing DSM activities. Created in 1994, it regulates activities in international waters, guided by its member nations plus the European Union (EU). The ISA is headquartered in Kingston, Jamaica, and has more than 150 state members. The supreme authority of the ISA is the assembly, in which all ISA members are represented. The assembly sets general policies, establishes budgets, and elects a 36-member council, which serves as the ISA's executive authority (Kung et al. 2021). The ISA is seeking to develop regulations in the form of a mining code but has come up against a deadline—what is called the "two-year rule".

In July 2021, Nauru made use of the two-year rule embedded in the United Nations Convention on the Law of the Sea (UNCLOS; United Nations 1982), which could allow mining to begin within two years in the Pacific's Clarion Clipperton Zone (CCZ) (Amon et al. 2022). The Metals Company (TMC), sponsored by Nauru, has provided assurances that it will work to ensure minimal environmental impact (The Metals Company 2023). In 2023, the company announced that it had finished testing its nodule collector vehicle in the North Sea and that trials would start in the CCZ. But how will the impact be checked? How can indigenous knowledge relevant to seabed mining be taken into account? Who will bear the liability for environmental harm? Many legitimate questions remain around TMC's plan (Blanchard et al. 2023).

The ISA has until 2025 to finalize regulations to dictate whether and how countries should pursue DSM involving the seabed and ocean floor and subsoil thereof in international waters.[1]

At this stage, whether to allow DSM—and if so, how—is still a core problem facing the ISA in international waters, and all countries within their own EEZs. The decision is initially best determined by an agreement based on a common objective and accepted principles, enforced in international and domestic law and regulations and in contracts with mining companies. Before proceeding to evaluate the best approach to regulation of DSM, it is important to first consider the policy objective.

C. **Net benefit to humankind**

UNCLOS is the constitutional document governing DSM in the seabed and ocean floor and subsoil thereof, beyond the limits of national jurisdiction—or "the area".[2] Article 136 of UNCLOS establishes the principle that the area and its resources are the "Common Heritage of Mankind" (Wang and Chang 2020). Article 137 of UNCLOS further states that "No State shall claim or exercise sovereignty or sovereign rights over any part of the Area or its resources" (UNCLOS Article 137(1)) and that instead "all rights in the resources of the Area are vested in mankind as a whole, on whose behalf the Authority shall act" (UNCLOS Article 137(2)). Article 140 of UNCLOS establishes a clear objective for the ISA (the authority regulating DSM in the area or in international waters) by requiring that DSM "shall be carried out for the benefit of mankind as a whole". This would be consistent with the United Nations commitment to sustainable development, as defined by the United Nations Brundtland Commission—namely, "Development that meets the needs of the present without

[1] The ISA began a lengthy conference on this issue in Jamaica on 10 July 2023. This ended on 28 July with more than 20 governments opposing fast-tracked licences. Brazil, Canada, Costa Rica, Chile, Finland, Germany, Portugal, Switzerland, and Vanuatu were among the 21 countries supporting a ban, moratorium, or precautionary pause on DSM. China, Norway, Nauru, Mexico, and the United Kingdom, meanwhile, supported the fast-tracking of licences for DSM. A growing number of countries concerned about the potential environmental impact suggested more scientific studies be done first (Symons, 2023). In December 2023, however, Norway's parliament agreed to allow seabed mineral exploration in the Arctic region, a key step towards full-scale ocean mining. Norway hopes to become the first country to make DSM happen on a commercial scale, despite the concerns over the environmental impact and the moratorium calls (see Klesty, 2023).

[2] See UNCLOS Article 1, which defines the "area" as meaning the seabed and ocean floor and subsoil thereof, beyond the limits of national jurisdiction. UNCLOS also establishes the ISA (also referred to as the Authority) to regulate DSM in this area.

compromising the ability of future generations to meet their own needs" (Bruntland Commission 1987, p. 37).[3]

The UNCLOS objective for DSM in international waters thus requires that an expected net benefit test be met or that the expected benefits of DSM be shown to exceed the expected costs to all humankind over time. By comparison, legally, in any country's EEZ it will be up to the country's government to decide whether a net benefit test is used, and if so, whether to consider the wellbeing of humankind as a whole over time or only the wellbeing of its own citizens (see also Crépin et al. 2012).

This raises the question of what would be the best regulatory framework for DSM given the overarching objective outlined above in UNCLOS Article 140. In international waters, a test of the net benefit to humanity over time must be applied not only before DSM proceeds (ex ante), but also after DSM is permitted (ex post) at regular intervals, subject to administrative and transaction costs. Ex ante regulation of international waters would determine at the outset whether DSM should proceed at all, and if so, on what terms, based on the expected net benefit test. Ex post regulation of international waters, on the other hand, would ensure that DSM is carried out only in accordance with the net benefit objective and that compensation is paid where it fails to meet expected standards. Mining companies should thus be subject to ex post regulation by courts to compensate for any environmental and social harm caused by mining (including oceanic and atmospheric pollution). They should have a legal duty to compensate those harmed by their activities, who in turn should have the right to sue mining companies to recover compensation for harm.

The following sections review key elements of the required ex ante and ex post regulatory framework for DSM in international waters, including:

- the net benefit test and how it might best be applied;
- standard cost–benefit analysis;
- environmental costs and benefits;
- risks, uncertainty, ignorance, and reversibility;
- regulatory budgets;
- financial assurance;
- the fiscal approach;
- mining trials;
- scientific information and transparency of process.

D. **The net benefit test**

In either international waters or EEZs, to compensate for risk and the inevitable uncertainty surrounding any expected net benefit estimate, the threshold for the required level of expected net benefit should not simply be set at zero (i.e., no expected net harm). Rather, a "risk-adjusted" net benefit test is required.

[3] The Brundtland Commission, formerly the World Commission on Environment and Development, was a sub-organization of the United Nations that aimed to unite countries in pursuit of sustainable development.

In this section, we first discuss the standard cost–benefit analysis required to evaluate whether any net benefit threshold test has been met. We then consider two key specific issues—namely, how environmental impacts will be evaluated and how to deal with the problem of risk and uncertainty in this regard.[4]

Standard cost–benefit analysis

The standard key elements of any economic cost–benefit analysis (CBA) methodology include:

1. Identify the counterfactual (or baseline) and DSM project to be compared.
2. Identify whose costs and benefits count, or who has standing in calculating costs and benefits. There is a clear distinction here between DSM in international waters and in EEZs.
3. Estimate and quantify project impacts, identify them as either costs or benefits, and assign units of measurement over the relevant time period. Costs and benefits are divided into two categories:

   a. **Private** costs/benefits, including impacts on direct participants, including participating mining companies and participating governments and citizens. The project will not proceed if it fails a commercial test for a mining company and should not proceed if it fails on private cost/benefit for relevant governments and citizens.
   b. **External** costs/benefits for any non-participants. This includes costs and benefits due to environmental, social, or cultural change. External costs and benefits, once added to a project's evaluation, may end up disqualifying a project that qualified on a private cost/benefit test or justifying a project that failed on a private cost/benefit test.

4. Monetize or assign monetary values (in a consistent currency) to each quantified impact, cost, and benefit.
5. Address time and discounting approach and apply discount rate to costs and benefits. This adjusts the costs and benefits that occur at various times throughout a project into a single time period so that they are directly comparable with one another. This process involves what economists call discounting, or calculating a present value (PV). Discounting traditionally places more weight on costs and benefits early on in a project than later (see also step 7 on sensitivity analysis).
6. Calculate the overall net present value (NPV) of the project proposed, including both private and social benefits and costs. This is equivalent to estimating the project's net social benefit (NSB). This is calculated as the PV of all benefits (PVB) minus the PV of all costs (PVC) (NSB = PVB − PVC). In this analysis, a net social benefit of greater than zero suggests the project has the potential to make global and/or host citizens better off. As noted, an NSB threshold above zero might be required.

---

[4] See also Krutilla et al. (2021), which focuses on how CBA can address uncertainty in the site-specific financial returns and financial risks associated with DSM contract applications to the ISA.

7. Perform sensitivity analysis. Where some uncertainty exists as to any key variables, the impact of changes in these variables can be evaluated. For example, sensitivity analysis might be performed on the appropriate rate of discount by considering a range of discount rates and evaluating the sensitivity of conclusions to them. The base case, against which the sensitivity of the results is tested, is usually a seven per cent discount rate (the rate suggested by the US Environmental Protection Agency's Guidelines for Preparing Economic Analyses in 2010).
8. Address risk and uncertainty. This is a key subject that is addressed further below.
9. Identify recommended decision on whether to conduct the DSM as proposed. This requires consideration of the proposed project's NSB, the sensitivity of NSB calculations, and any impacts that could not be quantified or monetized, including wider environmental and social impacts.

There have been no decisions by the ISA permitting DSM in international waters based on its net benefit for all humankind over time using CBA. However, CBA has been undertaken for DSM in EEZs that may provide lessons; we review this below. Two critical issues underlie estimates developed in the studies that we will focus on, namely the treatment of the environmental costs and benefits of DSM and of risk, uncertainty, and ignorance.

Environmental costs and benefits of DSM

Significant improvements have been made in the methodology of CBA to best incorporate environmental and social impacts (see Revesz and Livermore 2008; 2013). The concept of "ecosystem services" is defined as the benefits people obtain from the environment. Relevant ecosystem services are typically divided into four broad categories:

1. Provisioning services (e.g., material goods such as food, feed, fuel, and fibre) are associated with goods provided directly to people.
2. Regulating services (e.g., climate regulation, flood control, and water purification) control ecosystem processes that influence the wellbeing of humans.
3. Cultural services generate human wellbeing beyond any direct or indirect consumption of goods. Examples include recreational opportunities and "existence value" or wellbeing generated by the knowledge that an ecosystem exists in a certain state (including so-called spiritual value, e.g., the spiritual connection local or indigenous people have to their environs).
4. Supporting services (e.g., nutrient cycling and primary production) generate human wellbeing by facilitating the production of future provisioning, regulating, or cultural services.

An ecosystems services valuation (ESV) approach can then be used to value ecosystem services that might be lost due to DSM. This approach will work well where relevant costs and benefits are well known and relatively predictable. The critical problem with ESV of DSM impacts at the moment is the lack of information to enable the valuation of service impacts in deep seabeds. The returns to investment in more research or information to enable ESV of DSM therefore seem considerable.

This can be illustrated by considering three DSM cost–benefit studies undertaken by a partnership between the European Union (EU) and the Secretariat of the Pacific Community (SPC) under the Pacific Community's Deep Sea Minerals Project. The three DSM CBAs were prepared in 2016 in a report by consulting firm Cardno using an ESV approach (Cardno 2016).[5] They related to three different EEZ jurisdictions, and three different mineral deposits thought to have high potential for economic viability:

- Papua New Guinea (PNG) seafloor massive sulphide (SMS) deposits;
- Cook Islands polymetallic manganese nodules (MN);
- Marshall Islands ferromanganese cobalt-rich crusts (CRC).

Given that each project was in a different country's EEZ and not international waters, costs and benefits were assessed only from the perspective of citizens of the host country, based on the operation of a single mine site, and focused solely on:

- private costs and benefits to the host government, including administrative costs and revenues/royalty benefits;
- externalities or external costs and benefits incurred by the host country's citizens due only to social and environmental change.

Where costs and benefits could not be quantified and monetized, they were identified and discussed qualitatively. It was found that two of the DSM projects studied passed a net benefit test—the one in Cook Islands (where four metals were to be recovered and the mining company owned the operation and the processing facility in a country other than Cook Islands) offering a net benefit of $467 million, the one in Papua New Guinea (PNG) (involving seafloor massive sulphide mining) offering a net benefit of $82 million. Crust mining in Marshall Islands was determined to not be economically viable currently (under the two scenarios considered, due to present metal prices, expected ore recovery, and the cost of technology).

It is important to remember, however, that these estimates of local net social benefits excluded consideration of:

- private costs and benefits to foreign mining companies (including capital and operating costs and mining revenues), other than to the extent that they determined commercial viability;
- externalities to foreign-country governments and citizens.

This is critical, as even small per-person external costs and benefits from a DSM project that affect all people on the planet over time, both alive today and in the future, could add up to very large impacts that may well dwarf the social and private costs and benefits felt locally. For example, the Cardno report estimated that the total local net benefits from the two DSM projects with positive local net benefits (i.e., the one in Cook Islands and the other in PNG), when combined, would total $550 million. In mid-2015, when the report was published, the United Nations Department

[5] The authors of the Cardno (2016) report later summarized the work in a published journal article; see Wakefield and Myers (2018). For a review of both these publications see Krutilla et al (2021).

of Economic and Social Affairs estimated there were 7.3 billion people alive on the planet (UNDESA 2015). Focusing on environmental impacts alone, if these 7.3 billion people were on average willing to pay only eight (US) cents per person to preserve the natural state of the two local deep seabeds in Cook Islands and PNG and the two respective DSM projects were stopped, then the offsetting total global benefit from not proceeding with the DSM projects would have been \$584 million (0.08×7.3 billion). This would have more than offset the implied local cost of not proceeding of \$550 million estimated by Cardno, and would have been sufficient to justify stopping or delaying further progress on the two projects.

Thus, EEZ valuations like the one funded by EU/SPC clearly understate both the global benefits and the global costs of the DSM, including the global willingness to pay to stop or delay local DSM projects. It is worth reviewing the local EEZ studies, however, to appreciate the informational problem confronting the application of any (local or global) net benefit test. The local net benefit estimates might also usefully be seen as an estimate of the amount the global community might need to pay the local EEZ community to compensate them for the local cost of *not* mining or the cost to them of delay as a result of any agreement to stop or postpone local mining. The global community might consider paying for a delay or a moratorium if there were sufficient benefits from delaying in order to better evaluate options or to better minimize or mitigate any perceived harm.

Focusing on environmental impacts, Cardno (2016) drew on willingness-to-pay (WTP) and replacement-cost (RCM) methods to create a baseline estimate of the value of DSM-related changes in ecosystem service provision.

In all cases, Cardno (2016) claimed that conclusions were fairly robust to a reasonable range of uncertainty related to input values and discount rates. However, a close analysis of the information relied upon to conduct the ESV indicates that this is not the case. The poor informational foundations of the study highlight the need for more investment in research on ESV related to DSM.

To illustrate, we take the WTP estimate of the ESV provided by deep-sea vent habitats that the Cardno report states was used in the study. Cardno relied on Earth Economics (2015), which estimated ecological services provided by deep-sea vent habitats at \$1766 per hectare per annum (ph/a).[6] A close review of this report, however, reveals that Earth Economics did not itself develop a WTP measure of DSM ESV. Indeed, Earth Economics (2015, p. 80) correctly and explicitly noted that "ecosystem service valuation studies of deep seabed ecosystems do not yet exist".

Instead, Earth Economics derived its estimate from a relatively old report prepared for the New Jersey Department for Environmental Protection that tried to estimate the economic value of ecosystem services provided by New Jersey's natural capital (wetland, forests, rivers etc.) (Constanza et al. 2006). This study undertook a selective search of the ESV literature at the time and classified it into different types of studies in terms of quality, from highest (type A) to lowest (type C). Earth Economics appears to have relied on Constanza et al. review of type A studies, which were

[6] To see how this estimate was utilized in Cardno (2016), for the PNG see p. 3–28, for Cook Islands p. 4–35, and for Marshall Islands pp. 5–25 to 5–26.

peer-reviewed empirical analyses using conventional environmental economic techniques (e.g., travel cost, hedonic pricing, and contingent valuation) to elicit individual consumer preferences for environmental services. However, there are a number of problems with this approach.

Ninety-four type A studies were included in the New Jersey report, generating 163 estimates of ESV for 12 possible ecosystem services (e.g., gas and climate regulation, disturbance prevention, etc.), across 11 land cover types in New Jersey (e.g., fresh wetland, salty wetland, estuary, etc.). First, it is by no means clear that ESV estimates for these land cover types in New Jersey can be transferred, or used to accurately value deep-seabed ecosystem services in the Pacific.[7] There were also serious gaps in the available economic valuation estimates, as the 94 studies relied on provided only 32 ESV estimates, 24% of the total 132 possible ecological services by land type (12×11). There were so many gaps in the New Jersey report relied on by Earth Economics (2015) and Cardno (2016) that Constanza et al. themselves noted:

Given the gaps in the available economic valuation data, the results presented in this report should be treated as conservative estimates. In other words, the ESV results presented here are likely to underestimate, not overestimate the actual ecosystem goods and services valued by society in the State of New Jersey. (Constanza et al. 2006, p. 26).

The problem of gaps causing undervaluation is exacerbated by the fact that Earth Economics (2015) focused on, and Cardno (2016) in turn only used, ESV estimates from Constanza et al (2006) that were related to terrestrial forests to value DSM ecological services. This reduced the pool of studies used to nine and usable ESV estimates to only five out of the twelve possible ESVs from forests identified by Constanza et al. Of these five, Earth Economics (2015) and Cardno (2016) relied on just three as applicable to DSM.[8]

There are two other reasons that Cardno (2016) and Earth Economics (2015) are likely to have undervalued DSM ecological services. First, the valuation numbers they quote are in hectares while the numbers that they rely on from Constanza et al (2006) are per acre. Second, Constanza et al. valuations are in 2004 dollars. This highlights the scope for simple errors that can creep into the ESV of DSM when using transfer values found in studies of other ecosystems, such as terrestrial forests.[9]

As noted, for PNG Cardno (2016) relied heavily on the transfer values from WTP studies of terrestrial forests. For Cook Islands, they instead relied heavily on a "replacement cost" estimate using habitat equivalency analysis (HEA) rather than WTP estimates. HEA uses "service replacement cost"; however, because it was not technically feasible to replace the services provided by the deep-seabed ecosystem "in

[7] For a more general discussion of transfer error in value transfer studies. See Atkinson et al (2018, Chapter 6).

[8] There were estimates for only five forest ESVs (42 per cent), and two of these related to the categories "aesthetic and recreational" and "gas and climate change", which appear less relevant to DSM ecosystems.

[9] However, even if transfer values were trebled to account for the error of not translating acres to hectares and to include inflation, there would still have been a positive net benefit from the PNG and Cook Island DSM projects, according to Cardno (2016).

place", the deep-seabed HEA used by Cardno (2016) relied on ratios that equated composite service provided by deep seabeds with composite service provided by wetlands.[10] Once again, then, this was a "transfer value" approach posing similar problems to using WTP transfer values (see Atkinson et al. 2018, Chapter 6).

The higher the risk or uncertainty, the higher the net benefit threshold for evaluating any DSM needs to be. We therefore now turn to discussing risk, uncertainty, and ignorance and how they affect decision-making.

Risk, uncertainty, ignorance, and reversibility

The state of knowledge on ESV impacts of DSM can be classified on many levels. For example Knight (1921, p. 103) distinguished between "risk" and "uncertainty":

- "Risk" arises where the probabilities of alternative possible outcomes are measurable (either through calculation a priori or from statistics based on experience).
- "Uncertainty" arises where the probabilities of alternative possible outcomes are not measurable. More recent literature has suggested a further subcategory here, "deep uncertainty" or "fundamental uncertainty", where the alternative possible outcomes themselves are not even known, let alone their probabilities (see Lempert et al. 2003; Walker et al. 2013).

In the "risk" category, costs and benefits can be forecast and then deterministic sensitivity analysis or risk propagation methods used to address uncertainties. These are the techniques Cardno (2016) used in the CBA of DSM in each EEZ. The report included a separate sensitivity analysis post-calculation to test the sensitivity of the net benefits to variations in discount rates. Monte Carlo simulation[11] was used to evaluate the sensitivity of outcomes to risk associated with the proportion of the minerals recovered, the composition of material recovered from the seabed, the proportion recovered from processing, capital and operating expenses, and mineral prices.[12]

Risk analysis, however, was not applied to ESV by Cardno (2016). This was because ESV fell more into Knight's uncertainty category outlined above. Such uncertainty arises from the fact of ignorance, and the necessity of acting upon opinion rather than knowledge (Knight, 1921, p. 120). This is clearly the situation facing the ISA in relation to environmental impacts of DSM projects. Whether the ISA is

[10] The HEA metric is generally discounted service acre years (DSAYs), where one service acre year (SAY) represents a composite measure of all of the ecosystem services flowing over the course of a year from one acre of the habitat. Cardno (2016) estimated the total loss in Cook Islands to be 445,857 deep-seabed DSAYs; that a loss of 445,857 deep-seabed DSAYs would be offset by the creation of 2,196 wetland DSAYs; and that the cost of creating 2,196 wetland DSAYs would be $24,928,000, based on NOAA et al (2002). See Cardno (2016, pp. 4–36 to 4–37).

[11] A problem-solving technique used to approximate the probability of certain outcomes by running multiple trial runs (simulations) where inputs are drawn from a distribution using random variables. In Cardno (2016), the probability distribution was formed by generating a mean or average value for each input and bounding the mean from above and below (i.e., generating a high-end and a low-end value). The determination of the high and low values was based either on extremes found in the literature, or on a $+/-$ 50 per cent deviation from the mean.

[12] The technique's application to the DSM analyses is discussed in Cardno (2016, Sect. 2.3.4).

deciding to approve or decline regulations governing DSM or approve or decline a particular project, it appears likely that at the moment it would have to act from a state of ignorance about the environmental impacts of its choices or based on opinions rather than knowledge.

The nature and amount of information available for modelling or forecasting is a key determinant of the state of knowledge supporting such CBA at any point in time. The main reason Cardno was not able to undertake a risk analysis on the environmental impacts of DSM was the lack of information available to conduct such an analysis. Thus, as we have already highlighted, our state of knowledge needs to be improved before we can conduct reliable risk-adjusted CBA of the environmental impacts of DSM.

The literature on the value of information highlights that the scale and timing of decisions are conditioned on the availability of new information. Value-of-information approaches such as "real options" (see, among others, Brennan and Schwartz 1985; Insley 2017; Mason, 2001; Slade 2001) can be used to provide assessments of risk, as well as to address more fundamental uncertainty. A key dimension of the problem is the degree to which DSM environmental impacts are reversible. To the extent that they are, and that the cost of reversing the harm is less than that of enduring it, then the cost of avoiding the harm, or "avoided cost", can be used to value the impact of the harm. However, at least some of DSM's environmental impacts could clearly be very costly to reverse or even irreversible. Cardno (2016), in fact, repeatedly claims that "it is not technically feasible to replace the services provided by the deep seabed ecosystem 'in place' (that is, it is not technically feasible to create or restore deep seabed habitat)" (Cardno 2016, p. 3–30). Instead, Cardno (2016) examined how the ecosystem services lost by DSM could be replaced by ecosystems other than the site being mined.

Where major costs of a decision are irreversible or very costly to reverse, a "wait-and-see" approach still leaves the option of implementing DSM open later. The value of this option needs to be included in any CBA comparison of the net expected value of a "go versus no-go" decision on DSM at a specific time. Incorporating the value of information lost when development is undertaken may justify a conservative approach or the adoption of the precautionary principle where there is a high level of uncertainty and high irreversible costs (see Gollier and Treich 2003).

However, the value of future information does not always justify delay. Where information flow is endogenous, or is revealed through undertaking DSM, it may pay to approve DSM early. For example, early but small-scale trials of DSM technology may reveal information about the environmental impacts of DSM that enable better decisions on whether to expand the activity. Endogenous reduction of uncertainties through trial—or "try and see"—could also justify earlier commencement of DSM to gather information about whether it can benefit humankind over time. Finally, even where information flow is exogenous and not related to the activity, the value of investing early may offset the cost of lost information (Dixit and Pindyck 1994).

In summary, real-options value modelling enables better evaluation of the timing (now or later) and scale (small or large) of projects in a rational evaluation framework. Real-option value theory does not, however, predetermine the optimal timing or scale of investments. The type of uncertainty or information available about the nature and value of parameters in the decision model determines decision-making about whether, when, and how to proceed.

E. **Regulatory budgets**

The costs of DSM clearly depend on DSM activity levels—including the extent or level of the mining or the area and level of extraction activity. The interdependence of ecological systems means that CBA which focuses solely on impacts in a local area or on the local "partial" equilibrium, may miss effects on other related ecosystems and, therefore, more general-equilibrium or system-wide effects. This counsels against simple partial-equilibrium CBA.

Given these wider interdependencies and the uncertainty and potential costs of DSM already outlined, an appropriate legal approach to regulating DSM might be to start with a budget limiting the total area and/or amount of DSM ("total minable budget"). The total minable budget would be set to minimize the potential adverse impact of DSM over time, and perhaps would initially be limited to enable only trials to test and help quantify effects.

The right to access the limited amount of DSM available could be auctioned subject to certain due diligence requirements covering the financial, environmental, and social conditions to be by tenderers. The allocated mining rights could also be transferable to other licensed DSM companies, creating a secondary market for mining rights, greater financial liquidity in the market, and a greater ability to bear the legal burden and obligations being imposed on companies.

F. **Environmental financial assurance**

It is recommended that the mining company also be required to provide environmental financial assurance (EFA) by posting a bond or providing other financial assurance that would guarantee that the costs of environmental clean-up can be met, thereby minimizing the adverse costs of the risk of bankruptcy of the company.[13] A mining company bankruptcy has already occurred during a DSM project at the PNG Solwara site, involving the collapse of Nautilus Minerals (Doherty 2019; see also Stutt 2019). The cost of clean-up obligations, and therefore the value of any EFA or bond, would be estimated preferably before the auction of any rights, or the EFA requirement would at least be made a condition of any auction, with clean-up costs to be estimated and a bond posted before mining starts. Mining companies would thus be subject to a legal duty to clean up the environment affected by the DSM when they are finished in any area. It is unlikely to be possible to restore the area to its condition prior to mining, but rather, perhaps it could be required to be restored to a condition where the natural environment may be most able to recover over time. A relevant competent authority would monitor compliance.

[13] See Aghakazemjourabbafa and Insley (2021) and literature cited therein. Using a real-options approach, this paper studies the impacts of an environmental bond, which fully covers waste clean-up costs, on a mining firm's optimal actions over the full lifecycle of a terrestrial mine, when bankruptcy may shift clean-up costs to the government.

G. **Fiscal approach**

One of the ISA's responsibilities is to "provide for the equitable sharing of financial and other economic benefits derived from activities in the Area" (UNCLOS, Article 140(2)). In this regard, the proceeds of the proposed auctioning of DSM rights (subject to a total budget) could be used to fund research into the impact of the mining activity and compensate those adversely affected by it.

The ISA also has the right to design and administer the financial terms of contracts between itself and sponsored entities. For DSM, there are three main requirements mandated by the UNCLOS and the 1994 Implementing Agreement:

1. Article 140 of UNCLOS states: "The Area and its resources are the Common Heritage of Mankind" (CHM) and that DSM "shall be carried out for the benefit of mankind as a whole". UNCLOS Article137 (2) clearly implies that the ISA has an obligation to ensure DSM mining in the area occurs only if it would release net benefits to humankind as a whole over time. In addition, any DSM payment regime must fairly compensate humankind for the loss of resources which are the CHM. To realize this goal, the ISA must balance the following objectives: "(a) to ensure optimum revenues for the Authority from the proceeds of commercial production; (b) to attract investments and technology to the exploration and exploitation of the Area". This means any payment regime should generate as much revenue as possible for the ISA, subject to the need to attract investment.
2. Section 8(1)(b) of the Annex to the Implementation Agreement states: "The rates of payments under the system shall be within the range of those prevailing in respect of land-based mining of the same or similar minerals in order to avoid giving deep-seabed miners an artificial competitive advantage or imposing on them a competitive disadvantage". This is understood to mean that any DSM payment regime must not give, through a lower burden of taxation, a competitive economic advantage to DSM compared with land-based mining.
3. In addition to not disadvantaging land-based mining, any DSM payment regime must also generate sufficient revenues to compensate developing countries for any economic harm to their land-based mining sectors that can be attributed to DSM (see Article 151(10) of UNCLOS).

H. **Mining trials**

In October 2022, TMC, with its partner Allseas, lowered an 80-tonne robotic "collector" to the ocean floor in exploration trials. Fitted with tracks, the vehicle rolled along the seabed sucking up nodules and everything else in its path. The robotic collector vehicle stirred up sediment, creating large plumes, before the nodules travelled up a 4.5 km riser to the surface.

Allseas retrofitted a former deepwater drill ship—renamed *The Hidden Gem*—to undertake the trials. To obtain 3200 tonnes of rock, TMC was to vacuum the bottom of the sea in two parcels in the Clarion Clipperton Zone (CCZ), an area of 4.5 million square kilometres in the Pacific Ocean part-way between Mexico and Hawaii. There are potentially large profits in the CCZ, one of the richest areas for nodules in the world's oceans. However, this ecosystem took millions of years to form and has been untouched by human activity, and it may equally take millions of years for the ecosystem to come back.

More than 700 marine scientists and policy experts signed an open letter in 2021 stating: "we strongly recommend that the transition to the exploitation of mineral resources be paused".[14] The European Academies' Science Advisory Council has echoed the warning (EASAC 2023, p. 21).

In May 2023, scientists at the Natural History Museum in London released a database of new species discovered in the CCZ, including 5000 that had never before been formally identified, such as a mauve-coloured creature nicknamed "gummy squirrel". (Rabone Wiethase et al. 2023a, b; Rabone Horton et al. 2023). In a statement, museum researcher Adrian Glover (see Jones 2023) said, "It is imperative that we work with the companies looking to mine these resources to ensure any such activity is done in a way that limits its impact upon the natural world". He stated that TMC had spent $150 million so far on scientific research and assessing the environmental impact (Jones, 2023).

I. **Scientific information and transparency of process**

The use of "big data" is an important way to gain information on both mining activity and biodiversity impact. Due to the large size of streaming data, incorporating information from satellites, buoys, and ships, the system could be built on a cloud distribution platform using wireless communications networks between vessels and ports, as has been suggested for the use of big data in optimizing Arctic shipping routes in environments that are changing owing to climate change (Xu and Crabbe 2024; Zhang and Crabbe 2021).

Mining 500,000 km^2 (193,000 m^2) of the CCZ would impact an area three times larger than the combined area of Spain, Portugal, France, Belgium, and Germany—with associated noise and sediment plumes. Should we forge ahead with DSM in the midst of the climate crisis rather than look for alternative materials to build renewable energy technologies? Are we not, in trying to solve one problem, creating another new one? The next set of ISA meetings in 2024 will be critical in determining the direction of DSM.

One advance is that during its twenty-seventh Council session, the ISA decided to advance the development of environmental thresholds (ISBA/27/C/42) as binding standards and as part of the standards and guidelines being developed to support the development of draft regulations for the development of mineral resources in the Area (ISA 2022). The development of these environmental thresholds will be led by the Legal and Technical Commission of the ISA, supported by the scientific and technical expertise of the Intersessional Group of Experts. During the twenty-eighth session of the ISA, the Legal and Technical Commission considered the decisions and comments of the Council and developed and revised terms of reference for the establishment and operation of the Intersessional Group of Experts.

[14] Available at https://seabedminingsciencestatement.org (accessed: 11 February 2024).

This group will consist of three subgroups, namely: (i) the Toxicity Expert Group; (ii) the Expert Group on Turbidity and Sedimentation of Resuspended Sediments; and (iii) the Underwater Noise and Light Pollution Expert Group. Each will consist of a maximum of ten experts, selected primarily on the basis of scientific and technical expertise and experience, taking into account geographical representation and gender balance.

The objectives of each group include to:

1. synthesize and review existing information on environmental thresholds, potentially including:
   a. existing scientific literature and relevant baseline data (including natural variability of measured parameters), as well as guidance documents developed by national and international bodies
   b. available proxy information and experimental data on DSM-related activities (e.g., field testing of mining components)
   c. ecological analogues and assessment of their suitability to potentially affected species
   d. existing thresholds and experiences in other industries (e.g., shipping, oil and gas, dredging, and fisheries)
2. identify appropriate indicators to define threshold indicators;
3. define threshold levels, including early-warning thresholds; in doing so, expert groups may also consider, as appropriate, a range of threshold levels that should include uncertainties and confidence levels;
4. assess key knowledge gaps related to threshold determination and recommend future work needed.

The work of the intersessional expert group will focus on thresholds for polymetallic nodules, but it is expected that thresholds for cobalt-rich ferromanganese crusts and polymetallic sulphides resources will also be developed. The group will prepare a report as soon as possible for consideration by the Commissioners, which will be posted on the ISA website.

10.4 Policy Implications and Conclusions

For coastal waters and the coral reefs of PICTs, marine protection areas (MPAs) are one of the few management tools that governments and local communities can use to combat large-scale environmental impacts. These areas need to be no-take, well enforced, old (> 10 years), large (> 100 km^2), and isolated from each other by deep water or sand (see Crabbe 2019; Hall et al. 2023). However, success in saving coral reefs ultimately depends on the global community meeting or exceeding the science-based targets agreed to in Paris in December 2015 (see also Morgan et al. 2017). This will need more severe restrictions on fossil fuel burning than have currently been agreed internationally up to 2024.

To ensure that DSM in international waters is carried out for the benefit of humankind as a whole over time, the ISA needs to identify the net benefit to humankind as a whole over time from DSM. This can be achieved only through a full CBA of both regulatory and contractual arrangements governing DSM applications.

This chapter has focused on two critical issues thus facing the ISA: first, how to value the services to humankind provided by deep-sea ecosystems; second, the degree of uncertainty surrounding deep-seabed ESVs and how best to address it. Currently, there appear to be no detailed direct measures of the value of deep-sea ecosystem services. Instead, ESVs from terrestrial ecosystems have been used or transferred to value deep seabeds. On the assumption that deep-sea ecosystems are low-productivity, the transfer values used have been from low-productivity terrestrial ecosystems. However, we have explored in detail the transfer values used in the only major CBA study to date and concluded that they are unreliable. This lack of reliability is a general problem with transfer studies (Atkinson et al. 2018). Given the current high levels of uncertainty on ESV, and the irreversibility of any environmental damage, we recommend that the ISA adopt a real-options value approach to CBA. This supports a wait-and-see approach to allow more information to be obtained. To obtain the information required to reduce uncertainty, we recommend, in the meantime, proceeding with a limited number of mining trials with pure research objectives—what we call a "trial and see" approach.

We also recommend using regulatory budgets that cap total mining activity at a point where total net benefits are most likely to be maximized. In the initial period until more information is gathered, these budgets should limit activity to mining trials only. Ultimately, we further recommend the ISA use of auctions to award mining rights, with the revenue from such auctions being used to fund research, including ongoing mining trials; the monitoring and enforcement of standards, regulations and contract terms by the ISA; and the compensation of those harmed by loss of ecosystem services. We also recommend use of environmental financial assurance (EFA) to cover the costs of clean-up—as a prior condition of awarding a mining licence—common in terrestrial mining.

References

Aeby GS, Williams GJ, Franklin EC, Kenyon J, Cox EF, Coles S, Work TM (2011) Patterns of coral disease across the Hawaiian archipelago: relating disease to environment. PLoS ONE 6(5):e20370

Aeby GS, Howells E, Work T, Abrego D, Williams GJ, Wedding LM, Caldwell JM, Moritsch M, Burt JA (2020) Localized outbreaks of coral disease on Arabian reefs are linked to extreme temperatures and environmental stressors. Coral Reefs 39(3):829–846

Aghakazemjourabbafa S, Insley M (2021) Leaving your tailings behind: environmental bonds, bankruptcy and waste cleanup. Resour Energy Econ 65(C):101246

Amon DJ, Gollner S, Morato T, Smith CR, Chen C, Christiansen S, Currie B, Drazen JC, Fukushima T, Gianni M, Gjerde KM, Gooday AJ, Grillo GG, Haeckel M, Joyini T, Ju S-J, Levin LA, Metaxas A, Mianowicz K, Molodtsova TN, Narberhaus I, Orcutt BN, Swaddling A, Tuhumwire J, Palacio PU, Walker M, Weaver P, Xu X-W, Mulalap CY, Edwards PET, Pickens C (2022) Assessment

of scientific gaps related to the effective environmental management of deep-seabed mining. Mar Policy 138:105006
Anthony KRN, Marshall PA, Abdulla A, Beeden R, Bergh C, Black R, Eakin M, Game E, Gooch M, Graham NAJ, Green A, Heron SF, van Hooidonk R, Knowland C, Mangubhai S, Marshall N, Maynard JA, McGinnity P, Mcleod E, Mumby PJ, Nyström M, Obura D, Oliver J, Possingham HP, Pressey R, Rowlands G, Tamelander J, Wachenfeld D, Wear S (2015) Operationalizing resilience for adaptive coral reef management under global environmental change. Glob Change Biol 21(1):48–61
Atkinson G, Braathen NA, Groom B, Mourato S (2018) Cost benefit analysis and the environment: further developments and policy use. OECD, Paris
Blanchard C, Harrould-Kolieb E, Jones E, Taylor ML (2023) The current status of deep-sea mining governance at the International Seabed Authority. Mar Policy 147:105396
Bourne DG, Ainsworth TD, Pollock FJ, Willis BL (2015) Towards a better understanding of white syndromes and their causes on Indo-Pacific coral reefs. Coral Reefs 34(1):233–242
Brennan MJ, Schwartz ES (1985) Evaluating natural resource investments. J Bus 58(2):135–157
Commission B (1987) Our common future: report of the world commission on environment and development. Oxford University Press, Oxford
Cardno (2016) An assessment of the costs and benefits of mining deepsea minerals in the Pacific island region: deep-sea mining cost–benefit analysis. Pacific Community, Suva
CBD (Convention on Biological Diversity) (2010) Decision adopted by the conference of the parties to the convention on biological diversity at its tenth meeting: X/2 The strategic plan for biodiversity 2011–2020 and the Aichi biodiversity targets. Nagoya, 18–29 Oct 2010
Chen CC, Bourne DG, Drovandi CC, Mengersen K, Willis BL, Caley MJ, Sato Y (2017) Modelling environmental drivers of black band disease outbreaks in populations of foliose corals in the genus Montipora. PeerJ: Life Environ 5:e3438
Childs J (2018) 'Extraction in four dimensions: time, space and the emerging geo politics of deep-sea mining. Geopolitics 25(1):189–213
CITES (Convention on International Trade in Endangered Species of Wild Fauna and Flora) (2020) CITES Trade Database (Online). Available at: https://trade.cites.org. Accessed 2 Nov 2020
Clark MR, Durden JM, Christiansen S (2020) Environmental impact assessments for deep-sea mining: can we improve their future effectiveness? Mar Policy 114:103363
Comeros-Raynal MT, Brodie J, Bainbridge Z, Choat JH, Curtis M, Lewis S, Stevens T, Shuler CK, Sudek M, Hoey AS (2021) Catchment of sea connection: impacts of terrestrial run-off on benthic ecosystems in American Samoa. Mar Pollut Bull 169:112530
Constanza R, Wilson M, Troy A, Voinov A, Liu S, D'Agostino J (2006) The value of New Jersey's ecosystem services and natural capital. New Jersey Department of Environmental Protection, Trenton, NJ
Cordier T, Angeles IB, Henry N, Lejzerowicz F, Berney C, Morard R, Brandt A, Cambon-Bonavita M-A, Guidi L, Lombardi F, Martinez Arbizu P, Massana R, Orejas C, Poulain J, Smith CR, Wincker P, Arnaud-Haond S, Gooday AJ, De Vargas C, Pawlowski J (2022) Patterns of eukaryotic diversity from the surface to the deep-ocean sediment. Sci Adv 8(5):eabj9309
Crabbe MJC (2019) Adapting to extreme environments: can coral reefs adapt to climate change? Emerging Topics Life Sci 3:183–195
Crabbe MJC (2022) Deep sea mining for renewable technologies: a case study for using big data. Int J Big Data Min Glob Warming 4:2272001
Crépin AS, Biggs R, Polasky S, Troell M, de Zeeuw A (2012) Regime shifts and management. Ecol Econ 84(1):15–22
De'ath G, Fabricius KE, Sweatman H, Puotinen M (2012) The 27-year decline of coral cover on the Great Barrier Reef and its causes. Proc Natl Acad Sci 109(44):17995–17999
Dixit AK, Pindyck RS (1994) Investment under uncertainty. Princeton University Press, Princeton, NJ
Doherty B (2019) Collapse of PNG deep-sea mining venture sparks call for moratorium. Guardian

Eakin CM, Sweatman HPA, Brainard RE (2019) The 2014–2017 global-scale coral bleaching event: insights and impacts. Coral Reefs 38(4):539–545
Earth Economics (2015) Environmental and social benchmarking analysis of Nautilus Minerals Inc. Solwara 1 Project. Earth Economics, Tacoma, WA
EASAC (European Academies Science Advisory Council) (2023) Leading scientists urge moratorium on deep-sea mining: explore recycling and terrestrial resources first (Online). Available at: https://easac.eu/news/details/deep-sea-mining-press-release. Accessed 28 Dec 2023
Erftemeijer PL, Riegl B, Hoeksema BW, Todd PA (2012) Environmental impacts of dredging and other sediment disturbances on corals: a review. Mar Pollut Bull 64(9):1737–1765
Figueiredo C, Caetano M, Mil-Homens M, Tojeira I, Xavier JR, Rosa R, Raimundi J (2021) Rare earth and trace elements in deep-sea sponges of the North Atlantic. Mar Pollut Bull 166(7–8):112217
Gollier C, Treich N (2003) Decision-making under scientific uncertainty: the economics of the precautionary principle. J Risk Uncertain 27(1):77–103
Haapkylä J, Melbourne-Thomas J, Flavell M, Willis BL (2013) Disease outbreaks, bleaching and a cyclone drive changes in coral assemblages on an inshore reef of the Great Barrier Reef. Coral Reefs 32(3):815–824
Hall AE, Sievers KT, Kingsford MJ (2023) Conservation benefits of no-take marine reserves outweigh modest benefits of partially protected areas for targeted coral reef fishes. Coral Reefs 42:319–333
Heffernan O (2019) Deep-sea dilemma. Nature 571(7766):464–469
Hein JR, Koschinsky A, Kuhn T (2020) Deep-ocean polymetallic nodules as a resource for critical materials. Nature Rev Earth Environ 1:158–169
Hoegh-Guldberg O, Kennedy EV, Beyer HL, McClennen C, Possingham HP (2018) Securing a long-term future for coral reefs. Trends Ecol Evol 33(12):936–944
Hughes TP, Anderson KD, Connolly SR, Heron SF, Kerry JT, Lough JM, Baird AH, Baum JK, Berumen ML, Bridge TC, Claar DC, Eakin CM, Gilmour JP, Graham NAJ, Harrison H, Hobbs JPA, Hoey AS, Hoogenboom M, Lowe RJ, McCulloch MT, Pandolfi JM, Pratchett M, Schoepf V, Torda G, Wilson SK (2018) Spatial and temporal patterns of mass bleaching of corals in the anthropocene. Science 359(6371):80–83
Hughes TP, Kerry JT, Baird AH, Connolly SR, Chase TJ, Dietzel A, Hill T, Hoey AS, Hoogenboom MO, Jacobson M, Kerswell A, Madin JS, Mieog A, Paley AS, Pratchett MS, Torda G, Woods RM (2019) Global warming impairs stock–recruitment dynamics of corals. Nature 568(7752):387–390
Insley M (2017) Resource extraction with a carbon tax and regime switching prices: exercising your options. Energy Econ 67(C):1–16
IPCC (Intergovernmental Panel on Climate Change) (2018) Special report on the impacts of global warming of 1.5 °C: a summary for policymakers. IPCC Secretariat, Geneva
ISA (International Seabed Authority) (2022) The 27th session of the international seabed authority (Online). Available at: www.isa.org.jm/sessions/27th-session-20222. Accessed 14 Feb 2024
IUCN (International Union for the Conservation of Nature) (2016) IUCN resolutions, recommendations and other decisions. IUCN, Gland
Jacobson DM (2006) Fine scale temporal and spatial dynamics of a Marshall Islands coral disease outbreak: evidence for temperature forcing. EOS Trans Am Geophys Union 87(36):suppl
Jones DOB, Simon-Lledó E, Amon DJ, Bett BJ, Caulle C, Clément L, Connelly DP, Dahlgren TG, Durden JM, Drazen JC, Felden J, Gates AR, Georgieva MN, Glover AG, Gooday AJ, Hollingsworth AL, Horton T, James RH, Jeffreys RM, Laguionie-Marchaise C, Leitner AB, Lichtschlag A, Menendez A, Paterson GLJ, Peel K, Robert K, Schoening T, Shulga NA, Smith CR, Taboada S, Thurnherr AM, Wiklund H, Young CR, Huvenne VAI (2021) Environment, ecology, and potential effectiveness of an area protected from deep-sea mining (Clarion Clipperton Zone, abyssal Pacific). Prog Oceanogr 197:102653

Jones F (2023) Nearly 200 unique species are at risk from deep sea mining. Mining Technol. (Online). Available at: www.mining-technology.com/news/nealr-200-unique-species-are-at-risk-from-deep-sea-mining/?cf-view. Accessed 6 Jan 2024

Kensington N (2019) An assessment of the population of crown-of-thorns starfish (Acanthaster planci L.) around the island of Malapascua, Republic of the Philippines. M.Sc. thesis, The University of Dublin

Klesty V (2023) Norway parliament deal marks major step towards seabed mining. Reuters 5 Dec (Online). Available at: www.reuters.com/world/europe/norway-parliament-deal-advance-seabed-mining-2023-12-05. Accessed 14 Jan 2024

Knight FH (1921) Risk, uncertainty, and profit. Houghton Mifflin Company, Boston, MA

Krutilla K, Good D, Toman M, Arin T (2021) Addressing fundamental uncertainty in benefit–cost analysis: the case of deep seabed mining. J Benefit-Cost Anal 12(1):122–151

Kung A, Scobodova K, Lèbre E, Valenta R, Kemp D, Owen JR (2021) Governing deep sea mining in the face of uncertainty. J Environ Manage 279:111593

Lamb JB, Willis BL, Fiorenza EA, Couch CS, Howard R, Rader DN, True JD, Kelly LA, Ahmad A, Jompa J, Harvell CD (2018) Plastic waste associated with disease on coral reefs. Science 359(6374):460–462

Lempert RJ, Popper SW, Bankes SC (2003) Shaping the next one hundred years: new methods for quantitative, long-term policy analysis. RAND, Santa Monica, CA

Li B, Liang W, Liu Q-X, Fu S, Ma C, Chen Q, Su L, Craig NJ, Shi H (2021) Fish ingest microplastics unintentionally. Environ Sci Technol 55:10471–10479

Liew JH, Kho ZY, Lim RBH, Dingle C, Bonebrake TC, Sung YH, Dudgeon D (2021) International socioeconomic inequality drives trade patterns in the global wildlife market. Sci Adv 7(19):eabf7679

Mason CF (2001) Nonrenewable resources with switching costs. J Environ Econ Manag 42(1):65–81

Maire E, Cinner JE, Velez L, Huchery C, Mora C, Dagata S, Vigliola L, Wantiez L, Kulbicki M, Mouillot D (2016) How accessible are coral reefs to people? A global assessment based on travel time. Ecol Lett 19(4):351–360

Maynard J, Van Hooidonk R, Eakin CM, Puotinen M, Garren M, Williams G, Heron SF, Lamb J, Weil E, Willis B, Harvell CD (2015) Projections of climate conditions that increase coral disease susceptibility and pathogen abundance and virulence. Nat Clim Chang 5(7):688–694

McClanahan TR, Maina J (2003) Response of coral assemblages to the interaction between natural temperature variation and rare warm-water events. Ecosystems 6(6):551–563

McIlgorm A, Campbell HF, Rule MJ (2008) Understanding the economic benefits and costs of controlling marine debris in the APEC region. University of New England and Southern Cross University, Coffs Harbour

The Metals Company (2023) The metals company (Online). Available at: https://metals.co. Accessed 26 Dec 2023

Milinovic J, Rodrigues FJL, Barriga FJAS, Murton BJ (2021) Ocean-floor sediments as a resource of rare earth elements: an overview of recently studied sites. Minerals 11(2):142

Miller AW, Richardson LL (2015) Emerging coral diseases: a temperature-driven process? Mar Ecol 36(3):278–291

Morgan MG, Vaishnav P, Dowlatabadi H, Azevedo IL (2017) Rethinking the social cost of carbon dioxide. Issues Sci Technol 33(4):43–50

Muir PR, Marshall PA, Abdulla A, Aguirre JD (2017) 'Species identity and depth predict bleaching severity in reef-building corals: shall the deep inherit the reef?' Proc Roy Soc B: Biol Sci 284(1864):20171551

NOAA, MDNR, MDE, USFWS (2002) Final restoration plan and environmental assessment for the April 7, 2000 oil spill at chalk point on the Patuxent River, Maryland (Online). Available at: www.gc.noaa.gov/gc-rp/cp2107.pdf. Accessed 11 Feb 2024

Orcutt BN, Bradley JA, Brazelton WJ, Estes ER, Goordial JM, Huber JA, Jones RM, Mahmoudi N, Marlow JJ, Murdock S, Pachiadaki M (2020) Impacts of deep-sea mining on microbial ecosystem services. Limnol Oceanogr 65(7):1489–1510

Pandolfi JM, Connolly SR, Marshall DJ, Cohen AL (2011) Projecting coral reef futures under global warming and ocean acidification. Science 333(6041):418–423
Perrings C, Folke C, Mäler KG (1992) The ecology and economics of biodiversity loss: the research agenda. Ambio 21(3):201–211
Pollock FJ, Lamb JB, Field SN, Heron SF, Schaffelke B, Shedrawi G, Bourne DG, Willis BL (2014) Sediment and turbidity associated with offshore dredging increase coral disease prevalence on nearby reefs. PLoS ONE 9(7):e102498
Pratchett MS, Caballes CF, Rivera-Posada JA, Sweatman HPA (2014) Limits to understanding and managing outbreaks of crown-of-thorns starfish (Acanthaster spp.). Oceanogr Mar Biol 52:133–199
Puotinen M, Drost E, Lowe R, Depczynski M, Radford B, Heyward A, Gilmour J (2020) Towards modelling the future risk of cyclone wave damage to the world's coral reefs. Glob Change Biol 26(8):4302–4315
Rabone M, Horton T, Jones DOB, Simon-Ledo E, Glover AG (2023) A review of the international seabed authority database deepdata from a biological perspective: challenges and opportunities in the UN Ocean Decade. Database baad013
Rabone M, Wiethase JJ, Simon-Lido E, Emery AM, Jones DOB, Dahlgren TG, Bribiesca-Contreras G, Wiklund H, Horton T, Glover AB (2023b) How many metazoan species live in the world's largest mineral exploration region? Curr Biol 33(12):2383–2396
Revesz RL, Livermore M (2008) Retaking rationality: how cost–benefit analysis can better protect the environment and our health. Oxford University Press, New York
Revesz RL, Livermore M (2013) Globalisation of cost–benefit analysis in environmental policy. Oxford University Press, New York
Ruiz-Moreno D, Willis BL, Page AC, Weil E, Cróquer A, Vargas-Ángel B, Jordan-Garza AG, Jordán-Dahlgren E, Raymundo L, Harvell CD (2012) Global coral disease prevalence associated with sea temperature anomalies and local factors. Dis Aquat Org 100(3):249–261
Scoffin TP, Tudhope AW, Brown BE, Chansang H, Cheeney RF (1992) Patterns and possible environmental controls of skeletogenesis of Porites lutea, South Thailand. Coral Reefs 11(1):1–11
Skirving WJ, Heron SF, Marsh BL, Liu G, De La Cour JL, Geiger EF, Eakin CM (2019) The relentless march of mass coral bleaching: a global perspective of changing heat stress. Coral Reefs 38(4):547–557
Slade ME (2001) Valuing managerial flexibility: an application of real-option theory to mining investments. J Environ Econ Manag 41(2):193–233
SPREP (Secretariat of the Pacific Regional Environment Programme) (2018) Pacific marine action plan: marine litter 2018–2025. SPREP, Apia
Stutt A (2019) Nautilus Minerals officially sinks, shares still trading (Online). Available at: www.mining.com/nautilus-minerals-officially-sinks-shares-still-trading. Accessed: 11 Feb 2024
Sussman M, Willis BL, Victor S, Bourne DG (2008) Coral pathogens identified for white syndrome (WS) epizootics in the Indo-Pacific. PLoS ONE 3(6):e2393
Sutherland KP, Porter JW, Torres C (2004) Disease and immunity in Caribbean and Indo-Pacific zooxanthellate corals. Mar Ecol Prog Ser 266:273–302
Symons A (2023) 'Deep sea mining: here's which countries oppose and support the controversial practice', Euronews, 2 October (Online). Available at: www.euronews.com/green/2023/08/02/deep-sea-mining-heres-which-countries-oppose-and-support-the-controversial-practice. Accessed 26 Dec 2023
UNDESA (United Nations Department of Economic and Social Affairs) (2015) World population prospects: key findings and advance tables. United Nations, New York (Online). Available at: https://population.un.org/wpp/Publications/Files/Key_Findings_WPP_2015.pdf. Accessed 11 Feb 2024
UNEP (United Nations Environment Programme) (2005) Marine litter: an analytical overview. UNEP, Nairobi
UNEP (2009) Marine litter: a global challenge. UNEP, Nairobi

UNEP-WCMC (UNEP World Conservation Monitoring Centre) (2020) Speciesplus.net (Online). Available at: https://speciesplus.net/#/taxonconcepts/5595/legal. Accessed 26 Nov 2020
United Nations (1982) United Nations Convention on the Law of the Sea [Online]. www.un.org/depts/los/convention_agreements/texts/unclos/unclos_e.pdf. . Accessed 11 Feb 2024
Vargas-Ángel B, Huntington B, Brainard RE, Venegas R, Oliver T, Barkley H, Cohen A (2019) El Niño-associated catastrophic coral mortality at Jarvis Island, central Equatorial Pacific. Coral Reefs 38(6371):731–741
Vega Thurber RL, Burkepile DE, Fuchs C, Shantz AA, McMinds R, Zaneveld JR (2014) Chronic nutrient enrichment increases prevalence and severity of coral disease and bleaching. Glob Change Biol 20(2):544–554
Vercelloni J, Liquet B, Kennedy EV, González-Rivero M, Caley MJ, Peterson EE, Puotinen M, Hoegh-Guldberg O, Mengersen K (2020) Forecasting intensifying disturbance effects on coral reefs. Glob Change Biol 26(5):2785–2797
Vonnahme TR, Molari M, Janssen F, Wenzhöfer F, Haeckel M, Titschack J, Boetius A (2020) Effects of a deep-sea mining experiment on seafloor microbial communities and functions after 26 years. Sci Adv 6(18):eaaz5922
Wakefield JR, Myers K (2018) Social cost benefit analysis for deep sea minerals mining. Mar Policy 95:346–355
Walker WE, Lempert RJ, Kwakkel JH (2013) Deep uncertainty. In: Gass SI, Fu MC (eds) Encyclopedia of operations research and management science. Springer, Cham, pp 395–402
Wang C, Chang Y-C (2020) A new interpretation of the common heritage of mankind in the context of the international law of the sea. Ocean Coast Manag 191:105191
Weil E, Smith G, Gil-Agudelo DL (2006) Status and progress in coral reef disease research. Dis Aquat Org 69(1):1–7
Willis B, Page C, Dinsdale E (2004) Coral disease on the Great Barrier Reef. In: Rosenber E, Loya Y (eds) Coral health and disease. Springer, Berlin, pp 69–104
Xu L, Crabbe MJC (2024) Leading modes and feature zones of sea ice concentration in the North Pacific during spring seasons of 2000–2020. Int J Big Data Min Glob Warming 5:2350005
Zhang Z, Crabbe MJC (2021) Management of environmental streaming data to optimize Arctic shipping routes under climate change scenario. Arab J Geosci 14(15):1441

Chapter 11
The Present and Future of Micronesian Mangrove Forests in the Context of Rising Sea Levels

Kiyoshi Fujimoto, Shin Watanabe, Kenji Ono, and Keita Furukawa

Abstract In recent years, sea levels in the low latitudes of the north-western Pacific, including Micronesia, have risen much faster than the global mean. As a result, some mangrove communities on Pohnpei Island have already been visibly affected by surface erosion. On the other hand, *Rhizophora* communities, characterized by their prop roots, have barely maintained their habitat by producing and accumulating mangrove peat by themselves. Analysis of satellite imagery for Pohnpei, Kosrae, Chuuk and Yap shows no evidence thus far of simultaneous retreat of seaward forest margins or standing dead in surface erosion areas, but coastal erosion is already underway at some wave-sensitive sites. At the moderate rate of sea level rise predicted by the Intergovernmental Panel on Climate Change (IPCC) (approximately five millimetres per year), *Rhizophora* forests are likely to maintain their habitat. It is necessary to continue to monitor forest dynamics and to aggressively plant *Rhizophora* species on sites that have become bare land due to logging or trees being downed by typhoons.

K. Fujimoto (✉)
Nanzan University, Nagoya, Japan
e-mail: kfuji@nanzan-u.ac.jp

S. Watanabe
Tropical Biosphere Research Center, University of the Ryukyus, Taketomi, Japan
e-mail: nabeshin@lab.u-ryukyu.ac.jp

K. Ono
Tohoku Research Center, Forestry and Forest Products Research Institute, Morioka, Japan
e-mail: don@ffpri.affrc.go.jp

K. Furukawa
Association for Shore Environment Creation, Yokohama, Japan
e-mail: keita@meic.jp

E. Monaco and M. Abe (eds.), *Sustainable Development Across Pacific Islands*,
https://doi.org/10.1007/978-981-97-3629-4_11

11.1 Introduction

Mangrove forests are formed in the intertidal zone, which is the boundary between land and sea, and thus nurture a diverse ecosystem where land and sea creatures intermingle. This diverse ecosystem has been an important place for people living in the coastal zone to obtain various benefits essential to their daily lives, such as food, fuel-wood, and building materials. However, areas of mangrove forests have been rapidly decreasing worldwide in recent years due to development such as shrimp pond construction (FAO 2007). Under such situations, the mangrove forests in Federated States of Micronesia (FSM) are precious because they have maintained their environment as forests without being swallowed up by expanding development, although they have been somewhat affected by logging by the local people for daily use. However, they are in danger of extinction due to sea level rise caused by global warming, the rate of which has been steadily increasing in recent years.

According to the Intergovernmental Panel on Climate Change (IPCC)'s Sixth Assessment Report, the global mean rate of sea level rise was 1.73 mm per year over the long period of 1901–2018, but it was 2.33 mm per year between 1971 and 2018, 3.25 mm per year between 1993 and 2018, and 3.69 mm per year between 2006 and 2018, indicating an accelerating trend in recent years (IPCC 2021). The Fifth Assessment Report reported that sea level rose at a rate exceeding 10 mm per year during 1993–2012 in the low latitudes of the north-western Pacific Ocean from the Philippines to Micronesia (IPCC 2013).

Since 1994, the authors have conducted a long-term monitoring study of forest dynamics on Pohnpei Island, FSM, by establishing several fixed plots to evaluate the carbon storage ability of mangrove forests and to detect the effects of sea level rise (Fujimoto et al. 1995, 2013, 2023a; Nishino et al. 2015). In this chapter, we first extract the characteristics of mangrove forest dynamics in the four Micronesian islands—Pohnpei, Kosrae, Chuuk, and Yap—over the last 20 years using Google Earth satellite images. Next, we discuss the relationship between the forest dynamics found in satellite imagery and sea level rise, based on phenomena found in our long-term monitoring and multi-point surveys that may be the effects of sea level rise in mangrove forests. Based on these findings, we also predict possible future impacts on mangrove forests and make recommendations for mangrove forest management policies under sea level rise.

11.2 Mangroves in Micronesia

This section outlines the mangrove species distributed in Micronesia, the characteristics of mangrove habitats, and the current status of mangrove forests.

11.2.1 Mangrove Species and Communities

The area of mangrove forests in the four FSM states is estimated to be the largest on Pohnpei (5525 ha), followed by Kosrae (1562 ha), Yap (1117 ha), and Chuuk (306 ha) (MacLean et al. 1988). Eight true mangrove species, *Rhizophora stylosa, Rhizophora mucronata, Rhizophora apiculata, Sonneratia alba, Bruguiera gymnorrhiza, Xylocarpus granatum, Lumnitzera racemose*, and *Nypa fruticans*, are commonly distributed on the four islands. *Avicennia marina* and *Ceriops decandra* are found only on Yap, the westernmost part of FSM (Chapman 1976; Spalding et al. 2010). *R. stylosa* and *R. mucronata* are morphologically similar, and hybrids exist, so identification in the field is not easy (Mantiquilla et al. 2021). Therefore, most papers on Micronesian mangroves have described the two species together under the name of just one of the two. In this chapter, *R. stylosa* is used.

In Pohnpei, which has the largest distribution area, the major species are *R. stylosa, R. apiculata, S. alba, B. gymnorrhiza*, and *X. granatum* (Fujimoto et al. 2023b). In general, *R. stylosa* appears as a pioneer community on the seaward front, with a mixed community of *R. apiculata* and *B. gymnorrhiza* behind it, as well as *X. granatum* in addition to these on the most inland side (Fujimoto et al. 2015). *S. alba* occasionally forms pure forests in the forefront as pioneer communities (Fujimoto et al. 2015), but large-diameter trees (of more than one metre in diameter) are widely scattered throughout the forest (Fujimoto et al. 1995).

11.2.2 Geomorphological Setting of Mangrove Habitats and Sediments

Mangrove habitats can be classified into three types based on their geomorphological situations: delta/estuary type, located near the river mouths; back marsh/lagoon type, located in back marshes or lagoons behind coastal barriers, such as sandbars and beach ridges; and tidal flat/coral reef type, located on tidal flats and coral reefs where there is no river inflow (Miyagi 1993). Most of the mangrove forests in Micronesia are coral reef types, which are established on reef flats. A few estuarine types are found near the mouths of small rivers on Pohnpei (Fujimoto et al. 1995). On Kosrae, there are also small delta and back marsh/lagoon types (Fujimoto et al. 1996). The estuary type can also be seen on Yap via Google Earth satellite imagery.

Coral reef and back marsh/lagoon types have little sediment inflow from rivers, so the sediments are composed of mangrove peat (Fujimoto et al. 1995, 1999a, b, 2015). Mangrove peat has a primary matrix of very fine roots that are less than 0.5 mm in diameter (Ono et al. 2015, 2022), and more fibrous peat can be identified in *Rhizophora* communities (Fujimoto et al. 1999a, b; Ono et al. 2022). The thickness of mangrove peat layers in Micronesia generally reaches approximately two metres in coral-reef-type habitats (Fujimoto and Miyagi 1993; Fujimoto et al. 1996). Most mangrove peat layers on Chuuk are reported to be less than 50 cm thick, with a maximum thickness of 80 cm (Miyagi and Fujimoto 1989), but our field survey in 2003 identified mangrove peat with a layer thickness of 165 cm on Tol island. On Pohnpei, estuary-type habitats also consist of peaty sediments, but the amount of mixed-in inorganic matter is slightly higher, and the carbon content is lower, than in coral-reef-type habitats (Fujimoto et al. 1999a, b). The delta/estuary-type habitats on Kosrae also consist of mangrove peat in the present mangrove forest area, while the sediments of the *Nypa* and freshwater swamp forests in the interior consist of clayey sediments, with mangrove peat underlying the clay layers (Fujimoto et al. 1996).

Mangrove habitats consisting of mangrove peat are dependent on the productivity of the mangrove peat for their formation and maintenance, as little sediment flows in from the outside. In such habitats, mangrove forests have survived sea level rise by increasing the ground elevation, by producing and accumulating mangrove peat by themselves (Fujimoto and Miyagi 1993; Fujimoto et al. 1996). However, there are limits to this ability. No mangrove peat deposited during the early Holocene, when sea level rose more than 10 mm per year, has been found in any region of the world (Ellison and Stoddart 1991; Parkinson et al. 1994; Fujimoto et al. 1996, 1999b).

11.2.3 Status of Mangrove Forests and Disturbances

On Pohnpei, logging of mangroves is basically prohibited, leaving a well-preserved natural forest. Above-ground biomass reaches 327 megagames per hectare in the pioneer *R. stylosa* community and 895 megagames per hectare in the largest community (Fujimoto et al. 2023b). However, *B. gymnorrhiza*, with a diameter of approximately five centimetres, and *R. apiculate*, with a diameter of approximately 10 cm are sometimes cut down by local people as required to build work sheds, livestock sheds, etc. (Fujimoto et al. 2013). The proportion of human logging as a cause of mortality was slightly higher in mangrove forests adjacent to villages (35%) than in forests accessible only by boat away from villages (15%) (Fujimoto et al. 2013).

The mangrove forests of Kosrae are comparable to those of Pohnpei in tree size (MacLean et al. 1988). *Nypa* communities are much larger than the common South-East Asian communities that are often used as roofing material, with some communities reaching up to 10 m in leaf height. The impact of logging on Kosrae is greater in mangrove forests, excluding *Nypa* forests, than on Pohnpei, where 70% of the gap-forming factors are reportedly due to logging (Ewel et al. 1998).

Mangrove forests on Chuuk are dominated by *Rhizophora* species (Miyagi and Fujimoto 1989) and were heavily logged for fuel-wood at least until the early 2000s. According to our field survey in 2003, most of the trees on Weno, Tanowas, and Fefen Islands were less than seven metres tall. The mangrove forests on Tol Island had also been logged, but some of the seaward communities of *R. stylosa* were observed to have trees reaching a height of 10 m.

For Yap, although we have no field survey experience, there is a report of above-ground biomass ranging from 211 to 573 megagames per hectare (Kauffman and Cole 2010), which suggests that the tree size may be slightly smaller than that of

Pohnpei. Yap was hit by a very strong typhoon classified as Category 3 (1-min sustained winds of 50–58 m per s) in April 2004 (Prior and Guard 2005), which caused extensive damage to mangrove forests, especially in the south-eastern part of the island (Kauffman and Cole 2010).

11.3 Sea Level Rise in Micronesia

In FSM, continuous tide observations were conducted at Yap and Pohnpei. A record of sea level change for both islands, created using tide observation data from the Permanent Service for Mean Sea Level (PSMSL; www.psmsl.org), is shown in Fig. 11.1.

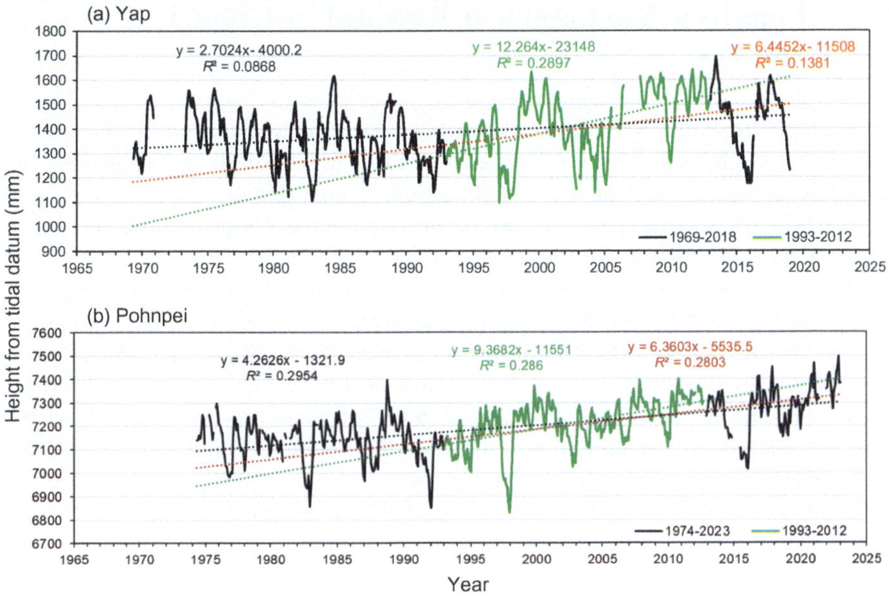

Fig. 11.1 Sea level records at **a** Yap and **b** Pohnpei. *Note* Pohnpei has two datasets, Pohnpei B (May 1974–December 2004) and Pohnpei C (January 2002–January 2023). Changes in **b** were combined in the two datasets by correcting the values of Pohnpei C to the relative height from the tidal datum of Pohnpei B, because changes in overlapping periods were very well synchronized. The solid black and green lines in **a** show the changes from May 1969 to December 2018 and January 1993 to December 2012, respectively. The solid black and green lines in **b** show the changes from May 1974 to January 2023 and January 1993 to December 2012, respectively. The dotted black, green, and red lines in **a** show the regression lines from May 1969 to December 2018, January 1993 to December 2012, and January 1993 to December 2018, respectively. The dotted black, green, and red lines in **b** show the regression lines from May 1974 to January 2023, January 1993 to December 2012, and January 1993 to January 2023, respectively. The slope of each regression equation indicates the average rate of sea level rise for each period

At Yap, the average rate of sea level rise between May 1969 and December 2018, which is the period for which data exists, was calculated to be 2.7 mm per year, compared with 12.3 mm per year between January 1993 and December 2012, when the IPCC (2013) reported a rapid sea level rise in this region (Fig. 11.1a). The average rate of sea level rise from 1993 to 2018 was calculated to be 6.4 mm per year, which is approximately twice the global mean.

At Pohnpei, the average rate of sea level rise between May 1974 and January 2023, the period for which data exists, was calculated to be 4.3 mm per year, 9.4 mm per year between January 1993 and December 2012, and 6.4 mm per year between January 1993 and January 2023 (Fig. 11.1b). Although the rate of sea level rise from 1993 to 2012 was slightly slower than that at Yap, it rose much faster than the global mean.

11.4 Impacts of Sea Level Rise Revealed by Ground Surveys

On Pohnpei, in *B. gymnorrhiza* communities where the tree density of *Rhizophora* species has decreased, knee roots are exposed to a height of 40 cm, suggesting the possibility of surface erosion associated with the recent rapid sea level rise (Fujimoto et al. 2023a, b). Surface erosion is also progressing in the *S. alba* community, which is one of the pioneer communities (Fujimoto et al. 2023a, b).

In contrast, *Rhizophora* communities increase ground elevation by accumulating mangrove peat and maintaining their habitat against sea level rise (Fujimoto et al. 2023b). However, aerial images taken by drones show that even in *Rhizophora* communities, trees with reduced leaves and declining vigour can be observed, suggesting that the rapid rise in sea level in recent years may be approaching the limit for *Rhizophora* communities to maintain their habitat (Fujimoto et al. 2023a).

Tidal creeks in mangrove forests have shown a sedimentation trend in recent years, suggesting that this phenomenon is associated with a rise in the base level of erosion due to sea level rise (Fujimoto et al. 2023b).

11.5 Mangrove Forest Dynamics from Satellite Images

To understand how mangrove forests have been spatially altered by recent sea level rise, four islands, Pohnpei, Kosrae, Chuuk, and Yap, were examined by comparing relatively clear multi-point temporal images from Google Earth high-resolution satellite imagery. Figure 11.2 shows a location map of the satellite images used for each island.

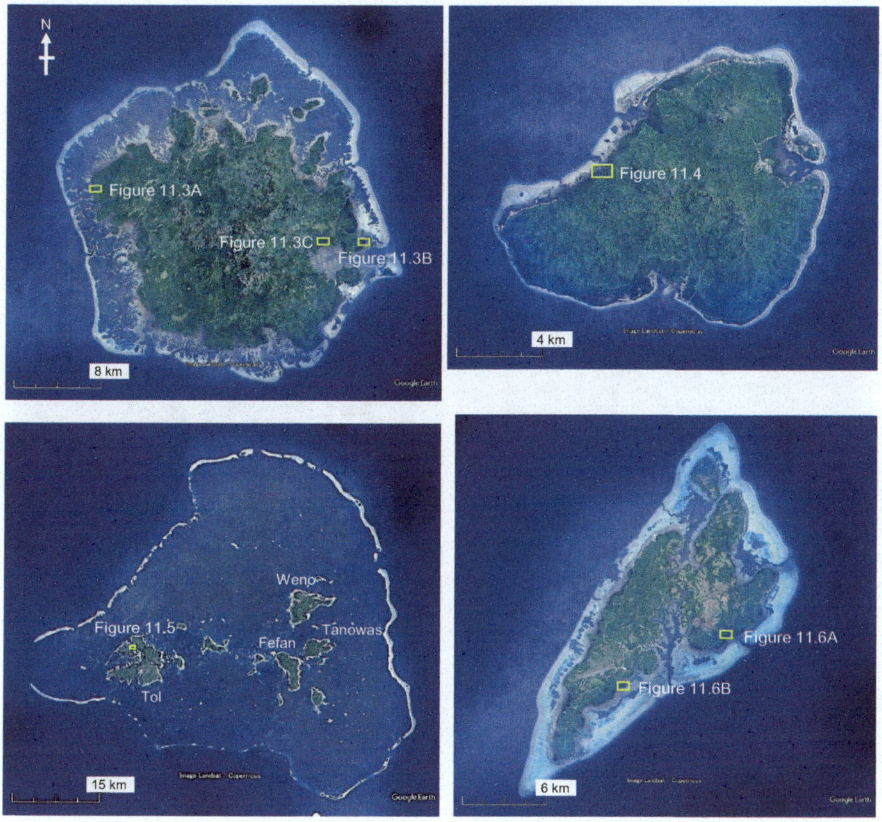

Fig. 11.2 Location map of satellite image coverage in Pohnpei, Kosrae, Chuuk, and Yap, shown in Figs. 11.3, 11.4, 11.5, and 11.6, respectively

For Pohnpei, images of coral-reef-type habitats in the western and eastern parts of the island (Fig. 11.3A and B, respectively) and estuarine type habitats in the eastern part (Fig. 11.3C) are used to discuss forest dynamics.

In the coral-reef-type habitats, there has been little seaward expansion of mangrove forests on the west side since 2005 (Fig. 11.3A(a) and A(b)), whereas significant expansion can be observed on the east side (Fig. 11.3B(a) and B(b)). Figure 11.3B shows one of the most rapidly expanding areas. On both the east and the west sides, brown sediments derived from mangrove peat were discharged and deposited on the reef flats in front of the mangrove forest (Fig. 11.3A and B). Nevertheless, the significant expansion of only the eastern shore suggests that mangrove peat that discharged to the eastern shore has been redeposited on the reef flat at a rate equal to or faster than the rate of sea level rise. This may be because the east coast is subject to waves generated by the north-east trade winds, and thus, the discharged mangrove peat is not carried far and is redeposited at the forest edge, whereas in the west the influence of waves is weaker, and thus the peat is discharged farther. The marked

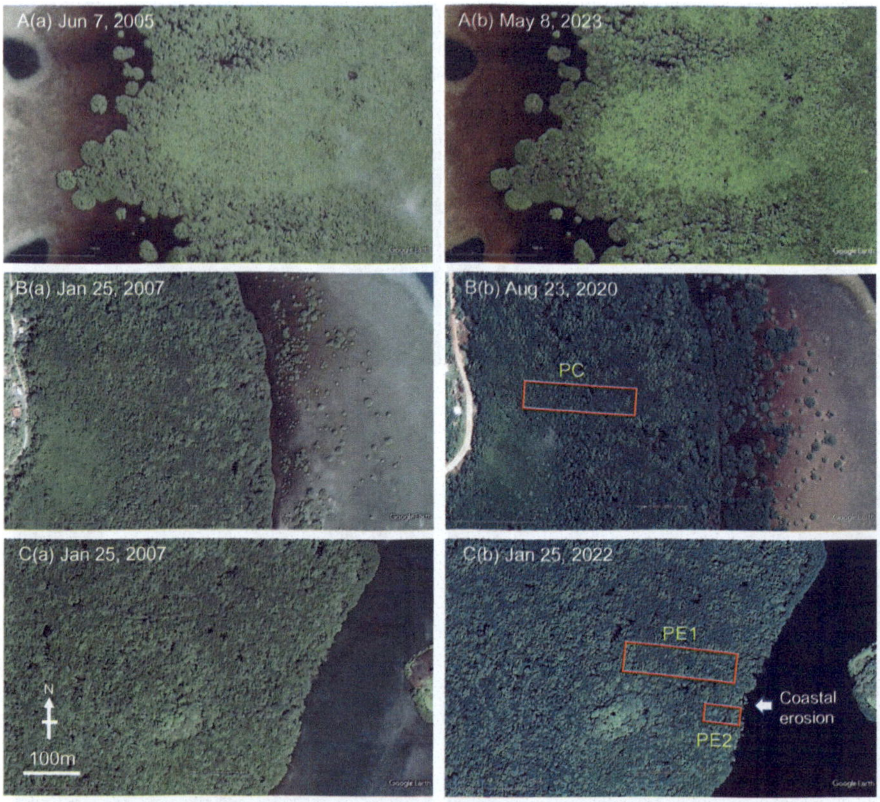

Fig. 11.3 Mangrove forest dynamics from Google Earth satellite imagery on Pohnpei. **A** A coral-reef-type habitat on the west coast (**a** © 2023 Maxar Technologies, **b** © 2023 Airbus). **B** A coral-reef-type habitat on the east coast (**a** © 2023 Maxar Technologies, **b** © 2023 CNES/Airbus). **C** An estuary-type habitat on the east coast (**a** © 2023 Maxar Technologies, **b** © 2023 CNES/Airbus). *Note* see Fig. 11.2 for these locations

expansion in the area shown in Fig. 11.3B may be because this area faces a tidal inlet of the outer reef and is more affected by waves, so in addition to the discharged peat, coral sand may also be supplied from the sea.

In addition, a long-term monitoring plot (plot code: PC, dominant species: *R. apiculata*) of 1 ha (width: 50 m, depth: 200 m), where we have observed forest dynamics since 1994, is located within the mangrove forest shown in Fig. 11.3B. It was reported there that the ground level has been increasing at a rate of 3.4 mm per year on the seaward side and 2.3 mm per year on the interior side (Fujimoto et al. 2023b). In other words, although peat is being discharged from the forest floor due to surface erosion caused by recent sea level rise, mangrove peat accumulates below ground to raise the ground level and maintain the habitat.

On the other hand, coastal erosion progresses in the mangrove forests facing the estuary, as shown in Fig. 11.3C(a) and C(b). Our long-term monitoring plots

Fig. 11.4 Mangrove forest dynamics from Google Earth satellite imagery of a coral-reef-type habitat on Kosrae. *Note* see Fig. 11.2 for these locations. *Source* **a** © 2023 Maxar Technologies; **b** © 2023 Airbus

(plot codes: PE1 and PE2) were also established in this mangrove forest (Fujimoto et al. 2023b). PE1 is located slightly inland from the shoreline, while PE2 faces the shoreline, and numerous fallen trees due to coastal erosion have been observed (Fujimoto et al. 2023b). This mangrove forest is located in an inner bay facing the same tidal inlet as in Fig. 11.3B (see Fig. 11.2). Because of the steep increase in water depth along the estuary, the mangrove forest is strongly affected by waves associated with north-east trade winds, and the wave force may be increasing due to recent sea level rise.

On Kosrae, satellite images do not show the seaward expansion of mangrove forests or their retreat due to erosion, as was observed on Pohnpei. However, the canopy gaps increased slightly between 2006 and 2023. The 2023 satellite image shows mangrove peat discharging from the forest (Fig. 11.4). Although the reasons for the increase in the gap are unidentified, recent sea level rise may lead to surface erosion in forests where the tree density of *Rhizophora* species has decreased, as was observed on Pohnpei.

On Chuuk, logging for fuel-wood was very prominent in the early 2000s. A comparison of satellite images from 2004, 2009, 2014, and 2023 shows that while vegetation has recovered in the areas that were bare in 2004, new bare land has expanded (Fig. 11.5), indicating that logging may still be ongoing. There are many waterways on the seaward side of the bare land (Fig. 11.5d), and forest restoration is delayed. On the seaward side of the bare land, forest recovery may have been delayed due to a decrease in ground elevation caused by surface erosion associated with recent sea level rise.

On Yap, the 2004 typhoon caused significant tree damage, mainly in the mangrove forests in the south-eastern part of the island (Fig. 11.6). Based on the recovery process, forests are gradually recovering in habitats facing estuaries where some sediment inflow is expected (Fig. 11.6A(a) to A(d)), but recovery is delayed in coral reef habitats (Fig. 11.6B(a) to B(d)). In habitats where large numbers of trees fell simultaneously and left bare land, surface erosion may have progressed due to sea level rise. In coral-reef-type habitats where no sediment inflow was expected, the

Fig. 11.5 Mangrove forest dynamics from Google Earth satellite imagery of a coral-reef-type habitat on Tol Island in Chuuk Atoll. *Note* see Fig. 11.2 for these locations. *Sources* **a** and **b** © 2023 Maxar Technologies; **c** © 2023 CNES/Airbus; **d** © 2023 Airbus

effects of surface erosion were particularly severe, and vegetation recovery may have been delayed.

11.6 Future of Mangrove Forests and Their Management

The mangrove habitat dynamics under sea level rise are determined by the relationship between the rate of sea level rise and the sum of the rate of ground-level change associated with sediment inflow from outside and sediment outflow from the forest, as well as the rate of ground-level rise associated with mangrove peat accumulation below ground.

In Micronesia, where sea level has been rising at a faster rate than the global mean in recent years, surface erosion is progressing in mangrove forests with reduced tree density of *Rhizophora* species, but there is no evidence of retreat of seaward forest margins due to coastal erosion, except in some wave-sensitive locations. In addition, no significant withering or falling of trees in the surface erosion area has occurred thus far.

However, surface erosion exceeding 40 cm has occurred in *B. gymnorrhiza* communities within 50 m of the seaward forest edge (Fujimoto et al. 2023a), indicating apparently low ground elevation and increased flooding time for the *B. gymnorrhiza* habitat. In such forests, withered and fallen trees are likely to increase in number

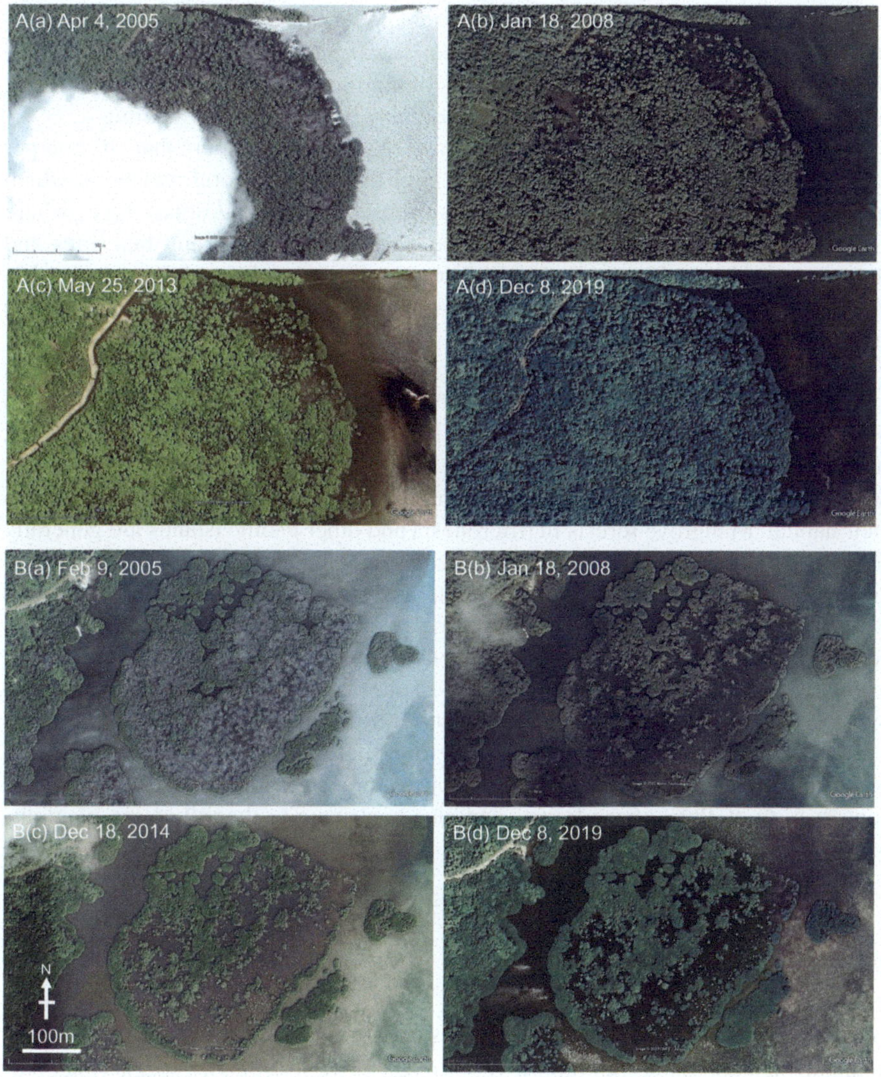

Fig. 11.6 Mangrove forest dynamics from Google Earth satellite imagery of Yap. **A** Estuary-type habitat. *Note* see Fig. 11.2 for these locations. *Sources* **a**, **b**, and **c** © 2023 Maxar Technologies; **d** © 2023 CNES/Airbus. **B** Coral-reef-type habitat. *Note* see Fig. 11.2 for these locations. *Sources* **a**, **b**, and **c** © 2023 Maxar Technologies; **d** © 2023 CNES/Airbus

in the near future. To monitor the changes, analysis using Google Earth satellite imagery, as shown in this paper, is effective.

On the other hand, *Rhizophora* communities are generally formed in seaward forest margins of coral-reef-type habitats, where mangrove peat accumulation raises the ground level and maintains the habitat against recent rapid sea level rise (Fujimoto 2023b). However, some trees in the *Rhizophora* communities of Pohnpei have been observed via drone imagery to be declining in vigour (Fujimoto et al. 2023a), suggesting that mangrove peat accumulation may be approaching its limits.

During the early Holocene, when sea level rose rapidly by more than 10 mm per year, no mangrove forests, including not only those of the coral reef type, which are maintained by mangrove peat, but also those of the delta/estuary-type, where a constant supply of sediment is expected, were able to maintain their sites and all retreated inland (Woodroffe 1992). The rate of sea level rise that progressed in Micronesia between 1993 and 2012 was comparable to the rate of sea level rise during the early Holocene.

The IPCC (2021) predicted a similar value for the global average maximum sea level rise rate by the end of this century. If similar rates of sea level rise continue in Micronesia in the future, mangrove forests in all habitats will likely be lost. However, at the moderate rate of sea level rise predicted by the IPCC (approximately five millimetres per year), *Rhizophora* communities are likely to be able to maintain their habitat. Mangrove forests in Micronesia and other Pacific islands are generally coral-reef-type forests dominated by *Rhizophora* species. Therefore, the first and most important step is to sustainably maintain *Rhizophora* forests without excessive logging. Logging is still in progress, especially on Chuuk, and immediate control is needed. Rapid surface erosion will occur on bare sites, resulting in no hope of forest recovery. Aggressive planting of *Rhizophora* species is needed on bare land created by logging on Chuuk and downed trees caused by typhoons on Yap.

Rhizophora forests have a high below-ground carbon fixation capacity compared with all other forests because of their ability to accumulate mangrove peat. The conservation of *Rhizophora* forests can also contribute to the mitigation of global warming.

11.7 Conclusion

Our previous series of studies has shown that mangrove forests in Micronesia can maintain their habitat in communities dominated by the *Rhizophora* species under the intermediate scenario of the IPCC sea level rise projections. However, in communities where vegetation succession has reduced the tree density of *Rhizophora* species, visible effects such as surface erosion are already appearing, and standing dead and fallen trees may increase in the future.

While no major anthropogenic disturbance to mangrove forests has been observed on Pohnpei, large-scale anthropogenic logging is still taking place in Chuuk, and surface erosion may be progressing in areas that are bare as a result of such logging. Although Kosrae has not seen large-scale logging like Chuuk, the impact of anthropogenic logging on gap formation may be greater than on Pohnpei. In Yap, the mangrove forests on the south-east coast were severely disturbed by the 2004 typhoon, and vegetation has not yet recovered in the coral-reef-type habitat. To sustain the mangrove ecosystem in Micronesia in the future, large-scale logging must be stopped as soon as possible. In addition, sites left bare by logging or typhoons should be immediately planted with *R. stylosa* or *R. mucronate*, which are pioneer species. Planting of these species can stop surface erosion and accelerate forest recovery.

Because of the ability of *Rhizophora* communities to accumulate mangrove peat and increase the ground level by themselves, they can maintain their habitat against sea level rise under the IPCC intermediate scenario, and they can also accumulate large amounts of carbon below ground. Developed countries that have released large amounts of carbon dioxide so far must urgently provide technical and financial support to encourage mangrove plantations in Micronesia and other oceanic islands.

References

Chapman VJ (1976) Mangrove vegetation. J. Cramer, Vaduz

Ellison AM, Stoddart DR (1991) Mangrove ecosystem collapse during predicted sea level rise: holocene analogues and implications. J Coast Res 7(1):151–165. Available at: https://journals.flvc.org/jcr/article/view/78431. Accessed: 11 Nov 2023

Ewel KC, Zheng S, Pinson ZS, Bourgeols JA (1998) Environmental effects of canopy gap formation in high-rainfall mangrove forests. Biotropica 30(4):510–518. Available at: https://doi.org/10.1111/j.1744-7429.1998.tb00091.x. Accessed: 11 Nov 2023

FAO (2007) The world's mangroves 1980–2005. FAO (Food and Agriculture Organization). For Paper 153 [Online]. Available at: www.fao.org/3/a1427e/a1427e00.htm. Accessed: 10 Nov 2023

Fujimoto K, Miyagi T (1993) Development process of tidal-flat type mangrove habitats and their zonation in the Pacific Ocean: a geomorphological study. Vegetatio 106(2):137–146. Available at: https://link.springer.com/article/10.1007/bf00045067. Accessed: 11 Nov 2023

Fujimoto K, Tabuchi R, Mori T, Murofushi T (1995) Site environments and stand structure of the mangrove forests on Pohnpei Island, Micronesia. Jpn Agric Res Quart 29(4):275–284. Available at: www.jircas.go.jp/sites/default/files/publication/jarq/29-4-275-284_0.pdf. Accessed: 10 Nov 2023

Fujimoto K, Miyagi T, Kikuchi T, Kawana T (1996) Mangrove habitat formation and response to Holocene sea-level changes on Kosrae Island, Micronesia. Mangrove Salt Marshes 1:47–57. Available at: https://doi.org/10.1023/a:1025994128221. Accessed: 10 Nov 2023

Fujimoto K, Imaya A, Tabuchi R, Kuramoto S, Utsugi H, Murofushi T (1999a) Belowground carbon storage of Micronesian mangrove forests. Ecol Res 14(4):409–413. Available at: https://doi.org/10.1046/j.1440-1703.1999.00313.x. Accessed: 10 Nov 2023

Fujimoto K, Miyagi T, Murofushi T, Mochida Y, Umitsu M, Adachi H, Pramojanee P (1999b) Mangrove habitat dynamics and Holocene sea-level changes in the southwestern coast of Thailand. Tropics 8(3):239–255. Available at: www.jstage.jst.go.jp/article/tropics/8/3/8_3_239/_article. Accessed: 11 Nov 2023

Fujimoto K, Tabuchi R, Hirata Y, Ono K, Taniguchi S, Lihpai S (2013) Aboveground dynamics and productivity of major mangrove communities on Pohnpei Island, Federated States of Micronesia. Glob Environ Res 17(2):207–214. Available at: www.airies.or.jp/journal_17-2eng.html. Accessed: 10 Nov 2023

Fujimoto K, Mochida Y, Kikuchi T, Tabuchi R, Hirata Y, Lihpai S (2015) The relationships among community type, peat layer thickness, belowground carbon storage and habitat age of mangrove forests in Pohnpei Island, Micronesia. Open J For 5(1):48–56. Available at: https://doi.org/10.4236/ojf.2015.51006. Accessed: 10 Nov 2023

Fujimoto K, Furukawa K, Ono K, Watanabe S, Eperiam E (2023a) Effects of sea-level rise on blue carbon stocks of mangrove ecosystems: insights from Pohnpei Island, Federated States of Micronesia. Carbon Footprints 2(15). Available at: www.oaepublish.com/articles/cf.2023.12. Accessed 22 Nov 2023

Fujimoto K, Ono K, Tabuchi R, Lihpai S (2023b) Findings from long-term monitoring studies of Micronesian mangrove forests with special reference to carbon sequestration and sea-level rise. Ecol Res 38(4):494–507. Available at: https://doi.org/10.1111/1440-1703.12346. Accessed: 10 Nov 2023

IPCC (2013) Climate change 2013: the physical science basis [Online]. Available at: www.ipcc.ch/report/ar5/wg1. Accessed: 10 Nov 2023

IPCC (2021) Climate change 2021: the physical science basis [Online]. Available at: www.ipcc.ch/report/ar6/wg1. Accessed: 10 Nov 2023

Kauffman JB, Cole TG (2010) Micronesian mangrove forest structure and tree responses to a severe typhoon. Wetlands 30(6):1077–1084. Available at: https://link.springer.com/article/10.1007/s13157-010-0114-y. Accessed: 11 Nov 2023

MacLean CD, Whitesell CD, Cole TG, McDuffie KE (1988) Timber resources of Kosrae, Pohnpei, Truk, and Yap, Federated States of Micronesia. In: Resource bulletin PSW-24. Pacific Southwest Forest and Range Experiment Station, USDA Forest Service

Mantiquilla JA, Shiao MS, Shih HC, Chen WH, Chiang YC (2021) A review on the genetic structure of ecologically and economically important mangrove species in the Indo-West Pacific. Ecol Genet Genom 18:100078 [Online]. Available at: https://doi.org/10.1016/j.egg.2020.100078. Accessed: 10 Nov 2023

Miyagi T (1993) Land conservation for sustainable land use of mangrove habitat. Trans Jpn Geomorphol Union 13(4):325–331

Miyagi T, Fujimoto K (1989) Geomorphological situation and stability of mangrove habitat of Truk Atoll and Ponape Island in the Federated States of Micronesia. Sci Rep Tohoku Univ Ser 7 (Geogr) 39(1):25–52. Available at: https://tohoku.repo.nii.ac.jp/records/11639. Accessed: 11 Nov 2023

Nishino Y, Fujimoto K, Tabuchi R, Hirata Y, Ono K, Taniguchi S, Ogawa T, Lihpai S (2015) Estimation of aboveground biomass in a Rhizophora stylosa forest with densely developed prop roots in Pohnpei Island, Federated States of Micronesia. Mangrove Sci 9:17–25. Available at: http://mangrove.or.jp/gakkai/Mangrove_Science/Vol.9/Mangrove_Science_Vol.9;17-25.2015.pdf. Accessed: 10 Nov 2023

Ono K, Hiradate S, Morita S, Hiraide M, Hirata Y, Fujimoto K, Tabuchi R, Lihpai S (2015) Assessing the carbon compositions and sources of mangrove peat in a tropical mangrove forests on Pohnpei Island, Federated States of Micronesia. Geoderma 245/246:11–20. Available at: https://doi.org/10.1016/j.geoderma.2015.01.008. Accessed: 11 Nov 2023

Ono K, Fujimoto K, Hairata Y, Tabuchi R, Taniguchi S, Furukawa K, Watanabe S, Suwa R, Lihpai S (2022) Total fine root production of several types of tropical mangrove forests evaluated by the continuous inflow estimation method in Pohnpei Island, Micronesia: large contribution of necromass production to the stocks of blue carbon originated from mangrove ecosystems. Ecol Res 37(1):33–52. Available at: https://doi.org/10.1111/1440-1703.12280. Accessed: 11 Nov 2023

Parkinson RW, DeLaune RD, White JR (1994) Holocene sea-level rise and the fate of mangrove forests within the wider Caribbean region. J Coast Res 10(4):1077–1086. Available at: https://journals.flvc.org/jcr/article/view/79480. Accessed: 11 Nov 2023

Prior SA, Guard CC (2005) In the wake of a destructive typhoon: cold water, low tides, and fog. Mariners Weather Log 49(1) [Online]. Available at: www.vos.noaa.gov/MWL/april_05/typhoon.shtml. Accessed: 11 Nov 2023

Spalding M, Kainuma M, Collins L (2010) World atlas of mangroves. Earthscan, London

Woodroffe C (1992) Mangrove sediments and geomorphology. In: Robertson AI, Alongi DM (eds) Tropical mangrove ecosystems. Coastal and estuarine studies, vol 41. American Geographical Union, Washington, pp 7–41. Available at: https://doi.org/10.1029/CE041p0007. Accessed: 15 Nov 2023

Chapter 12
Nature-based Solutions (NbS) for Sustainable Coastal Communities in the Pacific Island Countries and Territories

Akihiko Nonaka, Yoshimitsu Tajima, Tatsuhito Kono, Hiroya Yamano, Tomonori Orita, and Hajime Kayanne

Abstract In the Pacific island countries and territories (PICTs), flooding and erosion damage caused by sea level rise and high waves related to climate change are a major concern. However, PICTs have not widely installed effective counter-measures such as firm coastal levees and revetments due to the large number of affected areas and constraints on construction and maintenance costs. In addition, coral reef bleaching due to high water temperature and ocean acidification related to climate change not only causes loss of coastal ecosystems but also becomes a serious threat to the sustainability of the affected areas. It reduces the dissipative effect on wave energy and sediment production while diminishing the coastal ecosystem's crucial roles in the environment. Within this context, few studies have focused on the relationship between coral reef degradation and the safety of coastal areas, and for this reason, PICTs have not implemented many coral reef restoration projects. To address these issues,

A. Nonaka (✉)
Nikken Sekkei Ltd., Tokyo, Japan
e-mail: nonaka@nikken.jp

Y. Tajima · H. Yamano · H. Kayanne
The University of Tokyo, Tokyo, Japan
e-mail: yoshitaji@coastal.t.u-tokyo.ac.jp

H. Yamano
e-mail: hyamano@nies.go.jp

H. Kayanne
e-mail: kayanne@eps.s.u-tokyo.ac.jp

T. Kono
Tohoku University, Sendai, Japan
e-mail: kono@tohoku.ac.jp

H. Yamano
National Institute for Environmental Studies (NIES), Tsukuba, Japan

T. Orita
Ministry of the Environment of Japan (MOEJ), Tokyo, Japan

E. Monaco and M. Abe (eds.), *Sustainable Development Across Pacific Islands*,
https://doi.org/10.1007/978-981-97-3629-4_12

we propose here the concept of Nature-based Solutions (NbS) for coastal resilience and sustainability, consisting of various counter-measures against the impacts of climate change, such as coral reef restoration, coastal protection, and coastal zone management.

12.1 Introduction

Nearly 1.2 million people currently live in the Pacific island countries and territories (PICTs) (SPC, 2020), about 90 per cent living within one kilometre of the coast (Kumar, 2020). Houses are generally vulnerable and often cannot withstand the impacts of cyclones, floods, high winds, and storm surges (Nicholls et al., 2007, cited in Kumar, 2020). In the tropics, increased damage due to sea level rise and tropical cyclones, in turn due to the impact of climate change, threatens warm-water corals inhabiting coastal areas (IPCC, 2019). According to the United Nations Intergovernmental Panel on Climate Change (IPCC, 2021), the global average temperature has increased by about 1.09 °C from the pre-industrial times to between 2011 and 2020. Related to this, the global sea level rose by about 0.2 m between 1901 and 2018, and projected to rise by 0.44 to 0.76 m between about 2000 and 2100 under the intermediate climate change scenario SSP2−4.5 (among the Shared Socioeconomic Pathways set out in IPCC, 2021). Although levels of fossil CO_2 emissions in PICTs are low, accounting for less than 0.1 per cent of the global total (Crippa et al., 2022), these states are highly vulnerable to climate change due to the strong connection between people and the sea. In PICTs, the population has tended to concentrate in urban areas in recent years (Kumar, 2020, p .297). This trend intensifies the damage from flooding and coastal erosion due to land use change (Yamano et al., 2007) and also causes degradation of coastal ecosystems due to increased anthropogenic drainage and solid waste.

In this context, PICTs have adopted erosion counter-measures mainly to deal with coastal disasters, but in the future, flooding counter-measures against sea level rise and stronger waves will also be necessary. In many countries these measures are important actions in national adaptation plans (NAPs) or national determined contributions (NDCs), which are the policy documents on climate change. In Tuvalu and Marshall Islands, Green Climate Fund (GCF) coastal disaster risk reduction projects were adopted in 2015/16 and are currently underway. Other countries and regions will need to address similar issues in the future.

PICTs have adopted engineering measures mainly using materials such as stone and concrete blocks to protect their coastlines in the past, but these have been subject to damage from strong waves and have tended to become a heavy burden on the finances of the small island countries. For this reason, it has become important in recent years not only to rely on conventional engineering measures, but also to consider ecosystem-based adaptation measures and other options (IPCC, 2019). Based on this idea, the term "Nature-based Solutions" (NbS) describes measures using nature's functions in a sustainable manner to solve various socio-environmental issues (UNEA, 2022). In the context of coastal communities in PICTs, such NbS could be effective in actively harnessing the power of coral reef ecosystems. In this chapter, we propose NbS as a method for the restoration and conservation of coral reef ecosystems against bleaching damage and introduce the concept and planning method of a coastal protection project that optimally combines NbS with engineering measures, to make coastal communities in PICTs sustainable against the impacts of climate change.

12.2 Climate Change Impacts on the Coastal Area of PICTs

Climate change-induced sea level rise, changes in weather patterns, ocean warming, and ocean acidification pose threats to marine and terrestrial ecosystems, human health, infrastructure, coastal resources, freshwater availability, and the sustainability of agriculture, fisheries, forestry, and tourism (SPREP, 2020). IPCC (2021) and other sources describe the major impacts of climate change on the natural environment and the communities of the coasts of PICTs.

A. **Impact on weather and sea conditions**

If climate change continues under the intermediate scenario, sea level rise is projected to be 0.44–0.76 m between about 2000 and 2100, resulting in increased frequency and severity of coastal flooding in low-lying areas and erosion along most sandy coasts. Ocean warming due to climate change is also projected to be 2.4–4.8 times greater than the 1971–2018 change, and upper ocean stratification, ocean acidification, and ocean hypoxia are projected to increase during the twenty-first century.

B. **Ecosystem impacts (on warm-water corals)**

Ocean warming, including increased ocean heatwaves, acidification, anoxia, saltwater intrusion, and sea level rise, affects coastal ecosystems. In the future, climate change will more severely affect warm-water corals. A study that estimated remineralization rates from current coral distributions and examined the rate of upward sedimentation on reef crests has shown that most reefs are already in decline (see Fig. 12.1 for an example) and that reef crests will not be able to keep pace with future sea level rise (Perry et al., 2018).

C. **Impacts on coastal communities**

Climate change-induced sea level rise and severe storm surges and waves will cause flooding and erosion of coastal lands, houses, and infrastructure and threaten the livelihood, industry, and property of coastal communities by salinizing groundwater, a valuable source of fresh water, in atoll countries. Coral reef mortality due to bleaching reduces the effectiveness of wave dissipation and contributes to flooding damage, while a decrease in sediment supply causes beach erosion, leading to the gradual loss of land. In addition, the degradation of coral reef ecosystems reduces

Fig. 12.1 Bleaching and devastation of coral reefs, Fiji. *Source* The Ocean Agency (2016)

the value of the natural ecosystem itself, as well as fishery production, traditional culture, and tourism resources.

Coral communities form shallow and complex coral reef landforms offshore, which have a dissipative effect on waves arriving from the open ocean. Meta-analyses reveal that coral reefs provide substantial protection against natural hazards by reducing wave energy by an average of 97 per cent. Reef crests, the shallowest parts formed offshore, alone dissipate most of this energy (86 per cent) (Ferrario et al., 2014). Living corals grow upward and laterally to create shallow, undulating topography, but as coral reef ecosystems decline, coral reefs do not grow upward and the seafloor gradually flattens. This reduces the dissipation effect on wave energy and increases the risk of erosion and flooding in coastal areas (Reguero et al., 2019; Storlazzi et al., 2019, US EPA, 2022). When coral reefs are healthy, the rate of upward accretion of reef crests is estimated to be about 3–6 mm per year (Kayanne, 1992; Montaggioni, 2005), close to the 4.4–7.6 mm per year sea level rise assumed under the intermediate climate change scenario (SSP2−4.5) (IPCC, 2021), and it is likely that the wave-dissipating function will be retained because reef crests may catch up with sea level rises (Kayanne, 2016) (see Fig. 12.2).

D. **Impact on land formation**

Coral reefs produce coral gravel and foraminiferal sand as sediment, which waves and currents transport and deposit mainly along the shoreline (Kayanne et al., 2016). In atoll islands such as Kiribati, Marshall Islands, and Tuvalu, the production of sediment by coral reefs is an irreplaceable mechanism of land formation. Therefore, if the health of the coral reefs is compromised, this will threaten the sustainability of land in PICTs, especially in the atoll countries. Figure 12.3 illustrates the mechanisms of climate change-related problems and associated population concentrations affecting coastal communities and ecosystems in PICTs.

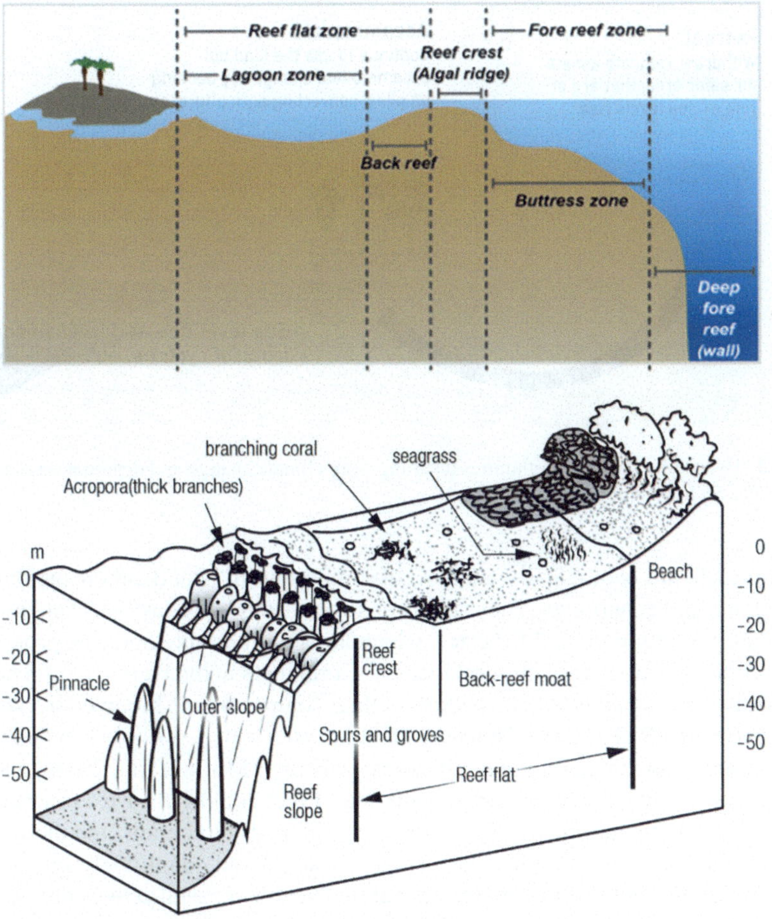

Fig. 12.2 Example of a coral reef topography. *Source* authors' illustration

12.3 Problem Analysis and Recommendations

A. Conventional counter-measures and their problems

To date, PICTs have adopted revetment systems using various materials such as concrete, stone, and sandbags as coastal protection measures. Among these measures, ageing or extremely high waves have destroyed even strong, durable concrete revetments (PaCE-SD, 2015). In some cases, waves rebounding from revetments increase the tendency towards erosion, and weak financial fundamentals in PICTs make coastal protection measures using engineering methods, which tend to be expensive, a heavy financial burden.

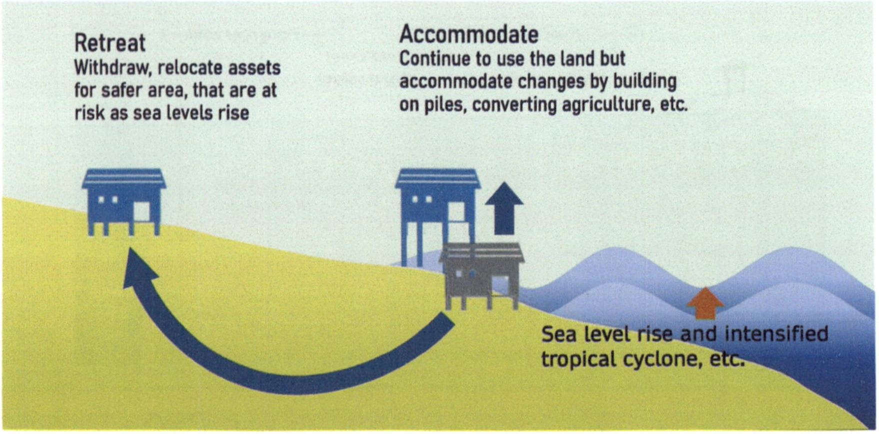

Fig. 12.3 Issues for coastal communities resulting from climate change and degradation of coastal ecosystems. *Source* authors' illustration

Coral reefs are ecologically and socially important to islands, their inhabitants, biodiversity, and economies. They supply sediment, stabilize coastlines, and provide income through tourism and fisheries, which are an important source of protein for many people and are part of cultural identity. Coral reefs in the Pacific region benefit not only the region but the world in terms of their contribution to biodiversity, habitat, and fisheries (SPREP, 2021). However, habitat disturbance, pollution, fishing, and climate change are damaging many Pacific coral reefs (Moritz et al., 2018), and this anthropogenic threat is increasing. In particular, PICT countries have a large coastal area; a complete picture of ecosystem damage is not easy to obtain, and the scale of restoration and conservation has been relatively small and quantitively insufficient. In addition, it has not been fully recognized that healthy coastal ecosystems play an important and indispensable role in disaster prevention and land formation, therefore the restoration and conservation of coastal ecosystems have not been positioned from the perspective of disaster prevention in NAPs and NDCs.

B. **Proposed solution: Coastal strengthening with Nature-based Solutions**

For the resilience of coastal communities in PICTs, we should consider not only conventional engineering coastal protection measures but also solutions that harness the power of healthy coastal ecosystems such as coral reefs, focusing on the role of coastal ecosystems in terms of wave-dissipation and sediment-supply effects. In recent years, problem-solving approaches that harness the power of nature have become known as Nature-based Solutions, or NbS. An IPCC report (2019) explains that ecosystem-based adaptation, which is similar to NbS, can also provide multiple benefits, such as carbon storage, improved water quality, and biodiversity conservation, if sufficient space is available for it and its long-term costs would be relatively low. Coral reef managers have also recently begun to consider reef restoration as a new tool for coastal protection and conservation (US EPA, 2022). Considering the above, in order to strengthen and sustain coastal communities in PICTs against the problems of sea level rise, flooding, and coastal erosion due to storm surge and high waves caused by climate change, we propose solutions that optimally combine (i) restoration and conservation of coastal ecosystems such as coral reefs, mangrove forests, and seagrass beds as NbS, (ii) engineering coastal protection measures, and (iii) institutions for disaster prevention and mitigation in local communities. Figure 12.4 illustrates this concept.

C. **Advantages of a Nature-based Solution**

Solution to multiple problems

The implementation of NbS in PICTs, utilizing coastal ecosystems, will not only strengthen coastal communities but also solve multiple problems at the same time, such as the preservation of ecosystems as sites for fisheries production, traditional culture, tourism resources, biodiversity, and local employment. The preservation of mangrove forests and seagrass beds contributes to decarbonization. It will also contribute to the achievement of the SDGs, including Goal 11, "Make cities inclusive, safe, resilient, and sustainable" and Goal 14, "Conserve and sustainably use the oceans, seas, and marine resources". This will contribute to the 2030 Mission and 2030 Global Targets of the Kunming-Montreal Global Biodiversity Framework.

Potential for lower project costs

Leveraging the ecosystems of coastal islands to achieve disaster prevention benefits can reduce the cost of engineering works in PICTs, which often require the importing of construction materials from remote areas, and lower the overall cost of the projects.

The impacts of climate change are expected to increase over time. Engineering measures such as coastal seawalls will become relatively less functional as sea levels rise, and their effectiveness will also decrease due to degradation over time. On the

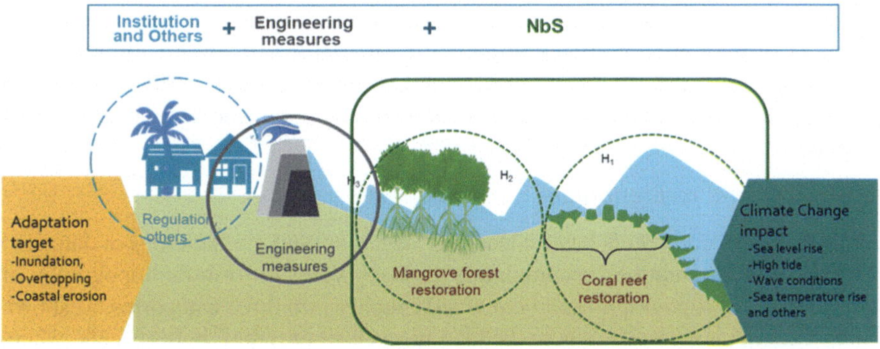

Fig. 12.4 The role of NbS in sustainable coastal communities in PICTs. *Source* authors' illustration

other hand, coastal ecosystems continue their wave-dissipation effect by growing upward as sea level rises.

Reduction of environmental impact

Engineering measures such as coastal levees degrade the coastal environment through the process of construction, and upright concrete levees may cause erosion of the sand in front of the levees by creating strong wave reflections. The introduction of NbS helps to reduce environmental impact by limiting the scale of engineering measures.

Domestic measures can be completed

Implementing and maintaining engineering works in PICTs may require the importation of cement, aggregates, reinforcing steel, and construction equipment. NbS, on the other hand, allows projects to be implemented and maintained by islanders who have acquired the necessary skills and tools.

Role in job creation

Ecosystem restoration can be carried out by skilled divers and vessels without the use of large quantities of construction equipment and imported materials. This can lead to the creation of local employment opportunities.

D. **Specific solution**

Coral reef restoration and conservation

In the past, there was a worldwide opinion that coral reef restoration was inefficient and not a realistic solution to the problem. In 1988, the Akajima Marine Science Laboratory (AMSL) was established in Japan as a research facility focusing on coral restoration, and many countries have conducted research on coral reef restoration since that time. In Japan, the Ministry of the Environment, the Japan Fisheries Agency (JFA), universities, and other institutions continue to conduct coral research and restoration projects, and in the United States, restoration projects for bleached coral reefs are underway in Florida, the Caribbean, and the Hawaiian islands. Australia has also expanded its coral research and restoration activities following large-scale bleaching of the Great Barrier Reef in 2016 and 2017, and several institutions in PICTs countries, such as Palau International Coral Reef Center (PICRC) and the University of the South Pacific (USP), are conducting coral research and restoration projects.

Location of coral reef restoration

Corals that form coral reefs have calcareous skeletons, and the skeletons of damaged or dead coral communities accumulate over many years to form the topography of coral reefs. This topography can be divided roughly into three categories, as shown in Fig. 12.5: fringing reefs, where the land meets the coral reef; barrier reefs, where there are lagoons between the land and the coral reef; and atolls, where coral reefs form in a ring-like formation. In all of these cases, the coral reef consists of a reef flat several hundred metres wide and a reef slope sloping down to the open ocean.

The reef flat is often composed of a reef crest that tends to appear above the water's surface at low tide and a back reef moat a few metres deep on the landward side of the crest.

From a coastal protection perspective, it is important to restore and conserve the health of the reef crest and its surrounding areas, where both wave-dissipation and sediment-supply functions are important (see Fig. 12.6). Reef crests and surrounding areas have been considered difficult to restore due to high waves and fast currents, but restoration and conservation efforts in these areas will become increasingly important in the future.

Selection of species to restore

The coral species to restore and conserve should be selected based on which species were originally dominant in and around the reef crests and which have been most severely degraded by bleaching or other factors. Among these species, those that are easy to restore or grow quickly should also be considered, to increase the certainty of restoration and accelerate the onset of effects. For example, it has been reported in Japan that *Goniastrea retiformis*, *Acropora degitifera*, *Acropora hyacinthus*, and other corymbose and tuberous species were abundant on reef crests and their edges (Hongo & Kayanne, 2010), and *Pocillopora eydouxi* and *Cyphastrea serailia*, among others, were abundant on the outer reef slope (MLIT, 2003). Since these species vary depending on the site, it is necessary to study the distribution of the species and the

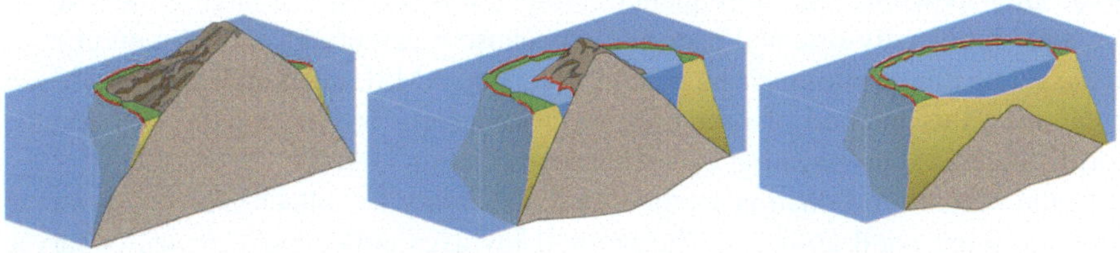

Fig. 12.5 Typical coral reef topography showing areas of particular importance (red) for coastal restoration and conservation. *Note* left to right: fringe reef, barrier reef, and atoll. *Source* authors' illustration

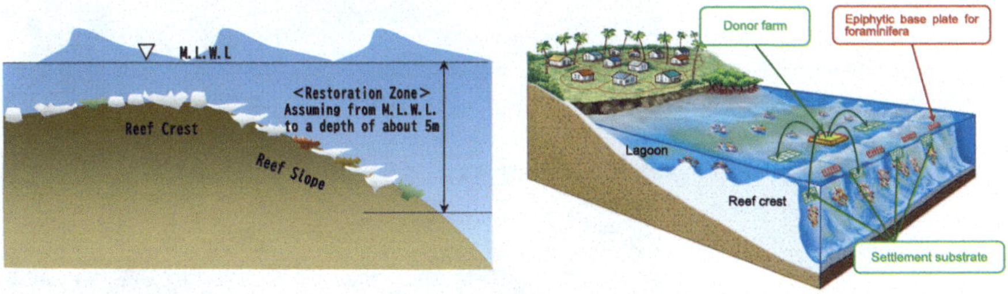

Fig. 12.6 Cross-section of coral reef topography near a reef crest (left) and location for the coral restoration (right). *Source* authors' illustration

state of devastation through a preliminary survey of a specific site before making a selection.

Conventional restoration technique (asexual reproduction method)

Asexual reproduction is a method of coral restoration in which divers remove small pieces of living coral or seedlings that have been growing in the sea for several years using glue or wire and transfer them to a restoration site. This method has been widely used because it replicates some of the natural restorative function of corals, and because it is relatively easy to implement, as some coral species reproduce repeatedly from fragments destroyed by waves (see Fig. 12.7).

However, because asexual reproduction requires taking small pieces from a living coral community, large-scale restoration could increase the stress on the coral community due to the large amount of small pieces required. Other problems include low genetic diversity due to clonal propagation (JFA, 2019) and the fact that many hermaphroditic corals do not fertilize between gametes of the same species, resulting in fewer larvae in the next generation, impacting on reef restoration (Omori, 2019).

New restoration technique (sexual reproduction method)

In contrast, there is a new restoration method that uses the mechanism of sexual reproduction, in which larvae called planulae, which are produced after the parent coral spawns and the eggs and sperm are fertilized, raised and used for restoration. Although this method requires highly specialized techniques to collect gametes and larvae after spawning and subsequent treatment, it is suitable for large-scale restoration and biodiversity-oriented restoration because it can produce a large number of larvae at one time while ensuring genetic diversity. AMSL in Okinawa, Japan, began researching this method of sexual reproduction early on, paving the way for the world's first coral propagation by sexual reproduction in 2005.

In the sexual reproduction method, it is necessary to collect gametes or larvae from surviving coral colonies. The method involves collecting gametes or larvae

Fig. 12.7 Coral transplantation in Okinawa Prefecture. *Source* photograph by a research group of Okinawa Prefecture in 2023; reproduced with permission

underwater, after spawning, with a larval-collecting device; collecting fertilized eggs or larvae floating on the sea's surface from a ship; or transferring parent corals to an aquarium on land and collecting gametes or larvae released therein. The method of collecting slicks floating on the sea surface has several problems: the survival rate of eggs or larvae is low, it is challenging to find slicks over a wide area of the sea, and it is difficult for dense slicks to form in areas where coral reefs have been degraded. The method of using a larval-collecting device underwater can efficiently collect millions of gametes or larvae at one time if the device is placed on the colonies before the spawning season (Suzuki et al., 2020). There are three main methods of implantation after the larvae are obtained:

- case 1: larvae are reared to seedlings in the sea for several years and then implanted to restoration site;
- case 2: substrate to which the larvae are attached is placed or spread onto the seabed;
- case 3: larvae are sprayed directly onto the seabed after being matured.

Because coral seedlings tend to decrease in survival rate after transplantation as their size decreases, the survival probability per larva is lower in cases 2 and 3 than in case 1. Conversely, in case 1 the effort and expense involved in rearing a single larva to a seedling is greater. Implanting seedlings one by one on the bedrock then requires a large number of divers for a large-scale restoration, and implanting in areas such as reef crests or outer reef slopes is not safe enough due to high waves and fast currents. For these reasons, the JFA and the Reef Restoration and Adaptation Program (RRAP) have adopted the case 2 and case 3 methods for large-scale restoration projects (JFA, 2022). Ideally, the entire restoration area should be immediately covered with transplanted coral larvae and coral spat, but this may be difficult due to the cost and lack of human resources for projects in extensive restoration areas. In such cases, a local coral larvae supply base could be established by intensively implanting coral seedlings into declining coral reefs (Omori, 2016).

Deployment to large-scale restoration

Until recently, the mainstream method for coral reef restoration was asexual reproduction targeting relatively small areas, but recently restoration projects that target large areas have been implemented. Japan and some other countries have applied cases 2 and 3 using the larval collection device shown in Fig. 12.8. Australia and other countries are experimenting with using ships to collect coral slicks floating on the sea surface over a wide area and then dispersing the slicks directly onto areas targeted for restoration (Doropoulos et al., 2019). The University of Hawaii has begun developing an artificial coral reef ecosystem for coastal protection with support from the US Defense Advanced Research Projects Agency (DARPA) (UoH, 2022).

In recent years, it has come to be considered that corals themselves may be genetically resistant to high temperatures (JFA, 2022). Based on this, studies on coral genes and high temperature tolerance report that certain genes are expressed under high water temperatures (Barshis et al., 2013; Dixon et al., 2015); *Acropora tenuis*, when experiencing short-term high water temperatures in summer, can sense the danger,

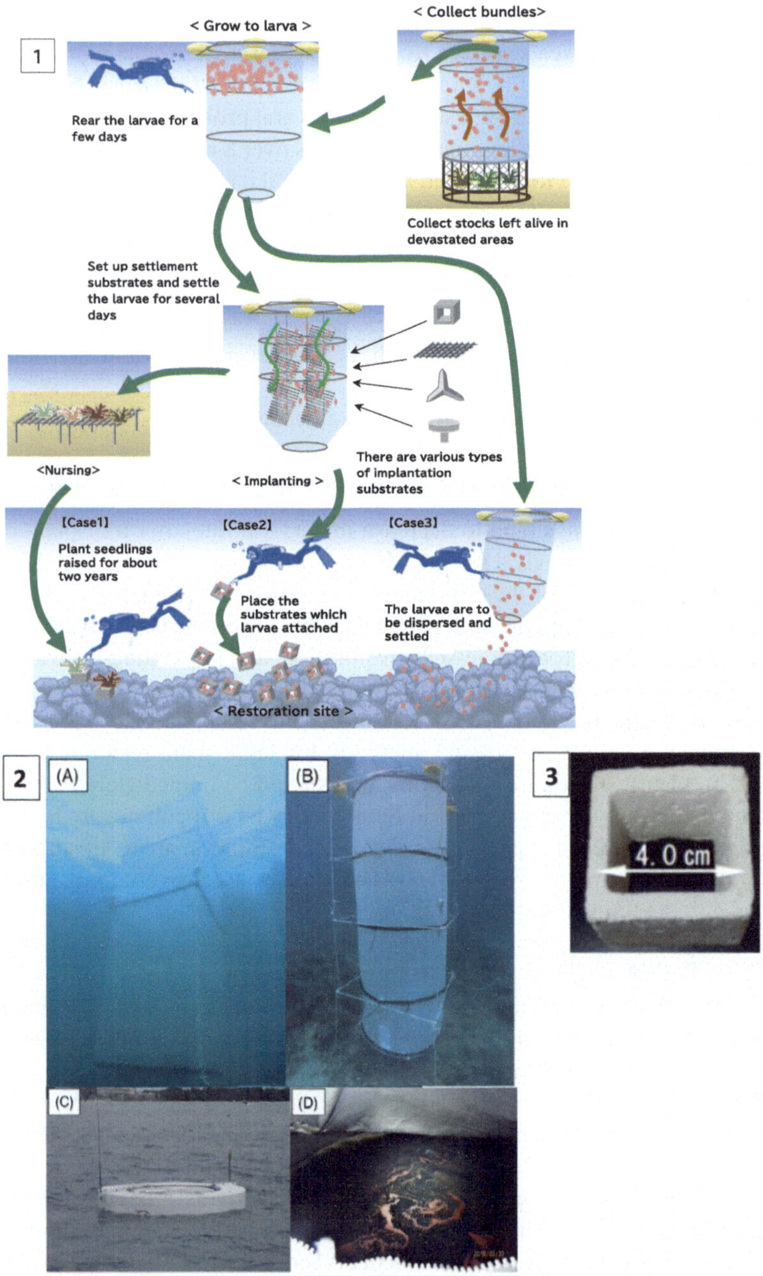

Fig. 12.8 (1) Examples of coral reef restoration methods (Source author's illustration); (2) the bundle collection system known as a "coral larval cradle (Suzuki et al., 2020)"; (3) substrate for placing coral (JFA, 2022)

and *Acropora tenuis* produce high numbers offspring tolerant of high water temperature in a year following high summer temperatures (Hazraty-Kari et al., 2022). The idea of transplanting coral spat produced by parents tolerant of high water temperature, selected by exposing corals to high water temperatures, to the ocean has also been proposed as a way to increase the regenerative capacity of coral communities in a context of high water temperatures (Humanes et al., 2021). In reef restoration under conditions of climate change, reproduction methods which take into account the newest knowledge as described above should be introduced to guard against the risk of future bleaching.

Preservation of water quality

Coral reef restoration requires the creation of an environment suitable for the habitat of the species to be restored, and water quality is a factor in this. In particular, polluted water discharged from population growth in coastal areas and increased soil particle content due to land development can threaten coral habitat. Therefore, the impact of water pollution from terrestrial sources must be assessed in order to restore and maintain healthy coral reefs. This issue is more important in enclosed lagoons than on reef ridges and outer reef slopes. Previous studies have proposed water quality guidelines for healthy coral growth, as shown in Table 12.1. In addition to measures to reduce wastewater at its source, it is desirable that basic measures be taken such as the collection and treatment of human waste and sewage by sewerage systems and treatment at the household level by septic tanks.

Sanitation facilities are already in place in densely populated areas of PICTs (e.g., Suva, Fiji; Tarawa, Kiribati; Koror, Palau), but in some cases sewer pipes are blocked, toilets and domestic wastewater are not connected to sewer pipes, and treatment plants are inadequately operated and discharge wastewater without adequate treatment. Urban wastewater treatment may be more expensive than coral restoration but is desirable from the standpoint of improving the sanitary environment for residents.

Engineering measures

Based on the characteristics of PICTs, including the limited variety of construction materials and relatively small economic scale, and the results of a review of construction methods used in the field, this section presents a perspective on and examples of engineering measures appropriate to the coastal protection of PICTs against the impact of climate change.

Basic approach

When NbS alone is not sufficient to address the impacts of climate change, conventional engineering coastal protection measures will be required. So far, PICTs have used revetments, which protect the coast from erosion and collapse, as the main coastal protection method. However, in the future, considering the sea level rise due to climate change and the occurrence of severe storm surges and tidal waves, levees/dikes and wave-absorbing facilities will also be required to prevent water and wave overtopping where the coast is prone to erosion (see Fig. 12.9).

Table 12.1 Water quality levels for healthy coral reefs (reference data)

Aspect of water quality	Unit	Site			
		Okinawa, Japan	Great Barrier Reef Australia	Florida Keys, United States	Mauritius
		Omija (2004)	De'ath and Fabricius (2008)	Thanopoulou et al. (2022)	MEHDE (1999)
Suspended solids (SS)	mg/L (milligrams per litre)	–	< 2.4 (summer) < 1.6 (winter)	–	< 5
Turbidity	NTU (Nephelometric Turbidity Units)	< 0.11	< 3.0	–	< 0.5
Total nitrogen	mg/L	< 0.1	–	–	–
Nitrate nitrogen	mg/L	< 0.01	–	–	< 0.2
Total phosphorus	mg/L	< 0.01	–	< 0.0032	–
Phosphoric acid phosphorus	mg/L	< 0.006	–	–	< 0.04

Source authors' construction based on stated sources

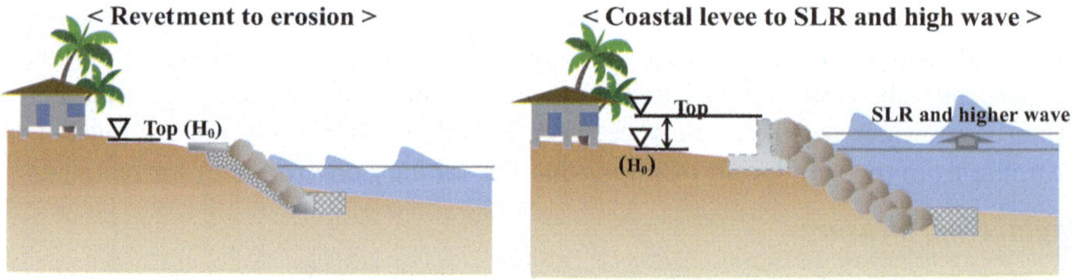

Fig. 12.9 Revetment (left) and coastal levee (right). *Source* authors' illustration

The main engineering counter-measures against storm surges, high waves, and beach erosion include not only coastal levees but also various other measures such as the installation of wave-dissipating blocks in front of or offshore of levees and beach nourishment with earth and sand to reduce waves and protect the beach. Here, however, we focus on the use of coastal levees to minimize damage to the marine environment.

Location and structure

Conventional coastal protection facilities often use concrete or masonry to protect the shoreline. On the other hand, in locations where land is available and there is no significant coastal erosion, onshore protection facilities can be installed at a lower cost and with less impact on the coastal environment. Figure 12.10 shows cross-sectional images of these two cases using rock. The use of rock is more suitable for volcanic islands, where the material is more readily available, while counter-measures on atoll islands, where rock is more difficult to obtain, can be similarly designed but using geotextile sandbags or concrete.

If more area is available on the land and terrestrial vegetation is present, a small-scale backstop seawall can be constructed near the target, such as a house, using this vegetation as a NbS to further reduce the cost and environmental impact of the counter-measure. Figure 12.11 shows an example of this method proposed in Marshall Islands, which use approximately 30–50 m' width of the vegetation zone.

In areas where coral and other biota are scarce from the shoreline to offshore, detached breakwaters can be installed to enhance the wave-dissipating effect and

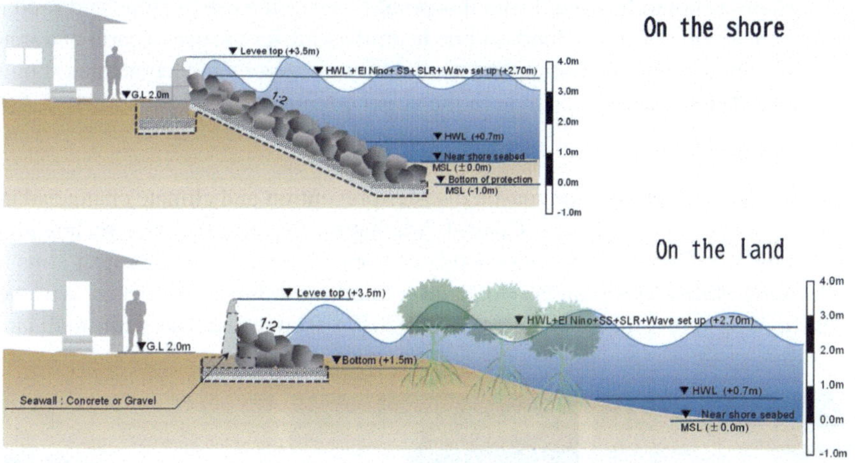

Fig. 12.10 Engineering counter-measures against storm surge and high waves (upper: volcanic island with no margin on the land side; lower: same condition with margin on the land side). *Source* authors' illustration

Fig. 12.11 NbS proposed in Marshall Islands against storm surge and high waves. *Source* authors' revision based on RMI (2020)

create a storage area for sediment supplied by the coral reef, thereby preventing sediment run-off.

Materials for coastal protection

By using materials that are readily available on the island, construction costs can be reduced and the landscape and ecosystem can be considered. Examples of materials used for coastal protection in PICTs include rocks, concrete, soil, sand, and sandbags, as shown in Fig. 12.12. PICTs have used different materials depending on the wave and tidal conditions in the target area, the size of the houses and infrastructure to be protected, the availability of materials on each island, and cost.

If the facility is to be climate-responsive, materials should be used that can cope with long-term changes and that are suitable for the local environment. In terms of transportation costs, materials that need to be transported from distant places should be avoided as much as possible, and materials that can be obtained as close to the site as possible should be used. From this point of view, the use of stone and sand is more beneficial on volcanic islands, while in atoll countries the use of earth and sand is more advantageous. In addition, the availability of cement and aggregates should be considered in the use of concrete in the target countries.

Coastal reclamation

In Tuvalu, the GCF project for coastal disaster prevention and climate change adaptation measures (TCAP, Tuvalu Coastal Adaptation Project) includes reclamation using dredged material on the lagoon side of Fongafale island. The project aims to reduce vulnerability to coastal flooding and erosion, including the effects of sea level rise due to long-term climate change (UNDP, 2017). Island countries with small land

Fig. 12.12 Examples of materials used in revetments and coastal embankments in PICTS. *Note* upper: flexible container, beach nourishment, rock-covered; lower: mortar bag, Fabrifoam concrete bag, reinforced concrete levee. *Source* photographs by authors, except for beach nourishment, reproduced with permission from Ohnaka et al (2017)

areas and low elevation, it is essential to create safe land by reclaiming sea areas and low marshlands as a means of protecting the lives and property of the population from the risk of inundation. However, the environmental impacts of reclamation, such as anoxia in dredged areas and changes in sediment dynamics in coastal areas, must be fully evaluated.

Institutional measures

For the resilience of coastal communities in PICTs, it is desirable to develop an integrated coastal zone management plan (ICZM) that includes coastal protection measures through the NbS and engineering measures described so far, and to position it within long-term governmental plans (Post & Lundink, 1996). Such a plan is particularly necessary where there is no adequate coastal protection plan or system. Furthermore, even assuming that coastal protection measures are effectively implemented, the effectiveness of coastal protection measures may not be fully realized if residential relocation to coastal societies with high inundation risk continues. For this reason, land use guidelines that restrict the construction of houses and other structures on high-risk land and promote the relocation of houses to safer areas, regional disaster prevention plans that stipulate the raising of low-lying land, and building codes, among other measures, should also be established where these are insufficient (see Fig. 12.13).

In addition to this, it is desirable that a coastal environment conservation policy, which includes the prohibition of fishing methods that damage coastal ecosystems and the establishment of ecosystem conservation zones, should also be included in the integrated plan. The overall planning method should be based on future (e.g., 20, 50, or 100 years) assumptions for coastal areas and should establish disaster prevention, environmental, and socioeconomic development goals, from which backcasting measures should be considered.

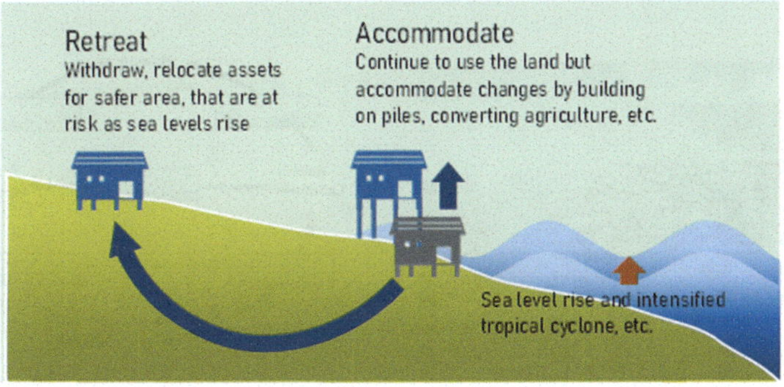

Fig. 12.13 Institution for disaster prevention systems in land-side housing relocation. *Source* authors' illustration

E. **Value of the project**

Coral restoration as an NbS has various advantages, including in coastal disaster prevention. Here, we present the economic values of coral restoration for coastal communities based on several previous studies.

The comprehensive value of coral reef restoration

Experts have assessed the value of coral reef restoration in relation to its impact on erosion protection, raw materials, genetic resources, ornamental resources, disaster prevention function, genetic diversity, aesthetic value, and educational value. Based on a report which collected results of studies from around the world, the average annual economic value of coral reefs per hectare is \$0.35 million (de Groot et al., 2012). However, reports limited to Pacific small island states indicate that the total economic value of coral reefs ranges from \$609 to \$17,873 per hectare annually (Laurans et al., 2013). These economic values vary widely depending on the characteristics of coastal communities and natural disasters, as well as fishing and tourism activities. By examining the area and individual uses of coral reefs in the proposed area, it is possible to estimate the value of reef restoration relatively accurately from these results. Figure 12.14 illustrates the diverse values of coral reefs, focusing primarily on the value of their ecosystem.

Value of coastal protection

The value of coastal protection measures is in the reduction or elimination of various types of damage caused by potential flooding and erosion. The benefits of this value are the sum of the value of assets such as houses, land, and social infrastructure protected in the assumed damage area, as well as a reduction in the amount of losses when individual businesses cannot operate. In particular, the value of erosion should be estimated in terms of the effect of preventing the loss of land itself. The damage

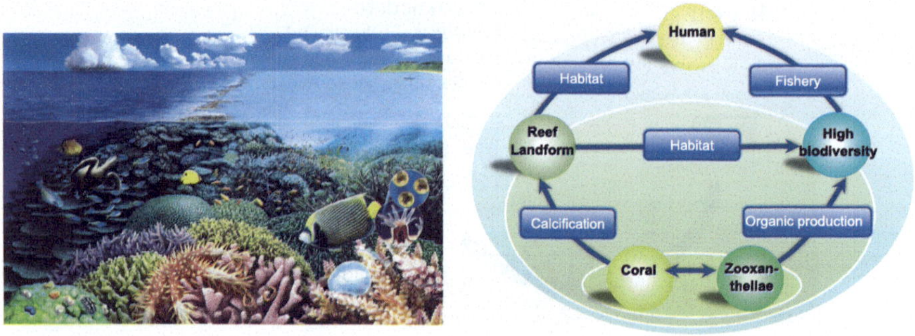

Fig. 12.14 Diverse ecosystems in coral reefs (left); various benefits to humans from symbiotic systems in coral reef topography (right). *Source* authors' illustration

caused by flooding and erosion must be assessed according to the coastal community in question, since the size of the damaged area, the degree of concentration of housing and infrastructure, and the value of assets vary greatly between coastal communities.

According to a report based on studies from around the world (de Groot et al., 2012), the highest economic value of disaster prevention in the form of coastal protection through coral reefs is estimated to be \$0.15 million per hectare annually. Fiji reports the economic value of coastal protection resulting from coral reef ecosystem services as \$350 per hectare annually (Laurans et al., 2013).

Value of land formation

Coral reefs in the tropics produce sediment from the rubble resulting from coral mortality and damage, as well as from the remains of foraminifera and calcareous algae. In addition to becoming sediment directly, these materials contribute to the sediment supply as excretions from fish, sea urchins, and other organisms that feed on them. The mechanism for the production and supply of sediment from coral reef ecosystems is described by Perry et al. (2023).

The amount of sediment produced by corals and foraminifera in a coral reef ecosystem is assumed to be about 2.5 kg/m^2 annually (Perry et al., 2023). Assumed the density of the sediment, including internal pores, is 2.0 g per cubic centimetre and the porosity between particles is 30 per cent, the apparent sediment production in coral reefs is estimated to be 1.8×10^{-4} m^3/m^2 annually (Takemori et al., 2015). Furthermore, if the main production site of the sediment in the coral reef topography has a width of 100 m in the offshore direction and all of the sediment produced there is washed ashore, the amount of sediment supplied can be estimated at about 0.18 m^3/m^2 of shoreline annually. Once this sediment reaches the shore, wind and waves transport it and deposit it on land, forming and maintaining atoll islands (Kayanne et al., 2016). These functions are the same on the coasts of volcanic islands.

F. **How to plan and evaluate counter-measures**

There have been few examples of climate change counter-measures based on NbS, and even fewer examples of counter-measure plans for coastal resilience that mix NbS and engineering measures. Therefore, we propose here a basic idea of how to formulate a counter-measure plan that includes NbS, and how to evaluate the plan in order to realize the coastal resilience of PICTs.

How to proceed with a counter-measure plan including NbS

It is necessary to develop a plan with the optimal method and scale for each measure, taking into account the cost, effectiveness, and environmental impact of the NbS and engineering measures described so far. The first step in this process is to study the characteristics of the area to be protected and the related policies and to establish the planning conditions. Next, an ICZM plan is developed, which consists of the community's protection goals against coastal disasters caused by sea level rise and extreme weather events, and the overall implementation policy for various measures. Subsequently, several promising experimental NbS, engineering, and institutional measures are developed to achieve the goals, and an examination of the feasibility of achieving the goals and the economic and environmental impact of each combination is narrowed down to a candidate plan. Finally, the combination of promising measures is evaluated with stakeholders to determine the optimal combination of measures. Figure 12.15 shows an example of this sequence of planning steps.

Evaluation method of the plan

For NbS to be sustainable, its economic aspects should also be given consideration. Long-term benefits should be weighed against short-term costs, and short-term actions against long-term goals and plans. If an NbS does not properly consider the economics of the plan, it runs the risk of ending up as a short-term project (IUCN, 2020). To this end, the entire plan, including NbS, should first be evaluated for the achievement of social goals and objectives related to disaster risk reduction and assessment of environmental impacts. If there are no problems, the economic potential of the entire plan should be evaluated through a cost–benefit analysis (CBA).

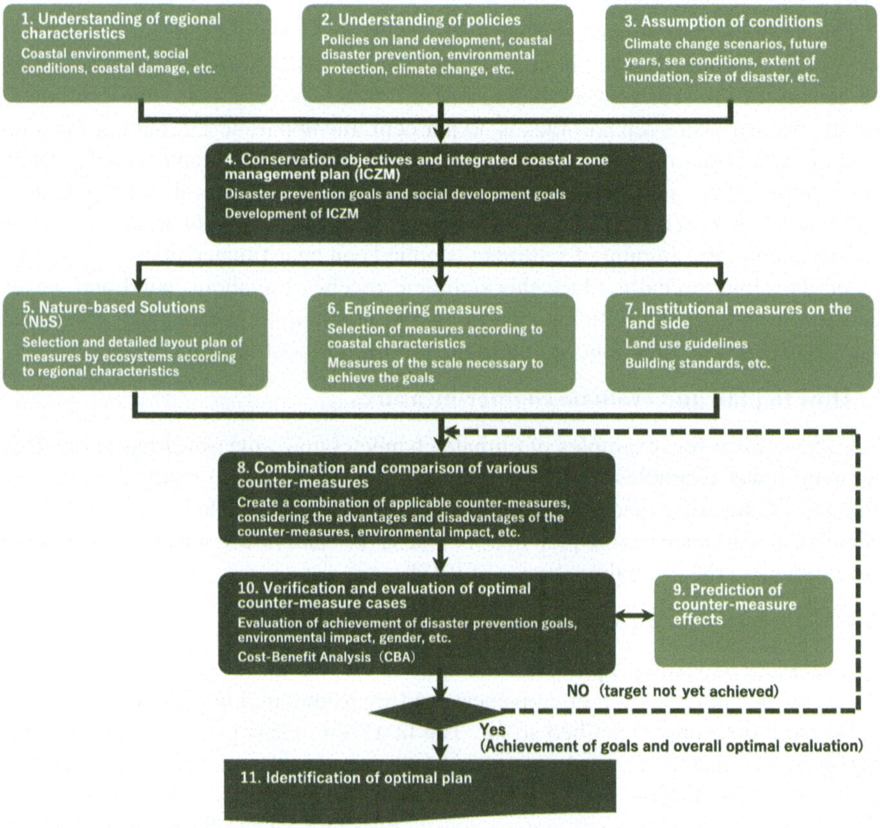

Fig. 12.15 How to proceed with a plan of action including NbS for the protection of coastal communities. *Source* authors' illustration

- takes into account all costs and benefits associated with the project;
- evaluates from the perspective of society as a whole, not from the perspective of individuals or specific groups;
- makes monetary assessments for every item possible in order to compare benefits and costs on an equal basis;
- aggregates and evaluates future costs and benefits within a single unit of time (dimension).

For this purpose, costs and benefits are calculated by year, unified into nominal values, converted into present values, and then added together over the planning period. To convert costs and benefits to present value, the social discount rate (the rate at which a society would be willing to trade present for future consumption) is applied. The total costs and benefits converted to present value are then evaluated as a single metric, such as net present value (NPV), i.e. the total benefits in terms of present value minus the total costs. The higher this value, the higher the economic value that the project brings. SPREP (2013) and others describe more-specific economic evaluation methodologies for projects in the Pacific.

12.4 Considerations for NbS Planning

Few examples exist of NbS action plans, and because NbS relies on the functioning of ecosystems, there are many uncertainties about their effectiveness and sustainability compared with conventional engineering measures. We list here a number of issues that need to be considered when planning NbS measures.

A. **Accurate understanding and analysis of the problem**

Media reports that low-elevation atolls have begun to be submerged due to sea level rise are the basis for appeals from island nations to the rest of the world. In many cases, however, the reported submerged areas were previously uninhabited, especially those at low elevations or facing the open ocean. In other cases, anthropogenic run-off from population growth and lifestyle changes enter coral reefs, killing the corals and foraminifera that would otherwise build the islands (Kayanne, 2022). The problems reported to be caused by climate change need to be properly analysed, and responses planned according to the mechanism of the problem, as direct effects, such as population concentration on islands and lifestyle changes, and indirect effects due to climate change are intricately linked.

B. **Accurate prediction of the effects of climate change**

To develop appropriate counter-measure plans for the long term, it is necessary to accurately predict the effects of climate change on marine phenomena and incorporate this into planning conditions. For example, typhoons such as Haiyan and Meranti, and cyclones such as Pam and Winston, which develop in low latitudes, often cause storm surges and storm surge disasters, but it is difficult to statistically assess future hazards in each region based on existing data alone. Therefore, it is necessary to predict future impacts using a stochastic typhoon model, developed for low latitude areas where typhoons are frequent but irregular, and a coastal inundation simulation model based on these results (Tajima et al., 2020).

C. **Consideration of time-varying factors**

While engineering structures such as coastal levees can provide their intended benefits immediately upon completion of construction, they cannot respond to long-term changes in external forces such as sea level rise, and their effectiveness tends to decline over time due to age-related deterioration and damage. On the other hand, ecosystem-based counter-measures are characterized by slow-acting effects that do not occur immediately after implementation but increase in effectiveness as organisms grow and reproduce. The effects of climate change increase over time. It is necessary to plan for the temporal characteristics of the effects of each measure and the changes in external factors such as the effects of climate change over time.

D. **Understanding the characteristics of NbS**

The specific properties of NbS can be understood as follows.

Slow-acting effects and evolution

Because the scale and shape of NbS change with the growth of biota, the time required for their effects to be fully expressed tends to be longer than for engineering measures. NbS should be designed with such delayed and evolving effects in mind.

Uncertainty of effects

Biological characteristics and environmental factors such as oceanographic and meteorological conditions can affect the rate of recovery and growth of an ecosystem. Where evaluable data is available, the planning of additional restoration methods and the additional effects of engineering measures should be considered in advance to respond to the probability of occurrence and consequences assumed for each scenario.

Sediment transport characteristics in coastal areas

In PICTs, the construction of causeways, harbours, and jetties connecting islands has impeded beach movement along the coast, and wave reflection from upright seawalls has changed the coast from a place of sand deposition to a place of erosion (Kayanne, 2022). In addition, coastal sediments move along the coastline and behave differently in terms of sedimentation and erosion at different locations. In particular, on atoll islands, the reefs on the open ocean side produce a large amount of sediment, which is transported in large quantities to the lagoon side through fractures in the island. To ensure that the installation of engineering works does not adversely affect sediment transport over the entire island, the sediment dynamics must be properly understood and planned for in advance.

12.5 Conclusions and Future Prospects

A. Conclusions

Coastal communities in PICTs have benefited greatly from coastal ecosystems such as coral reefs. However, the effects of climate change, such as rising sea levels and stronger waves threaten their security and sustainability. In addition to high water temperatures and acidification caused by climate change, anthropogenic discharges and destructive fishing practices degrade coastal ecosystems. Maintaining the sustainability of coastal communities and coastal ecosystems in PICTs, which are inherently more vulnerable to the effects of climate change, is therefore an important issue.

In response to these challenges, PICTs and other countries have used engineering coastal protection measures such as revetments and wave breakers for coastal protection, and coral reef and mangrove seedlings have been grown and transplanted to further support coastal ecosystem protection. Although the effectiveness of engineering coastal protection measures is highly reliable, the high cost of construction and the difficulty of repairing damage and deterioration over time have been obstacles to their widespread use, especially in PICTs. To solve this problem, the concept of NbS should be introduced, in which the ecosystem is actively used in terms of wave suppression and sediment supply.

In the application of NbS, it is important to evaluate the role of coral reefs as wave suppressors, sediment producers, fish and shellfish growers, and tourism resources, in addition to their role as wave suppressors. The application of NbS must also take into account the vulnerability of biota to rapid climate change and extreme external forces, as well as the time required for the effects of the intervention to manifest themselves. Therefore, the optimal combination of NbS and engineering coastal protection measures,, in terms of both time and space, should be considered. In addition to human drainage measures that complement NbS, social institutions on the land side, such as land use planning and building codes, should be added to help to reduce the costs and environmental impacts of hard measures. Ideally, these should be integrated into a unified perspective.

PICTs have so far mainly carried out the restoration of coral reefs, which is considered central in the use of NbS, on a relatively small scale. It is important at the next stage to seek to increase the size of the restoration area while reducing restoration costs and ensuring biodiversity, to implement an approach that applies a sexual reproduction method to a large area. In addition, a method should also be considered to increase the adaptive capacity of coral communities by studying those that have adapted to environmental changes in the warming ocean and selectively increasing the number of them.

B. Future prospects

Planning and implementing conservation measures for coastal communities and ecosystems, including NbS, requires human resources with interdisciplinary knowledge of the issues, but the relatively small populations and high proportion of people working abroad in PICTs means that there is likely to be a shortage of such personnel.

In addition, the relatively small economies of PICTs may not have sufficient domestic resources, not only for implementation but also for the research and planning phases. Therefore, PICTs may need to consider international support funds. But there is also concern about the lack of human resources capable of developing counter-measure plans, including NbS, properly evaluating their effectiveness and dealing with the complex process of applying for funds. To overcome this, PICTs must identify the problems to be solved and the goals to be achieved at an early stage; to establish a system of cooperation with countries and organizations that have the relevant knowledge, funds, and human resources; and to work together. These measures will reduce the risk of climate change-related disasters for coastal communities in PICTs and maximize the benefits of coastal ecosystems, thereby enhancing the sustainability of society and nature in PICTs.

References

Barshis DJ, Ladner JT, Oliver TA, Seneca FO, Traylor-Knowles N, Palumbi SR (2013) Genomic basis for coral resilience to climate change. Proc Natl Acad Sci 110(4):1387–1392

Crippa M, Guizzardi D, Banja M, Solazzo E, Muntean M, Schaaf E, Pagani F, Monforti-Ferrario F, Olivier JGJ, Quadrelli R, Grassi G, Rossi S, Oom D, Branco A, San-Miguel J, Vignati E (2022) CO_2 emissions of all world countries: 2022 report. Publications Office of the European Union, Luxembourg

De Groot R, Brander L, Van der Ploeg S, Costanza R, Bernard F, Braat L, Christie M, Crossman N, Ghermandi A, Hein L, Hussain S, Kumar P, McVittie A, Portela R, Rodriguez L, Ten Brink P, van Beukering P (2012) Global estimates of the value of ecosystems and their services in monetary units. Ecosyst Serv 1(1):50–61

De'ath G, Fabricius KE (2008) Water quality of the Great Barrier Reef: distributions, effects on reef biota and trigger values for the protection of ecosystem health. Final Report to the Great Barrier Reef Marine Park Authority. Australian Institute of Marine Science

Dixon GB, Davies SW, Aglyamova GV, Meyer E, Bay LK, Matz MV (2015) Genomic determinants of coral heat tolerance across latitudes. Science 348(6242):1460–1462

Doropoulos C, Vons F, Elzinga J, ter Hofstede R, Salee K, van Koningsveld M, Babcock RC (2019) Testing industrial-scale coral restoration techniques: harvesting and culturing wild coral-spawn slicks. Front Marine Sci 6(25 Oct)

Ferrario F, Beck MW, Storlazzi CD, Micheli F, Shepard CC, Airoldi L (2014) The effectiveness of coral reefs for coastal hazard risk reduction and adaptation. Nat Commun 5(1), article 3794

Hazraty-Kari S, Tavakoli-Kolour P, Kitanobo S, Nakamura T, Morita M (2022) Adaptations by the coral Acropora tenuis confer resilience to future thermal stress. Commun Biol 5(1371)

Hongo C, Kayanne H (2010) Holocene sea-level record from corals: reliability of paleodepth indicators at Ishigaki Island Ryukyu Islands, Japan. Palaeogeogr Palaeoclimatol Palaeoecol 287:143–151

Humanes A, Beauchamp EA, Bythell JC, Carl MK, Craggs JR, Edwards AJ, Golbuu Y, Lachs L, Martinez HM, Palmowski P, Paysinger F, Randle JL, van der Steeg E, Sweet M, Treumann A, Guest JR (2021) An experimental framework for selectively breeding corals for assisted evolution. Front Mar Sci 8:669995

IPCC (Intergovernmental Panel on Climate Change) (2019) Summary for policymakers. In: Pörtner H-O, Roberts DC, Masson-Delmotte V, Zhai P, Tignor M, Poloczanska E, Mintenbeck K, Alegría A, Nicolai M, Okem A, Petzold J, Rama B, Weye NM (eds) Special report on the ocean and cryosphere in a changing climate. Cambridge University Press, Cambridge and New York, pp 3–35

IPCC (2021) Summary for policymakers. In: Masson-Delmotte V, Zhai P, Pirani A, Connors SL, Péan C, Berger S, Caud N, Chen Y, Goldfarb L, Gomis MI, Huang M, Leitzell K, Lonnoy E, Matthews JBR, Maycock TK, Waterfield T, Yelekçi O, Yu R, Zhou B (eds) Climate change 2021: the physical science basis. Contribution of working group I to the sixth assessment report of the intergovernmental panel on climate change. Cambridge University Press, Cambridge and New York, pp 3–32

IUCN (International Union for Conservation of Nature and Natural Resources) (2020) IUCN global standard for nature-based solutions. IUCN, Gland

JFA (Japan Fisheries Agency) (2019) Revised: guide to coral propagation by sexual reproduction. JFA, Kasumigaseki

JFA (2022) Commissioned project to develop and demonstrate technologies for the conservation and restoration of coral reefs under severe environmental conditions [Online]. Available at: www.jfa.maff.go.jp/j/seibi/attach/pdf/sango_houkoku_h30-5.pdf. Accessed 1 Feb 2024

Kayanne H (1992) Deposition of calcium carbonate into Holocene reefs and its relation to sea-level rise and atmospheric CO_2. In: Proceedings of the 7th international coral reef symposium, no 1, pp 50–55

Kayanne H (2016) Response of coral reefs to global warming. In: Kayanne H (ed) Coral reef science: strategy for ecosystem symbiosis and coexistence with humans under multiple stresses. Springer, Cham, pp 81–94

Kayanne H (2022) Atoll submergence and Pacific marine environmental security. J World Aff 71:30

Kayanne H, Aoki K, Suzuki T, Hongo C, Yamano H, Ide Y, Iwatsuka Y, Takahashi K, Katayama H, Sekimoto T, Isobe M (2016) Eco-geomorphic processes that maintain a small coral reef island: Ballast Island in the Ryukyu Islands, Japan. Geomorphology 271:84–93

Kumar L (ed) (2020) Climate change and impacts in the Pacific. Springer Nature, Cham

Laurans Y, Pascal N, Binet T, Brander L, Clua E, David G, Rojat D, Seidl A (2013) Economic valuation of ecosystem services from coral reefs in the South Pacific: taking stock of recent experience. J Environ Manage 116:135–144

MEHDE (Ministry of Environment, Human Resource Development and Employment, Mauritius) (1999) Guidelines for coastal water quality, no 620/1999. MEHDE, Port Louis

MLIT (Ministry of Land, Infrastructure and Transportation, Japan) (2003) Marine nature restoration handbook, vol 4. MLIT, Tokyo

Montaggioni LF (2005) History of Indo-Pacific coral reef systems since the last glaciation: development patterns and controlling factors. Earth Sci Rev 71(1–2):1–75

Moritz C, Vii J, Lee Long W, Tamelander J, Thomassin A, Planes S (eds) (2018) Status and trends of coral reefs of the Pacific. Glob Coral Reef Monit Netw

Nicholls RJ, Wong PP, Burkett V, Codignotto J, Hay J, McLean R, Ragoonaden S, Woodroffe CD (2007) Coastal systems and low-lying areas. In: Parry ML, Canziani OF, Palutikof JP, van der Linden PJ, Hanson C (eds) Climate change 2007: impacts, adaptation and vulnerability. Contribution of working group II to the fourth assessment report of the intergovernmental panel on climate change. Cambridge University Press, Cambridge, pp 315–356

Ohnaka S, Ichikuwa S, Izumi M, Uda T, Hirano J, Sawada H (2017) Study on effectiveness of gravel beach nourishment in Tuvalu. J JSCE 73(2):528–533

Omija T (2004) Terrestrial inflow of soils and nutrients. In: Japanese Coral Reef Society and Ministry of the Environment (eds) Coral reefs of Japan. Ministry of the Environment, Japan, Tokyo, pp 64–68

Omori M (2016) A goal for >40% coral survival rate after 3 years out-planting: a reasonable requirement and prospect of active reef restoration. Midoriishi 27:1–4

Omori M (2019) Coral restoration research and technical developments: what we have learned so far. Mar Biol Res 15(7):377–409

PaCE-SD (Pacific Centre for Environment and Sustainable Development, University of the South Pacific) (2015) Coastal protection: best practices in the Pacific. USP, Suva. [Online]. Available at: http://repository.usp.ac.fj/8219/1/Paeniu_et_al._2015_Best_Practices_in_Coastal_Protection_for_the_Pacific.pdf. Accessed 1 Feb 2024

Perry CT, Alvarez-Filip L, Graham NAJ, Mumby PJ, Wilson SK, Kench PS, Manzello DP, Morgan KM, Slangen ABA, Thomson DP, Januchowski-Hartley F, Smithers SG, Steneck RS, Carlton R, Edinger EN, Enochs IC, Estrada-Saldívar N, Haywood MDE, Kolodziej G, Murphy GN, Pérez-Cervantes E, Suchley A, Valentino L, Boenish R, Wilson M, Macdonald C (2018) Loss of coral reef growth capacity to track future increases in sea level. Nature 558:396–400

Perry CT, Lange ID, Stuhr M (2023) Quantifying reef-derived sediment generation: introducing the SedBudget methodology to support tropical coastline and island vulnerability studies. Cambridge Prisms: Coastal Futures 1, e26

Post JC, Lundink CG (1996) Guidelines for integrated coastal zone management. World Bank, Washington, DC

Reguero BG, Secaira F, Toimil A, Escudero M, Díaz-Simal P, Beck MW, Rodolfo S, Storlazzi C, Losada IJ (2019) The risk reduction benefits of the Mesoamerican Reef in Mexico. Front Earth Sci 7, 28 May

RMI (Government of the Republic of Marshall Islands) (2020) Adaptation communication: Republic of the Marshall Islands (RMI). RMI, Majuro

RRAP (Reef Restoration and Adaptation Program) (no date) Coral seeding by automated aquaculture [Online]. Available at: https://gbrrestoration.org/program/coral-seeding-by-automated-aquaculture. Accessed 1 Feb 2023

SPC (The Pacific Community) (2020) Pacific island populations 2020 [Online]. Available at: https://pacificdata.org/story/pacific-island-populations-2020. Accessed 1 Feb 2024

SPREP (Secretariat of the Pacific Regional Environment Programme) (2013) Cost–benefit analysis for natural resource management in the Pacific: a guide. SPREP, Suva [Online]. Available at: https://pacific-data.sprep.org/system/files/cost-benefit-analysis-natural-resources-management-pacific.pdf. Accessed 1 Feb 2024

SPREP (2020) Pacific ecosystem-based adaptation to climate change. SPREP, Apia [Online]. Available at: www.sprep.org/sites/default/files/documents/publications/Pacific-Ecosystem-based-adaptation-climate-change.pdf. Accessed 1 Feb 2024

SPREP (2021) Pacific coral reef action plan 2021–2030. SPREP, Apia [Online]. Available at: https://library.sprep.org/content/pacific-coral-reef-action-plan-2021-2030. Accessed: 1 Feb 2024

Storlazzi CD, Reguero BG, Cole AD, Lowe E, Shope JB, Gibbs AE, Nickel BA, McCall RT, van Dongeren AR, Beck MW (2019) Rigorously valuing the role of U.S. coral reefs in coastal hazard risk reduction. US Geological Survey, Santa Cruz, CA

Suzuki G, Okada W, Yasutake Y, Yamamoto H, Tanita I, Yamashita H, Hayashibara T, Komatsu T, Kanyama T, Inoue M, Yamazaki M (2020) Enhancing coral larval supply and seedling production using a special bundle collection system "coral larval cradle" for large-scale coral restoration. Restor Ecol 28(5):1172–1182

Tajima Y, Shoji T, Taniguchi K (2020) Study on probabilistic inundation hazard along the coast of South Pacific islands: case study at Lakeba Island in Fiji. J JSCE: B2 (Coastal Engineering) 76(2):I_1231–I_1236

Takemori R, Tajima Y, Fujikawa H, Kayanne H (2015) Investigation on characteristics of local accumulation of coral gravels on an isolated reef. J JSCE: B2 (Coastal Eng) 71(2):I_721–I_726

Thanopoulou Z, Patus J, Sealey KS (2022) Water quality negatively impacts coral occurrence in eutrophic nearshore environments of the Florida Keys. Front Marine Sci 9:1005036

The Ocean Agency (2016) Ocean image bank [Online]. Available at: www.theoceanagency.org/search-result?img=YGcFGhMAACAAZd2L. Accessed 1 Feb 2024

UNDP (United Nations Development Programme) (2017) Project document template for directly implemented projects financed by the Green Climate Fund (GCF) [Online]. Available at: www.undp.org/sites/g/files/zskgke326/files/migration/pacific/5c6f1a9f1b85558d2815083ad2d275c6322c84a574571dff3803a196e298c92f.pdf. Accessed 1 Feb 2024

UNEA (United Nations Environment Assembly) (2022) Nature-based solutions for supporting sustainable development (UNEP/EA.5/Res.5) [Online]. Available at: https://wedocs.unep.org/bitstream/handle/20.500.11822/39752/K2200677%20-%20UNEP-EA.5-Res.5%20-%20Advance.pdf?sequence=1&isAllowed=y. Accessed 1 Feb 2024
UoH (University of Hawai'i) (2022) UH to develop living coastal-protection system inspired by coral reefs [Online]. Available at: www.hawaii.edu/news/2022/06/17/engineered-coral-reef-ecosystem. Accessed 1 Feb 2024
US EPA (United States Environmental Protection Agency) (2022) Action plan for restoration of coral reef coastal protection services: case study example and workbook. EPA, Washington, DC [Online]. Available at: https://icriforum.org/wp-content/uploads/2022/03/EPA_CORAL_REEF_RESTORATION_ACTION_PLAN_FEB2022.pdf. Accessed 1 Feb 2024
Yamano H, Kayanne H, Yamaguchi T, Kuwahara Y, Yokoki H, Shimazaki H, Chikamori M (2007) Atoll island vulnerability to flooding and inundation revealed by historical reconstruction: Fongafale Islet, Funafuti Atoll, Tuvalu. Global Planet Change 57:407–416

Part IV
Peace and Partnership

Chapter 13
Micronesian Unity at the Crossroads: Past Events and Future Perspectives

Maho Inomata and Masato Abe

Abstract This chapter examines the decoupling process of the six districts of the Trust Territory of the Pacific Islands (TTPI)—Northern Marianas, Palau, Yap, Truk, Ponape (including Kosrae), and Marshall Islands—during the 1960s and 1970s. The TTPI was a political entity created according to Micronesia's colonial history, its geographical and demographic characteristics, with diverse ethnic groups living in scarce populations on scattered tiny remote islands, economic gaps, and other internal factors determined by the United States' security interests. The decoupling process eventually led to the establishment of territory of the United States, the Commonwealth of the Northern Mariana Islands, and three sovereign nations: Palau, Federated States of Micronesia, and Marshall Islands. Some scholars claim that the United States failed to institute regional political unity within the TTPI, while others argue that it intentionally encouraged Micronesia's separationist sentiment. None of them, however, adequately address the Micronesians' reactions to the United States' geopolitical interests and actions. By assessing the primary sources mainly on the Micronesian side, this chapter presents the Micronesians' responses to the American policy towards the TTPI in the context of the dynamics of the Cold War in Asia and the Pacific and the wave of decolonization under the United Nations' supervision. It also investigates the historical crossroad for failed Micronesian unity that still affects today's Micronesia, comprehended in the context of the Compact of Free Association (CoFA) with the United States, a security, political, and economic framework of the bilateral relationship deeply embedded in the present issues.

M. Inomata (✉)
Embassy of Japan, Federated States of Micronesia, Kolonia, Micronesia
e-mail: maho.inomata@mofa.go.jp

M. Abe
United Nations Multi-Country Office for Micronesia, Kolonia, Federated States of Micronesia
e-mail: abem@un.org

E. Monaco and M. Abe (eds.), *Sustainable Development Across Pacific Islands*,
https://doi.org/10.1007/978-981-97-3629-4_13

13.1 Introduction

Micronesia literally means "tiny islands". Today the term refers to an area or subregion composed of five sovereign states (Palau, Federated States of Micronesia/FSM, Marshall Islands, Nauru, and Kiribati) within the 14 Pacific island countries and territories (PICTs) (United Nations Fiji, Solomon Islands, Tonga, Tuvalu, and Vanuatu 2023; United Nations Micronesia, no date). The term "PICTs" also covers Melanesia and Polynesia. In this chapter, the terms "Micronesia" and "Micronesian" refer to the area or subregion of the former Trust Territory of the Pacific Islands (TTPI) under the United Nations Trusteeship System in the Northern Pacific and its people, including Palau, FSM, Marshall Islands, and the Commonwealth of the Northern Mariana Islands (CNMI), and excluding Nauru and Kiribati.

The TTPI consisted of six districts: Northern Marianas, Palau, Yap, Truk (presently called Chuuk), Ponape (Pohnpei), and Marshall Islands. Kosrae (previously known as Kusaie) was separated from Ponape as the seventh district in 1977. After the negotiations between the TTPI and the United States, the CNMI and three states freely associated with the United States—Palau, FSM, and Marshall Islands—were eventually formed through the enforcement of their own constitutions. The United States established a Compact of Free Association (CoFA) with FSM and Marshall Islands in 1986 and Palau in 1994. The CoFAs provide these three countries with defence, economic assistance, and access to the social services of the United States.

A. ***Micronesia today***

Due to its geographical, demographic, and political characteristics, Micronesia faces multidimensional problems today. More than 2000 islands stretch across Micronesia (McHenry 1975). It is roughly the size of the continental United States, but its total land area is only about half the size of Rhode Island, the smallest state in the United States. Three archipelagos, namely the Mariana Islands, Caroline Islands, and Marshall Islands, constitute Micronesia (Meller 1985).[1] The subregion is located along the primary air and sea routes in the Northern Pacific. Its geographical characteristics of scattered and remote small islands make Micronesia vulnerable to international logistics and the risk of isolation from communications networks and imported goods and commodities. Socioeconomic activities in Micronesia have relied heavily on Guam and Hawaii as sources of higher education, advanced healthcare, regular transportation, and better employment.

---

[1] The Mariana Islands, located on the northern edge of the TTPI, is a single chain along a north–south line and constitutes the Northern Marianas district. Although it shares the common geological characteristics of limestone shelf and volcanic soil with Guam, the district excludes Guam. Guam has been under American rule since the Spanish–American War. The Caroline Islands, located in the south-west below the Mariana Islands and Guam and extending eastward over an arc towards Marshall Islands, consists of four TTPI districts, Palau, Yap, Truk, and Ponape (including Kosrae). Marshall Islands, located in the eastern TTPI, are scattered along two parallel north–south axes (the Ralik and Ratak chains) and constitute the Marshall district.

Population in Micronesia is sparse, and it has faced depopulation. It contains multiple cultural groups and even more languages and subdialects. People from Palau, FSM, and Marshall Islands can easily move to the United States without a visa (Hunt 2023). Young, ambitious, and even non-skilled labourers often migrate to the United States to seek better education and jobs or live with family members who have already settled there. Although these migrants often send remittances back home, the amounts have not been great in Micronesia (International Organization for Migration 2016). Small populations and depopulation have caused labour shortages and shrinking domestic markets in Micronesia (Economic and Social Commission for Asia and the Pacific 2007).

Even after the failed attempt to develop a single unified Micronesian country, political disunities continue among the former TTPI districts. Shortly after taking his oath of office in May 2023, the new FSM president, Wesley W. Simina, began formal visits to all four states of FSM: Yap, Chuuk, Pohnpei, and Kosrae. The primary purpose was to strengthen engagement and relationships between the federal government (based in Palikir on Pohnpei) and the four state governments, in accord with his new administration's motto, "Unity is our strength and prosperity" (Falcam 2023). The federal government and the four states have not entirely eradicated political disunities, which stem from long-standing disagreements and tensions driven by the history of Micronesia.

B. ***Micronesia's history***

From the time that Spanish explorer Ferdinand Magellan accidentally "discovered" Micronesia in 1520 until the early twentieth century, the islands were controlled by Spain and Germany (Micronesia Support Committee and Pacific Concerns Resource Center 1982, p. 6). Subsequently, Japan forced the capitulation of the islands without bloodshed when the First World War broke out in 1914 and started administrating Micronesia under the Mandates System established by the League of Nations in 1919. During the Second World War, some of the Micronesian islands turned into the bloodiest battlefields between the United States and Japan, and numerous people, including Micronesians, died. The Mandates System was replaced with the International Trusteeship System established by the United Nations in 1945. Because of the United States' permanent interest in the security of the Northern Pacific, it administered the TTPI as a "strategic area" exceptionally under the supervision of the United Nations Security Council, while other Trust Territories were administered under the supervision of the United States Trusteeship Council (McHenry 1975).

From the early 1960s, the United States' attitude toward the TTPI significantly changed because of its growing strategic interests in the Northern Pacific, contextualized by the Cold War and its reflection on the decolonization of the "Third World" under the United Nations' supervision. Along with these external influences, the internal unity of the TTPI was eroded partially because of its political separatism. Once TTPI districts began considering their future political status, existing differences, including hidden political goals, finally emerged through an extensive series of discussions. The 1978 plebiscite in the TTPI was a crucial crossroad that eventually led to the founding of three sovereign nations, Palau, FSM, and Marshall Islands; establishing the CoFAs with the United States.

C. ***Objectives***

Some scholars (Hezel 1978; Meller 1985) claim that the United States aimed to establish political unity among the TTPI districts as its ultimate goal, while others (Kiste 1986; McHenry 1975) argue that it intentionally encouraged separationist sentiment. However, none discuss sufficiently what the TTPI districts considered their future political status to be or how they approached the United States to achieve their political goals. Therefore, this chapter examines the decoupling process of the six districts and an additional district from the TTPI during the 1960s and 1970s in their quest to achieve self-governing status. By analysing the primary sources, mainly on the Micronesian side, the chapter assesses how the TTPI districts reacted against the United States' geopolitical interests, and what led to their unity in seeking to dissolve the Trust Territory. It suggests that the historical crossroad still affects today's Micronesia, particularly FSM, comprehending the CoFA as a framework of bilateral relationships and a political system deeply embedded in the subregion's socio-political and socioeconomic issues.

13.2 The Trust Territory of the Pacific Islands

The history of the US administration of the TTPI can be divided into two periods. As Kiste (1986) describes it, the first period began during the final stage of the war and lasted until the early 1960s; the second was from the inauguration of President John F. Kennedy to the late 1970s, with the advent of internal self-government. This section provides a brief overview these two periods.

A. ***First TTPI period (end of Second World War to early 1960s)***

On 26 July 1945, the Mandates System under the League of Nations was replaced with the International Trusteeship System, which embodied Chapter XII (12) of the Charter of the United Nations. Eleven Trust Territories were placed under the supervision of the International Trusteeship System by individual agreements with the administrators (Dag Hammarskjöld Library, no date; United Nations, no date).[2] However, because of the United States' solid military interests, the definition of "strategic area" in Articles 82 and 83 applied to Micronesia, exceptionally allowing

[2] The 11 Trust Territories were Western Samoa; Tanganyika; Rwanda-Urundi; Cameroons under British administration; Cameroons under French administration; Togoland under British administration; Togoland under French administration; New Guinea; Nauru; Strategic Trust Territory of the Pacific Islands; and Italian Somaliland. British-administered Togoland united with the Gold Coast (a non-self-governing territory) to form Ghana in March 1957. French-administered Cameroons became independent as Cameroon in January 1960. French-administered Togoland became independent as Togo in April 1960. Italian Somaliland, united with British Somaliland to form Somalia in July 1960. Following a plebiscite in British-administered Cameroons, the northern part of Cameroons joined Nigeria and its southern part joined Cameroon in February 1961. Tanganyika,

the United States to administrate the TTPI, then the Mandated Islands, under the supervision of the United Nations Security Council while other trusteeship arrangements were under the authority of the General Assembly (McHenry 1975). The Trusteeship Agreement for the Territory of the Pacific Islands was approved by the Security Council on 2 April 1947 and by the president of the United States on 18 July 1947. The agreement gave the administrating authority to the United States to "promote the development of the inhabitants of the trust territory towards self-governing or independence as may be appropriate to the particular circumstances of the trust territory and its peoples and the freely expressed wishes of the peoples concerned" (UNSC 1947, p. 18). It guided the overall direction of the United States in defining the future political status of the TTPI.

The early stage of the Cold War, however, affected the administrative authority to induce a new role for the TTPI in contributing to a global arms race, and the noble mission of advancing the wellbeing of the people of Micronesia. Kwajalein Atoll in Marshalls was initially developed as a naval site, later as a missile test site. Bikini and Eniwetok Atolls were used for numerous nuclear tests from 1946 to 1958 (McHenry 1975). The Central Intelligence Agency (CIA) used Saipan in the Northern Marianas district for training Nationalist Chinese troops from 1951 to 1962 (Kiste 1986).

The Department of the Interior replaced the navy as the administrator in 1951, and the TTPI administrative headquarters in Pearl Harbour in Hawaii was moved to Guam in 1954, then to Saipan in Northern Marianas in 1962. However, Saipan and Tinian in Northern Marianas were administered by the navy until 1962 because of military presence and restricted entry into these territories, which excluded foreigners from entering Micronesia because Northern Marianas was then the doorway to Micronesia (McHenry 1975). During that period, the United States administration employed a "benign neglect" or "ethnographic zoo [or museum]" policy to protect Micronesian economies and societies from outside influence (Kiste 1986, p. 128). Only authorized persons, mostly anthropologists or nuclear scientists, were allowed to visit Micronesia (Heine 1974). Under the military administration, efforts to bring Micronesians "towards self-government or independence", as the Trusteeship Agreement promised, were made tardily.

B. ***Second TTPI period (Kennedy administration to late 1970s)***

From the Kennedy administration in the early 1960s onwards, the United States' attitude towards the TTPI significantly changed because of its reflection on the decolonization of the developing world under United Nations supervision and its

under British administration, became independent in December 1961, and Tanganyika and Zanzibar united to form the United Republic of Tanzania in 1964. Western Samoa, under New Zealand administration, became independent in January 1962, changing its name to Samoa in 1997. Ruanda-Urundi, under Belgian administration, became the two independent and sovereign states of Rwanda and Burundi in July 1962. Nauru, administered by Australia on behalf of the administrating authorities of Australia, New Zealand, and the United Kingdom, became independent in January 1968. New Guinea, administered by Australia, united with the non-self-governing territory of Papua, also administered by Australia, to become the independent state of Papua New Guinea in September 1975. In the TTPI, administered by the United States, with no territories left on its agenda, the Trusteeship Council suspended its operations on 1 November 1994.

strategic interests in the Northern Pacific in the context of the Cold War throughout the Johnson and Nixon administrations until the late 1970s.

Evolving anti-colonalism in the United Nations

As the wave of anti-colonialism surged globally, the United States' policy towards the TTPI reached a turning point in the early 1960s. The United Nations General Assembly adopted Resolution 1514, the Declaration on the Granting of Independence to Colonial Countries and Peoples (also known as the Declaration on Decolonization) on 14 December 1960. It suggested three channels to achieving self-governance: (i) emergence as a sovereign independent state; (ii) free association with an independent state; and (iii) integration with an independent state (United Nations 1960). The Special Committee on the Situation with regard to the Implementation of the Declaration on the Granting of Independence to Colonial Countries and Peoples (also known as the Special Committee on Decolonization, or Committee 24) was established as the General Assembly's subsidiary organ specializing in the issue of decolonization, after Resolution 1654 was adopted on 27 November 1961. A United Nations mission visited the TTPI in 1951; after that, missions visited approximately every three years until the CoFA was approved by the plebiscite in Palau in November 1993.

The visiting mission of 1961 harshly criticized the fact that Saipan, still under navy administration, was benefiting from economic advantages and "(reverse) financial discrimination" (United Nations Visiting Mission to the Trust Territory of the Pacific Islands 1961, p. 3) because large US military expenditures had encouraged separatism between Northern Marianas and the other Micronesian districts. When the Trusteeship Council considered the visiting mission's report on 21 June 1961, U. Thant, a representative from Myanmar and later the third secretary general of the United Nations, pointed out that Saipan was still under military rule while the rest of the districts were under civilian authority (United Nations Trusteeship Council 1961). Saipan enjoyed privileges that could hamper the creation of a feeling of unity among Micronesian people.

The visiting mission of 1964 again cast doubt on political conditions in the TTPI, stating that Micronesians had not sufficiently considered the range of possibilities for their future political status. Almost all speakers in the district legislatures assumed that there were only two alternatives: independence, or integration with the United States. Since Micronesia would not be self-sufficient, at least in the foreseeable future, most people concluded that the only practical alternative was some form of integration with the United States as a part of Hawaii or the Territory of Guam instead of independence, which would mean that Micronesia would have to stand entirely by itself and that the United States would immediately cease, or significantly decrease, its aid (United Nations Visiting Mission to the Trust Territory of the Pacific Islands 1964).

Kennedy administration

Kennedy's sensitivity to colonialism drastically changed the United States' policy toward the TTPI after he assumed the presidency in early 1961. Responding to anti-colonialist criticism, his administration shed light on socioeconomic and political development in the TTPI by increasing the budget and conducting surveys led by economists, anthropologists, and military personnel.

Kennedy condemned all forms of colonialism at the United Nations General Assembly on 25 September 1961 (McHenry 1975). Consequently, his administration launched the first of a massive array of federal programmes and aid increases in 1962. By 1963, the Department of Interior's annual budget for the territory had tripled to $15 million. By 1978, the annual appropriation had reached $100 million, with an additional $30 million for federal programmes (Kiste 1986). The administration also launched education and health programmes, and many Americans, such as teachers and engineers, were deployed to Micronesia as Peace Corps volunteers (McHenry 1975).

The Kennedy administration also fundamentally transformed the United States' perspectives on its long-term relationship with Micronesia. On 18 April 1962, the president issued National Security Action Memoranda (NASM) No. 145, New Policy for the United States Trust Territory of the Pacific Islands. It states that the long-term goals of developing the TTPI are to establish a viable territory permanently associated with the United States and assure a standard of living consistent with such association (NSAM 1962a). The memorandum called for accelerated development of the area to bring its political, economic, and social standards into line with an eventual permanent association with the United States. The memorandum led to the establishment of a task force to consider what action might be taken to accomplish the United States' goals. The task force also aimed to provide policy and programme advice to the secretary of the interior, who was responsible for the administration of the TTPI. The task force consisted of representatives of the Departments of Interior, Defense, State, Health, Education, and Welfare, as well as observers from the National Security Council and the Bureau of the Budget. The memorandum proposed a survey mission to the TTPI to analyse the essential problems for TTPI's socioeconomic development (NSAM 1962a).

On 9 May 1962, President Kennedy issued NSAM No. 243, which appointed a survey mission headed by the Harvard economist Professor Anthony N. Solomon, later the assistant secretary of state for economic affairs, to assess conditions in the TTPI (NSAM 1962b). The Solomon Report was issued the following year (Solomon 1963). The report advised that if the United States aimed to keep the TTPI within its sphere of influence, it should ensure that Micronesians would desire a close and ongoing relationship with the United States. The report also recommended that the United States pay greater attention to socioeconomic development, especially in making improvements in agriculture, health, education, and capital. Lastly, the report recommended that a plebiscite be held to ensure Micronesians would opt for permanent association with the United States. The report clearly states that Micronesia is essential to the United States for security reasons. At the same time, it says that "time is running out for the United States in the sense that we may soon be the only nation left administrating a trust territory … when the pressures in the United Nations for a settlement of the status of Micronesia could become more than embarrassing" (Solomon 1963, p. 1). While the report admitted the United States' strategic interests in the TTPI and its importance as a priority, it also pressured administrators and policymakers to make progress in the TTPI to reflect the international moral standards.

Johnson administration

According to Gale (1979), under the Johnson administration many new programmes were extended to the TTPI but not in the programmatic manner suggested by the Solomon Report. Although the wars in Indo-China turned the administration's attention away from the TTPI, the "Great Society" programme[3] had a spillover effect on the TTPI and gradually led to the extension of federal education, health, and labour programmes to the TTPI. As a result, the number of personnel and the budget for the TTPI increased, and a precedent was set that the TTPI for considering a domestic matter (Gale 1979).

Nixon administration

Under the intensifying Cold War in the late 1960s, the shifting power correlation in Asia led the United States to reconsider its approach. The so-called "Nixon Doctrine" outlined the most critical aspects in July 1969. It did not declare the United States military withdrawal from Asia but provided vindication for reducing the United States military presence in Japan, Republic of Korea, the Philippines, Thailand, and Viet Nam. The military cited President Nixon's statement as a justification for activating the then vague contingency plans for the TTPI, such as the navy administration and the constant missile experiments (McHenry 1975).

The Nixon administration followed Nixon's predecessors' policy to create a new political status for the TTPI based on the examples of Guam as an unincorporated territory or Puerto Rico as a commonwealth. The task of the United States was to "meet minimal international standards for decolonization, guarantee the protection of strategic and economic interests, prove at least tolerable to Micronesians, conform to the rhetoric of the administration's human rights policies, and not open a Pandora's box encouraging Guam, American Samoa, Puerto Rico and the Virgin Islands, or the new Northern Marianas Commonwealth, to renegotiate their existent statuses of permanent affiliation in fundamental ways" (Gale 1978, pp. 429–430).[4]

13.3 The Birth of a Micronesian Political Entity

The grand strategy related to the Cold War affected the United States' overall policy towards the TTPI in a strategic manner, and officials in Washington still regarded the TTPI as a strategic security point in the Pacific. Nevertheless, the United States

[3] The "Great Society" is described as Johnson's vision to improve the standard of living in the United States by commitment to quality of life, affirmative action, and the government's role as stimulus and guarantor of social change (Zarefsky, 1979).

[4] Northern Marianas obtained commonwealth status with the United States in January 1978, separating from other Micronesian districts as the CNMI.

was also finally aware of the present socioeconomic problems in Micronesia and started considering the future political status of the TTPI. Scientific research and wise outlooks, such as the Solomon Report and the United Nations visiting missions' reports, guided the United States to an understanding of the local situation in the TTPI and to realize its international mandates. When the TTPI districts eagerly anticipated the negotiation for their future political status by the late 1960s, the United States was also ready to sit at the negotiation table.

A. ***The emergence of the Micronesian political entity***

The high commissioner, appointed by the president of the United States with the consent of the United States Senate, headed the executive branch of TTPI. As for the legislature branch, the leaders of the district legislatures participated in inter-district conferences to advise the high commissioner. They voted in 1958 to call themselves the Inter-District Advisory Committee to the High Commissioner. In 1961, they reconstituted themselves as the Council of Micronesia. By the following year, the Council of Micronesia had resolved to create a territory-wide legislature. It was apparent that "Micronesians had taken to heart the American notions about democracy and self-determination" (Kiste 1986, p. 131). In 1965, a bicameral legislature, the Congress of Micronesia (COM), was created, holding its first session in the same year. In 1967, the COM established its own Micronesian Political Status Commission (hereinafter called the Commission) to undertake four mandates: (i) to recommend procedures for and courses of political education in Micronesia; (ii) to study the range of political status alternatives open to Micronesians; (iii) to recommend ways of determining Micronesians' views on their future political status; and (iv) to undertake a comparative study of self-determination in Cook Islands, Puerto Rico, Western Samoa, and other territories (McHenry 1975). The Commission consisted of a representative from each of the six districts. Its chair, Senator Lazarus Salii, later the third president of Palau after its independence, was elected in the initial meeting. The Commission held three sessions, each lasting a week, and submitted its interim reports in 1968 and 1969.

B. ***A blueprint for future political status***

As Micronesians set their political goals and defined their ideal outcome, the first interim report of the Commission of 1968 could be seen as the first crystalized perspective on their future political status. The report suggested four political statuses: (i) independence; (ii) freely associated state; (iii) integration with a sovereign nation as a commonwealth or unincorporated territory; or (iv) remaining a Trust Territory (Micronesia Support Committee and Pacific Concerns Resource Center 1982).

The Commission report of 1969 was more decisive and explicit than that of 1968 in its recommendations. It clearly states that a self-governing state in free association with the United States was the most favourable future political option. The members of the Commission visited the Virgin Islands, Puerto Rico, American Samoa, Western Samoa, Fiji, and Papua New Guinea to consider suitable options for Micronesia's future political status. They also talked with the leaders of Nauru and Cook Islands and met with two members of a subcommittee of the United States Congress. The Commission members assessed political and economic development and determined the administrative and financial requirements for the TTPI. They also conducted public hearings in each district (Udui 1972). Based on their comparative analysis, the Commission finally recommended that the TTPI should be "constituted as a self-governing state and that this Micronesian state—internally self-governing and with Micronesian control of its branches, including the executive—negotiate entry into free association with the United States" (Congress of Micronesia 1969, p. 8). The Commission considered complete independence without any conditions the only alternative if the United States were unsatisfied with the free association option. However, Commission members admitted that independence might bring socioeconomic hardship and administrative difficulties (Congress of Micronesia 1969, p. 9).

The 1969 Commission report also criticized the perspectives of the United States on the Micronesian economy as the counterpart "lacked a clearly defined [economic] objective in Micronesia" (Congress of Micronesia 1969, p. 27). Furthermore, the report condemned Americans' common view that Micronesians should keep their way of life in a subsistence society and economy on islands where unexploded bombs and other debris of the Second World War remained or where the testing of nuclear weapons was conducted. The Commission observed that this view implied the "denial of the opportunity to rise to positions of responsibility in the modern world" (Congress of Micronesia 1969, p. 27).

Finally, the Commission report showed Micronesians' pragmatic self-reflection. It admitted that their land was the most valuable resource to Micronesia and Micronesians but also the only resource of value which Micronesians could offer the United States. The islands had strategic value in the Pacific, so the United States might require the use of some lands for security and military purposes. The report considered that "as a self-governing state in free association with the United States, [Micronesia] would accept the necessity of such military needs" (Congress of Micronesia 1969, p. 44).

C. ***Negotiations***

The Commission reports triggered Micronesians and Americans to sit at the negotiation table. Once the negotiations started, the two delegations were severely divided over the subjects of land control, unilateral termination of the agreement, and the future political status of the TTPI. In 1969, the American delegation did not agree with Micronesia's proposal for land control and unilateral termination. In the following year, the United States informally proposed unincorporated status, later toning down its proposal to Micronesia to commonwealth status. From 1971, the American delegation gradually accommodated its position towards Micronesia's original requests. It agreed on free association and that the United States would control external affairs and Micronesia control internal affairs. In the following year, the parties finally agreed on unilateral termination and a tentative draft of a CoFA. Despite the apparently steady progress of the bilateral negotiations between Micronesia and the United

States, separatism had infiltrated the TTPI, simultaneously caused by the geographical, environmental, and ethno-cultural nature and asymmetric economic development among the districts. Later, some districts, such as the Northern Marianas, Palau, and Marshalls, departed exclusively to separate negotiations with the United States.

1969

Secretary of interior Walter J. Hickel invited the Micronesian delegation to Washington in October 1969 to discuss the future political status of the TTPI. The United States delegation comprised the Departments of Interior, State, and Defense as well as observers from the Senate and House Committees on Interior and Insular Affairs. Harrison Loesch, assistant secretary of the Department of Interior, served as their chair. The Micronesian delegation prepared a list of 11 issues,[5] which the United States delegation was satisfied with, except for land control and unilateral termination of the agreement. The Micronesian delegation insisted that they should have unqualified control of land and that any use of land for military purposes should be subject to negotiation between the two governments, while the United States proposed a formula which would provide the president of the United States with the ultimate power to acquire land in Micronesia (Congress of Micronesia 1970).

Ultimately, the Micronesian delegation failed to reach an agreement with the United States, reporting four reasons to the COM afterwards. The first of these was the United States' "undiminished and inflexible strategic interest" in Micronesia as "the security situation in the Pacific ... remains essentially unchanged" since the end of the Second World War (Congress of Micronesia 1970, p. 45). Second, the United States leaned on its experiences with its territories and possessions, so it hesitated to consider a unique relationship with the TTPI. Third, while the Micronesian delegation centred discussions on the specific critical issues of reaching an agreement defining a new relationship of free association, the United States delegation centred discussions on a firm proposal based on their previous position. Finally, the American delegation implicitly believed that most Micronesians wanted to become American citizens and wanted their islands to become part of the United States. It was the Micronesian delegation's impression that the American delegation believed the future political

[5] The 11 topics were that (i) the people of Micronesia draft and adopt their own constitution; (ii) no confiscation of land and no military bases will be established without consultation and consent of the government of Micronesia and fair compensation, as well as land currently possessed by the United States being negotiated; (iii) the United States will conduct Micronesia's external affairs, provide protection from outside aggression, and consult with Micronesians entering into international obligation; (iv) Micronesia will agree not to allow any other country to enter into Micronesia for military purposes; (v) the United States will agree with an early settlement of Micronesia's post-war damage claims; (vi) the United States will remove all barriers to the free movement of Micronesians into the United States; (vii) same as the free movement of goods from Micronesia into the United States; (viii) the United States will fully consulate with Micronesia regarding shipping, civil aviation, and communication; (ix) the Micronesians will have access to the United States Ninth Circuit Court and the Supreme Court; (x) the Micronesians will continue to use the United States's banking facilities, currency, and postal services; and (xi) the United States will guarantee financial aid to Micronesia.

status of the TTPI should be determined by what the United States offered, rather than what Micronesians and their leaders chose (Congress of Micronesia 1970).

According to the analysis of Kaleb Udui, then legislative counsel to the COM and later the first president of the Senate of Palau, among the three federal departments which had responsibilities for Micronesia (i.e., Interior, State, and Defense), no single agency considered the subject of future political status as "falling within its immediate area of responsibility" (Udui 1972, p. 35). As a result, although there might have already been a broad consensus between Micronesia and the United States, a practical option that the United States might consider acceptable was not formulated. Therefore, it was concerned that "any change in the political status of the islands might jeopardize the eventual use of the islands by the United States for defence purposes [while equipped with no] guidelines by which to evaluate the status quo" (Udui 1972, p. 35).

1970

At the informal talks in January 1970, chair Harrison Loesch presented to the Micronesian delegation a proposal for unincorporated territory status, enabling the United States to gain permanent control and sovereignty over the TTPI. The Micronesian delegation argued that this arrangement might be against the Trusteeship Agreement and rejected the offer (Gale 1979). During the second negotiation round in Saipan in May, the United States delegation proposed that Micronesia become a permanent and self-governing member of the United States as a commonwealth (Congress of Micronesia 1970). The Micronesia delegation rejected this proposal too, because the United States insisted on retaining the right to expropriate land.

1971

In March 1971, President Nixon appointed Ambassador Franklin Haydn Williams, a former assistant secretary of defense, to negotiate over the future political status of Micronesia (Office of Micronesian Status Negotiations 1971b). In October, land control and unilateral termination were still under discussion during the third negotiation round in Hana, Maui, Hawaii. However, the two delegations agreed on a free association, which granted the United States control of defence and foreign affairs and of Micronesia's internal affairs. Also, Micronesians' ratification of the Compact agreement in a plebiscite was suggested as proof of the exercise of sovereignty, as guaranteed by the Charter of the United Nations and the Trusteeship Agreement (Office of Micronesian Status Negotiations 1971b).

The American delegation first publicly stated its future land requirements from the TTPI from a strategic point of view. This was the first crossroad towards Micronesian unity. Regarding land control, Ambassador Williams, in his opening statement on 4 October 1971, justified the United States' demand for land use in terms of international peace and security:

> The wide expanse of the Pacific embracing [Micronesia] is ... a strategic area [where t]he United States ... has an obligation for the maintenance of international peace and security and to guard against the Pacific Ocean area being used in the future as a base for aggression against the people of Micronesia or against other friends and allies. [The United States has]

real – but limited and definable – requirements for access to Micronesian land for these common defense purposes. (Office of Micronesian Status Negotiations 1971a, pp. 11–12)

On the same day, Captain William J. Crowe, Jr, Department of Defense, elaborated the specific requirements for land use in the TTPI: (i) continued use of the present military land holdings in Marshalls; (ii) additional land needs in the Northern Marianas; (iii) options for possible future use of some lands in Palau; and (iv) no need of land for military purposes in the other three districts, Yap, Truk, and Ponape (Office of Micronesian Status Negotiations 1971a). Drawing lines on the map of the TTPI arbitrarily seemed to have induced the differentiation of political goals afterwards. Along with the American strategic request, there was an unspoken guarantee that the United States would pay well for lease rights to the military bases. Considering the potential tax revenue from the American military or civilian population, the American strategic requests could be "an economic bonanza" (Hezel 1978, p. 206) for parts of the TTPI.

1972

During the fourth negotiation round in Koror, Palau, in April 1972, the American delegation finally accepted the Micronesians' unilateral agreement termination. However, some uncertainties about ratifying the Compact remained among Micronesians themselves. According to the TTPI's governmental system, endorsement by the Micronesian delegation could not bind the decision-making of the COM any more than the American delegation's recommendation could bind the president or Congress. While the American delegation was appointed by the executive branch of the administration and was ultimately accountable only to the president, the Micronesian delegation was composed of 33 members of equal power for the six districts, whose opinions might be taken quite differently internally. Although the Micronesian delegation mentioned that "Internal unanimity is not simple to command", they stressed their willingness to endorse the Compact and recommend it to the COM, which would adopt and certify it to the people of Micronesia in a plebiscite (Joint Committee on Future Status 1972, pp. 17–18). Nevertheless, the Northern Marianas representatives among the Micronesian delegation requested that Ambassador Williams enter talks separately, and the American delegation accepted their request (Micronesia Support Committee and Pacific Concerns Resource Center 1982). The Northern Mariana district had been economically more developed due to the American military bases in Saipan and Tinian. Abundant financial privileges could be expected. This was the second crossroad on the road to Micronesian unity.

Internal separatism eventually turned out to be inevitable. During the fifth round of negotiation in Washington from July to August, the two delegations finally reached a tentative agreement on a draft of the CoFA, including the preamble and the three titles, Internal Affairs, Foreign Affairs, and Defense (Congress of Micronesia 1972).

The Micronesian delegation returned home after the fifth negotiation round and recommended that the COM approve the Compact's agreed draft, and the Second Special Session of the Fourth COM in Ponape adopted Senate Joint Resolution No. 117 (Joint Committee on Future Status 1972). The Resolution said that the COM would instruct the Joint Committee on Future Status to negotiate with the United States regarding independence and continue negotiations toward a free association. It pointed out that the United Nations Trusteeship Agreement of 1947 suggested that independence should assure the development of the TTPI. Thus, independence could be the alternative to free association (Joint Committee on Future Status 1972). The members of the COM considered that a plebiscite should offer more than one option, so independence should also be negotiated as an alternative political status (Office of Micronesian Status Negotiations 1972).

As a result, in the sixth negotiation round in Naval Air Station Barbers Point, Oahu, Hawaii, from September to October 1972, the American delegation encountered an alternative idea—independence for the TTPI—which the Micronesian delegation brought up when kicking off the negotiations but implicitly withdrew quickly. The Micronesian delegation noted the growing sentiment within the TTPI in favour of independence and requested that this be reconsidered as the second option for future political status. To this revision of the Micronesians' existing position, the American delegation replied that the matter of independence was out of the question in the view of the United States because of the strategic importance of Micronesia. Ambassador Williams applied the brake, saying that even "one negotiating goal would be difficult enough" and "our common efforts have been directed solely toward Free Association and as a result of the US government has not addressed [independence]" (Office of Micronesian Status Negotiations 1972, pp. 25, 31). The government of the United States, he stated, might not agree with the termination of the trusteeship for an independence "which would in any way threaten stability in the area and which would in the opinion of the United States endanger international peace and security" (Office of Micronesian Status Negotiations 1972, p.31).

Salii's attitude became slightly more moderate on behalf of the Micronesian delegation, and he stated that "an effort to deal in depth with the alternative status of independence at this time would be diversionary and premature … [so] priority could be given to continued good faith efforts but both delegations to complete promptly a draft Compact of Free Association" (Office of Micronesian Status Negotiations 1972, p. 37). He reworded his caution to say that "no doubt that the pressures for the status of independence are growing and that continued delay in the development of a Compact of Free Association may make these pressures irresistible" (Office of Micronesian Status Negotiations 1972, p. 37). The discussion regarding Micronesian independence revealed that the COM's grip on convergence around a common future political goal among the six districts had been weakened, and the delegations had reached a deadlock.

1973

More than a year after the previous negotiation round, the seventh round was begun in Washington in November 1973. The discussion gradually shifted from the overall agenda to technical and specific aspects. At the same time, the erosion of the internal unity within the TTPI affected the substantial discussions. The negotiation broke down over the amount of financial assistance provided by the United States. The

Micronesian delegation insisted on negotiating for all six districts, while the American delegation insisted on negotiating for only five districts, excluding the Northern Marianas (McHenry 1975; Micronesia Support Committee and Pacific Concerns Resource Center 1982).

Until 1976

The Micronesian Constitutional Convention (ConCon) was established in July 1975, consisting of 56 delegations from all districts. Its mandate was to draft a constitution. The Constitution of the Federated States of Micronesia was signed by 52 of the ConCon delegations, including all of the delegates from Palau, Yap, Truk, Ponape, and Kosrae and a majority of those from the Northern Marianas and Marshalls, in November 1975 (Micronesia Support Committee and Pacific Concerns Resource Center 1982). The draft constitution set a plebiscite that would be held in July 1978 (Gale 1978).

Chair Salii and Ambassador Williams agreed on the text of the draft CoFA by initiating its preamble, 12 titles,[6] and three annexes[7] as the outcome document during the eighth negotiation round in Saipan, Northern Marianas, from May to June 1976 (Office of Micronesian Status Negotiations 1976). Following Northern Marianas, Marshalls and Palau sought separate negotiations with the United States. The TTPI disunity, which had been ongoing since the early 1970s, was accelerating as the planned all-district-wide plebiscite drew nearer.

13.4 The Crossroad of Micronesia's Future

The TTPI was a political entity created on the basis of colonial history. The people were divided among six cultures and spoke nine or more different languages. Heine (1974, p. 114) critically observed that the "history of Micronesian itself speaks clearly of the strong isolationism that has possessed the various ethnic groups throughout time and history. After many years of colonization by various power[s], the feeling of shared common interest and fraternity is still very weak." Udui (1972, p. 2) observed that Micronesia was "a historical accident" and its uniqueness consisted in huge differences "in culture, languages, religions, customs, and geographic insularity and dispersion".

Rapid modernization and transformation in the TTPI alienated the political leaders from their local followers, developing group antagonism within the TTPI. "The quest for political status, aggravated by lack of public participation … enlarged the gap between the Congress of Micronesia and the electorate" (Heine 1974, p. 120). As

[6] Title I (Internal Affairs), II (Foreign Affairs), III (Defense), IV (Finance), V (Applicable Laws), VI (Trade and Commerce), VII (Citizenship and Nationality), VIII (Immigration and Travel), IX (Representation and Consultation), X (Dispute and Settlement), XI (Amendment and Change of Status), and XII (Approval of the Compact and Effective Date).

[7] Annex A (Micronesia's International Activities), B (US Defense Land Needs), and C (Representational Provisions).

a result, Heine concluded, "regional loyalty has come to replace territorial loyalty" (Heine 1974, p. 120). Once the negotiations on future political status began in 1969, the Micronesian political entity gradually faded as different interest groups increasingly pursued their own goals. In other words, along with external factors, international anti-colonialism, and American strategic interests, internal factors impacting Micronesian political separatism stemmed from: (i) the geographical remoteness and dispersion of the tiny islands; (ii) the diversity of ethnic and cultural groups; (iii) growing economic gaps derived from the United States' military deployments in the selected islands; and (iv) distinct perspectives on private sector development. This section analyses the growing Micronesian disunity from the point of view of (i) the Northern Marianas, (ii) Marshalls, (iii) Palau, and (iv) other districts, as well as describing the final crossroad towards Micronesian unity for the future.

A. *Northern Marianas*

The internal discussions on the future political status of the TTPI had faded, especially since 1972 when the United States announced the start of separate negotiations with the Northern Marianas. The most developed TTPI district enjoyed financial and other economic advantages under naval administration after the Second World War. The high commissioner of the TTPI had been stationed in Saipan, the largest island of the Northern Marianas, since 1962 (Meller 1985). The Northern Marianas district is geologically, geographically, and ethnically part of the Mariana Islands, sharing many characteristics with Guam, located on the northern edge of the TTPI. Spanish rule over three centuries altered the Chamorro culture of the islands, which was hispanized to differentiate them from other Micronesians. Later, the islands were divided between the United States (Guam) and Germany (Northern Marianas); however, common language, kin, and culture continued to identify all Chamorro as an ethnic group (Meller 1985).

In the hearings in the Northern Mariana district from 29 May to 16 June 1969, conducted by the Commission of the COM, the Northern Marianas representatives of the COM expressed their wish to "immediately unite (or reintegrate) with the United States Territory of Guam" (Congress of Micronesia 1969, p. 33). During the third Northern Marianas district legislature in February 1971, members voted unanimously not to attend the special session of the COM in Truk, called by the high commissioner of the TTPI to begin on 3 May 1971. They wanted to separate Northern Marianas from the other five TTPI districts for permanent association with the United States (Congress of Micronesia 1971). During that time, the Department of Defense planned to construct a sizeable multi-service base in Tinian, expecting American troops to withdraw from Okinawa due to its reversion to Japanese control. The construction plan was eventually frozen, except for periodic amphibious exercises in Tinian (Gale 1978).

The Northern Marianas requested separate negotiations with the United States during the fourth negotiation round in April 1972. After that, a series of bilateral negotiations, the US–Marianas Status Negotiations, were conducted about every six months from December 1972 until December 1974. In 1975, the Northern Marianas and the United States finally agreed that the islands would become permanently affiliated with the United States under a commonwealth arrangement, comparable to that of Puerto Rico. The first elected governor took office in January 1978 when a new constitution was enacted. The CNMI became the first outright territorial acquisition of the United States since it had purchased the Virgin Islands in 1917 (Gale 1978).

B. ***Marshall Islands***

In addition to being the TTPI's most extensive copra production base, Marshalls enjoyed the largest tax revenues in the territory because of taxes levied on Kwajalein Atoll for the United States ballistic missile test site. Marshalls was in deep conflict with the COM over revenue-sharing. Eventually in April 1973, the Marshall Islands legislature, the Nitijela, established its own Marshall Islands Status Commission to begin separate negotiations with the United States (Kiste 1986; McHenry 1975). In March 1974, the legislature adopted a resolution informing the United Nations that Marshalls was unwilling to be a part of Micronesia after the termination of the Trusteeship Agreement and that it intended to start separate negotiations with the United States. However, the United States ignored these separatist movements, as it had not received a formal request from Marshalls (McHenry 1975). The referendum held in July 1977 in Marshalls showed that 62 per cent favoured separation from other TTPI districts (Hezel 1978).

C. ***Palau***

Palau had an even greater economic benefit in the foreseeable future, boosting its separatism. In 1975, Palauan political leaders were approached by Japanese business interests, the Nissho-Iwai Corporation and the Industrial Bank of Japan, with a proposal to build a $0.5 billion supertanker port and oil storage facility. The proposal would require the utilization of large tracts of land and would employ 12,000 people when in full operation. Palauan leaders were divided. The traditional leaders disagreed with the super-port plan due to the tremendous environmental and social effects it would have on the community. However, some political leaders who supported separation from the rest of the TTPI favoured the plan (Hezel 1978). The proposal became a controversial issue in Palau and was later dropped from public discussion (Kiste 1986). In April 1975, the Palau District Legislature created a political status commission (Micronesia Support Committee and Pacific Concerns Resource Center 1982). As in Marshalls, the referendum held in September 1976 showed that the majority—88 per cent—of Palauans favoured separation from the rest of the TTPI (Micronesia Support Committee and Pacific Concerns Resource Center 1982).

D. ***Other districts: Yap, Truck, Ponape, and Kosrae***

While certain ethnic groups of the islands within Truk attempted to break away from the larger units but failed, Kosrae, formerly a part of Ponape, successfully broke away and gained independent status as a district in 1977 (Hezel 1995; Kiste 1986). Ratification of the new constitution, which required the support of two-thirds of all districts, would have been impossible if Palau and Marshalls had rejected it. Thus, the Kosraeans' request to be an independent district was welcomed by the COM as a way to solve a legal deadlock. Even if Palau and Marshalls voted against it, the constitution would stand if all of the other four districts, Yap, Truk, Ponape, and Kosrae, voted in favour (Hezel 1995).

E. ***Final stage of the TTPI***

At the eighth negotiation round convened in Saipan in June 1976, negotiations between Micronesia and the United States delegations were in deadlock due to internal disunity among the TTPI districts. They resumed their negotiations informally within the "roundtable" arrangement in 1977 and later transitioned into formal negotiations from late 1977 to early 1978 (Micronesia Support Committee and Pacific Concerns Resource Center 1982). Participants were the United States, the Commission on Future Status and Transition from the COM, the Palau Political Status Commission (the Palau delegation), and the Marshall Islands Political Status Commission (the Marshall delegation).[8]

The first informal roundtable negotiation was held in Honolulu, Hawaii, in May 1977. The Marshall and Palau delegations expressed their desire for separate negotiations with the United States. The Palau delegation openly expressed their frustration, saying that:

> loosely-federated states of Micronesia ... evolved to become a national legislative body that is cumbersome and costly. Its lack of clearly defined policy and direction concerning the future well-being of the very diverse individual island groups of Micronesia unfairly gave advantage to those who for their own reasons advocate a strong centralized government. (Anien 1977, p. 3)

Thus, to continue a strong centralized government in the future "would only prolong and intensify the existing social and political disharmony throughout Micronesia and indeed within each district" (Anien 1977, pp. 3–4). The delegation concluded that "Palau is now totally united ... [with regard] to attaining a separate political status arrangement with the United States" (Anien 1977, p. 5). The Palau delegation cast deep doubts on Micronesian unity, asking: "How long must this pretence continue? How much more time and money can we waste on the failed experiment of 'Micronesian unity'?" (Anien 1977, p.7).

Compared with the Palau delegation, the Marshall delegation expressed a moderate position. Atlan Anien, speaker of the Marshall Islands legislature, stated, "historically, the Marshall Islands have not been regarded as an integral part of a single political or economic or social unit" (Anien 1977, p. 3). Amata Kabua, chair of the Marshalls delegation, noted:

> We have tried for thirty years to achieve Micronesian unity, and we are now convinced that such a goal is neither wise nor realistic ... the United States must recognize that it

[8] The Joint Committee on Future Status, established by the COM in 1972, was renamed the "Commission on Future Political Status and Transition" in June 1976 after the eighth round of negotiations. The new Commission's mandate was to negotiate the Compact into conformity with the Constitution of the Federated States of Micronesia. The Palau legislature created its own Palau Political Status Commission in April 1975. The Marshall Islands Nitijela created its own Marshall Islands Political Status Commission in April 1973 (see Micronesia Support Committee and Pacific Concerns Resource Center, 1982, pp. 19–21).

cannot impose unity where unity does not exist; it cannot wish away the determination of the Marshallese people to fashion their own destiny as a separate sovereign people. (Anien 1977, p. 1)

Although the Marshalls delegation did not explicitly support Micronesian unity, Kabua stated, "we do look forward to the time when we can sit down with other governments in the Pacific, including whatever entities emerge from the remainder of the Trust Territory, to examine without recognitions those areas of common interest, if any, that can be pursued cooperatively" (Anien 1977, pp. 1–2).

Despite separatist demands from the Palauans and the Marshallese, the United States publicly still encouraged the establishment of a common political entity for Micronesians. Robert Oakley, deputy assistant secretary of state, explained three benefits of Micronesian unity. If Micronesians chose to be separate entities instead of a common political entity: (i) they would face uncertainty because of the fact that the population numbered only 100,000 people in a vast area; (ii) it could be challenging to develop new administrative and functional services; and (iii) United States' financial aid, postal and weather services, and the services of the Federal Aviation Administration, could be complicated to provide (Oakley 1977).

To overcome the deadlock in the discussions, the United States proposed a two-level negotiation structure during the second informal roundtable conference in Guam in July 1977. While the bilateral negotiations would handle issues particular to individual districts, such as specific military land demands and financial aid, the multilateral negotiations would focus on topics common to all districts, such as defence, foreign relations, and free association status overall (Office of Micronesian Status Negotiations 1977).

Sam Falanruw from Yap stated that "Yap ... was committed to the unity of Micronesia and thus respectfully declined the invitation" to negotiate bilaterally with the United States. The delegation from Kosrae supported Yap's position. The Ponape delegation emphasized that "Ponape ... committed to the concept of unity ... and this unity should be promoted in all US and Micronesian approaches to the status issue and in the daily administration of the TTPI" (Office of Micronesian Status Negotiations 1977, pp. 13–14).

Nevertheless, the Palau delegates stated that they could no longer tolerate multilateral negotiations with other Micronesians because they had to "concentrate [their] resources on achieving a round bilateral [negotiations with the United States] obstructed by the intransigence of the Congress of Micronesia" (Office of Micronesian Status Negotiations 1977, pp. 28–29). They repeatedly declared that bilateral negotiations between Palau and the United States would be begun in order to achieve Palauans' self-governing political status exclusively.

Amata Kabua from Marshalls supported both bilateral and multilateral negotiations. He believed that the negotiations should consist of simultaneous bilateral negotiations between the United States and Marshalls, Palau, and the COM's Commission individually, representing "the four central Carolinian districts", as well as multilateral negotiations among the United States and all the districts regarding "possible future common links" (Office of Micronesian Status Negotiations 1977, pp. 30–31).

After informal roundtable negotiations had been held twice, the delegations held several formal roundtable negotiations from October 1977 to April 1978. The negotiation in Hilo, Hawaii, in April 1978 finally reached agreement to grant Micronesians control of foreign affairs and allow unilateral termination regarding the continuation of the United States' defence (Micronesia Support Committee and Pacific Concerns Resource Center 1982).

The plebiscite for the Constitution of the Federated States of Micronesia was held in all districts, including Kosrae but excluding Northern Mariana, on 12 July 1978. This was the last and most inevitable crossroad on the path to future Micronesian unity. While 55 per cent of Palauans and 60 per cent of Marshallese voted against the CoFA, a majority of four other districts voted in favour: Yap (95 per cent), Ponape (75 per cent), Truk (69 per cent), and Kosrae (61 per cent) (Micronesia Support Committee and Pacific Concerns Resource Center 1982). Cecil Andrus, secretary of interior, issued a Secretarial Order separating the districts by recognizing the COM as the Congress of the Federated States of Micronesia and the existing Palau and Marshalls legislatures as the primary legislatures for these new independent political entities (Micronesia Support Committee and Pacific Concerns Resource Center 1982).

Finally, one commonwealth territory of the United States and three countries freely associated with the United States had been formed by enforcing their constitutions by the beginning of the 1980s. The constitution of the CNMI took effect on 8 January 1978, that of the FSM on 10 May 1979, that of Marshall Islands on 1 May 1979, and that of Palau on 1 January 1981.

13.5 Conclusions

This chapter has examined the decoupling process of the TTPI districts, Northern Marianas, Palau, Yap, Truck, Ponape, and Marshalls (and additionally Kosrae), from the early 1960s to the late 1970s. While previous literature has focused primarily on the attitude of the United States in terms of its strategic intentions regarding the future political status of the TTPI, this chapter has investigated primary sources on the Micronesian side that enabled it to focus on attitudes in the TTPI itself towards its future political status. The chapter has also highlighted how Micronesians countered the United States' security interests to achieve their goals, although they failed to fully achieve Micronesian unity among the former TTPI districts.

A. *Summary*

First, it should be noted that, significantly, the TTPI voluntarily established its political entity, the COM, in the late 1960s and created a blueprint for its future political status as a self-governing state in free association with the United States. The blueprint was based on Micronesians' pragmatic self-reflection. They regarded their islands as valuable to themselves but also strategically crucial for the United States, which led them to consider accepting the United States' military needs.

Second, while the TTPI faced a series of future political status negotiations with the United States—which had been divided over land control, unilateral termination, and political status—it had also struggled with internal disharmony in the 1970s. The first crossroad of Micronesian unity was the announcement of the United States' land requirements with regard to the TTPI, based on the US strategic view in 1971. It envisaged the current and future economic gaps among the TTPI districts that led to their internal friction. The second junction was the decision of the Northern Marianas district to hold separate negotiations with the United States in 1972. The Palau and Marshalls districts followed Northern Marianas' separatism in the late 1970s because of their economic advantages compared with the rest of the districts. The stance of Palau was tempered by the plan to build a supertanker port and oil storage facility, while Marshalls was willing to maximize profits from tax revenues in Kwajalein Atoll. The regionwide plebiscite on 12 July 1978 was the final junction that eventually separated the TTPI districts into three sovereign nations. Eventually, the TTPI settled down in the form of one commonwealth territory of the United States and three countries freely associated with the United States.

Overall, external factors, the dynamics of the Cold War in Asia, and the wave of decolonization under United Nations supervision in the 1960s shaped US policy on the future political status of the TTPI. The United States had to meet the minimum international decolonization standards as well as safeguarding its security interests. The US strategic interest in Micronesia also suggested potential economic gaps among the TTPI districts, given existing military presence and future deployments. Furthermore, since the TTPI was a political entity based on colonial history, internal factors, including geographical and demographical characteristics, with diverse ethnic groups living in sparse populations on tiny, scattered, remote islands, separatist sentiments were awakened within the TTPI in the 1970s.

B. ***Implications***

The historical crossroad still affects the Micronesian countries, and the CoFA can be comprehended as a framework for their bilateral relationships and political systems deeply embedded in today's socio-political and socioeconomic issues. While this chapter is historically oriented, we suggest below ways that it can enrich future perspectives in Micronesia.

First, the Micronesian countries should enhance the efficiency of their governance by nurturing national unity. Given the sequence of the four districts combined, FSM has regularly faced friction between the federal and state governments. Cultivating national unity can be a key to strengthening efficient governance.

Second, the Micronesian countries should keep their regional ties and promote regional unity. Because of the CoFA, people from Palaua, FSM, and Marshall Islands are not required to have a visa to enter the United States. Depopulation has been a crucial issue in Micronesia. Micronesian regionalism is a heritage of the political negotiations during the 1960s and the 1970s, and further regional cooperation among the former TTPI districts, development partners, and various stakeholders can supplement existing solutions to help them overcome their vulnerabilities.

Finally, strengthening economic resilience is necessary for the Micronesian countries. Due to their similar geographical and demographical characteristics, the countries commonly profoundly depend on imports, skilled foreign labour, and only a few limited industries, such as fisheries and tourism, resulting in heavy fiscal reliance on financial aid via the Compact and other foreign sources. In this vein, Micronesian regionalism may also work well to develop regionwide solutions to enhance their islands' economic resilience and future prosperity.

Acknowledgements The authors appreciate the kind assistance provided by Lucy Oducado and Bruce Robert, the librarians of the College of Micronesia, who guided them in accessing valuable primary sources from the College's special Micronesian collections. The authors also appreciate the help of Makoto Abe, who edited and commented on an earlier version of the chapter. The opinions expressed in this chapter are those of the authors and do not necessarily reflect the views of the Ministry of Foreign Affairs of Japan and the United Nations.

References

Anien A (1977) Opening statement of Marshall Islands by Atlan Anien, Speaker, Marshall Islands Nitijela. In: Summary of record of U.S.–Micronesia roundtable conference, 18–21 May 1977, Honolulu, Hawaii

Congress of Micronesia (1969) Report: the future political status commission. Third congress, second session, July. Congress of Micronesia, Saipan

Congress of Micronesia (1970) Report of the political status delegation of the Congress of Micronesia. Third congress, third regular session, July. Congress of Micronesia, Saipan

Congress of Micronesia (1971) Journal of the senate of the congress of Micronesia. Fourth congress, fourth special session, May. Congress of Micronesia, Saipan

Congress of Micronesia (1972) Draft compact of free association presented by the joint committee on future status, fifth round of negotiations, Washington, D.C. Forth Congress, Second Special Session, August. Congress of Micronesia, Ponape

Dag Hammarskjöld Library (no date) UN Trusteeship Council documentation [Online]. Available at: https://research.un.org/en/docs/tc/intro. Accessed 26 Oct 2023

Economic and Social Commission for Asia and the Pacific (2007) Improving employment opportunities in Pacific island developing countries. Suva, United Nations [Online]. Available at: www.unescap.org/sites/default/files/Impoving-employment-opportunities-in-PIDCs.pdf. Accessed 11 Feb 2024

Falcam A (2023) President Simina and Vice President Palik pay official state visit to Chuuk State [Online]. Available at: https://gov.fm/index.php/component/content/article/35-pio-articles/news-and-updates/737-president-simina-vice-president-palik-pay-official-state-visit-to-chuuk-state?Itemid=177. Accessed 26 Oct 2023

Gale RW (1978) A new political status for Micronesia. Pac Aff 51(3):427–447

Gale, R.W. (1979) *The Americanization of Micronesia: a study of the consolidation of the U.S. rule in the Pacific*. Washington, DC: University Press of America.

Heine C (1974) Micronesia at the crossroads: a reappraisal of the Micronesian political dilemma. University of Hawaii Press, Honolulu

Hezel FX (1978) Looking ahead to the end of trusteeship, trust territory of the Pacific Islands. J Pacific Hist 13(4):204–210

Hezel FX (1995) Strangers in their own land: a century of colonial rule in the Caroline and Marshall Islands. University of Hawai'i Press, Honolulu

Hunt E (2023) Compact colonialism: U.S. neocolonialism in Micronesia in the early twenty-first century. Postcolonial Stud 5(1):1–29

International Organization for Migration (2016) Migration in the Federated States of Micronesia: a country profile 2015. International Organization for Migration, Geneva

Joint Committee on Future Status (1972) Future political status of the trust territory of the Pacific Islands Micronesia: proceedings of the sixth round of negotiations. Barbers Point, Oahu, Hawaii. 28 Sept–6 Oct 1972. Joint Committee on Future Status, Saipan

Kiste C (1986) Termination of the U.S. trusteeship in Micronesia. J Pacific Hist 21(3):127–138

McHenry DF (1975) Micronesia, trust betrayed: altruism vs self interest in American foreign policy. Carnegie Endowment for International Peace, New York

Meller N (1985) Constitutionalism in Micronesia. The University of Hawaii Press, Honolulu

Micronesia Support Committee and Pacific Concerns Resource Center (1982) From trusteeship to …? Micronesia and its future. Micronesia Support Committee and Pacific Concerns Resource Center, Honolulu

NSAM (National Security Action Memoranda) (1962a) New policy for the U.S. Trust Territory of the Pacific Islands (NSAM 145) [Online]. Available at: www.jfklibrary.org/asset-viewer/archives/JFKNSF/336/JFKNSF-336-001. Accessed 4 Feb 2024

NSAM (1962b) Survey Mission for the U.S. Trust Territory of the Pacific Islands (NSAM 243) [Online]. Available from: www.jfklibrary.org/asset-viewer/archives/jfknsf-341-003#?image_identifier=JFKNSF-341-003-p0001. Accessed 4 Feb 2024

Oakley R (1977) Remarks by deputy assistant secretary of State Robert Oakley. In: Summary of record of U.S.–Micronesia roundtable conference, 18–21 May 1977, Honolulu, Hawaii

Office of Micronesian Status Negotiations (1971a) The future political status: reported by president's personal representative for Micronesian status negotiations on the status talks held at Hana, Maui, Hawaii, on 4–12 Oct 1971. Office for Micronesian Status Negotiations, Washington, DC

Office of Micronesian Status Negotiations (1971b) The future political status of the Trust Territory of the Pacific Islands: Reported by president's personal representative for Micronesian status negotiations on the status talks held at Hana, Maui, Hawaii, on 4–12 Oct 1971. Office of Micronesian Status Negotiations, Washington, DC

Office of Micronesian Status Negotiations (1972) The future political status of the Trust Territory of the Pacific Islands: proceedings of the sixth round Micronesian status negotiations. Barbers Point Naval Air Station, Oahu, Hawaii. 28 Sept–6 Oct 1972. Office of Micronesian Status Negotiations, Washington, DC

Office of Micronesian Status Negotiations (1976) Micronesia status negotiations: eighth round of negotiations. Saipan, Northern Mariana Islands. 28 May–2 June 1976. Office of Micronesian Status Negotiations, Washington, DC

Office of Micronesian Status Negotiations (1977) The future political status of the Trust Territory of the Pacific Islands: summary record of U.S.–Micronesia Roundtable Conference. Guam. 25–27 July 1977. Office of Micronesian Status Negotiations, Washington, DC

Solomon AM (1963) A report by the U.S. government survey mission to the Trust Territory of the Pacific Islands. In: The Solomon Report: the U.S. Survey mission to the Trust Territory of the Pacific Islands headed by Anthony M. Solomon

Udui K (1972) Free Association: a political status option of self-determination in Micronesia. In: Smith FM (ed) Micronesian realities: political and economic. Center for South Pacific Studies, University of California, Santa Cruz, pp 31–46

United Nations (1960) Declaration on the granting of independence to colonial countries and peoples (Resolution/Decision: A/RES/1514(XV)) [Online]. Available at https://documents.un.org/doc/resolution/gen/nr0/152/88/pdf/nr015288.pdf?token=elLzy9GbFzoJ5v8jes&fe=true. Accessed 4 Feb 2024

United Nations (no date) International trusteeship system [Online]. Available at: www.un.org/dppa/decolonization/en/history/international-trusteeship-system-and-trust-territories. Accessed 26 Oct 2023

United Nations Fiji, Solomon Islands, Tonga, Tuvalu, and Vanuatu (2023) United Nations Pacific sustainable development framework 2023–2027 [Online]. Available at: https://pacific.un.org/en/237313-united-nations-pacific-sustainable-development-framework-2023-2027. Accessed 11 Feb 2024

United Nations Micronesia (no date) The United Nations in Micronesia [Online]. Available at https://micronesia.un.org/en/about/about-the-un. Accessed 11 Feb 2024

United Nations Trusteeship Council (1961) Trusteeship Council 27th session official records 1153rd meeting Wednesday, 21 June 1961, at 3.15 p.m. (T/SR.1153) [Online]. Available at https://digitallibrary.un.org/record/1637045?ln=en. Accessed 5 Feb 2024

United Nations Visiting Mission to the Trust Territory of the Pacific Islands (1961) Report of the United Nations Visiting Mission to the Trust Territory of the Pacific Islands, 1961: together with the relevant resolutions of the Trusteeship Council (T/1582; Resolution/Decision: T/RES/2104 (XXVII)) [Online]. Available at https://digitallibrary.un.org/record/1299087?ln=en. Accessed 5 Feb 2024

United Nations Visiting Mission to the Trust Territory of the Pacific Islands (1964) Report of the United Nations Visiting Mission to the Trust Territory of the Pacific Islands, 1964: together with the relevant resolution of the Trusteeship Council (T/1628; Resolution/Decision: T/RES/2141 (XXXI)) [Online]. Available at https://digitallibrary.un.org/record/1299092. Accessed 5 Feb 2024

UNSC (United Nations Security Council) (1947) Resolution of 2 April 1947 (S/RES/21) [Online]. Available at https://documents.un.org/doc/resolution/gen/nr0/042/17/pdf/nr004217.pdf?token=UaUVLo0PbgLKbOnz2h&fe=true. Accessed 11 Feb 2024

Zarefsky D (1979) The great society as a rhetorical proposition. Quarterly J Speech 65(4):364–378

Chapter 14
Revisiting Nuclear Legacy in Marshall Islands: The Implications of Transitional Justice and Trans-science

Yoshiki Narita and Masato Abe

Abstract In relation to Marshall Islands, "nuclear legacy" refers to the long-term environmental, health, and socio-cultural impacts of the United States' nuclear weapons programme conducted in the islands from 1946 to 1958. The legacy still takes a toll on the daily lives of the Marshallese. Bikini Atoll and Enewetak Atoll, two nuclear weapon testing sites, are still largely uninhabitable, and many cancer cases have occurred among the Marshallese exposed to fallout and residual radiation. Beginning with the first petition filed with the United Nations Trusteeship Council by members of the Marshallese Congress in 1954 (Marshall Islands and United Nations Trusteeship Council in Petition from Marshallese people concerning the Pacific Islands, 1954), for 70 years Marshall Islands has condemned the injustice of nuclear testing and advocated for the need to assist its affected sites and people. As a result of their continued efforts, the United Nations Human Rights Council adopted a resolution (A/HRC/RES/51/35) in October 2022, reaffirming the importance of the human rights of Marshallese people who have suffered from health and environmental damages and forced displacement. The resolution has influenced the international power balance regarding nuclear legacy issues. This chapter revisits Marshall Islands' nuclear legacy and examines its related diplomacy. The study also addresses emerging geopolitical and institutional frameworks regarding various nuclear tests in the Pacific. Recommendations as to the ways forward are made from the perspectives of human rights, science–social relations, and the roles of Marshall Islands and the United Nations Multi-Country Office for Micronesia, implying a nexus of transitional justice and trans-scientific issues with regard to the nuclear legacy in Marshall Islands.

Y. Narita (✉) · M. Abe
United Nations Multi-Country Office for Micronesia, Kolonia, Micronesia
e-mail: y.narita0607@gmail.com

M. Abe
e-mail: abem@un.org

E. Monaco and M. Abe (eds.), *Sustainable Development Across Pacific Islands*,
https://doi.org/10.1007/978-981-97-3629-4_14

14.1 Introduction

Marshall Islands experienced 67 known nuclear weapon tests detonated by the United States on Bikini Atoll and Enewetak Atoll from 1946 to 1958. These incidents are known as the dawn of the nuclear era. Marshall Islands has advocated the danger of nuclear weapons and their impacts on health, environment, and society since the first petition to the United Nations in 1954, which requested an end to nuclear testing in its territory. These long historical efforts bore fruit when the United Nations Human Rights Council (UNHRC) resolution (A/HRC/RES/51/35), entitled "Technical assistance and capacity-building to address the human rights implications of the nuclear legacy in the Marshall Islands" was adopted in 2022 (UNHRC 2022b). This resolution urges relevant United Nations agencies and other stakeholders to support Marshall Islands in improving its people's health and its environment.

This chapter revisits Marshall Islands' nuclear legacy and examines related diplomatic efforts in the international arena. Emerging geopolitical and institutional frameworks regarding nuclear tests in the Pacific are also addressed. Recommendations as to the ways forward are made from the perspectives of human rights, science–social relations, and the roles of Marshall Islands and the United Nations Multi-Country Office for Micronesia, implying a nexus of transitional justice and trans-scientific issues with regard to the nuclear legacy in Marshall Islands.

14.2 The History of the Nuclear Legacy

The nuclear weapon tests in Marshall Islands began soon after the end of the Second World War. This section summarizes the impacts and consequences of these tests and their aftermath for the environment and people of Marshall Islands.

14.2.1 Series of Nuclear Weapon Tests

The nuclear weapon testing in Marshall Islands was a direct result of the intense rivalry and arms race between the United States and the Soviet Union during the Cold War. Nuclear tests in Marshall Islands began in 1946 under "Operation Crossroads", with two atomic bombs that were detonated on Bikini Atoll under the United States military occupation (US Senate 2010). Prior to the tests, 167 Bikinians were displaced to Rongerik Atoll, 125 miles east of Bikini Atoll (Niedenthal 2013). In 1947, the newly formed United Nations granted the United States administrative authority over Marshall Islands as part of the Trust Territory of the Pacific Islands (TTPI). The TTPI allowed the United States to establish naval military and air bases, deploy armed forces, and provide security facilities and assistance in the Micronesia region, including Marshall Islands, which Japan had administered before the Second World

War. Subsequently, the United States, under the TTPI status, conducted the first nuclear tests at Enewetak Atoll in 1948 after the evacuation of about 145 people from the atoll to uninhabited Ujelang Atoll (Lazzari 2005). The United States continued nuclear tests until 1958, resulting in at least 67 nuclear bombs being exploded on Bikini Atoll and Enewetak Atoll.

The "Castle Bravo" nuclear test on Bikini Atoll in 1954 caused the largest radioactive contamination across Marshall Islands and neighbouring areas. The United States argued that this had happened because of the test's unpredicted high yield and adverse wind conditions.[1] First, people on Ailinginae Atoll (18 people), Rongelap Atoll (64 people), and Utirik Atoll (159 people) were evacuated to Kwajalein Atoll after directly experiencing radioactive fallout (US National Research Council 1994). The fallout also spread across Marshall Islands (Breslin and Cassidy 1955). Furthermore, the United States Defense Threat Reduction Information Center reported that gamma rays at fallout intensities were detected not only within Marshall Islands but also at Wake, Johnston, Kosrae, Ponape, Truk, Yap, Guam, and Iwo Jima (Kunkle and Byron 2013). The crew aboard the Japanese fishing boat *Daigo Fukuryu Maru* were exposed to the fallout 160 km away from "ground zero", outside of the "danger zone" announced by the United States (Takemine 2023). A couple of months after the Castle Bravo nuclear test, the Japanese survey ship *Shunkotu-Maru* investigated the radioactive status of the ocean and observed radionuclides produced by the nuclear tests 1000 km away from ground zero (Miyake 1972).

14.2.2 Impacts on the Islands

The nuclear tests severely damaged the environment of Marshall Islands, and people were often forcibly displaced due to severe health risks. The huge impacts of the tests continue to this day.

14.2.2.1 Environment

The nuclear experiments affected the environment through blasts and fallout. The tests were so powerful that they vaporized islands or carved out large craters on atolls. For example, the Castle Bravo crater, which was over two kilometres wide and 80 m deep, was created by six nuclear bomb explosions (Hughes et al. 2019; Kili, Bikini, and Ejit Local Government Council 2009). The fallout contaminated the land and the ocean by releasing radioactive materials, causing nearly irreversible

[1] There is scepticism about "the test's unpredicted high yield and adverse wind conditions" and the claim that the test occurred as intended. For instance, Edward Radford, a past chair of the United States National Academy of Science's Committee on Biological Effects of Ionizing Radiation, testified in 1994 that abnormally high radiation was observed at Kwajalein during the nuclear weapons tests in 1948, which is much further away from Bikini Atoll than Ailinginae Atoll, Rongelap Atoll, and Utrik Atoll (Johnson 2009).

damage. The radioactive particles from the tests entered the food chains, affecting a wide range of species. Fish and other marine life absorbed these materials, which were then passed down the food chains, affecting larger species and, ultimately, the human inhabitants who relied on these species for food (Renfro 1973).

Even after the United States conducted radiological surveys and remediation, the contamination remained a serious concern, especially for the people of Bikini, Enewetak, and Rongelap. The United States Atomic Energy Commission (AEC) conducted the first radiological survey on Bikini Atoll in 1967, finding caesium-137 in the soil to be the main concern in relation to resettlement (Tobin 1967). Following this, a joint AEC and the Defense and Security Accelerator taskforce began an intensive clean-up effort in 1969, before declaring Bikini Atoll safe for rehabilitation (Smith and Moore 1972). Several families moved back to Bikini Atoll, but the Bikini Council voted not to return as a community in 1972, unsatisfied with the AEC's assurances of Bikini's safety. In 1975, regular monitoring of the returned Bikini families revealed higher levels of radioactivity than initially thought (Kili, Bikini, and Ejit Local Government Council 2009).

The United States also surveyed Enewetak Atoll regularly after 1972 and found many radiation-affected species of fish and wildlife (Defense Nuclear Agency 1981). The clean-up efforts on Enewetak Atoll began in 1977, involving removing 100,000 cubic yards of radioactive soil and debris and dumping them in the "Cactus" bomb crater on Runit Island (DOE 2022). The concrete dome sealed over the radioactive waste is now called Runit Dome. In 1980, the United States proclaimed the completion of nuclear clean-up and rehabilitation efforts on Enewetak Atoll, declaring the southern islands within the atoll safe for habitation (Johnson 2009).[2] The northern islands, which were not included in the United States clean-up efforts, are still contaminated by radiation.

The case of Rongelap Atoll differed in that the islanders were returned to their home islands in 1957 before any clean-up efforts, based on a judgment of the AEC, which declared Rongelap safe for rehabilitation (DOE 1989). The community, especially young children exposed to radiation from the Bravo explosion, experienced serious thyroid cancer in the 1960s. The fear of residual radiation, which possibly caused cancer, urged Rongelap islanders to evacuate in 1985 via a Greenpeace vessel (Eknilang 2003). In response to the action of the Rongelap community, the US National Research Council (1994) reassessed the radiation status and concluded that the radiation dose was not high enough to deter resettlement. The Rongelap local government and the United States Department of the Interior (DOI) largely agreed upon clean-up guidelines, resettlement, and future monitoring in 1996 (Johnson 2009), but Rongelap refugees have yet to return to the atoll.

[2] According to the national census in 2021, there is no citizens living on Bikini Atoll while 296 people living in the southern part of Enewetak (Economic Policy, Planning, and Statistics Office and Pacific Community 2023).

14.2.2.2 Health

The nuclear tests impacted the health of the Marshallese through direct fallout from atmospheric tests, consumption of contaminated food and water, and contact with irradiated soil and ocean life (IAEA 2017). People on Ailinginae Atoll, Rongelap Atoll, and Utrik Atoll were exposed to the fallout from Castle Bravo as they were only evacuated a couple of days after the fallout reached these atolls. The immediate symptoms of heavy exposure were vomiting and diarrhoea, skin burns and hair loss. Numerous instances of reproductive cancers and birth defects have also been documented among women in Marshall Islands (Eknilang 2003).[3] On top of this, many children who were under the age of ten at the time of exposure developed thyroid tumours in later years, particularly in the early 1960s (Johnson 2009). It is also argued that nuclear testing has harmed people's health in the form of mental illness and non-communicable diseases (NCDs) (UNHRC 2012).

Although the United States has officially acknowledged only four atolls as exposed to fallout—the two nuclear test sites (Bikini and Enewetak) and the two atolls downwind from the Bravo test (Rongelap and Utrik)—the AEC report in 1955, which was declassified by the United States Department of Energy (DOE) in 1994, contradicted this claim by showing the degree to which six nuclear tests under Operation Castle affected 26 islands in terms of radiation doses (Breslin and Cassidy 1955). Furthermore, the affected lands still have residual radiation; therefore, the health risks were imposed on those who visited after the nuclear tests, such as the Marshallese returnees to Rongelap and workers for decontamination. The impact on health may be more severe than officially recognized by the United States. However, conducting comprehensive impact and risk assessments on health has not been possible due to limited available data (National Cancer Institute 2010).

14.2.2.3 Forced Displacement

As mentioned earlier, the nuclear tests created forced displacement of three groups: (i) those from Bikini Atoll, (ii) those from Enewetak Atoll, and (iii) those from Rongelap, Ailinginae, and Utrik Atolls. The first displacement occurred in 1946 under Operation Crossroads, with 167 citizens of Bikini Atoll. Bikinians initially relocated to Rongerik Atoll, a location ill suited to habitation due to its small landmass and lagoon (Niedenthal 2013). Suffering from food shortages there, the Bikinians moved again to Kwajalein Atoll in 1948, then to Kili Island, an isolated island more than 50 km away from the closest atoll, Jaluit, with no lagoon for fishing. In 1969, Bikinians were allowed to return to Bikini Atoll after the United States declared it safe from radiation following its clean-up efforts. However, as DOI officials revealed a significant increase of caesium-137 on Bikini Atoll, the returned Bikinians felt the

---

[3] Babies born without bones in their bodies and with transparent skin were seen on Rongelap and other atolls. This birth defect was called "jellyfish babies" (Eknilang 2003, p. 318).

health risks from the residual radiation and decided to evacuate from Bikini Atoll once again in 1978 (Kili, Bikini, and Ejit Local Government Council 2015).

The second displacement occurred on Enewetak Atoll in 1947, likewise, to make way for nuclear testing. An estimated 145 people were evacuated to Ujelang Atoll, about 200 km south-west of Enewetak. In total, 43 nuclear tests were conducted at Enewetak Atoll, and its land and ocean were severely contaminated. After decontamination efforts by the United States from 1977 to 1980, Enewetak islanders resettled on the southern part of the atoll (US Department of Veterans Affairs no date). According to the 2021 national census of Marshall Islands, the population on the atoll decreased to 137 citizens (Economic Policy, Planning, and Statistics Office and Pacific Community 2023). On the other hand, the northern part, including the Runit Dome, is still uninhabitable.

The largest and most devastating displacement happened following the 1954 Castle Bravo test on Bikini Atoll. The explosion yielded unexpected amounts of radioactive fallout,[4] which affected the people at Ailinginae, Rongelap, and Utirik Atolls. Nearly 250 people from these atolls were evacuated to Kwajalein Atoll (United States National Research Council 1994). After the United States declared them safe in 1957, the evacuated locals returned to their home atolls. However, as mentioned in the "Environment" subsection, with the fear of cancer caused by residual radiation, the Rongelap community decided to evacuate again from the atoll in 1985 (Johnson 2009).

14.2.3 Towards Full Settlements

The United States formed the TTPI Congress, or the Congress of Micronesia, in 1964, and the first elected Congress convened in 1965 (United Nations Department of Political Affairs 1980). The Congress comprised island groups such as Marshall Islands, the Northern Mariana Islands, Palau, and Micronesia (Yap, Chuuk, Ponape, and Kosrae). The Congress started considering their right to self-determination and established its own commission in 1969 to recommend becoming either a self-governing state in free association with the United States or independent (United Nations Department of Political Affairs 1980).

The Congress of Micronesia also played a role in formulating regional concerns about the nuclear legacy. For example, a special committee of the Congress sent out a group to assess the conditions at Rongelap Atoll in 1973. According to the committee report, despite almost two decades of medical consultations, the residents

[4] As mentioned in the previous subsection, the United States' claim about fallout levels being unexpected is disputed by the Marshallese, who believe that the yield and direction of the wind was expected and exposure to fallout was intentional (Johnson 2009). A medical study on the effects of radiation on the Marshallese took place alongside the provision of medical care. Known as Project 4.1, this study has been criticized in terms of the absence of informed consent from the participants (Atomic Heritage Foundation no date).

lacked comprehension regarding radiation and the potential impacts of exposure on their health, children's wellbeing, and the surroundings (Johnson 2009).

Marshall Islands left the Congress of Micronesia in 1978; the paramount chief, President Amata Kabua, declared independence one year later and began self-governing (CFE-DM 2022). In 1983, Marshall Islands signed the Compact of Free Association (CoFA) with the United States after a national referendum, which resulted in 58 per cent in favour of the agreement (Nohlen et al. 2002). The status as a sovereign state in free association with the United States went into effect in 1986, ending the trusteeship of the United States in Marshall Islands. Under the CoFA, the "agreement for the implementation of Section 177" was inked between Marshall Islands and the United States, which concluded the "full settlement of all claims with recognition of the United States' responsibility to address past, present and future consequences of the nuclear testing claims" (United States and Marshall Islands 1983, p. 12). This agreement assured a lump sum of $150 million for the establishment of compensation funds to address personal injury claims, property damage, and hardship suffered due to the nuclear tests, particularly the tests on Bikini and Enewetak Atolls (United States and Marshall Islands 1983). The Nuclear Claims Tribunal, an independent body to adjudicate claims and determine appropriate compensation for the nuclear test victims, was also established under the agreement.

In 1994, the DOE declassified documents relating to nuclear tests in Marshall Islands as part of a move towards increased transparency and openness in government, particularly concerning nuclear history (CRS 2005). The disclosure of the documents relating to the nuclear testing fuelled the discontent of the Marshallese with the "full settlements", based on previously inaccessible information revealed by these documents. In particular, a table in the Atomic Energy Commission's report (Breslin and Cassidy 1955) that summarized the relationships between the six nuclear tests conducted at Operation Castle and the cumulative dose on 26 islands undermined the US claim that only the four islands were affected by the nuclear tests.

In (2000), the Marshall Islands government submitted a changed circumstances petition (CCP) to the United States Congress, abiding by Article IX of the Nuclear Claims Settlement under Section 177 of the CoFA.[5] The CCP comprised five components: (i) funding to satisfy personal injury awards; (ii) funding to satisfy the Enewetak property damage award; (iii) funding to establish primary and secondary medical care infrastructure; (iv) fifty years of annual funding to support national healthcare programmes; and (v) expansion of the DOE medical monitoring programme to all exposed populations. More specifically, the petition insisted that the $150 million lump sum compensation was insufficient to cover claims filed fully and sought additional compensation from the United States. The United States Congress did not provide any response to the CCP, and the United States Department of State

[5] Article IX suggests that a change to the conditions of the compensation agreement could be considered "if loss or damage to property and person of the citizens of Marshall Islands, resulting from the Nuclear Testing Program, arises or is discovered after the effective date of this Agreement, and such injuries were not and could not reasonably have been identified as of the effective date of this Agreement, and if such injuries render the provisions of this Agreement manifestly inadequate" (United States and Marshall Islands 1983, p. 11).

(DOS) insisted that there was no basis for the Marshallese claims, given the assistance the United States had provided under the CoFA agreement (US Department of State 2004). On the contrary, the new agreement (Compact II), renewed in 2004 to extend the period to 2023, neither mentioned the CCP nor provided additional funds for nuclear testing compensation, describing "no changes to … Section 177 of the Compact" (United States and Marshall Islands 2003, p. 15).

The Republic of the Marshall Islands Supplemental Nuclear Compensation Act was introduced in the Senate of the United States in 2007 to provide supplemental ex gratia compensation to Marshall Islands for impacts of the nuclear testing programme for the communities of Enewetak, Kili, Mejatto, and Utrik from fiscal years 2007 to 2023. A substitute version of the same bill was prepared in the next year, 2008, and expanded the healthcare programme to include Ailuk, Likiep, Mejit, Wotho, Wotje, and Ujelang from 2009 to 2023 (US Senate 2007, 2008).

In 2022, a Senate joint resolution formally apologizing for the nuclear legacy of the United States in Marshall Islands was agreed (Senate of the United States 2022). In 2023, the Senate passed the Guam Host Community Compensation Act, expanding nuclear compensation to more Americans in the mainland United States and Guam (US House of Representatives 2023). Many Marshallese have expressed resentment since they were exposed to much higher radiation than the American downwinders, yet their request for expanded compensation has not been supported by the United States (Johnson 2023b).

The third CoFA agreement (Compact III) was signed in 2023, adding an extra 20-year period, to 2043, with over $700 million in trust funds contributions, while the Kwajalein development fund and others were reportedly not disclosed (Johnson 2023c). A fiscal procedures agreement governing the oversight and accountability of the United States grant funding was also signed to enhance financial management transparency. Even though Compact III does not include a change of clause on compensation for affected local communities, the agreement is intended to address the needs of the four affected atolls (NNC 2024).

14.2.4 Ongoing Matters

The multifaceted negative impacts of nuclear tests still cast a shadow in modern Marshallese society. The ongoing matters featured internationally and domestically are introduced below.

14.2.4.1 The Runit Dome

In 2019, United Nations Secretary General António Guterres raised concerns about the status of the Runit Dome regarding the leakage of radioactive materials into the ocean (Agence France-Presse 2019). The Runit Dome is a radioactive waste repository left by the United States after a series of nuclear tests (Fig. 14.1). In the same

Fig. 14.1 The Runit Dome. *Source* © Chewy Lin

year, the United States House Committee on Armed Services requested that the DOE submit a detailed report on the status of the Dome (DOE 2020). The DOE reported that: (i) the Runit Dome was not in any immediate danger of collapse or failure; (ii) the main risk the dome posed was derived from the flow of contaminated groundwater; (iii) internal exposure to fallout radionuclides was well below international standards for radiological protection of the public; (iv) the impact on the Runit Dome of rising sea levels was associated with the physical effects of storm surge and wave-driven flooding; and (v) a groundwater radiochemical analysis was needed. However, this report features only caesium-137 as a radioactive substance; strontium-90, another critical radionuclide, is largely ignored (Johnson 2023a). Also, an alleged 130 tonnes of polluted soil imported from the Nevada nuclear test site to the Runit Dome in the past recently became the subject of critical attention (Rust 2019).

14.2.4.2 Mismanaging Compensation Funds

There was also a matter on Marshall Islands' side in the form of the Kili, Bikini, and Ejit (KBE) Local Government Council's mismanagement of the Bikini Resettlement Trust Fund. The fund was managed based on the original Compact agreement to compensate those displaced from Bikini Atoll due to nuclear testing (United States and Marshall Islands 1983). In response to a request from the KBE in 2017, the

United States ended 35 years of oversight of trust fund use and authorized full decision-making power to the leaders of KBE, leading to the quick depletion of the resettlement trust fund (United States DOI 2017, 2023). The displaced Bikini community responded with severe demonstrations against the alleged mismanagement of the compensation funds in 2023. Consequently, the Marshall Islands government placed the KBE into receivership (Marshall Islands Journal 2023).

This mismanagement of compensation funds by the KBE also affected the lives of the settlers on Kili Island. The drying up of the fund meant the suspension of disbursements, leading to food and fuel shortages on the island. In January 2024, the newly elected president, Hilda Heine, declared a state of emergency for those living on Kili Island (Johnson 2024). Whereas local leaders have laid the foundation for nuclear legacy advocacy, given these incidents and the recently growing national government engagement, managing nuclear legacy issues may gradually shift from the local to the national level.[6]

14.2.4.3 Displaced People on Kili Island

Climate change is also a severe concern for people on Kili Island displaced by the first nuclear test at Bikini Atoll in 1946 because of the island's low land level (CFE-DM 2022). The current population in Kili is 415 (Economic Policy, Planning, and Statistics Office and Pacific Community 2023). The island experienced severe inundations caused by king tides in 2015 and 2016 (CFE-DM 2022). Climate change has already affected the lives of the displaced people and their families.

14.2.4.4 International Cooperation

Marshall Islands' nuclear legacy is politically sensitive and complicated. This is because despite compensation officially having been settled through the Compact agreement in 1983, Marshall Islands submitted the CCP in 2000. Furthermore, Marshall Islands' national finances are highly dependent on financial assistance from the United States under the Compact agreement. There is also the question of how to prove causality, such as in genetic effects, through successive generations of the communities affected by nuclear tests. Having said this, compensation can be seen as a human rights issue and hence, could potentially involve activating human rights mechanisms in the United Nations. Also, apart from the compensation, there could be specific areas where international cooperation can contribute, according to organizations' expertise and knowledge, to Marshall Islands' actions in relation to nuclear legacy provisions. The Marshall Islands National Nuclear Commission (NNC) (2019) strategizes the five critical pillars of nuclear justice: (i) full payment

[6] This point of view was based on discussion with Professor Seiichiro Takemine at Meisei University on 30 December 2023.

of awards of the Nuclear Claims Tribunal; (ii) quality healthcare; (iii) reduced radiation exposure risks in the environment; (iv) national capacity-building to monitor and understand radiation impacts; and (v) education and awareness regarding the nuclear legacy. The last four pillars are the areas where international organizations, including the United Nations agencies, can assist in addressing the nuclear legacy from the aspects of health, environment, capacity-building and preserving history.

14.3 Actions at the United Nations

Marshall Islands has advocated at the United Nations for the nuclear legacy to be addressed since the first petition was filed with the United Nations Trusteeship Council in 1954.[7] In response to the petition, the United Nations Trusteeship Council adopted a resolution to urge the administering authority, the United States, to give sympathetic attention to all claims made in the petition by the affected Marshall communities (United Nations Trusteeship Council 1954). However, direct intervention by the United Nations would have to wait until Marshall Islands was admitted to the United Nations in 1991. This section lists the island nation's achievements in the United Nations system to review how the nuclear legacy issues to the fore internationally.

14.3.1 International Atomic Energy Agency Investigation

Radiation surveys on affected islands and people in Marshall Islands have relied primarily on United States agencies such as the AEC and the DOE.[8] However, incidents caused by the United States' scientific decisions, such as the fallout from Castle Bravo and the premature return to Rongelap Atoll, led to Marshallese distrust of scientific investigations by the United States. Soon after Marshall Islands became a member state of the International Atomic Energy Agency (IAEA) in 1994, the nation requested an independent international review of the radiological status of Bikini Atoll. The IAEA report was formally submitted in 1997. The conclusion was that resettlement to the atoll was not recommended because of the risk of radioactive local foods, such as coconuts (Stegnar 1998). The report also suggested that no further survey on the radioactive status of the area would be required.

---

[7] To our knowledge, one more petition for the same purpose was submitted to the United Nations in 1956 from Marshall Islands (Marshall Islands and United Nations Trusteeship Council 1956).

[8] For example, the DOE launched a health studies and activities programme in 1977. This programme provided annual medical surveillance and care, environmental monitoring and characterization, and dose assessment for the peoples of the four "nuclear-affected atolls", namely Bikini, Enewetak, Rongelap, and Utrik (DOE no date).

14.3.2 UNESCO World Heritage

Marshall Islands obtained World Heritage status for the Bikini Atoll nuclear test site in 2010, recognizing its universal value as a distinctive part of twentieth-century history and representing the dawn of the nuclear age under the Cold War (UNESCO 2010). Accelerated by President Barack Obama's 2009 Prague announcement of a worldwide ban on all nuclear explosive weapons testing, the global nuclear disarmament movement supported Marshall Islands in obtaining the World Heritage status (Kurosaki 2013). Alongside this, there was a recognition that the nuclear test locations across Marshall Islands' vast ocean territory require careful planning and significant resources for research and management. In this vein, the World Heritage Committee approved international technical assistance in 2023 to survey shipwrecks within the Bikini Atoll nuclear test site (UNESCO 2023).

14.3.3 Nuclear Zero Lawsuits

"Nuclear zero lawsuits" refers to a series of legal actions filed by Marshall Islands in 2014 against nine nuclear-armed nations in the International Court of Justice (ICJ), accusing them of failure to meet their obligations under the Treaty on the Non-Proliferation of Nuclear Weapons (NPT) to work towards the cessation of the nuclear arms race at an early date and to nuclear disarmament (Nuclear Age Peace Foundation, no date). The nine nuclear powers include five NPT member states—China, France, the Russian Federation, the United Kingdom, and the United States—and four non-NPT member states—the Democratic People's Republic of Korea, India, Israel, and Pakistan. Only India, Pakistan, and the United Kingdom went forward at ICJ since they had already accepted the court's compulsory jurisdiction, while the other six had not, so trials had never happened. However, the ICJ upheld the first preliminary objection to jurisdiction raised by each of the three nuclear powers, based on the absence of a dispute between the parties, and found that it could not proceed to the case's merits (ICJ 2016a, b, c). Apart from the lawsuits with these nine nuclear powers, Marshall Islands also filed lawsuits against the United States in the United States Federal District Court in 2014 for the same purpose. The court dismissed the lawsuit based on jurisdictional grounds, concluding that the issue of nuclear disarmament under the NPT was a political question unsuitable for judicial resolution (Nuclear Age Peace Foundation 2017).

The late Marshallese foreign minister Tony deBrum led these historical lawsuits, which attracted worldwide attention, although local opinions were mixed (Takemine 2015). Some were concerned about the relationship with the United States; others pointed out that there would be no tangible merits for the citizens affected by the radiation damage. These reactions highlight Marshallese's broad and mixed attitudes regarding separating global nuclear disarmament and their nuclear legacy.

14.3.4 UNHRC Engagements

The United Nations General Assembly established the UNHRC in 2006 as the leading intergovernmental body responsible for strengthening the promotion and protection of human rights across the globe. The UNHRC has played a vital role in accelerating the discussion of Marshall Islands' nuclear legacy. The milestone achievements are the Special Rapporteur report in 2012 and the UNHRC resolution in 2022.

14.3.4.1 Special Rapporteur Report

UNHRC appoints Special Rapporteurs, independent experts, to examine, monitor, advise, and report on human rights situations in specific countries on major human rights themes. Special Rapporteurs are the largest body of independent experts in the United Nations human rights system, playing a pivotal role in the Human Rights Council's Special Procedures (UNHRC Special Procedures 2024). The Special Rapporteur's report highlighted the challenges faced by communities in Marshall Islands, particularly the forced displacement and long-term health effects due to the nuclear testing. Further, the Special Rapporteur stressed a particular concern about the impact of the hazardous substances and wastes in the dump site at the Runit Dome and suggested assessing the radiological conditions of Enewetak Atoll (UNHRC 2012). The report's recommendations also helped Marshall Islands to develop a national plan to pursue nuclear justice (UNHRC 2012).

14.3.4.2 UNHRC Resolution

In 2022, the UNHRC adopted a historic resolution entitled "Technical assistance and capacity-building to address the human rights impact of the nuclear legacy in the Marshall Islands" (UNHRC 2022b). This resolution "affirms the importance of addressing the adverse impact of the nuclear legacy on the realization and enjoyment of human rights by the people of the Marshall Islands" and "requests the Office of the United Nations High Commissioner for Human Rights (OHCHR) to cooperate with Marshall Islands in the field of human rights and to provide technical assistance and capacity-building to the National Nuclear Commission of the Marshall Islands in advancing its national strategy for nuclear justice and determining its technical assistance and capacity-building needs to pursue transitional justice in its efforts to address the nuclear legacy" (UNHRC 2022b, p. 3). In addition, it "recalls that addressing the nuclear legacy of Marshall Islands is a regional priority for the Pacific Islands Forum and has regional implications posing a serious environmental hazard to the Pacific region, with concerns regarding the integrity of the concrete dome containing nuclear and toxic wastes on Runit Island" (UNHRC 2022b, p. 3).

This resolution was adopted without voting,[9] while the United States announced its position on the resolution, insisting that the UNHRC and OHCHR were not appropriate bodies to opine or provide technical assistance on nuclear legacy issues since "science" is not their expertise (US Mission Geneva 2022). The United States was also concerned about fund sustainability, given the high costs and limited abilities and resources that the United Nations member states could provide. Furthermore, the United States indicated that some issues raised in the resolution had been settled bilaterally through binding international agreements, such as the Section 177 agreement, and expressed concern that the human rights approach downplayed compensation and settlements made in the past. As a rebuttal, the United States argued that scientific judgments should be made by the United Nations agencies suited to dealing with the nuclear legacy, such the IAEA and the United Nations Scientific Committee on the Effects of Atomic Radiation (UNSCEAR).[10]

14.3.5 The Treaty of Prohibition of Nuclear Weapons

In 2016, the United Nations hosted a conference to negotiate a legally binding instrument to prohibit nuclear weapons, leading towards their total elimination. The Treaty of Prohibition of Nuclear Weapons (TPNW) was adopted and entered into force with the support of 93 signatories and 70 parties in 2021 (United Nations 2017). Articles 6 and 7 of the TPNW are essential for the nuclear legacy, covering victim assistance, environmental remediation, and international cooperation and assistance. Marshall Islands has not yet signed or ratified the TPNW and has consistently abstained from TPNW-related resolutions (ICAN no date). The reason for this is regarded as because Marshall Islands received significant financial assistance in return for allowing the United States military to test intercontinental ballistic missiles in its territory, at Kwajalein Atoll. This practice is widely considered incompatible with the TPNW's prohibition on assisting with the development of nuclear weapons. Marshall Islands has also insisted that nuclear test-affected countries should not bear the cost of redressing the impacts of nuclear tests conducted by the nuclear powers, given the limited capacity of affected countries such as Marshall Islands (Hood 2023).

---

[9] In statements made before the decision, the representatives of India, Pakistan, and the United States briefly expressed concerns about whether OHCHR had the requisite expertise to address serious cross-cutting nuclear, environmental, and health matters (UNHRC 2022a). On the other hand, the representative from China firmly charged the United States with taking concrete measures to address its responsibility for the nuclear legacy and claimed to ratify the Protocols to the South Pacific Nuclear Free Zone Treaty without delay. This shows that nuclear legacy issues are intertwined with geopolitical tension in the Pacific between China and the United States.

[10] Similar diplomatic tension with the UNHRC Special Rapporteur has been observed in relation to the Fukushima Daiichi Nuclear Power Station accident. Japan expressed serious concern about the Special Rapporteur's claim that the planned water release would contain hazardous substances (Ministry of Foreign Affairs 2018).

Dealing with nuclear legacy issues, which the TPNW included in its terms, was also addressed in a resolution entitled "Addressing the legacy of nuclear weapons: providing victim assistance and environmental remediation to member states affected by the use or testing of nuclear weapons",[11] adopted by the United Nations General Assembly First Committee in 2023 (United Nations First Committee 2023a). The resolution encourages all parties to support victims and to assess and restore the environment contaminated by nuclear weapons and nuclear testing. Marshall Islands voted in favour this time, further suggesting the nation's position of distinguishing between nuclear disarmament and nuclear legacy issues. As a side note, the countries voting against were the Democratic People's Republic of Korea, France, the Russian Federation, and the United Kingdom, while China, Congo, India, Israel, Pakistan, and the United States abstained (United Nations First Committee 2023a, b). These were the same nations that Marshall Islands sued in the ICJ earlier, except for Congo, which supplies uranium to the nuclear powers.

14.4 Development of Regional Frameworks

This section examines the formation of regional cooperation frameworks related to the nuclear weapon tests in the Pacific. First, the history of nuclear weapon tests in the Pacific is overviewed. Then, the actions of Pacific Island countries in formulating regional cooperation frameworks are reviewed, including recent actions of the Pacific Islands Forum (PIF) and the Pacific Small Island Developing States (SIDS) on nuclear issues.

14.4.1 Nuclear Tests in the Pacific

From 1946 to 1996, France, the United Kingdom, and the United States detonated over 320 nuclear devices under their jurisdiction in the Pacific, whose specific areas including: Marshall Islands (Bikini and Enewetak Atolls), the United States (Amchitka and Johnston Islands), Australia (Maralinga, Monte Bello Islands), Kiribati (Kiritimati and Malden Islands), and French Polynesia (Moruroa and Fangataufa Atolls).

After nuclear tests in Marshall Islands, 23 times at Bikini Atoll and 44 times at Enewetak Atoll from 1946 to 1956, the United States conducted nuclear tests at Kiritimati Island and Johnston Island 24 times and 14 times, respectively, as a part of Operation Dominic in 1962. Nuclear testing sites then moved to Polynesia, where France conducted 193 nuclear bomb tests from 1966 to 1996 in the air and later underground (Henley 2021). The United Kingdom also conducted 21 nuclear

[11] Kazakhstan and Kiribati, both nuclear test-affected countries, took a lead on this resolution among others (United Nations First Committee 2023b).

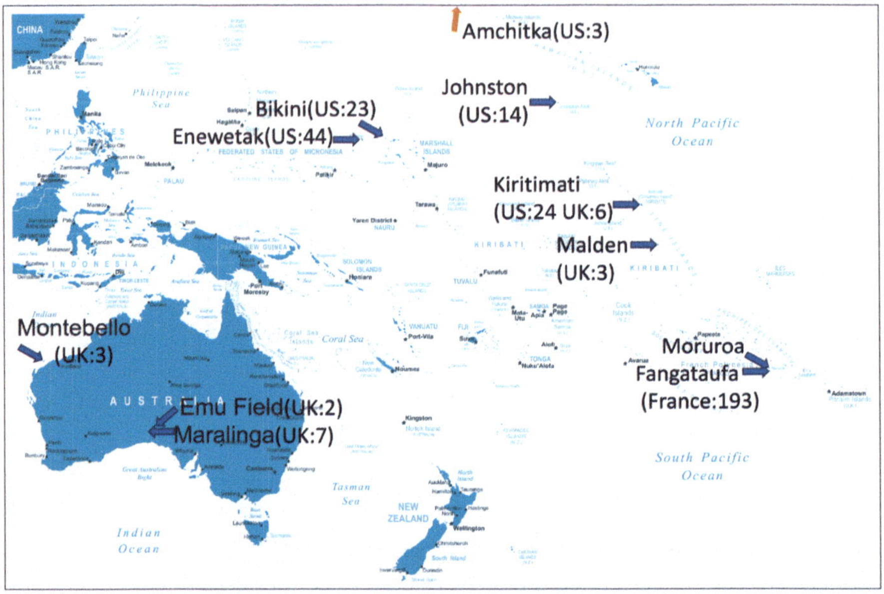

Fig. 14.2 Nuclear weapon tests in the Pacific. *Note* numbers in parentheses indicate number of nuclear weapon tests at the sites. *Source* authors' illustration based on a map purchased from Adobe Stock

weapon tests in Australia and Polynesia (Donaldson et al. 2022). Figure 14.2 provides a regionwide overview.

The nuclear tests by France, the United Kingdom, and the United States dispersed fallout beyond the test sites throughout the Pacific, detected in Cook Islands, Fiji, New Zealand, Niue, Samoa, Tokelau, Tonga, and Tuvalu (International Disarmament Institute no date). The impact of the nuclear tests also extended beyond people in these areas, affecting the significant number of military and civilian personnel from Australia, Fiji, France, New Zealand, the United Kingdom, and the United States who had participated in the testing. These nuclear tests and the dispersal of the fallout in the Pacific have left devastating incidents of sickness, anxiety, displacement, radiation, and environmental damage.

14.4.2 Regional Cooperation in the Pacific

Given the prolonged nuclear testing in the Pacific, island nations gradually shifted their efforts towards fostering a stronger regional cooperation framework. This subsection examines such regional development in detail.

14.4.2.1 Emerging Regional Cooperation Against Nuclear Testing

The nuclear tests in the Pacific influenced the shape of the regional cooperation frameworks. The first regional group formulated in the Pacific was the South Pacific Commission (SPC), established in 1947, comprising countries with sovereign or administrative territories in the Pacific: Australia, France, the Netherlands, New Zealand, the United Kingdom, and the United States. Representatives of Pacific islands could participate in the South Pacific Conference, an advisory committee of the SPC established in 1950. However, political matters are outside the scope of the SPC (Kurosaki 2012). In the 1960s, Pacific island nations developed serious concerns about the newly planned nuclear tests and the consequences of nuclear tests already conducted (Ogashiwa 1992). Although representatives of Cook Islands requested the adoption of a resolution to oppose nuclear tests planned by France at the 1965 South Pacific Conference, this proposal was rejected based on the SPC's principle (Ogashiwa 2000).

These grave concerns about the nuclear tests and discontent with the SPC led to the formulation of the South Pacific Forum (SPF) by seven states in 1971.[12] The increasing number of independent Pacific countries in this period supported the establishment of the forum (Kurosaki 2012). At the first meeting in New Zealand, the SPF adopted a resolution to express deep regret over France's nuclear tests (Ogashiwa 2000).[13] In 1979, the plan of Japan's Nuclear Safety Commission to dump low-level radioactive waste in a trench at a depth of 6200 m off the Ogasawara Islands also stimulated the non-nuclear movement in the Pacific (Takemine 2023).[14] Then, the SPF reacted to this plan by adopting a resolution condemning it at the forum held in Kiribati in 1980 (Ogashiwa 2000). In 1985, the forum approved the South Pacific Nuclear Free Zone Treaty, known as the Treaty of Rarotonga, enacted the following year for nuclear disarmament in the South Pacific (SPEC 1985). The treaty prohibits nuclear explosive devices in the territory of a state party and the dumping of radioactive materials into the region's ocean. When France planned to resume nuclear testing in the 1990s, SPF again opposed the plan, and France finally ceased the nuclear weapon tests in the South Pacific in 1996. Subsequently, France, the United Kingdom, and the United States signed the treaty protocols in 1996, although the United States has not ratified this yet. As a side note, Marshall Islands, along with Palau and Federated States of Micronesia (FSM), did not sign the treaty, because of

---

[12] Those seven original member states comprised Australia, Cook Islands, Fiji, Nauru, New Zealand, Tonga, and Western Samoa (now known as Samoa).

[13] In 1973, Australia and New Zealand also separately filed a lawsuit with the ICJ against France to stop its nuclear testing in the South Pacific. This lawsuit concluded in 1974 that the objectives had been achieved because France publicly announced that it would cease aerial testing and revert to underground testing (Herman 1976).

[14] Ocean dumping of radioactive waste was a common international practice at that time. As a result of such opposition in the Pacific, Japan became the first country to stop ocean dumping for nuclear waste in the Pacific Ocean, ahead of other countries such as New Zealand, the Republic of Korea, the Russian Federation (then the Soviet Union), and the United States (Sjoblom and Linsley 1994).

its late admission to the SPF in 1987 and probable consideration of the United States military presence in the North Pacific.[15]

14.4.2.2 Pacific Islands Forum

With the increased number of SPF member states and efforts to address common issues in the Pacific, such as climate change and marine resource management, the forum has increased its presence internationally (Kurosaki 2016). The SPF was renamed the Pacific Islands Forum (PIF) in 1999 because of the growing participation of the North Pacific countries. The PIF's interest in nuclear issues was relatively low for a while: the PIF strategic plan 2050 recognizes climate change as "the region's single greatest threat to security", mentioned more than 30 times, while it only mentions nuclear issues once in the context of nuclear contamination (PIF 2022, pp. 21–27).

The 51st PIF leaders meeting communique in 2023 rebooted the forum's attention to nuclear issues (PIF 2023b). The main concern at the conference was Japan's advanced liquid processing system (ALPS) treated water discharge.[16] The ALPS-treated water discharge plan was formulated in response to the 2011 Great East Japan Earthquake and the Fukushima Daiichi Nuclear Power Plant accident. It involves treating and gradually releasing water used to cool the damaged reactors and has since been stored on-site, into the ocean after removing most radioactive materials, except tritium (Ministry of the Environment 2023). The IAEA has assessed this plan, acknowledging Japan's efforts to ensure that the discharge meets international safety standards and poses minimal environmental and public health risks (IAEA 2023).

However, the PIF secretary general and several members, including Marshall Islands,[17] were suspicious of the IAEA assessment and opposed the discharge plan based on the advice of the PIF expert panel, which raised questions about the IAEA report (PIF 2023a, c). Even after intensive and ongoing dialogues with Japan and the IAEA, the PIF leaders were concerned about the potential threat of nuclear contamination to the health and security of the Pacific, stating a "nuclear wastewater issue"

[15] The Treaty of Rarotonga is accessible at: https://web.archive.org/web/20160304084144/, http://www.forumsec.org/resources/uploads/attachments/documents/SPNFZ%20Status%20Report.pdf. (Accessed: 2 March 2024).

[16] In addition to the discharge of the ALPS-treated water, the Australia–United Kingdom–United States (AUKUS) trilateral security agreement on Australia's purchase of nuclear submarines was on the agenda, concluding that "[PIF leaders] welcome the transparency of Australia's efforts and its commitment to comply with international law" (PIF 2023b, p. 9).

[17] The Marshall Islands Parliament (Nitijela) passed a resolution on 24 March 2023, "expressing grave concerns over Japan's plans and decisions to dump radioactive wastewater from the Fukushima Nuclear Plant into the Pacific Ocean and urging Japan to consider safer alternative plan to dispose the radioactive wastewater then releasing into the Pacific Ocean" (Marshall Islands Parliament 2023, p. 1).

in the 51st PIF leaders meeting communique (PIF 2023b, p. 7).[18] The nuclear legacy and the Rarotonga Treaty were also brought up to emphasize transgenerational and transboundary risks, although they are not legally binding to water discharge authorization.[19] Notably, the communique also recognized "the sovereignty of member states to determine their national positions on the water discharge" (PIF 2023b, p. 7), and a certain number of state leaders affirmed the safety of the discharge plan. Although the PIF has been sensitive to nuclear issues, it is not necessarily true that it represents the opinions of all Pacific island nations.[20]

14.4.2.3 Pacific Small Island Developing States at the United Nations

The PIF is not only the entity to advocate its interests on the global stage. Pacific Small Island Developing States (SIDS) is a United Nations-specific group among Pacific island nations based in New York. SIDS' call for "new Pacific diplomacy" originated in the early 1990s during the global sustainable development dialogues of the Rio + 20 United Nations Conference process (Fry and Tarte 2015, p. 7). In 2009, SIDS took over representing Pacific countries from the PIF at the United Nations.[21] This shift happened because of the differing interests of the Pacific islands from Australia and New Zealand, exemplified in Fiji's suspension from the PIF membership in 2009 (Manoa 2015). The member states of SIDS are those of the PIF minus the two regional powers that strongly support the Fiji-led initiative (Fry and Tarte 2015). Most notably, the SIDS, in collaboration with Australia and New Zealand, drafted the UNHRC's 2022a, b resolution on the nuclear legacy in Marshall Islands (Ministry of Foreign Affairs of Marshall Islands 2022).[22] Pacific Island countries seem to be using the three positions in the different diplomatic channels—SIDS for the United Nations systems, PIF for regional frameworks, and sovereignty country status for bilateral diplomacy—for their own particular interests.

[18] A list of political dialogues and briefing sessions for PIF members and secretariat is accessible at the Ministry of Economy, Trade, and Industry of Japan's website (Ministry of Economy, Trade, and Industry 2023).

[19] The Rarotonga Treaty covers only the ocean territory of its member states.

[20] This point of view was first presented by Professor Takehiro Kurosaki, Tokay University, and Hideyuki Shiozawa, Sasagawa Peace Foundation, at a seminar organized by Sasagawa Peace Foundation on 16 November 2023. For example, President David Panuelo of FSM officially visited Japan in February 2023 and showed an understanding of the discharge of the ALPS-treated water (Ishii 2023). Also, President Surangel Whipps Jr. of Palau expressed his confidence in the Japanese management of the treated water during his visit to Fukushima in June 2023 (Ministry of Foreign Affairs 2021).

[21] However, PIF gained observer status in the United Nations at its sixth committee in 71st session without a vote. See www.un.org/en/ga/sixth/71/pacific_island.shtml.

[22] The authors of the draft resolution were Australia, Fiji, Marshall Islands, Nauru, New Zealand, Samoa, and Vanuatu.

14.5 Possible Ways Forward

The listed events in the previous sections, the history of the nuclear legacy, actions at the United Nations, and emerging regional frameworks suggest a shift in the balance of power on nuclear legacy issues in terms of human rights, science–social relations, and the roles of Marshall Islands and the United Nations. This section explores these domains and suggests ways forward to address the issues of nuclear legacy.

14.5.1 Transitional Justice

The international arena has rethought human rights violations against the Marshallese as part of the nuclear legacy in terms of emerging transitional justice. The term "transitional justice" suggests the full range of judicial and non-judicial measures associated with a society's attempt to ensure accountability, serve justice, and achieve reconciliation in the context of large-scale past conflict, repression, violations, and abuses (UNSC 2004). This concept was developed in the 1990s, focusing on regime change and peacebuilding within a country, and expanded during the 2000s to encompass historical injustices against indigenous peoples and others (Hirai 2017). The typical extended transitional justice examples are the cases of "settler states" like Australia and New Zealand retrieving the rights of indigenous people (Balint and Evans 2011). In this context, applying transitional justice to the nuclear legacy is considered another conceptual expansion, because the UNHRC's historic resolution in 2022 aims to strengthen Marshall Islands' strategy for nuclear justice and pursuit of transitional justice in the nation's efforts to address the nuclear legacy (UNHRC 2022a).

On Majuro in March 2024, OHCHR held the first international workshop on transitional justice to address the nuclear legacy in Marshall Islands in accordance with the UNHRC resolution. The workshop's goal was to sensitize participants based on the latest Guidance Note on Transitional Justice (OHCHR 2024), as well as capacity-building of Marshallese stakeholders such as NNC staff, government officials in various departments, affected communities, and relevant civil society members. The participatory sessions focused on key elements of comprehensive transitional justice processes: consultations, truth-seeking, criminal justice, reparation, and guarantees of non-recurrence. The objectives and key features of the new guidance note were also explained in the sessions.[23]

Considering the OHCHR engagement and recent favourable trends in international society in relation to nuclear legacy issues, transitional justice on nuclear legacy may explored further despite the possibility of a backlash from the United

[23] The guidance note was designed to help overcome the challenges identified for a traditional transitional justice framework. It is oriented towards a more comprehensive approach from a long perspective, encompassing the five key features: normative, strategic, inclusive, gender-responsive, and transformative (United Nations Secretary General 2023).

States.[24] The human rights approach could be effective particularly in providing redress for the non-radiological consequences of nuclear legacies, such as compensation, forced displacement, and remembrance. However, the validity of judgments on compensation in light of the lack of scientific data would remain a central point of argument, and how to interpret limited scientific facts and incorporate them into a truth-seeking mechanism might also be controversial.[25] In addition, the situation of displaced people from Bikini Atoll, Enewetak Atoll, and Rongelap Atoll has begun to be reviewed, since internally displaced people were the central concern from a human rights perspective (International Center for Transitional Justice 2012; United Nations Economic and Social Council 1998). The human rights violation is also being examined from the climate change perspective, given the low-lying islands to which displaced people were forced to move. Furthermore, the role of remembrance in relation to the nuclear legacy is also spotlighted today. In 2024, ahead of the International Day for Disarmament and Non-Proliferation, the 14 United Nations human rights experts issued a statement that stressed the importance of remembrance, paying tribute to past and present victims of past human rights violations in confronting the nuclear legacy from the Pacific to West Asia, from Central Asia to North Africa (UNHRC Special Procedures 2024).[26]

Having said this, the radiological consequences of nuclear legacy are also critical for the people of Marshall Islands, considering the ongoing direct impact of residual radiation and fear of the transgenerational impact on health. However, Marshall Islands does not have enough scientific capacity to monitor the status of radiation issues alone, thus relying to a large extent on evidence and reports provided by the United States. Further, due to inadequate science literacy in the country, there are difficulties in comprehending the status and actual risk to health of radiation. Giff Johnson, the editor of *Marshall Islands Journal*, emphasized at the workshop that the fundamental problem of the nuclear test legacy in Marshall Islands was the islands' lack of understanding of the many layers of the impact of the 67 US nuclear tests, and a lack of control of this legacy because all of the studies, data, and information about it are owned and controlled by the US government.[27] Until Marshall Islands owns the nuclear legacy by engaging independent scientists and doctors to perform studies that address all aspects of it, many of them as yet unstudied or poorly understood, and develops its own capacity to manage the legacy, it will remain largely a bystander to the most significant problem affecting the nation, unable to address the legacy needs as a result of lack of information and knowledge. In such a situation, it is even more difficult for the Marshall Islanders to consider the use or restoration of a nuclear test site when they are not assured of its safety. In the guidance notes to the United

[24] The opinion in this paragraph is developed at the workshop based on the original ideas of the authors.

[25] The involvement of science in the pursuit of transitional justice may be analogous to the situation regarding the application of scientific evidence in the general judiciary or courts.

[26] A digital archive was implemented to record nuclear testing history (Marshall Islands Journal 2021). see at https://marshall.reearth.io/?fbclid=IwAR0MMTHNK73375ROoulqxJvDypu0vc9NM2F6sfLncMEpN1Zvwr4Mx2pVuf8.

[27] Giff Johnson gave permission at the workshop for his comments to be cited in this chapter.

Nations transitional justice approach, ownership is recognized as a key characteristic of "inclusiveness". Thus, building scientific capacity to manage nuclear legacies is an essential component in pursuing transitional justice with respect to such legacies.

14.5.2 *Trans-scientific Issues*

In 1972, United States nuclear physicist Alvin Weinberg conceptualized "trans-scientific issues", a domain of inquiry where scientific questions are raised but cannot be conclusively answered by science alone (Weinberg 1972, p. 218).[28] Regarding the nuclear legacy in Marshall Islands, scientific assessment can be conducted through radiation surveys of health and the environment. However, how best to address the issues identified by the survey is shaped not only by science but also by various other factors, such as socioeconomic and environmental issues and public policies. Thus, nuclear legacy issues are fundamentally trans-science issues.

Science and technology studies (STS) could provide insights to help address trans-science issues. STS is an interdisciplinary academic field that examines the relationships between science and society and produces insights from the point of view of social science, including philosophy, ethics, history, and sociology (Merton 1993; Stilgoe and Guston 2017). STS covers issues such as the uncertainty of science, secrecy, and ignorance seen in the nuclear legacy in Marshall Islands (Vogel et al. 2017). This approach is expected to bridge the gaps in science-related issues between different sectors—such as science and technology, citizenry, politics, and regulations—by analysing their interactions and proposing a dialogue platform (Horst, Davies, and Irwin 2017; Stilgoe and Guston 2017).

From its inception to the present, nuclear testing and its legacy have entailed gaps between scientific judgement and public concerns. Such discrepancies are particularly large in Marshall Islands because scientific mistreatment has created huge resentment among the public. The Marshallese are also dissatisfied with how scientific facts about the nuclear legacy are shared. Since the nuclear legacy in Marshall Islands involves various sectors and issues, cross-disciplinary perspectives are also essential. Therefore, the role of a coordinator who connects science and local society is vital to facilitate discussion aiming towards consensus and design collaborations among different sectors on nuclear legacy issues.[29]

---

[28] Trans-science views are sometimes criticized in that conventional scientific methodologies encounter limitations due to their intrinsic values and uncertainties when confronted with multi-faceted and ambiguous queries like those around environmental hazards. This compels scientists to extend their analysis beyond empirical evidence to reach conclusions (Carolan 2006).

[29] Harry Collins, a sociologist of science, defined a specialist who has scientific knowledge and can talk about scientific issues with scientists in academia as "interactional expertise" (Collins 2014, p. 87). The coordinator in nuclear legacy issues here may not have to be at such a level of expertise but would need to know the conventions and values of science well enough to be able to publicly discuss scientific aspects of nuclear legacy.

To date, scientific findings on nuclear legacy have tended to be communicated one-sidedly in reports and official meetings, with limited participation of stakeholders. The insight provided by STS may help to inspire outreach activities to establish mutual understanding between scientists and the public in a two-way dialogue approach.[30] Such outreach efforts seem not to have been adequately made in Marshall Islands in the past but are necessary to get all stakeholders, including local people, on the same page.

However, the level of science literacy in Marshall Islands will challenge attempts to advance the STS approach. In the Marshall Islands Standards Assessment Test 2023, the proportion of students meeting the expectation for the grade level in Grade 12 is just nine per cent while that in English is also low, at 18 per cent (Ministry of Education, Sports, and Training 2023). This implies difficulties in acquiring scientific understanding considering that English is a second language and science education texts are normally written in English. Ideally, policies in education should be improved, particularly in science and mathematics, since this development gap affects not only nuclear legacy but also developing Marshallese skilled workers. Another option would be to prioritize intensive long-term training for a few Marshallese scientists to develop future Marshallese experts in scientific aspects of nuclear legacy while creating Marshallese-friendly tools for better public understanding of nuclear science using infographics or arts.

Interestingly, when discussing nuclear legacy, the social responsibility[31] of scientists is rarely on the agenda. Even though nuclear scientists in modern international academia are not directly responsible for nuclear testing, scientific research addressing the problems of nuclear legacy is within their research scope, which is presumably based to an extent on the research developed at nuclear weapon tests in the past. Although nuclear science academia may remain political in relation to nuclear powers, it might be an option to expand research institutes so that they can be relied on to provide further research and national capacity-building in nuclear science.[32]

---

[30] Such actions can be considered a part of "science communication" (Horst et al. 2017, p. 881).

[31] John Forge, a philosopher of science, defines "social responsibility" as the norm of being "aware that [one's] work may carry consequences beyond the boundaries of [one's] institution or community and then [acting] accordingly" (Forge 2008, p. 16). In the case that scientists engaged in the nuclear tests of the past had envisaged the consequences for the environment and the health of local people, the nuclear legacy would be considered the result of scientists' absence of social responsibility.

[32] Nuclear science institutes include others besides the MOE and IAEA. For example, Bernd Grambow, a scientist in radiochemistry and incumbent president of the expert committee of the International Institute of Nuclear Energy (France), proposed integrated programming of nuclear legacy clean-up research at the international level (Grambow 2017). No progress has been made on this as far as the authors can see. If such cooperation were realized, it would be a prerequisite to contribute to scientific capacity-building or public understanding to understand nuclear science to avoid "parachute science", a practice where researchers conduct fieldwork in foreign communities to collect data and then leave without engaging with the local communities and researchers (Odeny and Bosurgi 2022).

14.5.3 A New Phase in Marshall Islands' Nuclear Legacy

In reviewing recent developments, Marshall Islands' nuclear legacy has required expanding the national government's role from advocation to coordination. The Marshall Islands National Strategic Plan (NSP) 2020 to 2030 defines nuclear justice as cross-cutting issues over the nation's five critical pillars: (i) society and culture; (ii) development and resilience; (iii) infrastructure; (iv) economic development; and (v) governance (Economic Policy, Planning and Statistics Office 2020). Given Marshall Islands' limited resources and capacities, a holistic approach across sectors with effective coordination is key to successfully addressing the nuclear legacy.

The NNC, established in 2017, has become the entity that responds to the needs and coordinates among various stakeholders. It appears to be the vehicle for the government's recent activities on the issues of nuclear legacy. NNC's initiatives include information dissemination, awareness-raising, and youth education, mostly featuring the history of nuclear tests and their consequences (NNC 2024). With the tangible support of OHCHR, the nuclear legacy has begun to be addressed from a human rights aspect recently, including the establishment of NNC. This momentum would continue to restore the human rights of affected individuals and communities beyond generations, especially concerning compensation, displacement, and remembrance. The NNC is expected to lead in facilitating this movement with policymakers and the public.

However, it also showed that the scientific capacity of the country and its people is insufficient for obtaining true ownership of the nuclear legacy, meaning control and management of radiation issues based on evidence-based intelligence. Thus, NNC may be encouraged to make efforts to incorporate science education into its activities in the future by seeking assistance from experts in science. Also, though it is a mandate of the national government, the formulation of projects to develop Marshallese experts in nuclear science would be necessary to build national capacity in nuclear legacy issues and improve science education.

As projects to address the nuclear legacy are implemented, Marshall Islands' responsibility in coordinating tasks and resources with various stakeholders is increasing to change the lives of affected communities. In addition, as projects progress, there will be an additional role to bring its insights and lessons learned to the international and the regional forums as a pioneering example.

14.5.4 United Nations Multi-Country Office for Micronesia

Perhaps the most desirable change in Micronesia's development coordination in recent years has been the establishment of the United Nations Multi-Country Office (UNMCO) in 2021. This office coordinates the United Nations entities and agencies in the North Pacific, which comprises Marshall Islands, Palau, FSM, Nauru, and Kiribati, aiming to enhance the United Nations system's engagement in the five

Small Island Developing States (SIDS). Hence, Marshall Islands' nuclear legacy is also included in its scope.

The involvement of UNMCO is essential to address the country's nuclear legacy, given the lack of human resources and coordination capacity. For example, there are limited numbers of skilled workers for basic public services relating to various nuclear legacy issues, such as health, education, and utilities, and in this context, the United Nations system can provide a range of technical assistance to enhance capacity. Given the politically sensitive nature of nuclear legacy issues, the involvement of the United Nations system is also highly desirable to gain international expertise in specific areas, such as nuclear science and human rights. Furthermore, as mentioned in previous sections, addressing nuclear legacy requires collaboration across different disciplines, sectors, and groups. Marshall Islands is not fully equipped with the capacity to facilitate this, so UNMCO's support, facilitation, and coordination—especially among the United Nations entities and agencies—are vital to the success of Marshall Islands' nuclear legacy campaigns. To this end, new officers have recently been deployed, including the Human Rights Officer at the OHCHR Pacific Regional Office in Micronesia and the Country Coordination Officer at a satellite office in Marshall Islands, who are also involved in nuclear legacy issues. Although it is still the beginning, close collaboration between Marshall Islands and UNMCO is expected to affect their nuclear legacy significantly.

14.6 Conclusions

This chapter has revisited Marshall Islands' nuclear legacy and examined related diplomatic efforts in the international arena. Emerging international frameworks regarding nuclear tests and regional organizations in the Pacific have also been addressed. These bilateral, regional, and international histories illustrate the transition of power balance on nuclear legacy issues. As Marshall Islands has gradually gained the power to raise concerns about the nuclear legacy by enhancing its geopolitical position and growing regional frameworks, the shifting of responsibility from local to national levels and the possible conflict between human rights and scientific approaches to nuclear legacy have been observed.

Recommendations were made regarding human rights, science–social relations, and the role of Marshall Islands and the United Nations Multi-Country Office for Micronesia. Recent developments on nuclear legacy issues have been guided by a human rights approach, particularly a comprehensive approach to transitional justice. This approach to the non-radiological consequences provides an opportunity to rethink issues related to reparations, forced displacement, and memorialization from the perspective of the affected communities. On the other hand, national capacity-building to monitor and understand the radiological status of the nuclear legacy in terms of health and the environment is also important in pursuit of transitional justice. This is because such capacity restores Marshall Islands' ownership over the nuclear legacy. The trans-scientific view of nuclear legacy issues suggests the application of STS knowledge. Considering the multidisciplinary nature of nuclear legacy issues and the inadequate scientific capacity of Marshall Islands, the role of the coordinator is to bridge different experts and stakeholders, including scientists and local Marshallese. The need for tailored science communication for Marshall Islands may also be worth considering. In addition, it is suggested that the role of scientific academia be considered as a possible option to expand scientific support in addressing nuclear legacy issues. To address the issues raised by the transitional justice and trans-science perspectives, the role of Marshall Islands is in expanding from advocacy to coordination, with the likely addition of a role in sharing lessons learned with the international community. In order to respond to these developments, the role of the United Nations Multi-Country Office for Micronesia in developing and complementing Marshall Islands' coordination and resource capacity becomes imperative.

The nuclear legacy in Marshall Islands is attracting international attention again after nearly 80 years have passed since the first nuclear test on Bikini Atoll. The human rights approach is now a vehicle through which to review the issues of nuclear legacy. However, the scientific aspects of nuclear legacy still pose challenges. In this sense, the nexus between transitional justice and trans-science is key to advancing solutions to the issues. Marshall Islands' continued advocacy and coordination efforts, with the tangible cooperation of international society, are also essential. These recent developments suggest that Marshall Islands' nuclear legacy issues have entered a new phase in their history.

Acknowledgements The authors appreciate institutional support provided by the United Nations Volunteers. They also thank Shishin Kawamoto and his staff at the Science Communication Laboratory of Hokkaido University and Seiichiro Takemine at Meisei University for their substantive and thoughtful advice. Special thanks are also due to Diego Valadares Vasconcelos Neto and Raphael Pangalangan, the Human Rights Officers of OHCHR, and Giff Johnson, the editor of the *Marshall Islands Journal*, for their expert advice. Makoto Abe read an earlier version of this chapter, providing substantive comments that enhanced its relevance. The authors partially utilized ChatGPT-4 to shape the outline of the chapter and draft its manuscript, following the *Principles for the ethical use of artificial intelligence in the United Nations system* (CEB 2022).

References

Agence France-Presse (2019) Nuclear "coffin" may be leaking radioactive material into Pacific Ocean, U.N. chief says. CBS NEWS, 16 May 2019 [Online]. Available at: www.cbsnews.com/news/enewetak-atoll-dome-un-antonio-guterres-concerns-marshall-islands-structure-leaking-radioactive-material-pacific. Accessed: 15 Feb 2024

Atomic Heritage Foundation (no date) Marshall Islands [Online]. Available at: https://ahf.nuclearmuseum.org/ahf/location/marshall-islands. Accessed: 7 Mar 2024

Balint J, Evans J (2011) Transitional justice and settler states. Paper presented at ANZCCC: the Australian and New Zealand critical criminology conference 2010. Institute of Criminology, Sydney Law School, University of Sydney, Sydney

Breslin AJ, Cassidy ME (1955) Radioactive debris from operation castle: islands of the mid-Pacific. Atomic Energy Commission (AEC), New York

Carolan M (2006) Science, expertise, and the democratization of the decision-making process. Soc Nat Resour 19:661–668

CEB (Chief Executives Board for Coordination) (2022) Principles for the ethical use of artificial intelligence in the United Nations system. Advanced unedited version, High-Level Committee on Programmes (HLCP), Inter-Agency Working Group on Artificial Intelligence, 20 Sept 2022 [Online]. Available at: https://unsceb.org/sites/default/files/2022-09/Principles%20for%20the%20Ethical%20Use%20of%20AI%20in%20the%20UN%20System_1.pdf. Accessed: 15 Feb 2024

CFE-DM (Center for Excellence in Disaster Management and Humanitarian Assistance) (2022) Republic of the Marshall Islands: disaster management reference handbook. CEE-DM, Pearl Harbor, HA

Collins H (2014) Are we all scientific experts now? Polity Press, Cambridge

CRS (Congressional Research Service, US) (2005) Republic of the Marshall Islands changed circumstances petition to congress. In: CRS report for congress, order code RL32811. CRS, Washington, DC

Defense Nuclear Agency (US) (1981) The radiological cleanup of Enewetak Atoll. Defense Nuclear Agency, Fort Belvoir, VA

DOE (Department of Energy, US) (1989) Rongelap reassessment project report. In: Report to president and congress, corrected edn. DOE, Washington, DC

DOE (2020) Report on the status of the Runit Dome in the Marshall Islands. In: Report to congress. DOE, Washington, DC

DOE (2022) Report on the visual study and groundwater analysis of the Cactus Crater containment structure on Runit Island, Republic of the Marshall Islands. In: Report to congress. DOE, Washington, DC

DOE (no date) International health studies and activities [Online]. Available at: www.energy.gov/ehss/international-health-studies-and-activities. Accessed: 15 Feb 2024

DOI (Department of Interior, US) (2017) Interior authorizes full decision-making power to Bikini leaders over annual budget of the Bikini resettlement trust fund. OIA News, 29 Nov 2017 [Online]. Available at: www.doi.gov/oia/interior-authorizes-full-decision-making-power-bikini-leaders-over-annual-budget-bikini. Accessed: 15 Feb 2024

DOI (2023) Statement on the Kili Bikini Ejit resettlement trust fund. OIA News, 5 May 2023 [Online]. Available at: www.doi.gov/oia/press/Statement-on-the-Kili-Bikini-Ejit-Resettlement-Trust-Fund. Accessed: 15 Feb 2024

Donaldson B, Minor E, Martin AB, Bolton BM (2022) Addressing British nuclear tests in Kiribati: a new opportunity for victim assistance and environmental remediation. UNA-UK and Article 36, London

Economic Policy, Planning and Statistics Office (Marshall Islands) (2020) National strategic plan 2020–2030: Republic of the Marshall Islands

Economic Policy, Planning, and Statistics Office (Marshal Islands) and Pacific Community (2023) Republic of the Marshall Islands 2021 Census report, volume 1: basic tables and administrative report. EPSSO and Nouméa: Pacific Community, Majuro

Eknilang L (2003) Learning from Rongelap's pain. Seattle J Soc Just 2(1):315–321

Forge J (2008) The responsible scientist: a philosophical inquiry. University of Pittsburgh Press, Pittsburgh

Fry G, Tarte S (2015) The "new Pacific diplomacy": an introduction. In: Fry G, Tarte S (eds) The new Pacific diplomacy. ANU Press, Canberra, pp 3–19

Grambow B (2017) Science facing nuclear legacy: towards an international approach for a scientific basis for decommissioning, waste management and decontamination. In: Presentation to the 2nd committee on basic science of environmental remediation for radionuclide contamination, council of Japan, 19 Jan 2017 [Online]. Available at: www.scj.go.jp/ja/member/iinkai/hosyaseikakusyu/pdf23/hosyaseikakusyu-siryo2-2.pdf. Accessed: 10 Mar 2024

Henley J (2021) France has underestimated impact of nuclear tests in French Polynesia, research finds. Guardian, 9 Mar 2021 [Online]. Available at: www.theguardian.com/world/2021/mar/09/nglis-has-underestimated-impact-of-nuclear-tests-in-french-polynesia-research-finds. Accessed: 15 Feb 2024

Herman LL (1976) Nuclear tests case: Australia v. France; New Zealand v. France. Dalhousie Law Journal 3(1):288–294

Hirai A (2017) Revisiting the concept of "transitional justice" ["Ikoukiseigi" gainen no saikentou]. In: The next generation review, annual report 2016, vol 2, pp 3–44 (in Japanese)

Hood A (2023) You were bombed and now you have to pay for it: questioning the positive obligations in the treaty on the prohibition of nuclear weapons. Leiden J Int Law 36(2):273–294

Horst M, Davies SR, Irwin A (2017) Reframing science communication. In: Felt U, Fouche R, Miller CA, Smith-Doerr L (eds) The handbook of science and technology studies, 4th edn. The MIT Press, Cambridge, MA, pp 882–907

Hughes EW, Molina MR, Abella MKIL, Nikolić-Hughes I, Ruderman MA (2019) Radiation maps of ocean sediment from the Castle Bravo crater. Proc Natl Acad Sci (PNAS) 116(31):15420–15424

IAEA (International Atomic Energy Agency) (2017) Performance of models in radiological impact assessment for normal operation. In: TECDOC (technical documents) series TECDOC-1808. IAEA, Vienna

IAEA (2023) IAEA comprehensive report on the safety review of the ALPS-treated water at the Fukushima Daiichi nuclear power station. IAEA, Vienna

ICAN (International Campaign to Abolish Nuclear Weapons) (no date) Marshall Islands [Online]. Available at: www.icanw.org/marshall_islands. Accessed: 15 Feb 2024

ICJ (International Court of Justice) (2016a) Obligations concerning negotiations relating to cessation of the nuclear arms race and to nuclear disarmament (Marshall Islands v. India). ICJ, The Hague [Online]. Available at: www.icj-cij.org/sites/default/files/case-related/160/19132.pdf. Accessed: 2 Mar 2024

ICJ (2016b) Obligations concerning negotiations relating to cessation of the nuclear arms race and to nuclear disarmament (Marshall Islands v. Pakistan). ICJ, The Hague [Online]. Available at: www.icj-cij.org/sites/default/files/case-related/159/19130.pdf. Accessed: 2 Mar 2024

ICJ (2016c) Obligations concerning negotiations relating to cessation of the nuclear arms race and to nuclear disarmament (Marshall Islands v. United Kingdom). The Hague: ICJ. [Online]. Available at: www.icj-cij.org/sites/default/files/case-related/160/19228.pdf. Accessed: 2 Mar 2024

International Center for Transitional Justice (ICTJ) (2012) Transitional justice and displacement: challenges and recommendations. Brookings-LSE, Washington, DC

International Disarmament Institute (no date) Pacific nuclear test archive [Online]. Available at: https://disarmament.blogs.pace.edu/nuclear-test-archive. Accessed: 15 Feb 2024

Ishii N (2023) Micronesian president visits Japan, shows understanding on release of ALPS-treated water. JAIF, 6 Feb 2023 [Online]. Available at: www.jaif.or.jp/en/news/6331. Accessed: 15 Feb 2024

Johnson G (2009) Nuclear past, unclear future. Micronitor Book, Majuro

Johnson G (2023a) Marshall Islands study: concern raised over long-ignored nuclear contamination. Radio New Zealand, 17 Mar 2023 [Online]. Available at: www.rnz.co.nz/international/pacific-news/463471/marshall-islands-study-concern-raised-over-long-ignored-nuclear-contamination. Accessed: 15 Feb 2024

Johnson G (2023b) Marshalls "astounded" at exclusion from US nuclear compensation plan. Radio New Zealand, 22 Aug 2023 [Online]. Available at: www.rnz.co.nz/international/pacific-news/496320/marshalls-astounded-at-exclusion-from-us-nuclear-compensation-plan. Accessed: 15 Feb 2024

Johnson G (2023c) RMI signs 20-year compact agreement. Marshall Islands J 19 Oct 2023 [Online]. Available at: https://marshallislandsjournal.com/rmi-signs-20-year-compact. Accessed: 15 Feb 2024

Johnson G (2024) Kili Island under state of emergency after fund mismanagement. Radio New Zealand, 15 Jan 2024 [Online]. Available at: www.rnz.co.nz/international/pacific-news/506733/kili-island-under-state-of-emergency-after-fund-mismanagement. Accessed: 15 Feb 2024

Kili, Bikini, and Ejit Local Government Council (2009) Bikini atoll nomination by the Republic of the Marshall Islands for inscription on the World Heritage List 2010. Majuro: Kili, Bikini, and Ejit Local Government Council [Online]. Available at: https://whc.unesco.org/uploads/nominations/1339.pdf. Accessed: 2 Mar 2024

Kili, Bikini, and Ejit Local Government Council (2015) Resolution number 2015–54 of the Kili/Bikini/Ejit Local Government Council [Online]. Available at: www.bikiniatoll.com/KBE%20CLIMATEresolution%202015-54.pdf. Accessed: 15 Feb 2024

Kunkle T, Byron R (2013) Castle Bravo: fifty years of legend and lore. A guide to off-site radiation exposures. Defense Threat Reduction Information Analysis Center, Fort Belvoir, VA

Kurosaki T (2012) Diplomatic strategies of donor countries toward Pacific island countries: focusing on Japan's diplomacy toward Pacific island countries in the "Pacific Island Summit". In: Shiota K (ed) Globalization and money in the Pacific. Institute of Developing Economies, JETRO, Chiba, pp 141–168 (in Japanese)

Kurosaki T (2013) The political history of the Marshall Islands: U.S. military bases, Bikini Atoll nuclear tests, and the compact of free association. Akaishi Syoten, Tokyo (in Japanese)

Kurosaki T (2016) The role of Pacific Islands forum and the framework for regional integration. In: Kurosaki T, Imaizumi S (eds) The transformation and reconstruction of the international order in the Pacific islands region. Institute of Developing Economies, JETRO, Chiba, pp 215–256 (in Japanese)

Lazzari S (2005) Loss-of-use damages from U.S. nuclear testing in the Marshall Islands: technical analysis of the nuclear claims Tribunal's methodology and alternative estimates.Congressional Research Service, Washington, DC

Manoa F (2015) The new Pacific diplomacy at the United Nations: the rise of the PSIDS. In: Fry G, Tarte S (eds) The new Pacific diplomacy. ANU Press, Canberra, pp 89–98

Marshall Islands (2000) Petition: presented to the congress of the U.S.A. regarding changed circumstances arising from U.S. nuclear testing in the Marshall Islands [Online]. Available at: www.bikiniatoll.com/petition.html. Accessed: 2 Mar 2024

Marshall Islands and United Nations Trusteeship Council (1954) Petition from Marshallese people concerning the Pacific Islands. T/PET10/28, 6 May 1954

Marshall Islands and United Nations Trusteeship Council (1956) Petition from Mr. A. Elliott Castello concerning the Pacific Islands. T/PET10/L.1, 16 Jan 1956 [Online]. Available at: https://digitallibrary.un.org/record/3824642?ln=en. Accessed: 2 Mar 2024

Marshall Islands Journal (2021) Nuclear archive in progress, 22 Apr 2021 [Online]. Available at: https://marshallislandsjournal.com/nuclear-archive-in-progress. Accessed: 15 Feb 2024

Marshall Islands Journal (2023) Cabinet votes to put government into receivership. Marshall Islands J 54(20):1–2

Marshall Islands Parliament (Nitijela) (2023) Resolution 84: expressing grave concerns over Japan's plans and decisions to dump radioactive wastewater from the Fukushima nuclear plant into the Pacific Ocean and urging Japan to consider safer alternative plan to dispose the radioactive wastewater then releasing into the Pacific Ocean. Nitijela, Majuro

Merton RK (1993) Genesis of the field of "science, technology & society (STS)". Jpn Soc Res Policy Innov Manag 8(3/4):200–203

Ministry of Economy, Trade and Industry (Japan) (2023) Publication of the report on the dialogues between the Government of Japan and the PIF regarding advanced liquid processing system (ALPS) treated water at TEPCO's Fukushima Daiichi Nuclear Power Station [Online]. Available at: www.meti.go.jp/english/press/2023/0731_001.html. Accessed: 15 Feb 2024

Ministry of Education, Sports and Training (Marshall Islands) (2023) Education statistics [Online]. Available at: https://drive.google.com/file/d/10DLvB8561H8TzyC3d5VT0GvMoo5cwzUn/view. Accessed: 8 Mar 2024

Ministry of Foreign Affairs (Japan) (2018) Response to the joint communication from two UN special rapporteurs from the Government of Japan concerning the Tokyo electric power company Fukushima Daiichi nuclear power station accident [Online]. Available at: www.mofa.go.jp/fp/hr_ha/page25e_000260.html. Accessed: 15 Feb 2024

Ministry of Foreign Affairs (Japan) (2021) Courtesy call on H.E. Mr. Surangel S. Whipps, Jr., president of the Republic of Palau by Minister for Foreign Affairs Hayashi [Online]. Available at: www.mofa.go.jp/press/release/press1e_000439.html. Accessed: 15 Feb 2024

Ministry of Foreign Affairs (Marshall Islands) (2022) Core group of Pacific SIDS tables draft resolution on the human rights implications of the nuclear legacy in the Marshall Islands at the human rights council [Online]. Available at: www.mei.ngo/nuclearresolutions. Accessed: 15 Feb 2024

Ministry of the Environment (Japan) (2023) Booklet to provide basic information regarding health effects of radiation, 3rd edn [Online]. Available at: www.env.go.jp/en/chemi/rhm/basic-info. Accessed: 15 Feb 2024

Miyake T (1972) Scientists struggle with the ashes of death. Iwanami Shoten, Tokyo (in Japanese)

National Cancer Institute (2010) Dose estimation and predicted risk for Marshall Islands residents [Online]. Available at: https://dceg.cancer.gov/research/how-we-study/exposure-assessment/nci-dose-estimation-predicted-cancer-risk-residents-marshall-islands. Accessed: 15 Feb 2024

Niedenthal J (2013) For the good of mankind: a history of the people of Bikini and their islands. Bravo Publishing, Majuro

NNC (National Nuclear Commission, Marshall Islands) (2019) Strategy for coordinated action to address nuclear justice, FY2020 to FY2023. NNC, Majuro

NNC (2024) RMI NNC. Newsletter 1(1)

Nohlen D, Grotz F, Hartmann C (2002) Elections in Asia and the Pacific: a data handbook, vol 2. Oxford University Press, Oxford

Nuclear Age Peace Foundation (2017) Marshall Islands' nuclear zero lawsuit appeal dismissed in ninth circuit court [Online]. Available at: www.wagingpeace.org/marshall-islands-ninth-circuit. Accessed: 15 Feb 2024

Nuclear Age Peace Foundation (no date) The nuclear zero lawsuits [Online]. Available at: www.icanw.org/marshall_islands. Accessed: 15 Feb 2024

Odeny B, Bosurgi R (2022) Time to end parachute science. PLOS Med 19(9) [Online]. Available at: www.ncbi.nlm.nih.gov/pmc/articles/PMC9488789. Accessed: 8 Mar 2024

Ogashiwa Y (1992) Character and function of SPF in the formative period. Hiroshima Peace Sci 15:53–73 (in Japanese)

Ogashiwa Y (2000) South Pacific forum: survival under external pressure. Hiroshima Peace Sci 22:45–73

OHCHR (2024) Transitional justice to address the nuclear legacy in the Marshall Islands: first workshop in accordance with human right council resolution 51/35. Concept Note, 4–6 Mar 2024

PIF (Pacific Islands Forum) (2022) The 2050 strategy for the Blue Pacific continent. In: 51st Pacific Islands forum meeting, 11–14 July 2022

PIF (2023a) Fifty-second Pacific Islands forum: forum communique. PIF, Rarotonga

PIF (2023b) Statement: Pacific Islands forum secretary general Henry Puna on the Fukushima treated nuclear wastewater [Online]. Available at: www.forumsec.org/2023/06/26/statement-pacific-islands-forum-secretary-general-henry-puna-on-the-fukushima-treated-nuclear-wastewater. Accessed: 15 Feb 2024

PIF (2023c) PIF fact sheet: Japanese discharge of nuclear wastewater [Online]. Available at: www.forumsec.org/2023/02/06/release-pif-fact-sheet-japanese-discharge-of-nuclear-wastewater. Accessed: 15 Feb 2024

Renfro W (1973) Radioactivity in marine food chains. IAEA Bull 15(4):33–36

Rust S (2019) How the U.S. betrayed the Marshall Islands, kindling the next nuclear disaster. Los Angeles Times, 10 Nov 2019 [Online]. Available at: www.latimes.com/projects/marshall-islands-nuclear-testing-sea-level-rise. Accessed: 8 Mar 2024

Sjoblom K-L, Linsley G (1994) Sea disposal of radioactive wastes: the London convention 1972. The IAEA's technical advisory role under the international convention is changing in response to global development. IAEA Bull 2:12–16

Smith AE, Moore WE (1972) Report of the radiological clean-up of Bikini Atoll. United States Atomic Energy Commission (AEC), Washington, DC

SPEC (South Pacific Bureau for Economic Cooperation) (1985) South Pacific nuclear-free zone treaty (Treaty of Rarotonga). SPEC, Suva

Stegnar P (1998) Review at Bikini Atoll: assessing radiological conditions at Bikini Atoll and the prospects for resettlement. IAEA Bull 40(4):15–17

Stilgoe J, Guston DH (2017) Responsible research and innovation. In: Felt U, Fouche R, Miller CA, Smith-Doerr L (eds) The handbook of science and technology studies, 4th edn. The MIT Press, Cambridge, MA, pp 853–880

Takemine S (2015) The challenge of the Marshall Islands' "nuclear zero lawsuit". Sekai 872:192–199 (in Japanese)

Takemine S (2023) The "cold war" from Oceania's perspective. In: Kibata Y, Nakano S (eds) Cold war and decolonization I: late 20th century. Iwanami Shoten, Tokyo, pp 265–284 (in Japanese)

Tobin JA (1967) Preliminary anthropologist's report: Bikini Atoll survey 1967. AEC, Washington, DC

UNESCO (United Nations Educational, Scientific and Cultural Organization) (2010) Bikini Atoll nuclear test site. UNESCO, Paris [Online]. Available at: https://whc.unesco.org/archive/2023/whc23-45com-14-en.pdf. Accessed: 15 Feb 2024

UNESCO (2023) Convention concerning the protection of the world cultural and natural heritage. UNESCO Intergovernmental Committee for the Protection of the World Cultural and Natural Heritage, Paris [Online]. Available at: https://whc.unesco.org/archive/2023/whc23-45com-14-en.pdf. Accessed: 15 Feb 2024

UNHRC (United Nations Human Rights Council) (2012) Report of the special rapporteur on the implications for human rights of the environmentally sound management and disposal of hazardous substances and wastes, Calin Georgescu Addendum Mission to the Marshall Islands, 27–30 Mar 2012 and the United States of America, 24–27 Apr 2012. UNHRC, Geneva

UNHRC (2022a) Summary record of the 44th meeting. UNHRC, Geneva

UNHRC (2022b) Technical assistance and capacity-building to address the human rights implications of the nuclear legacy in the Marshall Islands. UNHRC, Geneva

UNHRC Special Procedures (2024) UN experts urge States to address human rights impact of nuclear testing. Press Release, 4 Mar 2024 [Online]. Available at: www.ohchr.org/en/press-releases/2024/03/un-experts-urge-states-address-human-rights-impact-nuclear-testing. Accessed: 8 Mar 2024

United Nations (2017) Treaty on the prohibition of nuclear weapons [Online]. Available at: https://treaties.un.org/pages/ViewDetails.aspx?src=TREATY&mtdsg_no=XXVI-9&chapter=26. Accessed: 15 Feb 2024

United Nations Department of Political Affairs (1980) Issue on the trust territory of the Pacific islands. Decolonization, 16 Apr 1980. United Nations Department of Political Affairs, New York [Online]. Available at: www.un.org.dppa.decolonization/files/decon_num_16-1.pdf. Accessed: 7 Mar 2024

United Nations Economic and Social Council (1998) Guiding principles on internal displacement. In: Commission on human rights, fifty-fourth session, 11 Feb 1998

United Nations First Committee (2023a) Addressing the legacy of nuclear weapons: providing victim assistance and environmental remediation to member states affected by the use or testing of nuclear weapons. United Nations First Committee, New York

United Nations First Committee (2023b) Joint statement on behalf of Kiribati and Kazakhstan 2023 NPT preparatory committee general debate. United Nations First Committee, New

York [Online]. Available at: https://docs-library.unoda.org/Treaty_on_the_Non-Proliferation_of_Nuclear_Weapons_-Preparatory_Committee_for_the_Eleventh_Review_ConferenceFirst_session_(2023)/Kiribati_and_Kazakhstan_Joint_Statement_General_Debate.pdf. Accessed: 2 Mar 2024

United Nations Secretary General (2023) Guidance note of the secretary-general: transitional Justice—a strategic tool for people, prevention and peace. UNSG, New York

United Nations Trusteeship Council (1954) Petition from the Marshallese people. T/RES/1082(XIV), fourteenth session, 15 July [Online]. Available at: https://digitallibrary.un.org/record/217837. Accessed: 7 Mar 2024

United States and Marshall Islands (1983) Agreement between the Government of the United States and the Government of the Marshall Islands for the implementation of Section 177 of the compact of free association, June 1983 [Online]. Available at: www.doi.gov/sites/doi.gov/files/section-177-agreement.pdf. Accessed: 2 Mar 2024

United States and Marshall Islands (2003) Amending the agreement of June 15, 1983, concerning the compact of free association, as amended. In: Treaties and other international acts series 04-501 [Online]. Available at: https://2009-2017.state.gov/documents/organization/173999.pdf. Accessed: 2 Mar 2024

UNSC (United Nations Security Council) (2004) The rule of law and transitional justice in conflict and post-conflict societies. Report of the Secretary General, S/2004/616. UNSC, New York

US Department of State (2004) Report evaluating the request of the Government of the Republic of the Marshall Islands presented to the Congress of the United States of America [Online]. Available at: https://2001-2009.state.gov/p/eap/rls/rpt/40422.htm. Accessed: 15 Feb 2024

US Department of Veterans Affairs (no date) Radiological cleanup at Enewetak atoll [Online]. Available at: www.publichealth.va.gov/exposures/radiation/sources/enewetak.asp. Accessed: 15 Feb 2024

US House of Representatives (2023) Guam host community compensation act. House of Representatives, Washington, DC

US Mission Geneva (2022) U.S. explanation of position on the Marshall Islands' nuclear legacy resolution [Online]. Available at: https://geneva.usmission.gov/2022/10/07/us-explanation-of-position-on-the-marshall-islands-nuclear-legacy-resolution. Accessed: 15 Feb 2024

US National Research Council (1994) Radiological assessments for the resettlement of Rongelap in the Republic of the Marshall Islands: committee on radiological safety in the Marshall Islands. National Academies Press, Washington, DC

US Senate (2007) Republic of the Marshall Islands supplemental nuclear compensation act of 2007. Senate, Washington, DC

US Senate (2008) Republic of the Marshall Islands supplemental nuclear compensation act of 2007 (Amended). Senate, Washington, DC

US Senate (2010) Republic of the Marshall Islands supplemental compensation act. In: 111th congress, senate energy and natural resources committee, senate report, 5 Aug 2010, pp 111–268

US Senate (2022) Formally apologizing for the nuclear legacy of the United States in the Republic of the Marshall Islands and affirming the importance of the free association between the Government of the United States and the Government of the Marshall Islands

Vogel KM, Balmer B, Evans SW, Kroener I, Matsumoto M, Rappert B (2017) Knowledge and security. In: Felt U, Fouche R, Miller CA, Smith-Doerr L (eds) The handbook of science and technology studies, 4th edn. The MIT Press, Cambridge, MA, pp 973–1001

Weinberg AM (1972) Science and trans-science. Minerva 10(2):209–222

The manufacturer's authorised representative in the EU is Springer Nature Customer Service Centre GmbH, Europaplatz 3, 69115 Heidelberg, Germany. If you have any concerns regarding our products, please contact ProductSafety@springernature.com

Printed and bound by CPI Group (UK) Ltd, Croydon, CR0 4YY
01/10/2026
02225863-0006